Understanding
THOMAS MANN

Understanding Modern
European and Latin American
Literature

James Hardin, *Series Editor*

volumes on

Ingeborg Bachmann
Samuel Beckett
Thomas Bernhard
Johannes Bobrowski
Heinrich Böll
Italo Calvino
Albert Camus
Elias Canetti
Camilo José Cela
Céline
Julio Cortázar
Isak Dinesen
José Donoso
Friedrich Dürrenmatt
Rainer Werner Fassbinder
Max Frisch
Federico García Lorca
Gabriel García Márquez
Juan Goytisolo
Günter Grass
Gerhart Hauptmann

Christoph Hein
Hermann Hesse
Eugène Ionesco
Uwe Johnson
Milan Kundera
Primo Levi
Thomas Mann
Boris Pasternak
Octavio Paz
Luigi Pirandello
Graciliano Ramos
Erich Maria Remarque
Alain Robbe-Grillet
Joseph Roth
Jean-Paul Sartre
W. G. Sebald
Claude Simon
Mario Vargas Llosa
Peter Weiss
Franz Werfel
Christa Wolf

UNDERSTANDING

THOMAS
MANN

HANNELORE MUNDT

UNIVERSITY OF SOUTH CAROLINA PRESS

© 2004 University of South Carolina

Published in Columbia, South Carolina, by the
University of South Carolina Press

Manufactured in the United States of America

08 07 06 05 04   5 4 3 2 1

Library of Congress Cataloging-in-Publication Data

Mundt, Hannelore.
  Understanding Thomas Mann / Hannelore Mundt.
    p. cm. — (Understanding modern European and Latin American
  literature)
  Includes bibliographical references and index.
    ISBN 1-57003-537-7 (cloth : alk. paper)
    1. Mann, Thomas, 1875–1955—Criticism and interpretation. I. Title.
  II. Series.
    PT2625.A44Z7496 2004

  833'.912—dc22

                                                          2003025456

For my husband, Derek Montague, and our children, Tanja and Dennis

Contents

Editor's Preface

Understanding Modern European and Latin American Literature has been planned as a series of guides for undergraduate and graduate students and nonacademic readers. Like the volumes in its companion series *Understanding Contemporary American Literature,* these books provide introductions to the lives and writings of prominent modern authors and explicate their most important works.

Modern literature makes special demands, and this is particularly true of foreign literature, in which the reader must contend not only with unfamiliar, often arcane artistic conventions and philosophical concepts, but also with the handicap of reading the literature in translation. It is a truism that the nuances of one language can be rendered in another only imperfectly (and this problem is especially acute in fiction), but the fact that the works of European and Latin American writers are situated in a historical and cultural setting quite different from our own can be as great a hindrance to the understanding of these works as the linguistic barrier. For this reason the *UMELL* series emphasizes the sociological and historical background of the writers treated. The philosophical and cultural traditions peculiar to a given culture may be particularly important for an understanding of certain authors, and these are taken up in the introductory chapter and also in the discussion of those works to which this information is relevant. Beyond this, the books treat the specifically literary aspects of the author under discussion and attempt to explain the complexities of contemporary literature lucidly. The books are conceived as introductions to the authors covered, not as comprehensive analyses. They do not provide detailed summaries of plot because they are meant to be used in conjunction with the books they treat, not as a substitute for study of the original works. The purpose of the books is to provide information and judicious literary assessment of the major works in the most compact, readable form. It is our hope that the *UMELL* series will help increase knowledge and understanding of European and Latin American cultures and will serve to make the literature of those cultures more accessible.

J. H.

Acknowledgments

I am grateful to the University of Wyoming for the Flittie sabbatical award and a sabbatical leave that enabled me to begin the research for this book. I am also indebted to my colleagues from the English department at the University of Wyoming, Sandra Clark, Susan Frye, Cedric Reverand, Eric Sandeen, and Robert Torry, for providing helpful comments and advice on content and diction. Thanks also to series editor James Hardin and project editor Scott Evan Burgess for their advice in preparing the manuscript. Special thanks are due to Martha Hanscom, a librarian at the University of Wyoming, who made many thoughtful suggestions in her reading of the manuscript and under whose auspices our library collection on Thomas Mann grew considerably. I am deeply grateful to my husband Derek Montague for his thorough editorial reading of the final draft. Last but not least, I owe a very special debt to my friend and fellow Thomas Mann scholar Herbert Lehnert for his invaluable critical comments, lucid insights, and encouragement.

Chronology

1875   Paul Thomas Mann is born on 6 June in Lübeck, an old Hanseatic town on the Baltic Sea. His father, owner of a grain business and senator of Lübeck, is Thomas Johann Heinrich Mann; his mother is Julia née da Silva Bruhns. Their other children are Luiz Heinrich (b. 1871), Julia (b. 1877), Carla (b. 1881), and Viktor (b. 1890).

1891   Mann's father dies. The family business is liquidated, and the family house sold. An annual allowance provides Heinrich and Thomas Mann with the opportunity to pursue their artistic careers. Julia Mann moves with her children Julia, Carla, and Victor to Munich while Thomas stays in Lübeck to finish school. With his friend Otto Grautoff, he publishes the periodical *Frühlingssturm* (Spring storm). Publication ceases after two issues. Thomas joins his family in Munich, where he works as an unpaid apprentice at an insurance company. Publishes his first story, "Gefallen" (Fallen).

1895   Publishes "Der Wille zum Glück" ("The Will to Happiness") in the journal *Simplicissimus*. Makes first visit to Italy, with his brother Heinrich.

1897   Visits Rome and Palestrina, Italy. Writes stories to be published the following year.

1898   Publishes first collection of short stories, *Der kleine Herr Friedemann* (*Little Herr Friedemann*).

1900   Completes first novel, *Buddenbrooks*. Serves briefly in the military, and is discharged on medical grounds. Begins friendship with Paul Ehrenberg.

1901   *Buddenbrooks: Decline of a Family* (*Buddenbrooks: Verfall einer Familie*) published in two volumes.

1903   Publishes second collection of short stories and novellas, *Tristan: Six Novellas*. Among them is one of Mann's most famous novellas, *Tonio Kröger*. Mann suffers from repressed homosexual desires and outsider existence.

1904   Gets engaged to Katia Pringsheim, the daughter of a wealthy Jewish professor in Munich.

1905   Marries Katia on 11 February. First daughter, Erika, is born. Publishes his drama *Fiorenza* (first performance in 1907).

1906   "Wälsungenblut" ("The Blood of the Walsungs") printed for *Die Neue Rundschau*, but withdrawn from publication. A private edition appears in 1921. First son, Klaus, is born. Work on *Königliche Hoheit* (*Royal Highness*) begins.

1908   Visits Venice. Builds summer house in Bad Tölz, Bavaria.

1909   *Royal Highness* published; second son, Golo, is born. Plans for the novel *Bekenntnisse des Hochstablers Felix Krull* (*Confessions of Felix Krull, Confidence Man*) and for the essay "Geist und Kunst" (Intellect and art).

1910   Mann's sister Carla commits suicide; Mann continues work on *Confessions*. Second daughter, Monika, is born.

1911   Visits Venice again. Publishes first essay on Wagner titled "Auseinandersetzung mit Wagner" (Taking issue with Wagner), and continues work on *Death in Venice*.

1912   Visits Katia in Davos where she stays at a sanatorium. Completes and publishes *Death in Venice*.

1913   Begins *Der Zauberberg* (*The Magic Mountain*).

1914   Moves to new house on Poschinger Strasse in Munich. First World War begins. Mann joins in the widespread enthusiasm at the outbreak of war and writes "Gedanken im Kriege" ("Thoughts in War") and "Friedrich und die große Koalition" ("Frederick and the Grand Coalition"). Discord with Heinrich.

1915   Begins *Betrachtungen eines Unpolitischen* (*Reflections of a Nonpolitical Man*).

1918   Publishes *Reflections of a Nonpolitical Man*. Third daughter, Elisabeth, is born. After the end of First World War, Kaiser Wilhelm II abdicates. Germany is proclaimed a republic.

1919   Publishes *Herr und Hund* (*A Man and His Dog*) and *Gesang vom Kindchen* (*Song of a Child*), both idyllic texts that reflect Mann's retreat from political debates after *Reflections*. Receives honorary doctorate of the University of Bonn. Third son, Michael, is born. Resumes work on *The Magic Mountain*

1921   Lectures on "Goethe und Tolstoy" ("Goethe and Tolstoy"). Secures steady income through lecture tours and readings from his fictional works.

1922   Reconciles with his brother Heinrich. Supports the Weimar Republic with his speech "Von deutscher Republik" ("The German Republic").

1924   Publishes *The Magic Mountain.*

1925   Publishes *Unordnung und frühes Leid* (*Disorder and Early Sorrow*).

1926   Travels extensively in Europe; begins work on *Joseph* tetralogy.

1927   Meets Klaus Heuser. Sister Julia commits suicide.

1929   Receives the Nobel Prize for Literature. Becomes a member of the Rotary Club (until 1933) and delivers numerous lectures, among them: "Rede über Lessing" ("Speech on Lessing") and "Die Stellung Freuds in der modernen Geistesgeschichte" ("Freud's Position in the History of Modern Thought").

1930   Travels to Egypt and Palestine. Publishes *Mario und der Zauberer* (*Mario and the Magician*) and *Lebensabriß* (*A Sketch of My Life*). Delivers speech titled "Deutsche Ansprache: Ein Apell an die Vernunft" ("An Appeal to Reason") and warns against antihumanistic forces in Germany.

1932   Delivers speech "Goethe als Repräsentant des bürgerlichen Zeitalters" ("Goethe as Representative of the Bourgeois Age").

1933   Hitler becomes Chancellor of Germany in January. After Mann's 10 February 1933 speech on Wagner titled "Leiden und Größe Richard Wagners" ("The Sufferings and Greatness of Richard Wagner"), the Manns travel abroad for a lecture tour to The Netherlands and France, followed by a vacation in Switzerland. They do not return to Germany, deciding instead to settle in Switzerland. Publishes *Die Geschichten Jakobs* (*The Tales of Jacob*), the first volume of the *Joseph* tetralogy, in Germany.

1934   Publishes second volume of the *Joseph* tetralogy, *Der junge Joseph* (*Young Joseph*), in Germany while opposition to Hitler's growing regime of terror is crushed. Mann makes first visit to the United States.

1935   Second visit to the United States. Mann awarded honorary doctorate from Harvard University.

1936   Publishes third volume of the *Joseph* tetralogy, *Joseph in Ägypten* (*Joseph in Egypt*). Mann publicly voices his opposition to Nazi Germany with his speech "Achtung, Europa!" ("Europe Beware"). Becomes a Czech citizen. Consequently, loses German citizenship and honorary doctorate of the University of Bonn.

1938   Annexation of Austria. Mann decides to immigrate to the United States. Lives in Princeton and becomes lecturer in the humanities at Princeton University.

1939   Publishes *Lotte in Weimar* (*Lotte in Weimar: The Beloved Returns*). Second World War begins in September.

1940 Begins monthly Radio broadcasts with BBC to Germany (reports continue until 1945). Publishes *Die vertauschten Köpfe* (*The Transposed Heads: A Legend of India*). Delivers Princeton lecture titled "On Myself."

1941 Invited to the White House. Begins lecture tour on "The War and the Future." Moves to Pacific Palisades near Los Angeles.

1943 Publishes last volume of tetralogy *Joseph der Ernäher* (*Joseph the Provider*) in Stockholm. Publishes *Das Gesetz* (*The Tables of the Law*) in the United States. Begins *Doktor Faustus* (*Doctor Faustus*).

1944 Becomes U.S. citizen and supports Roosevelt during the elections.

1945 Second World War ends. Delivers lecture on "Deutschland und die Deutschen" ("Germany and the Germans").

1946 Diagnosed with lung cancer; successful treatment in Chicago.

1947 Publishes *Doctor Faustus*, a novel that links German culture and its adherents to the descent of Germany into barbarism and irrationality. Begins lecture tour on "Nietzsches Philosophie im Lichte unserer Erfahrung" ("Nietzsche's Philosophy in the Light of Contemporary Events") in the United States, then in various European countries, but not in Germany.

1948 Publishes *Die Entstehung des Doktor Faustus: Roman eines Romans* (*The Story of a Novel: The Genesis of "Dr. Faustus"*).

1949 Begins another lecture tour in Europe, visiting both West and East Germany, where Mann is honored with the Goethe Prize in Frankfurt and Weimar, respectively. Son Klaus commits suicide in Cannes.

1950 Heinrich Mann dies in March in Los Angeles. Mann visits Switzerland, meets the waiter Franz Westermeier in Zurich.

1951 Publishes *Der Erwählte* (*The Holy Sinner*). Resumes work on *Confessions*.

1952 Move to Switzerland due to McCarthyism in the United States and the wish to spend his final years in Switzerland.

1953 Publishes *Die Betrogene* (*The Black Swan*). Audience with Pope Pius XII in Rome.

1954 Publishes *Bekenntnisse des Hochstaplers Felix Krull* (*Confessions of Felix Krull, Confidence Man*), his last novel, which remains a fragment. Moves to Kilchberg near Zurich. Plans for play on Luther's marriage.

1955 Presents essay on Schiller, in a shorter version, in his hometown Lübeck. Dies 12 August in Zurich of arteriosclerosis.

Abbreviations and Editions

Quotations from or references to Mann's primary writings and correspondence will be cited parenthetically in the text and abbreviated as indicated below. All translations from the German texts listed below, as well as other secondary German sources quoted in the book, are my own.

B   *Buddenbrooks: The Decline of a Family.* Translated by John E. Woods. New York: Alfred Knopf, 1993.

Br 1   *Briefe, 1889–1936.* Edited by Erika Mann. Frankfurt am Main: Fischer, 1962.

Br 2   *Briefe, 1937–1947.* Edited by Erika Mann. Frankfurt am Main: Fischer, 1963.

Br 3   *Briefe, 1948–1955 und Nachlese.* Edited by Erika Mann. Frankfurt am Main: Fischer, 1961–1965.

BS   *The Black Swan.* Translated by Willard R. Trask. New York: Alfred Knopf, 1954.

DF   *Doctor Faustus: The Life of the German Composer Adrian Leverkühn As Told by a Friend.* Translated by John E. Woods. New York: Vintage International, 1999.

DüD   *1–3 Dichter über ihre Dichtungen*, 3 vols. Edited by Hans Wysling and assisted by M. Fischer. Munich: Heimeran, and Frankfurt am Main: S. Fischer, 1975–1981.

E 1–6   *Essays,* 6 vols. Edited by Hermann Kurzke and Stephan Stachorski. Frankfurt am Main: S. Fischer, 1993–1997.

ETD   *Essays of Three Decades.* Translated by H. T. Lowe-Porter. New York: Alfred Knopf, 1948.

FK   *Confessions of Felix Krull, Confidence Man.* Translated by Denver Lindley. New York: Vintage International, 1992.

GW 1–13 *Gesammelte Werke in Dreizehn Bänden*, Frankfurt am Main: S. Fischer, 1974.

HM/TM   *Letters of Heinrich and Thomas Mann, 1900–1946.* Translated by Don Reneau with additional translations by Richard and Clara Winston,

	edited by Hans Wysling. Berkeley and Los Angeles: University of California Press, 1998.
HS	*The Holy Sinner*. Translated by H. T. Lowe-Porter. New York: Alfred Knopf, 1951
JB	*Joseph and His Brothers*. Translated by H. T. Lowe-Porter. New York: Alfred Knopf, 1948.
Letters	*Letters of Thomas Mann, 1889–1955*. Selected and translated by Richard and Clara Winston. New York: Alfred Knopf, 1971.
LiW	*Lotte in Weimar: The Beloved Returns*. Translated by H. T. Lowe-Porter, Introduction by Hayden White. Berkeley and Los Angeles: University of California Press, 1990.
MM	*The Magic Mountain*. Translated by John E. Woods. New York: Alfred Knopf, 1999.
NB 1–6	*Notizbücher 1–6*. Edited by Hans Wysling and Yvonne Schmidlin. Frankfurt am Main: S. Fischer, 1991.
NB 7–14	*Notizbücher 7–14*. Edited by Hans Wysling and Yvonne Schmidlin. Frankfurt am Main: S. Fischer, 1992.
OD	*Order of the Day*. Translated by H. T. Lowe-Porter, Agnes E. Meyer, and Eric Sutton. New York: Alfred Knopf, 1937; Reprint 1969.
R	*Reflections of a Nonpolitical Man*. Trans. Walter D. Morris. New York: Frederick Ungar, 1983.
RH	*Royal Highness*. Translated by A. Cecil Curtis. London: Minerva, 1997.
TM/OG	*Briefe an Otto Grautoff 1894–1901 und Ida Boy-Ed, 1903–1928*. Frankfurt am Main: S. Fischer, 1975.
TB	*Tagebücher 1918–1921. 1933–1934. 1935–1936. 1937–1939. 1940–1943*. Edited by Peter de Mendelssohn. *Tagebücher 1944–1946. 1946–1048. 1949–1950. 1951–1952. 1953–1955*. Edited by Inge Jens. Frankfurt am Main: S. Fischer 1977–1995.
Stories	*Death in Venice and Other Stories by Thomas Mann*. Translated by David Luke. New York: Bantam Books, 1988.
SN	*The Story of a Novel: The Genesis of "Dr. Faustus."* Translated by Richard and Clara Winston. New York: Alfred Knopf, 1961.
Tables	*The Tables of the Law*. Translated by H. T. Lowe-Porter. New York: Alfred Knopf, 1945.
Tales	*Death in Venice and Other Tales*. Translated by Joachim Neugroschel. New York: Penguin Books, 1999.

CHAPTER 1

Introduction

Over the last two decades, a significant surge of interest in Thomas Mann's life and œuvre has taken place, made apparent by a wave of numerous new studies and translations of his major works. The main reason for this widespread attention to Mann lies in the publication of his diaries, opened twenty years after his death in 1975 and published in ten volumes between 1977 and 1995. What, one must ask, could those diaries, written between 1918 and 1921, and 1933 and 1955, contain to cause such a stir?[1] Mann himself speculated that they would bring "cheery discoveries." "Let the world know me," he said, "but not until all are dead" (*TB 1949–1950* 278). What he wanted the world to discover was his most vigilantly guarded secret: his homosexual disposition. But why this need to set the record "straight"?

In all probability, Mann feared that readers and scholars might turn toward more contemporary and experimental writers, whose stars were rising while Mann was still alive, and that his works might be all but forgotten within a few decades after his death. Indeed, since the 1950s Mann's popularity had been overshadowed by new talents in German literature—Max Frisch, Günter Grass, Heinrich Böll, and Christa Wolf. For many, Mann had come to embody the aloof, bourgeois writer, known for form and decorum and a vast body of literature belonging to a bygone world. When Mann decided to have his diaries published a hundred years after his birth, he counted on the enormous impact they would engender, leading to a revival in the interest in his works. His timing could not have been better. Of course, he could not have anticipated that, initiated by the feminist movement of the 1970s, the academic disciplines of women's and gender studies, and a general interest in the representation and sublimation of stigmatized and repressed sexuality, would flourish concurrent with the period in which his diaries were published. Testifying to Mann's secret desires, his hopes and fears, and to a life hidden behind masks and a bourgeois facade, these diaries were soon embraced as new keys to the interpretation of his life and works.

It should be mentioned that the diaries, amounting to over 4,500 printed pages, contain only a few, albeit revealing, passages about Mann's homosexual desires and his suffering from the fetters of conventional morality. Nonetheless, these passages are, in their honesty and candidness, an appeal against sexual repression, and thus a call for the acceptance of difference, for tolerance and humanity. Self-exposure and rebellion against the narrow-mindedness of bourgeois-Christian morality are but one aspect of the diaries. In presenting countless minutiae of Mann's everyday life, they disclose the life of a narcissistic, creative outsider protected by his wife and, late in life, by his eldest daughter. Furthermore, and equally essential in understanding Mann and his works, they reveal Mann's human side, his desire to go beyond his self-centered self, and his need to communicate with the world beyond his fiction, essays, speeches, and thousands of letters. From these diaries emerges an individual who rebelled against the human community, but who, simultaneously, yearned for it and was deeply concerned about its progress and survival. This concern for humanity fostered another important dimension of the diaries: Mann's reflections upon critical periods of German history—after the First World War; during Nazi Germany; the years of the Second World War and its aftermath; and the beginnings of the cold war.

The diaries are used in this book particularly where they enhance and augment our understanding of Mann's fiction and the person and the times behind Mann the writer. The central source for understanding Mann remain the fictional works themselves, their major themes, their artistic presentations, and their multifaceted meanings. And rather than exclusively understanding Mann and his works as representative of twentieth-century German, as well as European, art and cultural history, which they undoubtedly are, I instead approach Mann as a man of letters, whose writings, though influenced by nineteenth-century German culture and its venerated masters, primarily Schopenhauer, Wagner, and Nietzsche, are strikingly and surprisingly contemporary today, despite the fact that well over on hundred years have passed since his first publications appeared. While many of his famous works are set in the German world of the nineteenth and twentieth century (e.g., *Buddenbrooks*, *Tonio Kröger*, *Doctor Faustus*), many also reach beyond it (e.g., *Der Tod in Venedig* [*Death in Venice*], *Der Zauberberg* [*The Magic Mountain*] and his epic *Joseph* tetralogy, *Joseph und seine Brüder* [*Joseph and His Brothers*]). What all these novels and stories have in common, and what makes them timeless, current, and universally appealing, is their concern with sexual repression, conformity, and the individual's responsibilities in society. Mann's fiction tells about human defeats, victories, and achievements, the destructive and constructive side of creativity, and last but by no means least, about the power and danger of ideologies. Known for his ambiguities and irony, Mann refused to accept any definite and binding interpretation of the human

2

condition or to embrace any fixed belief, as he felt that rigid and dogmatic thinking breeds intolerance. Today, in an age when mankind must find a way to accept differences in order to live together peacefully, Mann's non-commitment as an expression of his humanity assumes more value than ever before. This humanity is the foundation of his writings, as Mann suggested in his essay "Der Künstler und die Gesellschaft" ("The Artist and Society") in 1952, contemplating the intrinsic worth of his life's work—his art: "It is connected with the good, at its foundation lies kindness, which is related to wisdom, and even closer to love" (*E* 6 235).

Paul Thomas Mann was born on Sunday, 6 June 1875, in the Hanseatic city of Lübeck, an old seaport famous for its medieval brick churches and gabled houses. Lübeck, an independent republic, or *Freistaat*, was governed by a merchant aristocracy to which the Mann family belonged. Thomas Mann's father, Thomas Johann Heinrich Mann (1840–1891), owned a third-generation grain business and, as one of the city's most respected citizens, became a senator of the independent republic of Lübeck in 1877. His mother, Julia née da Silva Bruhns (1851–1923), was the daughter of the German owner of a plantation near Rio de Janeiro whose wife was Portuguese-Creole-Brazilian. After her mother's death, Julia was brought to Lübeck by her father, who left her there to obtain a German education. In *Lebensabriß* (*A Sketch of My Life*), from 1930, Mann describes how his parents had shaped his life. From his mother, a beautiful, musical woman, he had inherited his artistic side and from his father, his bourgeois discipline and strong work ethic. These different natures account for one of the major tensions in Mann's life and in his fiction: that between art and bourgeois life.

Together with his older brother, Luiz Heinrich (1871–1950) and his three other siblings, Julia (1877–1927), Carla (1881–1910), and Viktor (1890–1949), Thomas enjoyed a carefree and happy childhood. Summer vacations were spent at the Baltic seaside town of Travemünde. Thomas, an imaginative child, staged puppet shows, played with marionettes, and enjoyed acting. He also learned to play the violin and the piano. These outlets for his creative talents enabled him to transcend the world in which he grew up through use of his creativity and imagination. Thomas looked up to his older brother Heinrich with a mixture of admiration and envy because Heinrich was not afraid to rebel against his bourgeois background. Single-mindedly Heinrich pursued a literary career and even had early successes in publishing stories in newspapers. Against his father's wishes, Heinrich dropped out of school. He soon got a job as a bookseller's apprentice in Dresden, and shortly thereafter secured another apprenticeship in Berlin for the new (and now famous) publishing house, Samuel Fischer. The senator now put all his hopes in his second son as his successor in the firm—but this, too, would be in vain. Thomas, who hated school and only managed to finish after repeating grades several times, also had literary, rather than mercantile, ambitions. When the senator became seriously ill in July 1891, he drew up his will, instructing the guardians of his estate to liquidate his business, to oppose Heinrich's literary ambitions, and to situate Thomas in a practical profession. He died of cancer of the bladder in October, leaving his wife and children an annual income sufficient to permit them to lead a privileged existence—and, ironically, to allow Heinrich and Thomas to pursue their literary careers.

The brothers were encouraged by their artistically inclined mother, who was proud of her sons' literary ambitions and understood how restricted they felt in Lübeck. After her husband's death, she would herself move to Munich in 1893 to enjoy the city's diverse cultural and social life, leaving Thomas in Lübeck to finish school. While a student at the local high school, the *Katharineum-Gymnasium*, Mann began writing poetry. Among the literary figures he admired were famous nineteenth-century Germans such as Heinrich Heine (1797–1856), with his ironic, antibourgeois stance, and Theodor Storm (1817–1888), known for his literary realism and detailed, atmospheric depiction of northern Germany. In the 1890s Mann also read the German philosophers Friedrich Nietzsche (1844–1900) and Arthur Schopenhauer (1788–1860). During that period he also developed a lifelong fascination for the music of Richard Wagner (1813–1883). Mann's intellectual and artistic interests set him apart from many of his classmates. As he was also rather aloof and refused to take part in the childish antics of his schoolmates, he did not make friends easily. We know of one friend, Otto Grautoff, a bookseller's son and Mann's social inferior. Their friendship evolved from a mutual interest in literature. With Grautoff and others he edited a student journal, *Frühlingssturm* (Spring storm), of which only two issues were printed. In the submissions to the journal, Mann used the nom-de-plume Paul Thomas (his two given names). Interestingly, in this pseudonym, Mann simultaneously conceals and reveals his own identity, a paradoxical impulse that comes to form a distinguishing mark of Mann's fiction.

The unlikely friendship between Grautoff and Mann deserves further comment. Grautoff (1876–1937) was not from one of the patrician families of Lübeck. His father's small business went bankrupt, the family became poorer, and in 1891 Grautoff's father committed suicide. Grautoff resented his socially inferior life and yearned for recognition, which he hoped to attain through his friendship with Mann. Taken aback by Grautoff's unattractive, slovenly appearance, Mann would at times distance himself from Grautoff. But he never spurned Grautoff, as did other sons of the mercantile aristocracy, because Grautoff's loyalty and admiration provided a counterbalance to Heinrich's devastating criticism of Thomas's early poems, which had left him with feelings of inferiority.

Thomas Mann's letters to Grautoff, written after Mann's graduation from school in 1894 and his move to Munich where he joined his family, have fortunately not been lost. Given that his diaries from this period have been destroyed, these letters, dating from 1894 to 1901, provide valuable insights into Mann's private life at that time. They also simultaneously present a mystery: In a letter from April 1895, Mann inquired whether Grautoff had, as promised, destroyed the seventh volume, probably a diary, some time ago (*TM/OG* 39–40). It appears that this volume contained a secret Thomas Mann wished to conceal. Mann's inquiry suggests Grautoff was Mann's confidante and that he knew "intimate" details about Mann which, as a loyal friend, he never revealed (*TM/OG* 37). Perhaps they were details of such a nature that Mann did not dare put them on paper subsequently. Did they pertain to a secret homosexual love? Did Mann tell Grautoff about his clandestine first love—Mann's classmate Armin Martens— whom he later immortalized in the figure of Tonio Kröger, and about his frustrations? Possibly, but we cannot know for sure. What can be ascertained from these letters, however, are Mann's doubts about his artistic ambitions. He wrote to Grautoff that the artist is a "good-for-nothing" (*TM/OG* 47) whose libertine, outsider existence he could not adopt for himself: "Perhaps one needs a firm hold, an orderly occupation in order not to fall into idle ways" (*TM/OG* 48).

Mann found just such an activity when he joined a fire-insurance company in Munich, a practical profession that did not interest him at all. During work hours he wrote his first story about sorrowful love, "Gefallen" (Fallen), which was immediately accepted for publication by the journal *Die Gesellschaft*. Two years later, the journal *Simplicissimus* published *"Der Wille zum Glück"* ("The Will to Happiness"). Mann convinced his mother of his talents, and then resigned from his monotonous job at the insurance company and began auditing lectures at the Technical University in Munich. Luckily, neither Thomas nor Heinrich needed to work for a living. Their father's death provided both brothers economic freedom. Their inheritance allowed them to live modestly yet comfortably, and in 1895, both left for Italy. It was from Italy that Thomas Mann would send his first major story, which camouflaged the repression of his own homosexual desires, "Little Herr Friedemann," to the magazine *Neue Rundschau,* owned and edited by Samuel Fischer. There it was published in 1897. What readers of the story did not realize, either then or more recently, is that the secret theme of forbidden love was at the heart of Mann's creativity. Recognizing the young author's talents, Fischer not only wanted Mann to write a collection of stories for him, but also requested a longer prose work. So it was that Mann began

Buddenbrooks, his first and most successful novel. This in turn marked the beginning of the collaboration between Mann and the Fischer publishing house that would last until the author's death and beyond—even today, Fischer remains the principal publisher for Mann's texts.

Begun in Palestrina, Italy, in 1898, *Buddenbrooks* was finished in Munich in May 1900. When Mann sent the manuscript to Fischer, he insured the package for 1000 Marks, as it was the only copy in existence. Initially Fischer did not want to publish such a lengthy book, but the author refused to compromise on length. *Buddenbrooks* appeared initially in two volumes in 1901. More than one million copies were sold in a little over a year. Being a writer might bring an extraordinary, privileged existence, but fame and artistic talent did not free Mann from ordinary life and the concomitant social responsibilities. Mann had to begin his obligatory military service in October 1900. However, after only three weeks of service with an infantry regiment, he ended up in the barracks hospital, suffering from foot pain that resulted from having fallen arches. He was discharged from military service by the end of the year, based on the testimony he secured from his mother's doctor, and settled down in Munich where he was to have his primary residence for the next three decades.

One year earlier, at the end of 1899, Mann had met the brothers Carl and Paul Ehrenberg. His affection for the younger Paul, a painter, lasted until 1903. That Mann was attracted to him and suffered secretly from unfulfilled desires, sexual frustrations, and his submission to bourgeois morality, is indicated in notebook entries. From a letter to Heinrich Mann we know that at the beginning of 1901 Mann was unhappy: "Really dreadful depression with quite serious plans for self-elimination have alternated with an indescribable, pure, and unexpected inner joy, with experiences that cannot be told" (*HM/TM* 46). That Mann was attempting to resist his homosexual disposition became apparent when he spent April 1901 with his brother Heinrich in Italy. During that time he met Mary Smith, an English woman whom he, albeit briefly, considered as a candidate for marriage. Was Paul Ehrenberg the obstacle to commitment, or was it Miss Smith's lack of money and social status? Mann expressed doubts about marrying a foreigner. But these doubts might have been nothing more than a pretense for shunning a conventional relationship.[2] Mann's literary production of the early 1900s echoes his feeling of exclusion from a normal life. Again, notebook entries from that time, which markedly establish connections between fictional characters and Mann himself, provide invaluable insights into his technique of privately disclosing while publically concealing his homosexuality. The relationship to Paul Ehrenberg had cooled off by the summer of 1903. Contact was infrequent and brief over the subsequent decades, but Mann never forgot his infatuation.

6

Paul Ehrenberg will surface in the fictional character of Rudi Schwerdtfeger in *Doctor Faustus*.

By the end of 1903, the success of *Buddenbrooks* had assured Mann a steady income. He was established as a respected, well-known author. Life took a new direction when he met the twenty-year-old Katia Pringsheim, the daughter of the wealthy mathematics professor Alfred Pringsheim and his wife Hedwig. Katia attended university and studied mathematics, unusual for a woman in those days. She had even planned to pursue her doctorate when Mann appeared in her life and fell in love with her. He called her his queen, and pursued her unrelentingly. Initially reluctant to commit herself, she finally agreed to marry him, because, as she later pointed out in her memoirs, she wished to have children. After a brief engagement they were married in February 1905. Whether Mann would have wooed the intelligent, beautiful Katia had she not been the daughter of a wealthy and well-known family, is debatable. With the generous financial help of his father-in-law the newlyweds were able to live a comfortable life. Their marriage, which lasted until Mann's death, allowed him to enter the world of Germany's educated middle class and reconciled him with the world of his father. It brought him a form of bourgeois integration that was to protect him against a socially marginalized existence. However, this marriage, which between 1905 and 1919 resulted in the birth of six children, came at a high price: his renunciation of homosexual love. Why did Mann pay the price of love for a bourgeois life that was, to some extent, a facade? The reward for his submission to a conventional existence was the appeasement of his bourgeois conscience, fame, and, ultimately, recognition as the national representative of the arts for all of Germany.

Mann's commitment to a bourgeois life brought further tensions with his older brother. Heinrich saw in his brother's need for bourgeois recognition, his discipline, and in his marriage to Katia Pringsheim and its ensuing bourgeois life-style, a betrayal of his art. The fact that he did not attend Thomas's and Katia's wedding is a telling one. Thomas countered Heinrich's disapproval by questioning his brother's artistic discipline and his frequent, detailed depictions of sexuality as a means to boost his literary success. At the same time, Thomas agreed to some extent with Heinrich's criticisms. In stories written right after his marriage, "Wälsungenblut" ("The Blood of the Walsungs") and "Schwere Stunde" ("Harsh Hour"), Thomas expressed his doubts about bourgeois existence, and wondered what negative impact it might have upon his artistic creativity. He also voiced these doubts to Heinrich in a letter dated June 1906: "Without a wife and child things would go better [artistically]" (*HM/TM* 83). But we cannot always trust Mann's statements in his letters. For example, in this particular case, he seems to have been trying to strike a conciliatory tone. Mann's relationship to his bourgeois world and family life was always ambivalent. During the first few years of his marriage, Mann often experienced poor health, but the symptoms indicate psychosomatic causes and an inner rebellion against his new life. Nonetheless, seeming to confirm his commitment to just such a life, more children arrived in the following years: Klaus in 1906, Golo in 1909, and Monika in 1910.

Suffering from sexual repression and the search for liberation from that suffering were an essential part of Mann's flight into art when he began writing. Writing compensated for what life denied him. Moreover, Mann wanted the world, though unaware of his secrets, to love and admire him, and respect the outsider. Fulfillment of these ambitions would require extraordinary artistic achievements—and these did not come easily. Mann's artistic creativity was in a crisis after the completion of *Tonio Kröger* as he felt challenged to match or even surpass the high artistic level of *Buddenbrooks*. Plans abounded. A novel about German society, tentatively entitled "Maya" or "The Beloved" and inspired by Mann's problematic relationship to Paul Ehrenberg, never developed beyond preliminary notes. *Fiorenza*, Mann's only drama, completed briefly before his marriage and centering on the theme of the outsider's exclusion from life, was a failure. Mann wanted to write a "masterpiece," as he had mentioned to his brother Heinrich at the end of 1905 (*HM/TM* 76), and had contemplated writing a novel on Frederick the Great that he hoped would gain him the position of national poet laureate. A few notes from early 1906 suggest a project about a homoerotic, unmarried king distanced from life. The novel would thus serve as a counterpoint to Mann's own integrated, married bourgeois life. It was never written. Instead he turned to *Royal Highness*, which he had begun planning as early as 1903 and which would be one of Mann's few narratives that appears to end happily. An essay on aesthetics, "Geist und Kunst" (Intellect and art) written mostly in 1909 and conceived as an ambitious project in the vein of Friedrich von Schiller's *On the Naïve and Sentimental in Poetry*, never made it past a collection of notes. The next project, the novel *Bekenntnisse des Hochstaplers Felix Krull* (*Confessions of Felix Krull, Confidence Man*), begun in 1910, remained a fragment. The intended masterpiece would came, finally, with *Der Tod in Venedig*.

Doubts about his life as husband, father, and artist can be traced throughout Mann's work from the first decade of the 1900s. But in these works there is also a sense that, for the sake of art, he had made the right choice. In *Royal Highness*, when the heir to the throne bestows his representational duties upon the younger brother, one can discern Mann's own feelings of superiority toward his brother.

By 1910 Mann had achieved eminence as a writer; he could count on steady royalties from his work and, from an external perspective, he led a fulfilled, integrated existence as husband and father. His life was highly disciplined, structured around a set, daily routine. He wrote in the mornings from nine o'clock to noon, then took a walk with his dog, then read and kept up with his correspondence in the afternoons. Interruptions were not tolerated in the mornings and not welcomed in the afternoons. A more social life followed in the evenings. Frequently Mann read to family and visitors from his works. The invention of the gramophone allowed him to devote many of his evenings listening to music, above all to Wagner. To his children he was a loving yet remote father. While not involved in their everyday lives and tasks, he liked to play games with them and entertain them with stories. Running the household was left to Katia.

Bad news came in 1910 when Mann's mother, who was by then living a secluded life in Polling, a small Bavarian town, called to inform Mann that his sister Carla had committed suicide. Carla was twenty-nine and had ended her life after several failed attempts to become an actress and the end of a relationship from which she had expected to acquire a respected, bourgeois life. Her fate later reappears in *Doctor Faustus* in that of the fictional character Inez Rodde. Unlike his sister, Thomas enjoyed the stability and bourgeois security of the summer house in Bad Tölz, a luxurious apartment in Munich, and a big household with four children and three servants. By 1910 he was a respected author with a schedule kept busy by demands for public appearances. Mann could meet these demands because Katia freed him from domestic and other daily concerns. But, with the birth of four children in five years, her health had suffered. Consequently, Mann decided to take her on a vacation in 1911 that would take them first to a seaside resort along the Dalmatian coast and then to Venice, a vacation that inspired Mann to write his most famous novella, *Death in Venice*. A longer visit to a Davos sanatorium in 1912 would serve as further rest from her daily duties— and would lead to another of Mann's fictional texts, *The Magic Mountain*. When Katia spent the beginning of 1914 in Arosa, Switzerland, Mann himself had to oversee the move into the new house on Poschinger Strasse in Munich, a stately home representative of his bourgeois success, a residence that his father would have surely been proud of.

In the meantime, the tensions in the troubled relationship between Thomas and Heinrich were heightened with the outbreak of the First World War. Mann defended bourgeois humanistic culture and the German administrative political system, while his older brother had become a staunch defender of French bourgeois democracy. Indirectly, Thomas accused Heinrich of dogmatism in an essay written at the beginning of the war, "Gedanken im Kriege" ("Thoughts in War")

(1914). Heinrich responded with "Zola" (1915), an essay on the French writer Emile Zola (1840–1902) and a defense of western-style democracies. This essay deepened the gap between them. During the following years the brothers avoided all contact with each other, even when in the same room. Their reconciliation in 1922, brought about when Heinrich became seriously ill, could only partially patch up the long-lasting discord between the two brothers.

The years between 1914 and 1918 are marked by the absence of literary publication. Thomas Mann was occupied with *Betrachtungen eines Unpolitischen* (*Reflections of a Nonpolitical Man*), a defense of German culture. The novels he had begun before the war, *Confessions of Felix Krull* and *The Magic Mountain*, would have to wait. Coming to terms with his own beliefs and orientation was one reason for writing *Reflections* in a time when the future of his world was no longer certain. Being the spokesperson for bourgeois culture and a representative of his time was another reason. When the end of the war came, and with it the collapse of the German monarchy, Mann took temporary refuge in writing fiction, the humorous work *Herr und Hund* (*A Man and His Dog*). Events in his personal life promoted another diversion. In 1918, Katia gave birth to their third daughter, Elisabeth, who inspired Mann to write the idyllic short narrative *Gesang vom Kindchen* (*Song of a Child*), written in verse form. This late and unexpected return to fatherhood, which brought Mann immense happiness, was followed by another birth, that of his son Michael in 1919.

Germany's defeat in 1918 did not result in the end of bourgeois culture in Germany despite various attempts to establish left-wing governments. During this period Mann's prestige grew, perhaps a sign both of the Germans' need for ideological security and of a recognition of the values of bourgeois-humanistic culture in those politically chaotic times. Mann was awarded an honorary doctorate by the University of Bonn in 1919. The diaries from 1918–1921 reveal a multifaceted personality. Mann hovered between nihilism, ideological noncommitment, emotional outbursts against western-style democracies, and for Russian communism (*TB 1918–1921* 178). But conservative leanings also resonate throughout these diaries. Noticeably, they express no nostalgia about the loss of monarchy, thus indicating Mann's openness to the new world that came with the creation of the Weimar Republic. Triggered by the assassination of Germany's foreign minister Walther Rathenau in 1922, Mann recognized the importance of a plea for humanism and democracy. The speech "Von deutscher Republik" ("The German Republic") is such a plea. While politically vague, full of literary references, and certainly not written to appeal to the general public but rather to Mann's peers, its intention is clear: to support the young republic and a democratic Germany guided by the principles of bourgeois humanism and culture, as represented by Goethe and the Age of Enlightenment, and whose carriers Mann saw in the educated German middle class.

By the second half of the 1920s, largely due to the critical success of *The Magic Mountain*, Mann, now in his fifties, was recognized nationally and internationally as Germany's leading writer. To fortify his preeminent position and reputation, Mann undertook many public appearances, read from his works, and gave numerous speeches throughout Germany and in neighboring European countries. He observed with concern the growing support for National Socialism. Mann saw himself as a critical voice and guiding light for his nation, an authority that was reinforced when he became the recipient of the Nobel Prize for Literature in 1929. In 1930 he used his authority as the preeminent representative of German culture to make yet another strong political statement. In *"Deutsche Ansprache: Ein Apell an die Vernunft"* ("An Appeal to Reason") he argued that art can show the way to a better society, but that this leadership no longer suffices to battle the antihumanistic, irrational movement of the National Socialists. He told his audience "that the political place of the German citizen is today with the Social-Democratic Party" if Germany is to have any hope of guaranteeing the survival of "freedom, culture, or intellectual well-being" (*OD* 67). This sentence marks a drastic departure from *Reflections*, in which Mann had presented an aristocratic-conservative German world as the sole guarantor of German culture. However, his goal remained the same: the preservation of bourgeois culture. Is it selfishness that made him defend a social-democratic agenda? Is it his contempt for what he denounced in 1931 as the "ruinous power of the mob" (*GW 12* 661) or his political sensibility that made him recognize the dangers of National Socialism and the need for political action? All of the above can be considered valid reasons.

After his lecture titled "Leiden und Größe Richard Wagners" ("The Sufferings and Greatness of Richard Wagner"), delivered on 10 February 1933, commemorating the fiftieth anniversary of the composer's death, Mann left with Katia on a lecture tour that took him to Amsterdam, Brussels, and Paris. It ended with a vacation in Arosa, Switzerland, where the couple arrived on 24 February. News about arrests and violence in Munich following Hitler's rise to power on 30 January 1933, coupled with warnings from Erika and Klaus and friends in Germany not to return back home for a while, led the Manns to decide to extend their stay in Switzerland. What they did not know at this time was that their long exile had now begun. A search of Mann's house in Poschinger Strasse took place in April, and his cars were taken by Nazi authorities. From an extant letter to an official dated July 1933 and signed by Reinhard Heydrich (at that time chief of the political police in Munich), we know that an arrest order for Mann's deportation to the concentration camp at Dachau had been issued by the Munich political police, probably in April. In August the Manns' house was confiscated. The painful loss of home, and with it the loss of many dear personal items, would be followed three years later by a loss of German national identity. Mann and his family were stripped of their German citizenship in 1936.

When it became obvious that their return to Germany was not in their best interests, Mann was shocked, depressed, and angry. The life he had constructed so carefully and with so much self-denial, was being dismantled. The forces of antireason and regression, against which he had fought for a decade, had won out. Support from his main audience, the educated middle class, had dissipated. He felt betrayed when some of them turned publicly against him in an editorial from the newspaper *Münchner Neuesten Nachrichten* titled "Protest der Richard-Wagner-Stadt München" ("Protest from Richard Wagner's City of Munich"), accusing him of belittling Wagner in his lecture. Among those signing the protest were highly respected representatives of German cultural life: the conductor, and instigator of the protest, Hans Knappertsbusch, and the composers Hans Pfitzner and Richard Strauss. Deeply hurt and in despair, Mann nonetheless did not respond openly at that time. He had good reasons for not doing so. His fate and that of his family remained uncertain. The Nazi authorities had not officially banned him from Germany. His house then was still his; the first part of the *Joseph* tetralogy was scheduled for publication in Germany. Mann did not want to lose those readers awaiting his new work.

Yet, fearing for the worst, actions were initiated to salvage whatever they could from their home in Munich. Erika, still in Munich at the time, was able to retrieve the manuscripts of the Joseph novels, as well as some other materials, and bring them to Switzerland. Some of their furniture, such as Mann's desk and most of the other items from his study—including Ludwig von Hofmann's *Die Quelle* (The fountain), an oil painting of three nude young men bathing in a fountain that hung in Mann's various studies from 1914 until his death—were brought to Switzerland. Mann was in agony; the family's German passports were set to expire on 3 April, valuable documents were still at Poschinger Strasse: above all his diaries written over decades, none of which he intended to ever be read by any of his family members and which he was anxious should not fall into the hands of the Nazis. Golo was sent to the house with instructions not to open the diaries and to pack them up. He heeded his father's request, but the Manns' chauffeur—unbeknownst to them, a spy for the Nazis—took charge of the suitcase containing the valuable cargo. Whether it was inspected by Nazi officials in Munich is unclear. It was, however, opened at the Swiss border, and some documents—contracts with Mann's publisher—were sent to Munich for investigation before the suitcase was returned. The diaries were deemed manuscripts, and thus of no political importance. Finally, a month after Golo had entrusted the suitcase to the chauffeur, it arrived in Switzerland, to Mann's great relief.

The beginning of the Manns' long exile was restless and full of uncertainties. After a brief stay in France where other German writers and intellectuals had found refuge—among them Lion Feuchtwanger, Walter Benjamin, and Heinrich Mann—Thomas and Katia Mann returned to Switzerland, their youngest children with them. The older ones were also safe outside Germany. Financially, the Manns were, unlike many other émigrés, financially secure, as some of their money, including half of the sum received for the Nobel Prize, had been deposited in a Swiss bank account before 1933. Their loss, in the end, amounted to about half of their pre-1933 assets. They were able to rent a stately house in Küsnacht near Zurich. Soon they could even afford a car and maids, and were able to recreate the world to which they were accustomed. With some of his furniture and books from Munich retrieved, Mann was able to resume his daily routine and life as a man of letters, in an environment similar to the one he had been forced to leave behind. The Manns lived in Küsnacht for nearly five years. Despite all uncertainties and upheavals, the loss of security and an unknown future, Mann finished the third volume of the *Joseph* tetralogy by 1936. He had lost his home in Munich, much of his audience, and the dream of the German nation he had imagined in his speeches would become a reality during the Weimar Republic. But he could once again cling to the world dearest to him: he found a home in writing, in both his fiction and in the daily devotion to his diary.

Even his busy life as a public speaker continued. At the suggestion of his American publisher, Alfred Knopf, Mann undertook his first visit to the United States in May 1934. Other engagements, taking him to Prague and Vienna, followed. An invitation from Harvard University to bestow an honorary doctorate of letters on him led to a second voyage to America in June 1935. In the laudation Mann was praised as "one of the few contemporary guardians of the great tradition of German culture."[3] Eschewed in Germany, the exiled, homeless author must have found this international accolade particularly gratifying, especially since it was followed by an invitation from the White House and a meeting with President Franklin Roosevelt and his wife Eleanor. But, while being celebrated as Germany's most famous exiled citizen, Mann came increasingly under attack from other exiled writers, and even from his older children, Erika and Klaus, because he did not publicly condemn Hitler's regime and its reign of terror and intolerance. When Mann finally broke his silence, he did so cautiously at first. His criticism, voiced against the regime among family and friends and in his diaries, became public in "Achtung, Europa" ("Europe Beware"),[4] a speech he had planned to present in Nice in April 1935. Instead, he asked that it be read in his absence in French, because he neither wanted to compromise his German publisher nor endanger the publication of his works in Germany and so lose contact with his loyal readers. He still cherished hopes that his literature, voicing the need for love, humanity, and tolerance, might be a force of resistance to the reign of irrationality and antihumanism in Nazi Germany.

"Europe Beware" never mentions German National Socialism or Hitler; but, as Mann had anticipated, his criticism of primitive mass movements, irrationalism, and anti-intellectualism, of the perversion of truth and morality, was received as a critique of Nazi Germany. Hence, in an open letter from February 1936, published in a Zurich newspaper, Mann no longer shied away from explicitly mentioning Germany as a nation from which, in its present state, no good could come. He concluded the letter with a quotation from a poem by August Graf von Platen (1796–1835): "Better far to quit one's land for ever / Than under sway of breed so infantine / To tolerate the yoke of blind mob hate."[5] This was an unequivocal affirmation of exile and clear separation from Germany, underscored by Mann's acceptance of Czech citizenship in November 1936, a formal national identity that allowed him to travel. As expected, Mann's German citizenship was officially revoked by German authorities soon thereafter. In response to the retraction of his honorary doctorate from the University of Bonn in December 1936, following his expatriation, Mann expressed his pride at having been recognized by others to represent "the high dignity of German culture" (*GW 12* 786). Distancing himself from a bellicose Germany under National Socialism, Mann accused the dean of the University of Bonn: "You have the unbelievable audacity to mistake yourself for Germany!" (*GW 12* 789) Germany was now wherever Mann was.

After this open break with Nazi Germany, Mann no longer had to hide his opinions of the Nazi regime, and he made sure to voice them during the years that followed in hundreds of public speeches and lectures, prefaces to various works, diverse statements, and in radio addresses to German listeners broadcast by the BBC between October 1940 and the end of 1945.[6] Mann, now in his sixties, had no intention of withdrawing from public life, as had Herman Hesse (1877–1962) and other émigrés who had found refuge in Switzerland. After two further stays in the United States in April 1937 and February 1938, the Manns decided to move there in September 1938. They could rely on the help of Mann's admirer, Agnes E. Meyer, wife of the wealthy, influential publisher and owner of the *Washington Post*, Eugene Meyer. Her connections became a vital asset to Mann. She arranged for him to secure a post as lecturer in the humanities at

Princeton University from 1938 to 1940, a duty that obliged him to give a few lectures in exchange for a modest salary. Most of his income at that time came from speeches that he gave in Europe and throughout North America. Without a doubt, Mann became the most visible and famous German émigré, and was invited to the White House again in January 1941. In the same year he was offered the position of Consultant in German Literature at the Library in Congress in Washington, D.C., a position that he held from 1941 to 1944.

After initially residing in Princeton, the Manns decided to move to Pacific Palisades, near Los Angeles, in 1941. There they joined familiar company. The Los Angeles area had become a sanctuary for many exiled German writers and intellectuals, including Theodor W. Adorno (1903–1969), who a few years later would advise Mann on musical theory for his novel *Doctor Faustus*. Building a new, spacious house to make up for the loss of their Munich residence and becoming American citizens in 1944 were part of the Manns' reconstruction of a new existence. Mann liked America for its openness, its wide landscapes, its youthful mentality, and its democracy.[7] Conversely, America liked and welcomed him wherever he appeared. The loss of his audience at home was compensated by the enormous crowds that would be drawn to his public lectures after his arrival in the United States. The well-filled auditoriums, such as the Wilshire Theater in Los Angeles and Madison Square Garden in New York, gave Mann a satisfaction that compensated for his betrayal by the educated burghers in Germany. He spoke out against Nazi Germany and against anti-Semitism. For example, his speech "The Fall of the European Jews," in which he drew attention to the ongoing extermination of European Jewry, attracted an audience of ten thousand in San Francisco in June 1943. Mann enjoyed the attention, but his diary entries also reveal that he sometimes undertook the strenuous lecture series with reluctance.

Fulfilling his numerous social obligations and public engagements, organizing his lecture tours, and keeping his financial accounts was no easy task. For the more mundane aspects of his life Mann had a reliable staff that was recruited mainly from his own family, and who selflessly served his needs.[8] Above all, he could count on the support of his wife Katia and his daughter Erika, which allowed him to live his representational existence as Germany's most honored émigré.[9] Occasionally, Katia even had to fill in as driver. Also of assistance was Golo Mann, who had joined them after an adventurous escape from France over the Pyrenees via Spain to Portugal with Mann's brother Heinrich in late summer 1940.[10] Exile brought the family together. All of Mann's six children were able to enter the United States. Heinrich came to live near Thomas Mann in western Los Angeles. Yet their relationship, while friendly on the outside, continued to be strained on Thomas's side despite the fact that their common enemy, Nazi Germany, had closed some of the ideological gaps that had separated them for decades.

Heinrich Mann's fate was less fortunate than that of his famous brother. Given his limited command of English, there was little he could do professionally in America. His initial contract as a screenwriter for Hollywood productions was not renewed. His novels and stories were unknown outside Europe, and his leftist ideas did not find public appeal. Financially, he was dependent upon Thomas. Neither Thomas nor Katia sought his company, to some extent a result of their dislike of Heinrich's wife Nelly, who lacked social graces and was an alcoholic. Thomas could never understand how Heinrich could love Nelly, who was clearly his intellectual and social inferior. Nelly's suicide in December 1944 left Thomas partially relieved, as the financial support he provided for Heinrich was no longer spent by Nelly on alcohol, and because Heinrich was freed from his wife's embarrassing and sometimes cruel behavior. Nonetheless, Heinrich suffered from his solitary existence. It was to come to an end, however, six years later when he was planning to leave for East Berlin to become the president of the Berlin Academy of Arts. The promise of a new life with the concomitant honor and steady income was cut short by a stroke that killed him on 11 March 1951. Thomas, who had lost the rival of his early literary career, was saddened by his brother's death but saw it as the "most merciful solution" (*TB 1949–1950* 175), as Heinrich was by then in very poor health.

As the apparent proponent and defender of German culture, in particular its humanism, in exile, Thomas Mann was recognized as the antithesis of Nazi Germany. However, the extent to which he truly believed in the values of German culture and the level of his engagement for humanism and democracy in the early years of his exile remains unknown. To his diary he divulged: "Democratic idealism. Do I believe in it? Don't I just fancy myself playing a role?" (*TB 1937–1939* 135) In "Bruder Hitler" ("Brother Hitler") from 1939, he invited a comparison between Hitler and the bourgeois artist, i.e. himself. Moreover the fiction from his exile years presents an ambivalent assessment of the artist and his relationship to the world. *Lotte in Weimar* is a highly self-critical novel in which Mann depicts an artist's exploitation of those around him for the sake of his art. It also recaptures an earlier theme and reason for his writing: the sacrifice of love for the sake of art. The guilt of the bourgeois artist lies also at the core of *Doctor Faustus*, a novel specifically about Germany and its descent into National Socialism. It is striking that, despite the many years Mann spent in exile in the United States, none of his fiction, either written there or later back in Europe, includes a story about his American experiences. The young and vast nation, as Mann commented, "is alien to people, provides few cleaving impressions."[11]

Despite doubts about the artist's morality and his failure to establish a better world, Mann did not falter in his public exhortation of democratic and humanistic principles. Relentlessly he called upon Germans during the Second World War to distance themselves from their inhuman leadership. Mann's engagement reflects his underlying belief in the artist as a person of influence, despite his expressed skepticism. In "Schicksal und Aufgabe"—later delivered in a shorten English form as "The War and the Future"—he presents himself as an artist in the service of "the idea of democracy, of humanity, of peace, and of human freedom and dignity."[12] His pledge is noticeably free of political, ideological rhetoric. He did, however, support Roosevelt's reelection as U.S. president in 1944. But this step was the exception rather than the norm. When asked to participate in the "Council for a Democratic Germany," an initiative proposed by the well-respected theologian Paul Tillich, Mann declined. Partaking in a collective endeavor was never to his liking as he primarily wished to voice his own opinions, not those of others, and because he held on to the conviction, expressed earlier in *Reflections*, that humanistic principles can be betrayed all too easily by political goals.

With the end of the war, Mann did not return to his homeland. He was skeptical about de-Nazification and the seemingly instantaneous ideological conversion of the Germans. A lack of interest in personally seeing the physical destruction of Germany and its human cost is also a likely reason for his continuing stay in Southern California. In September 1945, four months after the surrender of Germany, he accused, in an open letter, German writers who had stayed in Nazi Germany of passivity and of indirect complicity. The letter was first published in the New York–based, German-language publication *Aufbau* as "Why I Won't Return to Germany," a title not chosen by Mann. In it, he emphasized that his exile had caused him much suffering—a position that was not understood by the majority of Germans in war-ravaged Germany, most of whom felt themselves to be enduring far greater misery. Neither did the letter find much sympathy among fellow émigrés in the United States.

Mann remained in Pacific Palisades and continued working on *Doctor Faustus*. In contrast, most Germans wanted to forget their recent history. The novel took its toll on Mann. He was emotionally and physically drained; sleeplessness and overall exhaustion plagued him. But his ill health was caused by more than the stress brought on by the novel. In April 1946 he was diagnosed with lung cancer. He was transferred to Billings Hospital in Chicago where he underwent a potentially life-threatening operation. Now nearly seventy-one, he recuperated from the surgery, which cost him a rib and two-thirds of his right lung, amazingly quickly, and was soon able to resume work on the novel, which he finished by the end of January 1947. He did not rest, however. A lecture, "Nietzches Philosophie im Lichte unserer Erfahrung" ("Nietzsche's Philosophy in the Light of Contemporary Events"), first presented in English at the Library of Congress in April 1947, and then in New York, provided the impetus and opportunity for a lecture tour to various cities in Europe. Germany, however, was not on the travel agenda. He did not receive an official invitation, a snub that must have been painful as he had proven his loyalty to Germany throughout his exile. Mann could have visited Germany privately, but he chose not to. The tour ended with a two-month stay in Switzerland where he met many old friends and where both his lecture on Nietzsche and a reading from *Doctor Faustus* were enthusiastically received.

In September 1947 Mann returned to the United States where the anti-communist witch-hunt, initiated by the House Un-American Activities Committee, had begun. Unbeknownst to Mann, he too was on the committee's black list. The following year, 1948, was relatively quiet for Mann. To defend himself against accusations that the passages on music in *Doctor Faustus* were mainly conceived by Theodor W. Adorno, Mann embarked on unfolding the genesis of the novel in *Die Entstehung des Doktor Faustus: Roman eines Romans* (*The Story of a Novel: The Genesis of "Dr. Faustus"*). Later that year, he started a new project, *Der Erwählte* (*The Holy Sinner*). Progress was slow. Diary entries and letters reveal that after the completion of *Doctor Faustus* Mann doubted that he could rekindle the artistic inspiration and creativity that had brought about his masterpieces. Skepticism regarding the new project, coupled with numerous external, disconcerting occurrences made writing difficult. The first disruption came with Mann's decision to visit Europe again. When he planned his lecture tour for 1949, he considered several European nations, including England, Sweden, Denmark, and Switzerland; but the divided Germany was still excluded. When both Frankfurt in West Germany and Weimar in East Germany offered to bestow the Goethe Prize on him, he was initially undecided whether he should accept the honors. His reticence to visit Frankfurt was fueled by the hostility of many West German critics that had resulted in part because he had looked upon those artists and intellectuals who had stayed in Germany during the Nazi years with suspicion, and had presented Germany as a devilish nation in *Doctor Faustus*. Travel to Weimar in the East of the divided nation was equally unappealing because, in the prevailing climate of anticommunist hysteria in the United States, it would further American criticism against him. In the end, he went to both cities.

Another disconcerting event slowed down work on *The Holy Sinner*. While in Sweden, on 21 May, Thomas and Katia Mann received the news that their son Klaus had committed suicide in Cannes. The diary entry marking this tragic death reports: "He should not have done that to them" (*TB 1949–1950* 57). "Them" refers to Katia and Erika. Mann judged his son's suicide as an act of cruelty, of irresponsibility, and lack of consideration toward others. Klaus's repeated suicide attempts, his drug addiction, and other personal problems had burdened the family for years. Mann did not disrupt his lecture plans, and only their son Michael attended the funeral.

Reminiscent of the admiration Mann enjoyed as national poet laureate during the Weimar Republic, large and cheering crowds came to welcome him in Frankfurt and Weimar. But after an absence of sixteen years, the honors he received and the success of his lectures could not erase the fact that he had become alienated from the nation that had turned against him in 1933. Doubts concerning the success of de-Nazification in the West, and misgivings about totalitarian communism in the name of humanism in the East amplified his feelings of distance from both Germanys. But when Mann returned to the United States, a sense of alienation and disenchantment about American democracy also became gradually apparent. The frantic hunt for communists and communist sympathizers had increasingly poisoned the political atmosphere. Mann's visit to East Germany had raised suspicions, leading to his denouncement as a communist. He was angered and became frightened by the misunderstandings, reoccurring suspicions, and denunciations, and especially by the hearings and investigations by the FBI and the House Un-American Activities Committee, whose existence he deemed to reflect a growing fascist mentality. With the rising political tensions between East and West and the onset of the cold war era, Mann felt forced to curtail public expressions of his political views.

Nonetheless, he continued to make plans for lectures in the United States and Europe. But the Library of Congress, where Mann intended to give his by now traditional annual speech, turned him down. The FBI dossier on Mann, growing ever more extensive since his visit to the GDR, made the Library of Congress fearful that Mann's lecture would alienate members of Congress and thus compromise the reputation of the library. Mann was, however, welcomed at the University of Chicago, and a few days later in New York, where he called upon the United States to take the initiative for a global peace conference. After New York, the Manns left for Europe. Successful appearances in Scandinavia and France were followed by a long vacation in Switzerland. In July 1950 Mann stayed in the Hotel Dolder in Zurich, near the clinic where Katia Mann would receive treatment for varicose veins. There he would encounter the waiter Franz

Westermeier, and this encounter would provide a welcome diversion from the political and ideological conflicts on both sides of the Atlantic Ocean. A diary entry testifies to the unexpected resurgence of Mann's homosexual desires. Mann did not show his emotions, aware of the necessity to keep the secret (*TB 1949–50* 213–15). Nonetheless, Mann would add Westermeier to the gallery of clandestine beloved (along with Paul Ehrenberg and others)—a gallery now opened to the public through the publication of the diaries. At that time Mann was still unsure whether he should destroy the diaries and reveal his secret, or whether to take it to his grave (*TB 1949–1950* 255). His need to tell the world, as we know, won out over his bourgeois concerns.

The Manns soon returned to the United States, where Mann resumed his daily regimen of writing. His "enthusiasm for the young-masculine" (*TB 1949–50* 257) dominated his thoughts: "complete preoccupation with passions, heartache that can only be relieved through fiction somewhat" (*TB 1949–50* 253). His escape into fiction—the novel *The Holy Sinner*—to compensate for what he was forced to deny himself throughout his whole life, could, however, not eliminate his worries about the hunt for communists under Senator Joseph McCarthy, about imperialistic American foreign policies, the threat of nuclear war, and the U.S. involvement in southeast Asia. The Manns considered selling their house in Pacific Palisades and moving once again, this time to Switzerland. The appearance of his name on a list published by the House Un-American Activities Committee in April 1951, only renewed these considerations. In June, the Manns left for an extended visit to Europe, returning to Southern California in October. The following year, at the end of June 1952, they again left for Europe, this time never to return.

One decisive factor in their decision to resettle in Switzerland was Erika's precarious situation. Because of her radical views, the U.S. government was unlikely to grant her, a British citizen, an extension of her visa. Thomas and Katia Mann did not want to live without their oldest child.[13] Over the years, Erika had become involved in her father's work as editor, adjutant, administrator, and manager of his affairs. Mann's thoughts about his death and his wish to be buried in Switzerland were another factor. Arriving in Switzerland, the Manns lived in various places until they settled down in their final residence at Kilchberg near Zurich in 1954.

Between 1952 and his death in August 1955, Mann finished *Die Betrogene* (*The Black Swan*), published the fragmentary novel *Confessions of Felix Krull, Confidence Man* (hereafter referred to as *Confessions*), and made plans for a play on Martin Luther's marriage. Unremittingly, Mann kept up his customary daily schedule: creative writing in the mornings; correspondence, reading, and listening to recorded music in the afternoons and evenings. Public readings and appearances, speeches, and ceremonies to receive national and international awards kept his life full of activities until the end. His diary reveals that he often suffered from exhaustion, depression, and doubts about his creative powers. A sense of loneliness gripped him at times, as all his siblings and many of his friends from his exile years, including Alfred Einstein (1880–1952), were dead.

His last completed work was an essay on Friedrich Schiller. A shorter version was presented as a lecture in Stuttgart and in Weimar in May 1955 to commemorate the 150th anniversary of Schiller's death. After Weimar, Mann's hometown Lübeck was the next travel destination. At the beginning of his speech there, he could not refrain from ribbing his audience by pointing out that he had not forgotten the criticism *Buddenbrooks* had garnered in the city, but that he nevertheless felt honored to be able to return to his roots. He went on to voice his regrets that most of his friends, teachers, and acquaintances were no longer alive, but, above all, that his father, who was so concerned that his son might not become a valuable and productive citizen, could not witness how he, Thomas Mann, the internationally renowned man of letters, was now being honored by the city of Lübeck. In evoking his father's image more than sixty years after his death, Mann once again underscored his closeness to the bourgeois world, whose humanistic values, discipline, and work ethic he endorsed all his life by sub-scribing to a life of self-discipline and self-denial, even while simultaneously rebelling against it through his art. For his eightieth birthday celebration Mann returned to Kilchberg, where all the members of his family gathered for the last time to honor their patriarch. Over one thousand telegrams, letters, and gifts arrived. A few weeks later, while on vacation in The Netherlands, Mann took ill with thrombosis and was flown to a hospital in Zurich. There he died of compli-cations from arteriosclerosis on 12 August 1955.

CHAPTER 2

Early Stories

When Mann's first collection of short stories, titled *Der kleine Herr Friedemann* (*Little Herr Friedemann*), was published in 1898, the young author was praised for his precise language and his detailed psychological portraits of his characters and of their social milieu.[1] Yet some critics were disturbed by the rebellious character of the stories that stirred readers up from their comfortable lives and challenged their beliefs and orientations. Characters who are sick or crippled, emotionally and physically dysfunctional, often ridiculous figures sarcastically drawn to undermine bourgeois values populate Mann's early literary landscape. Wretched or unrequited love and alienation from society were themes with which Mann articulated the experiences of his youth, and simultaneously his generation's growing pains and resentments against the world of their fathers. Critics disagreed on the literary merits of these early stories, but everybody sensed the arrival of a new voice in the German literary world.

In 1893, at the age of eighteen, Mann published his first prose, a brief sketch titled "Vision" (Vision), in a school paper he himself edited. The first person narrator, most likely a writer, feels the warm evening air entering his room. Stimulated by his senses, he has a vision of a dazzling tablecloth embellished with leaves and flowers atop of which stands a crystal goblet with golden ornaments, a hand resting around its bottom. The hand brings up painful memories of bygone love and passion. The vision fades, but its powerful impact remains. Mann's narrator has regenerated his knowledge that he once was loved by a woman; furthermore, he has regained the ability to cry. The vision, referred to as an "accidental artwork" (*GW 8* 9), has a cathartic function.

In fact, this sketch about early sorrows and Mann's fascination for the creative imagination, surprisingly well written for a beginner, deserves mention because it provides valuable insights into Mann's response to the literary climate at the time and his search for his own literary voice. He dedicated "Vision" to Hermann Bahr (1863–1934), the outstanding exponent of Viennese modernism in the 1890s, whose essays on the French symbolists and whose call for a new, antinaturalistic literature impressed young writers of the day. Bahr asserted that the bourgeois age of time-honored values and traditions was over and that sensibility should replace rationality. One of Bahr's central themes, presented in his 1890 essay "Zur Kritik der Moderne" (Criticism of modernism) and the subsequent 1891 essay "Die Überwindung des Naturalismus" (Overcoming Naturalism), is the suspension of the chasm between *Geist* (spirit or intellect) and *Leben* (life), a chasm Mann would make his primary theme throughout his literary career. According to Bahr, this suspension is possible if the artist practices what he calls *Nervenkunst* (nerve art). Nerves are transmitters and the most sensitive seismograph of the outside world. The artist must allow the nerves, which receive and transmit messages from life around the artist to the artist, to function as a bridge that connects reality with the intellect. Mann's "Vision" is a fictional rendering of this process.

The antibourgeois attitude of the symbolists intrigued Mann. It supported him in his own resistance against the mundane world of his Hanseatic merchant ancestors, a world driven by economic concerns and a stern morality. Over four decades later, in his Princeton lecture "On Myself," Mann referred to the strong influence of the Viennese school of symbolism on his first literary experiments. However, what Mann does not mention is that "Vision" is inspired by yet another source, the 1892 poem "Die Hand" (The hand) by his brother Heinrich. Mann's adaptation of identical phrases and images for his sketch is not, as one might assume, an indication that he plagiarized his older brother's work due to his own lack of creative talent. More likely, it is an homage to his brother's admired artistic talents. Also, and more importantly, the younger Thomas sends a signal to Heinrich that he, Thomas, can improve on the same aesthetic subject.[2] Respect and disrespect for his brother's talent are thus intertwined.

While Mann continued to share the antibourgeois sentiments of the symbolists, he freed himself soon from Bahr's *Nervenkunst* as his first short story "Gefallen" (Fallen), originally published in the journal *Die Gesellschaft* in late 1894, attests. He wrote the story while working as an unpaid trainee at an insurance company in Munich. "Gefallen" follows in the footsteps of bourgeois realism and is written in a narrative style that tells a story within a story, a style Mann was certainly familiar with from tales by the German writer Theodor Storm (1817–1888) and the Swiss author Conrad Ferdinand Meyer (1825–1898). The story, which functions as a framing device, introduces us to a segment of German society that will provide the core of Mann's fiction thereafter: artists and the educated German burghers. In "Gefallen," a group of four men—the artist Meysenberg, the liberal economist Laube, the physician Dr. Selten, and an unidentified first person narrator—gather at Meysenberg's art studio whose oriental carpets and faded silk drapes indicate a bourgeois setting with a bohemian atmosphere, a world somewhere between bourgeois respectability and antibourgeois rebellion.

The story juxtaposes Selten, a cynic whose experiences have left him with nothing but ironic contempt for the world, with the economist Laube, whose name recalls to mind the liberal writer Heinrich Rudolf Laube (1806–1884). Laube is an idealistic liberal who lashes out at the rigid, nonemancipatory norms and misogynist conventions of bourgeois society. In reaction to Laube's criticism that men can take sexual licenses while sexually free women are ostracized as "fallen" women, Selten tells his three friends a story about a good-hearted, twenty-year-old man.

The story starts out as one about sexual frustrations and unfulfilled love. The young man is controlled by his secret passions for the actress Irma Weltner. He finally dares to approach her; a love affair ensues. Mann has the young man briefly contemplate whether he is a "scoundrel" (*GW 8* 30) as he is enjoying his noncommittal affair with the actress. His love for her comes to an abrupt end when he finds in her apartment an old man whose drooling mouth and overall physical unattractiveness are the very first testimony to Mann's talent for satire and mockery of bourgeois society. The young man realizes that Irma Welten sells her body to upper class men. He leaves, his love turned into hate and cynicism. After Selten has finished his story, he identifies himself as the young man of the story.

With Selten, Mann unmasks the double standards of bourgeois society. Selten accepts a woman's sexual emancipation as long as he is its beneficiary. The readers recognize Selten's blind spot. He applies patriarchal standards with his claim that his lover is his object of desire exclusively, while it is only the freedom from these standards that make his uncommitted relationship to Irma Welten possible. The lesson Selten wants to convey with his story is: "When a woman today falls for love, tomorrow she will fall for money" (*GW 8* 42). This is not the lesson that Mann wants his readers to learn, as he challenges Selten's judgment with an array of perspectives. Irma Welten justifies her prostitution with economic necessity. She argues that only the rich can have morality, while she cannot afford to be a "saint" (*GW 8* 40). Does "Gefallen," therefore, endorse a woman's sexual emancipation? Yes and no. We are encouraged to share the young man's aversion of the old, drooling, revolting client and to condemn the actress who sells herself to someone like him. The story suggests then that sexual emancipation is debatable. Laube's liberal views, that women should obtain the same sexual freedom as men and his correct assessment that society is full of prejudices against women, seem to take the message of the story in the opposite direction. Yet, Mann undermines Laube's authority as well. He presents his spokesperson for emancipation with humor and distance. Laube's ideological fervor makes him appear biased. Ultimately, a dubious light is thrown on sexual emancipation by its own consequences—the destruction of romantic love—rather than by Mann's ambivalent portrait of Laube.

The title "Gefallen" refers not only to the "fallen woman" who sells her body for money, but also to Selten. His love for Irma Welten is the romantic, idealistic first love of a young man. When his longing for love is fulfilled, he believes in a benevolent God and a supportive, beautiful nature. He regards a lilac bush growing underneath the actress's window as symbolic for this passion and requited love. But when Selten feels betrayed, he turns against God by raising his fist to the sky and by tearing at the lilacs. The bush continues distributing its enticing scent even as love comes and goes. Mann shows that nature is indifferent to the sufferings and disillusionment of the young man. This indifference marks the influence of the anti-idealistic, nihilistic philosophy of Arthur Schopenhauer upon Mann. Like nature, Selten becomes indifferent. He "falls" from a romantic view of love to cynicism.

To reveal Selten's nihilistic perspective, Mann seats his character on a large pew in Meysenberg's art studio. Selten scoffs at this pew continually, underscoring his loss of belief. But, while Selten's story is aimed at explaining and justifying his cynical detachment, his contempt for the world and rejection of love forever, his body language at the end of the story unmask a man quite capable of emotions. After he has told his story, he walks to a vase of lilacs in the studio and inhales their scent. With an "embittered, sad brutality" (*GW 8* 42) he destroys the flowers. This act underlines Selten's turning away from love and emotion, but also uncovers that he is still emotionally involved in the world.

The characterization of the young man's obsessive passion and theatrical behavior are indicative of an inexperienced young writer. However, Mann's evocation of romantic literature with the obvious erotic symbolism of the lilacs and his simultaneous refusal to participate in the optimistic interpretation of the world, typical of romantic literature, disclose both his conscious play with literary tradition and departure from it. Furthermore, "Gefallen" displays central aspects of his later works, such as the play with perspectives, his mocking depiction of the bourgeois world, the clash of bourgeois and antibourgeois values, and the affirmation and renunciation of nihilism. The narrator is part of this fictional world that denies ideological fixation. He remains the most enigmatic character in the story. Always detached, he sides neither with the idealistic Laube nor with the disillusioned Selten, who used to be, in his own words, a perfectly "good fellow" (*GW 8* 14). The narrator is curious to know the facts, and he admires the simplicity and truthfulness of Selten's narrative. But can we trust his judgment when he comments about Selten at the end of the story that traces of the former "good fellow" no longer exist? Selten's crushing of the flowers undermines his words.

The openness with which the narrative ends will become a trademark of Mann's writing.

While "Gefallen" displays the influence of Schopenhauer, it is uncertain to what extent Mann was familiar in the mid-1890s with Schopenhauer's work beyond its principal tenets. Schopenhauer's philosophy, as presented in *The World As Will and Representation* from 1819, is a pessimistic and nihilistic assessment of existence. Existence has no deeper meaning. The driving force of life and the universe is a blind, self-perpetuating will. This cosmic will has power over rationality and intellect and is embodied in sexual desire; it is, as Mann explains later in his Schopenhauer essay from 1938, "unrest, a striving for *something*—it is want, craving, avidity, demand, suffering; and a world of will can be nothing else but a world of suffering" (*ETD* 381). Death can bring relief from this suffering as it erases individual existence, Schopenhauer's *principium individuationis*. The only other possible escape from this suffering is through an aesthetic and ascetic life that negates the power of the will, i.e. the desire for life. Besides Schopenhauer's nihilistic approach, it is the escape from a meaningless existence into art that must have intrigued a rebellious young man like Mann.

The other two cultural masterminds of the time, Friedrich Nietzsche and Richard Wagner, also influenced Mann from early on. He read Nietzsche as early as 1894, possibly even earlier. Although Mann made the point that he adopted "the idea of life" *R* 58) from Nietzsche's writings, the author's statement must be taken with caution. After all, later in *Lebenabriß* (*A Sketch of My Life*) he mentioned that he hardly believed anything Nietzsche wrote. It is safe to say that Mann used bits and pieces from his works and toyed with them. Mann was less interested in Nietzsche, the prophet of the new, strong life and the *Übermensch* (superman), of the life-affirming, Dionysian existence. Rather, he appreciated Nietzsche's play with perspectives, Nietzsche as the critic of the artist and art as illusion and, above all, the critic of bourgeois values and morals and forecaster of bourgeois decadence. Nietzsche, the skeptic of orientations with a nihilistic trend and the other Nietzsche, the affirmer of the will to life and power, provided Mann with a paradoxical perception of life and the intellectual tools to oscillate between orientations.

Last, but by no means least, in this group of the "triple constellation of eternally united spirits" (*R* 54), whose influence upon Mann's work appears throughout his literary career, is Richard Wagner. His operas, notably *Lohengrin* (1848), and his music dramas, including *Tristan and Isolde* (1859) and the epic, monumental tetralogy *The Ring of the Nibelung* (1854–1874), introduced Mann to the illusionary world of art and its escapist function. In particular, he was intrigued by Wagner's use of leitmotifs, particularly as a means of bringing organization and structure to a fictional world characterized by decline and chaos, degeneration and dissolution. Nietzsche's essay "The Case of Wagner" (1888), taught Mann to distrust Wagner's art. But Mann's passion for Wagner's music never faded; rather, it was merely tempered by "enthusiastic ambivalence" (*GW 10* 928).

Mann never made a secret of Nietzsche's influence as the title of Mann's second story reveals. "The Will to Happiness" is an obvious reference to Nietzsche's fragment *The Will to Power* (1887/88). The story was first published in *Simplicissimus* in 1896. In a letter to his friend Grautoff he wrote that the story will bring him "honor" (*TM/OG* 64). It is Mann's first story about an artist's problematic existence. An unnamed first person narrator, an educated burgher and art lover who expects the artist to remain aloof from society and the entrapment of life, recounts the life of his former school friend Paolo Hofman, the son of a German merchant and a South American mother. Paolo's early life is based on Mann's own life, underscored by the name Paolo (Paul) Hofman (Mann). The character nevertheless cannot be identified with the author. As the story unfolds, Paolo's life becomes very different from that of his creator. Suffering from a weak heart, Paolo falls in love with the beautiful Baroness Ada von Stein. Rejected by her parents as a suitable husband for their daughter, he moves to Italy where for the next five years his will to be united with Ada reigns over his physical debilitation. Ada, determined not to marry anybody else but Paolo, is finally granted her wish. In the early morning after their wedding night, the artist dies.

It is not only the title, "The Will to Happiness," that suggests the influence of Nietzschean thoughts on Mann's second story. Their presence is also reflected by the relationship between art and disease established by Nietzsche in "The Case of Wagner" and personified in the artist figure of Paolo. He is a weak child; light-blue veins are visible in his temples and cheeks, a symbol of decadence and an aesthetic and outsider existence. Furthermore, Paolo's "Solemnity of Distance" (*Tales* 4) is a reference to Nietzsche's *Beyond Good and Evil*, from 1886, and *The Genealogy of Morals*, from 1887. "The Will to Happiness" is Mann's first text to address the conflict between bourgeois and artistic existence, between life and spirit, embodied in Paolo's love for Ada. With Paolo, Mann creates an artist figure who wants to break through to life. The narrator assumes that his frail health has made Paolo desire life, represented in the story by women and their sexuality. In school, Paolo once had drawn the portrait of a naked woman to express his unfulfilled sexual desires; he again finds consolation in art when Ada is denied to him. But he wants life, rather than its sublimation in art, and, consequently, he is punished by Mann.

Mann has Paolo die the moment he realizes a life of sexuality and, simultaneously, of a sanctified bourgeois existence as a husband and integrated member of society. That death is imminent is signaled by a scene that takes place the night before Paolo leaves Rome for his wedding. The narrator offers Paolo a glass of water from the Trevi fountain, because superstition holds that if you drink the water before leaving the city, you will return. Before Paolo can drink, the glass is shattered by a sudden bolt of lightning. He dies the morning after the wedding night. On the realistic level of the story, Mann rewards the patient Paolo by permitting him to experience the triumph of happiness through the fulfillment, albeit short-lived, of his desire to embrace life. On the symbolic level, with this death Mann punishes the artist who makes the wrong choice by preferring life over art, and thereby giving up his distance.

Mann ends the story with the narrator commenting that Ada, who, rather than being devastated by the death of her husband, stands at the head of his coffin, her face radiating with "the grave and powerful solemnity of triumph" (*Tales* 20). Her triumph lies in the fact that her sexual desires have been fulfilled. Like Irma in "Fallen," Ada is portrayed as a sexually active woman. But she is also a counter figure to Irma. She is not promiscuous and morally questionable, and is not a target of the narrator's irony or mockery. But underneath this positive female identity, remarkably unpatriarchal for its time, lies a more conservative construction that belongs to a misogynist discourse. Ada is associated with the sphere of destruction and death. Paolo's embrace of life results in his immediate, untimely death. Thus a woman's sexuality becomes the subversive, even destructive force that Christian tradition has established.

Mann's next story, "Der Tod" ("Death"), from 1897, can be seen as an antidote to "The Will to Happiness." The mild climate of Italy has been replaced by a northern, gloomy coastal land, reminiscent of Theodor Storm's harsh landscapes. "Death" consists of sixteen diary entries written between 10 September and 11 October by a forty-year-old Count awaiting his imminent death, which subsequently occurs on 12 October. In the tradition of the literature of decadence, Mann depicts the Count as a neurasthenic, whose nervous debility forces him to spend days at a time lying in his room. We are to understand his disability as a metaphor for his abhorrence of everyday life. In the vein of Schopenhauer's philosophy, the Count believes in the meaningless of life. Approximately twenty years ago, he had himself foretold the specific date of his own death; he thus wills himself to die on this day, believing that he has power over death. In contrast to the Nietzschean "will to life," embodied in the previous story by Paolo, the Count displays Schopenhauer's thoughts on the yearning for death and his assumption that with death comes the dissolution of the individual into an "infinite, muffled and roaring darkness" (*GW 8* 74); in other words, the escape from the *principium individuationis*.

Neither his love for a beautiful Portuguese woman, who had died in childbirth, nor his affection for his twelve-year-old daughter, Asuncion, diverts him from his yearning for death. But before he can die, he also wills Asuncion to die because he cannot bear the thought of leaving a suffering orphan behind. Coincidentally, and realistically, Asuncion dies of heart failure. Symbolically, and in the Count's mind, "fine and mysterious happenings" (*GW 8* 75) have led to his daughter's death. Has he been successful in willing her death, as he will be successful in willing his own? With this incident Mann addresses the asocial behavior of the outsider whose self-interest is destructive to others, yet he leaves open the question of whether the Count is actually guilty.

The Count expects death to be "grand and beautiful and of wild majesty" and "a moment of enrapture and unspeakable sweetness" (*GW 8* 74). On 10 October, just two days before his predicted death, the Count believes that the figure of Death visits him at night. Rather than a grand figure who will bring an elating experience, Death turns out to be a ridiculous figure, resembling a dentist, who proclaims, "Best to get it over with" (*GW 8* 74). The Count is shocked by the mundane, bourgeois nature of death: "Never have I known a colder and more scornful feeling of disillusionment" (*GW 8* 75). The Count now awaits death, no longer sustaining the illusion that it will be majestic.

"Death" illustrates Mann's probing into Schopenhauer's philosophy and, most significantly, into the impact of the imagination upon reality. Its destructive and self-destructive side are testimony to Mann's early criticism of aestheticism. An innocent child is dead; the Count's notion of death as an exotic, grandiose experience is a disappointing delusion. That death is a "last disappointment" (*GW 8* 105) is also a point Mann raises in his story "Enttäuschung" (Disillusionment), written during his stay in Italy in 1895. The story was not published until 1898 in the collection *Little Herr Friedemann*. In it, a narrator, whose name and background remain unknown, observes the life that is happening at the Piazza de San Marco in Venice. His attention is drawn in particular to one man, a stranger who is hunched over and holding a cane with both hands behind his back. The man walks back and forth on the piazza every day, often talking to himself while shaking his head and smiling. One day the stranger starts talking to him without intermission, and without allowing the narrator to respond to his rhetorical questions; then he leaves.

With the stranger's diatribe Mann interweaves thoughts on the power of language with disillusionment in life. The stranger blames the language of religion and literature for conjuring up worlds of extremes and evoking experiences that surpass reality: "Language . . . is rich, is exuberantly rich in comparison to the meagerness and the limitations of life" (*GW 8* 103). Mann's story suggests that there is an overwhelming abundance of language, that whoever enters the realm of creative language understands the chasm between what is and what could be and must therefore be disappointed by life. This exactly is the fate of the stranger. Alienated from a world he deems to be despicable and full of "cowardness and lies" (*GW 8* 104), he is now lonely, unhappy, and somewhat deranged. Disillusioned by the knowledge that his life can never match fiction and that even the experience of his death will be a disappointment, he leaves the narrator with an "Adieu" (*GW 8* 105).

First impressions suggest that "Enttäuschung" is about the recognition of the banality and worthlessness of reality. The story contains many references to Schopenhauer; he speaks through the voice of the stranger, who even bears a physical resemblance to him.[3] The stranger wants to escape reality. He speaks about his favorite activity, looking at the stars so he can distance himself from reality and life. He wonders if it is not best "to dream of a liberated life, in which reality is absorbed in my great ideas without the tormenting remnants of disillusionment? Of a life without any horizons?" (*GW 8* 105) Who and what can offer such a life in which the desire stays alive while reaching the goal is inevitably accompanied by disillusionment? The answer for the stranger lies in dreams, and in the creative mind. Imagination, Mann is telling us here, is a liberating force.

But it is a liberating force with ambiguous consequences. Creativity opens up a world denied to us by reality and makes us aware of the banality of existence. But it also leads us away from the security and comfort of a stable world, and replaces firm beliefs with doubts. Through the stranger, who seems totally resigned to a life without goals or purpose, Mann addresses the alienating, psychologically burdening effect that creativity can have upon the individual. Mann poses, yet leaves unanswered, the question whether we should not simply stay away from the power and magic of words, and thus embrace a secure, yet banal life. It is telling that he does not give his narrator the opportunity to either affirm or explicitly contradict the stranger's diatribe about his pessimistic assessment of life and critical comments on creativity. The narrator seems himself to be skeptical about the authority of words when he doubts whether his retelling can capture the impression the stranger has made on him. By implying that reality is much richer than language alone can convey, Mann introduces a reversal of the point of view of the stranger. Yet, immediately after this statement the narrator presents a detailed description of the Piazza San Marco and its "miraculous buildings whose luscious and fairytale like contours and golden ornaments stand out against a gentle, light blue sky in delightful clarity" (*GW 8* 99). This highly poetic description suggests that language not only has the power to captivate life, but that it can evoke a world that is otherwise inaccessible, beyond that which is visible.

"Little Herr Friedemann" first appeared in the magazine *Neue Deutsche Rundschau* in May 1897. The story is based on an earlier, unpublished story, written in 1894, titled "Der kleine Professor" (The little professor). The revised version is the first milestone in Mann's long and productive literary career. It established his lifelong connection with the Samuel Fischer publishing house, which, after having published the novella in its literary journal, asked Mann for a collection of short stories and, subsequently, for the novel that would launch his international literary fame, *Buddenbrooks*. Mann knew by the time that he had completed the novella that this story surpassed everything he had written so far—that he had found his own literary voice.

"Little Herr Friedemann" is the first of Mann's stories that takes place in a town that can be identified with Lübeck. The descriptions of the city walls and the buildings, as well as the autobiographical elements such as a father who had been a Dutch Consul before his death and the three unmarried daughters of Johann Siegmund Mann, enter the realm of fiction. The story comprises fifteen chapters. Mann devotes the first five of these to the early years in the life of his protagonist, Johannes Friedemann. A fall, caused by a negligent wet nurse, leaves Friedemann permanently crippled. Quite possibly Mann was influenced by Nietzsche's treatise "What Is the Meaning of Ascetic Ideals?" in *The Genealogy of Morals*, in which Nietzsche argues that the strong desire for beauty and art is a result of suffering, destitution, and melancholy, when he (Mann) turns his cripple, who is excluded from a normal life, into an epicurean. Friedemann becomes a lover of art and leads an uneventful, dispassionate life. The protagonist's last name, which means "man of peace," underscores his contemplative, passive existence. Mann's character turns everything into an aesthetic delight, even the death of his mother. He is physically shaken when attending Wagner's opera *Lohengrin*. Love of art and his aesthetically triggered emotions become his substitute for real love and life; art provides, to use a modern term, a virtual reality in which he completely immerses himself.[4]

With the arrival of Gerda von Rinnlingen, the wife of the new local commandant, passion enters the monotonous, controlled life of Friedemann. In the next five chapters of the narrative, Mann shows how fragile the construction of an ascetic and aesthetic identity can be. Everything that Friedemann had sublimated since his youth resurfaces. Despite the knowledge that passion will bring misery and destruction, he is "obedient to the invincible, sweetly tormenting power from which there is no escape" (*Stories* 22). Possibly influenced by Nietzsche's thoughts on the powerful forces of life, Mann has Friedemann completely submit to these forces in the last five chapters. Shaking and quivering, Friedemann lets Gerda von Rinnlingen know with an "inhuman" stammering voice that he is in love with her; she pushes him away with a "short, proud, scornful laugh" (*Stories* 26). Aware that he has lived a life of self-denial and lies, he becomes so self-disgusted and disillusioned that he drowns himself. Nature, the quintessential force of life, becomes the site of his suicide. This tragic ending of a human life, ostracized, mocked, never holding any promise, is followed by the laconic, dispassionate comment: "The splash had silenced the crickets for a moment. Now they began their chirping as before, the park rustled softly and down the long avenue came the muted sound of laughter" (*Stories* 27). With the indifference of nature to the suffering of Friedemann, Mann reiterates a perspective presented in "Gefallen": a non-idealistic and unsentimental perception of existence, influenced by Schopenhauer's atheistic, nihilistic philosophy.

The last sentences of "Little Herr Friedemann" make us wonder where the narrator, who seems to be so indifferent, like nature itself, to the sufferings of the crippled protagonist, is ideologically positioned. He hovers above the fictional world and has detailed knowledge about the inhabitants of the town, thus identifying himself as belonging to this world. He unmasks weaknesses, for example Frau Friedemann's negligence when she leaves her newborn son with the alcoholic wet nurse, and points out the hypocrisy and narrow-mindedness of the community with their reactions to the arrival of the nonconventional Gerda von Rinnlingen. He tends to ridicule and caricature the bourgeoisie. For example, he draws attention to Friedemann's ugly, spinster sisters, one of whom always has spittle in the corner of her mouth and trembles in an odd fashion when speaking. His perspective is that of a distanced, ironic observer. We are given no reason to doubt his observations and judgments, including those that reflect unkindly upon Johannes Friedemann. The cripple's escape into aestheticism is understandable, but his reactions to music are exaggerated. In pointing out Friedemann's dilating nostrils and his contorted face, the narrator does not spare him from ironic treatment either. In fact, Friedemann's inability to cope with life is told with clinical coldness, even though a tacit empathy accompanies the narrator's presentation of the little hunchback's predicament.

Inaccessible to the narrator are the innermost thoughts of one character: the enigmatic Gerda von Rinnlingen. With her, Mann undermines the gender stereotypes of the late-nineteenth-century bourgeois world. She is married, yet childless. Her emancipated, masculine behavior and lack of submissive, feminine body language raise eyebrows among the bourgeois women and pose a threat to patriarchal structures. Her coldness and snobbish behavior are juxtaposed in her conversation with Friedemann. She reveals a caring personality and a feminine sensitivity when she inquires with a "soft, gentle, pensive voice" (*Stories* 25) about Friedemann's physical condition. What this conversation also reveals is her own otherness. She mentions to Friedemann that she is often ill, that she suffers from a nerve condition, and that she knows what it means to be unhappy. Here Mann sends various signals—attributes such as the dark shadows under her eyes and her light-blue veins, her own love for art—that she belongs to the world of the outsider, the world of decadence.

There is another dimension to her otherness. On the surface level, she pushes Friedemann away and humiliates him, even driving him towards suicide when he approaches her, because he turns out to be just another heterosexual man making ordinary sexual advances. She fits the traditional image of *la belle dame sans merci* that had flooded nineteenth-century art. On a deeper, symbolic level, her cruelty toward the cripple represents the arrogance and rejection of life characteristic of Mann's artist figures. Imposing traditional male attributes to Gerda von Rinnlingen, including smoking, riding, and driving a carriage through town, is Mann's narrative device for telling a story that cannot be told: that of his own homosexual inclinations. In a letter to his friend Otto Grautoff, written in Rome in April 1897, Mann confessed: "Since 'Little Herr Friedemann' I am suddenly able to find the direct forms and masks in which I can be among people with my experiences" (*TM/OG* 90). And a little later he wrote that he had found "novelistic and publicly acceptable masks, to express my love, my hatred, my compassion, my loathing, my pride, my mockery and my accusations" (*TM/OG* 97). In light of later diary entries, which attest to Mann's homosexual disposition, Gerda von Rinnlingen can be understood as a "mask," as a projection of hidden and unspeakable desires, as Mann's narrative tool for transferring homosexuality to a heterosexual character.[5] Her renunciation of Friedemann's advances is a secret code for Mann's own renunciation of stigmatized desires.

"Der Bajazzo" ("The Joker"), based on an earlier unpublished manuscript entitled "Walter Weiler," first appeared in September 1897 in the magazine *Neue Deutsche Rundschau*. The story never found the author's unequivocal approval. Heeding Mann's own wish, his American publisher Alfred Knopf did not include it in the first American collection of his stories, *Children and Fools* (1928). A new translation (in *Death in Venice and Other Stories*) acknowledges that it deserves attention. The protagonist, an unnamed, thirty-year-old, first person narrator, starts by confessing his disgust with life and his suicidal thoughts, and follows with a retrospective summation of his alienated, unhappy existence. He recounts how, when a child and as a young man, he did not cultivate his artistic inclinations, instead merely dabbling in artistic endeavors and just imitating others. Having recognized that his son will not raise above the "talent of a kind of mimicking buffoon or joker" (*Stories* 37), his father makes him work as an apprentice in a hardware store. As in Mann's own life, his father's death results in liberation. The inheritance he receives allows the "joker" to lead an idle, dilettante existence in a midsized, German town. The contempt that a young woman and an old friend, both integrated in bourgeois life, display toward him, confronts him with the uselessness of his existence.

A joker is a buffoon and imitator of others. Ruggero Leoncavallo's then popular Italian opera *Pagliacci*, composed in 1892 and performed under the German title *Der Bajazzo*, might have influenced Mann in the characterization of his protagonist. The narrator also matches the traits of the modern, late-nineteenth-century dilettante as characterized and criticized in Paul Bourget's novel *Cosmopolis* and his *Essais de psychologie contemporaine*, both from 1893. To be a dilettante means to be unfit for a productive life. Mann's dilettante despises the world of bourgeois work ethics and subscribes to a futile, hedonistic existence. He is drawn toward aestheticism, yet does not have the talent to produce great art himself. With this character, Mann addresses a paradoxical existence. On the one hand, the narrator rejects the values of what he deems to be a dull and uncreative bourgeois world and justifies his detachment. On the other hand, the outsider envies the "children of light" (*Stories* 48–49), the integrated human beings, and their happiness. He suffers from his loss of orientation and a valid structure that could bestow meaning upon his empty life. Escape from a bourgeois existence results in boredom and a life without purpose and goals. Does "The Joker" suggest that it is not worth rebelling against a mundane life and that one is better off being a conformist? Certainly not, as the story illustrates the dangers of being on the outside, and questions an asocial, antibourgeois life without praising a life within the social community.

It should be noted that the narrator's abhorrence of the world is an existential problem. It is not rooted in political or social deficiencies. In fact, the narrator's idle, privileged existence is facilitated by the capitalist nature of bourgeois society. He lives off the profits of his father's business and investments, and craves the applause and approval of the same people he despises. While loathing the world around him, he is simultaneously disgusted by his own alienation and the disrespect society shows him. The narrator's dislike for people without imagination and his desire to escape from a limiting, dull, bourgeois existence certainly reflect Thomas Mann's, as well as his brother Heinrich's, need for an artistic, creative life freed from the fetters of bourgeois expectations. The story also conveys the doubts associated with leaving a respected world, entering the uncertain world of creativity, and the outsider's fears of rejection and of marginalization.

There are other autobiographical elements to the story. The town and the house in which the joker grows up resemble Lübeck and Mann's home. The narrator's father, a businessman after whose death the company is liquidated, and his tender, musically inclined mother, evoke Mann's parents. Mann's playing with marionettes, his dislike for school and the business world, and his trips to Italy arc all integrated into the narrative. This self-referential quality is extended to include references to his own literature. "The Joker" contains narrative elements that can also be found in "Little Herr Friedemann." Both the joker and Friedemann grow up in the same town, indicated by the fact that Mann has both work in the hardware store of Herr Schlievogt. Both have mothers who read fairy tales to them. Both see a young, attractive woman steering a horse carriage, whom they also observe during the performance of a Wagner opera. This young woman's existence makes their own lives unbearable. These similarities make the dissimilarity of the endings of the two stories all the more striking. While the thirty-year-old Friedemann commits suicide, the thirty-year-old joker continues to suffer from life. In one story, passion for life and the inability to participate in life result in death; in the other, disgust with life leads to a lifeless, empty existence. The correspondences between both stories indicate that during this time Mann viewed the outsider existence from various angles, that he produced variations to explore the chasm between life and art, a chasm that he felt himself, as the autobiographical elements of the stories suggest. Playing with variations subsequently became a pattern that he continued, refined, and mastered throughout his literary career.

"Tobias Mindernickel," written in the summer of 1897 and first published in the *Neue Deutsche Rundschau* in January 1898, was the last story to be added to the collection of novellas. Mann, whose initials are, strikingly, identical with those of the story's protagonist, Tobias Mindernickel, never commented on this short text. Tobias Mindernickel, whose clothes and furniture reveal a middle-class background, has obviously endured declining fortunes; he now lives alone in a run-down neighborhood. The narrator, commenting on the strange behavior of this lonely, rather shy character, attributes Mindernickel's social demotion to an inability to cope with life. One day, Tobias helps a young, injured boy. This act of compassion reveals not only Tobias's longing for life, but also his longing for control over it. That Tobias compensates his exclusion from life with a compassion for life, driven by a secret will to power, is further illustrated when he buys a young hunting dog that he names "Esau." In contrast to the biblical figure of Tobias, who treats his dog kindly, Mann's character exercises a strict and cruel control over his playful dog, who merely acts in accordance with his natural instincts. Mindernickel only displays loving care for the creature when Esau accidentally runs into his master's bread knife. Healed, Esau again displays his lively, instinct-driven nature and defies his master's strict commands. In order to regain total control, Mindernickel intentionally stabs the dog to subdue him and, quite by accident, wounds him fatally. The narrative initially evokes our sympathy for this wretched, ridiculous figure, but simultaneously asks that we distance ourselves when his rejection by society and his feebleness engender violence. This short story can be understood as a play with perspectives, and as a challenge to Mann's bourgeois world not to condemn the outsider too hastily.

Mann's early stories can be seen as a dialogue with the major literary and philosophical voices of the late nineteenth century. They are indicative of his oscillation between recognition and deliberate distance from them in order to find and articulate his own voice. Intertextual references to Nietzsche's and Schopenhauer's works point to Mann's toying with their ideas and concepts, rather than providing a clear-cut affirmation or renunciation of them. It is this juggling of ideas and perspectives, a refusal to take a firm position, that also informs Mann's narrative strategies. Underlying his stories is a condescending attitude toward bourgeois life, its trifling expectations and oppressive conventions, even contempt for a world that brings suffering and sexual frustrations. Nonetheless, Mann does not glorify the escape from this world, be it into death or into the realm of art and aestheticism. Renunciation of bourgeois life and mores is juxtaposed with yearning for a respectable, integrated existence.

Since the publication of Mann's diaries, much attention has been given to the autobiographical dimension of Mann's works, particularly in regard to his secret homosexual frustrations. Doubtless, autobiographical elements are everywhere in his early stories. Besides specific correlations between Mann's characters and himself, the milieu is mainly that of Mann's own upbringing: small, old towns with narrow, crooked streets and gabled houses; places such as Munich and Venice; stories about men who have to choose between art and life; being on the outside versus living an honorable, bourgeois existence in a boring world. Reading between the lines, one can sense Mann's justification for leaving what he perceived as a philistine world after his father's death, as well as elements of guilt for looking down upon bourgeois society with which he, like some of his outsider characters, had a parasitic relationship. This desire to write about himself in numerous variations might explain the noticeable absence of German history and politics from these early stories. It is a world within, yet outside, immediate political and historical events. Granted, Mann's narratives are a tool for self-representation.[6] Simultaneously, however, they hold universal appeal, specifically because they ignore particular social and political events, and address the individual's problematic existence in a world that demands conformity. As Mann proposes in a diary entry on 10 January 1919, "The most intimate . . . is the most universal and most human" (*TB 1918–1921* 131).

CHAPTER 3

Buddenbrooks

In 1897, Samuel Fischer offered to publish a novel-length work of Mann's to follow the publication of his collection of short stories in 1898. Most certainly this proposition must have flattered the twenty-two-year-old Mann, whose stories had so far yielded only modest success. When he would begin work on his novel *Buddenbrooks: Decline of a Family* in October 1897, he had grand ambitions; he was striving for greatness, both to demonstrate that his literary talents exceeded those of his brother Heinrich and to secure a place in literary history. Later Mann commented that with *Buddenbrooks* he had intended to write "a society novel disguised as a family saga" (*GW 11* 554), thus a novel in the tradition of the great European realistic novels of the nineteenth century. Not only did Mann surpass his brother's reputation, but in the end he managed to create one of the great novels about nineteenth-century German society. On the way to fame, he had to overcome one major hurdle. Fischer requested that the thousand pages of handwritten manuscript Mann submitted be shortened by fifty percent. The young author answered Fischer's request with a firm "no," an indication of how essential Mann felt all the many details in the novel to be. While he had to wait months for Fischer's final decision on the fate of the manuscript, he half-jokingly wrote to Heinrich that, should the novel not be published, he intended to become a bank clerk. Fischer's eventual positive decision spared him from a life behind a banker's desk. *Buddenbrooks* was published in two volumes in October 1901; a more affordable, one-volume edition followed in 1903. Despite its epic length, it rapidly gained widespread popularity and brought its author national as well as international recognition, culminating in 1929 with the highest honor that can be bestowed upon a writer: the Nobel Prize for Literature.

The novel follows the lives of four generations of the Buddenbrooks, a bourgeois family residing in an unnamed town on the Baltic Sea, and covers more than forty years, from 1835 until 1877. The prosperity of the family is founded on a wholesale grain business, headed first by the family patriarch Johann Buddenbrook, then by his son Johann Jr.—also called Jean in the novel—and finally by Thomas Buddenbrook, after whose death the firm is dissolved. This prosperity allows the family to purchase a stately house in 1835, and *Buddenbrooks* opens with a family gathering to consecrate it—one of many gatherings to follow in the novel. This happy occasion is overshadowed, however, by tensions caused by the absent Gotthold, the senior Buddenbrook's son from his first marriage. Gotthold had married for love and below his station, and had thus provoked his father's anger. In the interest of the family, Johann Buddenbrook Sr. had remarried for money, not love, and is now demanding respect for his sacrifice. He feels that his sons and others in the family's circle should follow his example. Gotthold's punishment for disregarding these demands is exclusion from the family. The pressure to commit to a life sacrificed to bourgeois success and conventions, with the accompanying renunciation of individual fulfillment, is the pivotal theme in the novel from the very beginning. It becomes the focus of Mann's depiction of Thomas and Tony Buddenbrook, the children of Johann Buddenbrook Jr., the central characters of the novel.

In the name of the family, individual happiness must be sacrificed again and again. Thomas Buddenbrook, representing the family's third generation, marries the cold-hearted, artistically inclined Gerda in 1857. The birth of their only child, their sickly son Hanno, occurs in 1861. Thomas's sister Tony, although in love with a student, marries the unsympathetic businessman Grünlich for money and for her family's prestige, but divorces him four years later in 1850, when he turns out to be a bankrupt fraud. In 1857, Tony marries again for the sake of her family, this time to a Bavarian businessman who is more interested in beer and the couple's maid than in Tony. Their unhappy marriage ends when Tony demands a divorce two years later. Also ill-fated are the lives of Johann (Jean) Buddenbrook's other two children, Christian and Clara. Christian is the black sheep of the family. A sickly dilettante, he marries for love, but his wife, a former courtesan, subsequently has him committed to an insane asylum. Clara marries a fortune-hunter and dies at the young age of twenty-six.

The Buddenbrooks' unhappy marriages, accompanied by detrimental business decisions, an inner resistance to devote their lives to the reputation of the family, and failing health, bring about the decline of the family. Thomas Buddenbrook, physically and psychologically fragile, dies in 1875 from a stroke brought on by an infected tooth. The liquidation of the family business follows. His son Hanno, alienated both from his father's world and life in general, and devoted instead to music, dies of typhoid fever at the age of sixteen in 1877. The family saga concludes with a family gathering, held to reminisce about the Buddenbrooks' glorious past. The only persons present are Tony, together with her daughter, several female members of the Buddenbrook family, and an old teacher, all dressed in black.

This précis suggests, as does the novel's subtitle "The Decline of a Family," that *Buddenbrooks* is about degeneration and death, a family's emphasis on money rather than love, and that the novel thus expresses Mann's detachment from his bourgeois world. What this brief summary of *Buddenbrooks* cannot convey is one of the fascinating facets of Mann's first novel and of his fiction in general: the author's love for detail and humorous depiction of this world. Like perhaps no other German novel, *Buddenbrooks* captures the atmosphere of nineteenth-century bourgeois society. The meticulous descriptions of rooms and buildings, numerous family gatherings, even instructions on how to poach carp in red wine, provide today's reader with insights into the lifestyle and ambiance of this bygone bourgeois world. The novel contains an abundance of brief moments of every-day existence within this luxurious and affluent world, making it come alive and drawing us in, while at the same time keeping us at a critical distance. Such a scene is that in which a maid waddles down the hall to give Madame Budden-brook a visitor's calling card. The description adds to the humorous dimension of the novel while simultaneously reminding the reader of the privileged, formal existence enjoyed by upper-middle-class women. In contrast to our expectations, Mann suggests that it is not the hardworking maid who deserves our sympathy, but her mistress. The narrator's comment that the maid encounters Madame Bud-denbrook spending her time "crocheting with two large wooden needles—a shawl, a blanket, or *something of that sort*" (*B* 286; italics mine) is intended to raise our skepticism about this luxurious world. What Madame Buddenbrook intends to create with her needlework is depicted as unimportant. With a seemingly trivial observation the author takes a critical stance that he develops further in the depiction of Tony Buddenbrook: upper-class women are predestined to an idle, domestic life and excluded from a meaningful existence.

Mann does not restrict his detailed account to the upper-class world. Often, seemingly superfluous information that introduces nameless lower-class charac-ters or situations without developing them further diverts from the lives of the Buddenbrooks. When, for example, Consul Buddenbrook asks his barber, Wen-zel, about the weather, Wenzel informs him about the fog and snow outside as well as about some trifling implications: "The boys have fixed themselves up another slide, good thirty foot long, out in front of St. Jakob's, and I almost took a tumble as I was leaving the mayor's house. Damn those kids" (*B* 314). Not only does Mann add, through Wenzel's comment, a human touch to his weather report, he also stirs our imagination about the playing and laughing children and good-natured, sympathetically drawn Wenzel slipping and sliding. The casual, small-talk nature of this comment contains a deeper, hidden meaning, as it reflects a central motif of the novel: downfall. Later, Thomas Buddenbrook will fall in the street, and the family itself will fall from the heights of its success to its end.

The many trivial details and brief images indicate that the novel holds a fas-cination, even compassion for life. Thus, they are a vital part of the novel. This compassion provides a counterbalance to the story of frustrated lives, decadence, and death that propel the plot of the novel forward. Both a fascination for and a critical detachment from the bourgeois world are transmitted through Mann's narrator. He invites us to witness this world, draws us into the story with questions, and hints at events to come to rouse our interest: "And what was going on here? Something horrible, ghastly" (*B* 381). The narrator has an intimate knowledge of this world and participates in its joys and sorrows. For example, the birth of Thomas Buddenbrook's son elates him—"A firstborn son, a Buddenbrook! Can anyone understand what that means?" (*B* 348) He voices concern that perhaps not enough food will be available for the christening party. After all, the reputation of the Buddenbrook family is at stake, and thus that of the narrator's own world. That Mann does not employ an objective, unbiased narrator becomes very noticeable in his presentation of "poor Tony" (as the narrator repeatedly refers to her). In other cases, he can hide his compassion. In detached, clinical terms the narrator informs us about the symptoms of typhoid and the painful death it causes in general, rather than directly about Hanno Buddenbrook's suffering from the deadly disease. He leaves it to the reader's imagination to fill in the blanks.

On the other hand, Mann's narrator foregoes his emotional involvement and looks upon this bourgeois world with humor and ironic distance, often with a touch of condescension. It is a world that makes us laugh, where all-too-gaunt and all-too-tall people exist next to terribly short and fat ones, where a nearly toothless banker can make a sound that reminds us of the clang of a Chinese gong, and where a hunchbacked teacher, Sesemi Weichbrodt by name, exaggerates vowels and is remembered by her phrase "Be heppy, you *good* chawld!" (*B* 146, 313) Ironically, her wish that Tony Buddenbrook will find happiness will not come true. Often the narrator positions himself as an educated burgher who mocks the less educated, such as the citizen Herr Stuht who says "iffamy" instead of "infamy" (*B* 165), and who refers to Thomas Buddenbrook as having "the least provincial mind of any of the men around him" (*B* 317–18). In presenting the flaws and idiosyncrasies of this small world, Mann curtails our emotional investment in the story and wants us to take an ambivalent, skeptical stance. Furthermore, he provides comical relief from the gloomy dimension of the novel, the Buddenbrooks' decline.

As Mann was only twenty-two years old when he began to write *Buddenbrooks*, one wonders how he had learned to conjure up this world so rich in detail and atmosphere. Mann drew most heavily upon one direct source: the world he grew up in. *Buddenbrooks* is so realistic in many parts that many readers, upon its publication, saw it as a roman à clef about recognizable, reputable citizens of

Lübeck and the author's own family, forcing Mann to lecture his readers about the difference between fiction and reality.[1] Certainly, autobiographical details abound. The unnamed town in the novel is Mann's hometown of Lübeck. While this north German town is never mentioned by name, its street names and places are authentic. Mann consulted his own family history and papers; his sister Julia sent an account of aunt Elisabeth Haag-Mann's life that shaped the character Tony Buddenbrook. The novel's main male character, Thomas Buddenbrook, dies the year his author and namesake was born. Mann resorts to some of his family's first names: Thomas, Johannes, and Elisabeth. Mann's father, Thomas Johann Heinrich Mann, held the largely honorary position of Royal Netherlands Consul in the city, and was elected senator in 1877. Gerda Buddenbrook, née Arnoldsen, shares with Mann's mother Julia her well-known beauty and musical talent. Tony's move to Munich after marrying her second husband reflects Mann's own residence in the southern German town. Mann's own disappointing experience with the German school system finds its way into the school episode towards the end of the novel. However, the central theme of *Buddenbrooks*, the decline of a family ending in the death of the last male and the liquidation of the firm, is certainly not autobiographical. Mann's father chose to liquidate his family business when he realized that his sons Thomas and Heinrich were not in the least interested in taking it over. Neither did their artistic sensibility and striving to become artists, reflected in the novel by Hanno, kill them.[2]

The world of *Buddenbrooks* is the one neither Thomas nor Heinrich Mann cared to join, that of the German burghers, the well-to-do patrician families of the Hanseatic city of Lübeck who held property as well as political power and privileges. The novel spans German history, from Napoleon's conquest of the German states to the *Gründerzeit*, the founding of a unified German Empire under Bismarck. While the Buddenbrooks' decline is embedded in a turbulent time of German history, the changing political and social climate has little if any significant impact upon them. During the war against Denmark in 1864, Prussian officers take up residence at the Buddenbrooks'. History thus appears in the shape of a brief private inconvenience. Historical and political changes in 1871, vaguely addressed as "the shocks and upheavals of the war just ended" (*B* 485), leave no decisive mark on the family's economic fate and political standings. Mann provides a brief window on the bourgeois-liberal movement of the mid–nineteenth century through the character of the medical student, Morten Schwarzkopf. The progressive ideas he introduces to Tony Buddenbrook focus on oppression of the middle class by the aristocracy. Being beyond her experience, they mean little to Tony who grew up in the Lübeck, where tradition held that Hanseatic families controlled both commerce and society, and no one gave much thought to class conflict. Both Morten and progressive politics in general become a target of Mann's humor, as the young student's rebellious thoughts echo those of the members of his fraternity in Göttingen. Indirectly Mann points out that Morten does not whole-heartedly stand behind them, because he conceals from his father his questioning of authority.

Also full of humor are two scenes in which the Buddenbrooks' servants rebel. In the first of these, the cook Trina, who had been introduced to leftist ideas by a butcher's apprentice, ironically referred to by the narrator as a "bloody fellow," responds when Madame Buddenbrook complains about a sauce, that soon she, Trina, will be sitting on Madame Buddenbrook's sofa wearing her silk dress and being served. Trina, whom the novel ridicules because she misunderstands the leftist goals for a classless society as merely being a reversal of social status and privileges, makes this prediction with her hands on her hips, expressing a sense of power. Her gesture of power is immediately undermined: "It went without saying that she had been let go at once" (*B* 158). Because the narrator belongs to the bourgeois world, it does not occur to him to question the Buddenbrooks' decision to dismiss her immediately. In the second scene, rioters, among them the Buddenbrooks' warehouse worker Corl Smolt, advocate a revolution because Berlin and "Peree," (*B* 170), the uneducated workers' name for Paris, have one! When Consul Buddenbrook, upon Smolt's demand for a republic, responds that they already have one in Lübeck, Smolt is ridiculed. The whole group of "insurrectionists" (*B* 169), some of whom are tired or uninterested in revolution, disperses. The scene ends with a subservient Smolt fetching the horse carriage for Consul Buddenbrook's father-in-law.

Buddenbrooks pokes fun at those who, in the radical political climate of 1848, tentatively, but without deep political convictions or sufficient political knowledge, subscribe to political orientations and ideological promises. Mann turns their revolutionary aspirations into a harmless, even ridiculous undertaking, thereby taking sides with the educated burghers and his own social class in a time of radical political and social changes. Is *Buddenbrooks* thus a work attesting to the author's "political sleepiness," as Mann had suggested himself in a half-serious tone (*GW 12* 140). The answer must be "no," as it was not Mann's goal to write a historical and political novel with *Buddenbrooks*; rather, as his depiction of Morten Schwarzkopf and the members of the working class illustrates, he questions belief in ideologies, be they socialist or bourgeois. Mann uses the sociopolitical climate of the time as a backdrop to provide an intimate look at the hopes and disappointments, as well as the strengths and weaknesses, of a family that is constrained by their bourgeois ideology. In writing *Buddenbrooks*, as Mann would later explain, he was interested in the psychological profile of the family: "The psychological-human element was my main interest; I included the socio-political one only half subconsciously; it did not preoccupy me much" (*R* 99).[3]

Various frameworks for bourgeois family novels existed when Mann wrote *Buddenbrooks*. He was familiar with contemporary social novels, in particular those by the Norwegians Alexander Kielland and Jonas Lie (*GW 11* 550), the French novel *Renée Mauperin*, from 1864, by the Goncourt brothers, Emile Zola's *Les Rougon-Macquart*, from 1871–1893, and Theodor Fontane's *The Poggenpuhls*, from 1896. Perhaps the most important influence, however, was not a novel, but Wagner's *The Ring of the Nibelung*, from 1854–1874. In transposing Wagner's mythological world of Germanic gods onto an everyday, bourgeois world, Mann parodies Wagner's epic music drama.[4] The beginning of *Buddenbrooks*, the move into the new house, is reminiscent of the gods' move into Walhalla in the first part of *The Ring: The Rhinegold*. Another striking parallel between Wagner's and Mann's texts lies in the denial of love. The Nibelung Alberich forswears love to possess the ring, riches, and power, but, as subsequent events demonstrate, all of this he does in vain. The Buddenbrooks renounce love for bourgeois success but cannot find happiness. Wagner's family patriarch, Wotan, the representative of power and order, is entangled in a constricting net of obligations, controlled by fate, deceit, and self-deceit. He loses his power and knows that he and the gods are doomed. Wagner's demise of the gods is mirrored in the degeneration and end of the Buddenbrook family.[5]

Despite his parodistic response to *The Ring*, Mann pays homage to Wagner's artistic achievements by adopting Wagner's technique of leitmotifs. Fate and decline are central, reoccurring motifs in *Buddenbrooks* and not restricted to the Buddenbrook family. The Ratenkamp family, whose house the Buddenbrooks have purchased at the beginning of the novel, are also subject to decline. Ratenkamp's demise was, according to Consul Johann Buddenbrook Jr., "inevitable—fate simply took its course. He must have acted under the pressure of implacable necessity. Ah, I'm convinced that he halfway knew about his partner's dealings, that he was not totally ignorant of what state his warehouse was in. But he was immobilized" (*B* 19). This comment suggests that fate, which hinders Ratenkamp from acting, is a mysterious force outside individual control, but it also points to Ratenkamp's poor business decisions, a view Mann underscores with Johann Buddenbrook Sr.'s rejection of his son's fatalistic notions as "idées" (*B* 19). Throughout *Buddenbrooks*, fate and individual choice, powerlessness and individual responsibility, are at work simultaneously. Bad business decisions plague the Buddenbrooks and bring them to the brink of bankruptcy; forces beyond their control, such as a hailstorm that destroys their crops, accelerate their economic decline. The novel suggests that even the initial successful rise of the bourgeois newcomer and entrepreneur Hageström, the Buddenbrooks' competitor, will be followed by decline. Purchasing the former Buddenbrooks house on Meng Strasse is but one example of the parallel pattern that will ultimately lead to their demise. The correspondence between these three families suggests that *Buddenbrooks* contains a fatalistic notion of life as a continual process of rise and decline, and insinuates that people are trapped in mythical patterns and cannot therefore be held responsible for their actions. Conversely and simultaneously, the decline of both the Buddenbrooks and the other families is presented as self-inflicted, the result of realistic, logically explainable causes.

"Secret powers"[6] appear throughout the novel and are ascribed to characters such as Tony's devilish husband Grünlich, the banker Kesselmeyer and the harpy-like figures of the three Buddenbrook cousins. The following brief, amusing episode illustrates the extent to which these powers are explicitly invoked and at the same time undermined. Thomas and his brother Christian have the tailor, who made them suits, send their father a bill for eighty marks although the suits cost only seventy marks. The boys receive the difference of ten marks in cash from the tailor—not, as the narrator notes, particularly unusual for a small business transaction. But their scheme to augment their allowances takes an unforeseen turn, commented on ironically by the narrator: "By the hand of some dark fate the entire matter came to light" (*B* 59). Did the tailor divulge the secret? Did Johann Buddenbrook check the tailor's bill? In any case, an ominous fate is reduced to an accidental or maybe deliberate uncovering of the truth, and, unexpectedly, a blessing, as Johann Buddenbrook then raises his sons' allowance. Less benevolent is the power of fate in the case of Madame Antoinette Buddenbrook's death. She dies of natural causes, in old age, of an indefinable illness that she does not have the resilience to fight off. "Something new, alien, extraordinary thing seemed to have made an appearance, a secret" (*B* 60). Fate and secret agents, the mysterious forces of life coupled with real causes—later in the novel stroke and typhoid—accompany the decline of the Buddenbrooks until the end of the novel.[7]

Besides fate, degeneration plays a significant part in the Buddenbrooks' decline. Physical degeneration was a central theme of naturalistic literature in the 1890s, represented mainly by the works of Zola in France, and by those of Hauptmann, Holz, and Schlaf in Germany. From Bourget and Nietzsche, Mann learned about decadence as a psychological phenomenon. In the section "What Is the Meaning of Ascetic Ideals?" from *The Genealogy of Morals*, Nietzsche makes the point that tiredness, nineteenth-century *Weltschmerz*, and pessimism subvert Western cultures and nations, resulting in physical and psychological degeneration, nihilism, and a yearning for death. In *Buddenbrooks*, physical and psychological decline bring about a lack of viable male heirs, and thus the end of the family. Because of the inferior social status of bourgeois women at the time, the survival of female family members is inconsequential to the family's fortunes.

The novel opens with a healthy Johann Buddenbrook, and closes with a sickly, weak great-grandson Hanno, who dies at the age of sixteen. In the course of the novel the male representatives of the family die at a younger and younger age. Simultaneously, there is not only a decline in birthrates, but a dearth of male offspring. The physical decline of male members of the family is indicated by weak teeth. Thomas Buddenbrook's teeth are small and yellow; the extraction of a molar brings about a deadly stroke. Hanno suffers terribly while teething as a baby, and the extraction of several of his back teeth at the age of eight develops into a life-threatening situation. A similar affliction is visited upon the Hagenström family. For example, Moritz Hagenström, the brother of the Buddenbrooks' business rival, shares Thomas Buddenbrook's bad teeth as well as his devotion to aesthetic rather than economic interests. This physical as well as psychological decline suggests that the Hagenströms, too, are following a path that is leading unerringly toward their ultimate demise. With the Hagenströms' purchase of the Buddenbrooks' house on Meng Strasse, Mann underscores the commonalities between the two families.

The psychological decline of the Buddenbrooks takes place over their last three generations. The yardstick with which to measure the decline is provided by Mann's portrayal of Johann Buddenbrook Sr. During the dinner party scene at the beginning of the novel, Mann introduces him as a religious skeptic from the age of Goethe. Although he had bought a house on whose threshold was inscribed *Dominus providebit* ("The Lord will provide"), he prefers to trust his own abilities and entrepreneurial skills. Johann Buddenbrook's belief in self-reliance and a bourgeois work ethic reveals the presence of religion in his new house to be a mere convention. He takes pride in being an enlightened person with an individualistic and humanistic orientation, and therefore resents the growth of inhuman materialism and capitalism, illustrated by his criticism of the rise of trade and technical schools which seems to push aside the ideas of the Enlightenment: "Grammar schools and classical education are suddenly all foolishness, and the whole world has nothing in its head but coal mines and factories and making money" (*B* 23). But Johann Buddenbrook's humanism has limitations as Mann clearly reveals. Gotthold's "mésalliance" (*B* 41) has led to his being ostracized. Money reigns over love and human compassion.

While Johann Buddenbrook Sr. believes that the individual forges his own destiny and identifies with his work, his son, the Consul Johann Buddenbrook, sees his business involvement as a duty. In contrast to his father, who puts religion into the service of bourgeois mercantile interests, the less self-assertive, pessimistic son is a sentimentalist and presents himself as a devout Christian who believes in providence. As the narrator points out, he "was probably the first of his lineage to know and cultivate feelings that were out of the ordinary, more differentiated, alien to his solid middle-class heritage" (*B* 229). This comment must be viewed with skepticism. Consul Johann Buddenbrook often suspends his Christian feelings when conducting business so that it frequently becomes a ruthless, cold-hearted undertaking that assures survival of the firm at the expense of the interest of individual family member. Mann therefore exposes as hypocritical his behavior towards his avowed beliefs. For the most part the Consul ignores his responsibility for his daughter's unhappiness, brought about by his insistence on her marriage to Grünlich. At one point, however, he does briefly acknowledge his guilt, but escapes from the burden of individual responsibility by referring to divine will. Mann sends various signals that it is not an unfathomable plan from above, but rather the Consul's poor judgment and belief that all must make sacrifices to serve the firm. These bring about both Tony's unhappiness and financial burdens for the family. Costly dowries for marriages that end in divorce or death reduce the family's wealth. This decrease in the family's fortunes comes at an inopportune time, as under the Consul's stewardship business stagnates.

What differentiates Johann Buddenbrook's son, Thomas, from his father and grandfather are imagination and idealism that fuel his desire to achieve honor, recognition, and prestige in his city. To aggrandize his family's name, he enters city politics. But beneath this ambitious exterior, Mann reveals a man without self-identity. Thomas Buddenbrook regrets that when faced with difficult decisions he cannot find existential assurance in prayer like his father. In common with his grandfather, he subscribes to a Protestant work ethic and sense of responsibility, but he lacks his grandfather's self-reliance and "comfortable superficialities" (*B* 563), qualities that allowed the senior Johann not only to never be concerned by questions on eternity and immortality, but to find self-fulfillment in what amounts in Thomas Buddenbrook's mind to "insignificant, small-scale, pennywise transactions" (*B* 414). To combat his inner emptiness, Thomas Buddenbrook adopts a facade he feels projects an identity expected of him by society. Adjunct to this construction is the building of a new house, a symbol of self-representation and bourgeois success. Well groomed and impeccably dressed, his carefully crafted, immaculate outward appearance masks his alienation and growing physical weakness. He has become an actor, his life a continual performance on the stage of bourgeois representation: "He was empty inside" (*B* 531).

With Christian Buddenbrook, Thomas's brother, Mann presents a contrasting, but similarly decadent, character. Christian, a hypochondriac, attempts to integrate himself into the mercantile world and to be a dutiful son. He works for various firms abroad, yet his sensibility and aesthetic interests identify him as a bourgeois outsider. In this character, Mann continues to explore the same inner conflicts experienced by his dilettante in "The Joker." Yearning for a home and bourgeois existence are juxtaposed with Christian's inability to exist within the confines of bourgeois conventions. He is unable to lead a false existence and to pretend to be a burgher like his brother. Christian's contempt for his brother's work ethic and criticism of his reserved life, one without spontaneity and love but full of poise and dignity and calculated movements, is not unfounded. Yet the novel does not propose his outsider existence as an alternative to his brother's decadent world. His marriage to a courtesan ruins his life. Rather than providing him with the "home" and the loving care (*B* 503) he hopes for, she has him declared insane, thereby inheriting his money.

With Hanno Buddenbrook, Thomas Buddenbrook's only child, the decline of the family reaches its final stage. Hanno is contemptuous of his family's bourgeois world. Christian religion has no meaning for him; the Bible is nothing but "lines of print fusing into a black muddle" (*B* 616). What is left? Hanno becomes fully enmeshed in the world of art. Music, soon his all-encompassing passion, leads him away from life and takes on the function of a substitute religion, as Mann indicates when music brings "peace, bliss, heaven itself" (*B* 443) to Hanno. It is highly asocial, "gnawed away at your courage and fitness for daily life" (*B* 606) and gives him a willingness to embrace "doom" (*B* 641).

As in the story "Little Herr Friedemann" and subsequent works, Mann continues to link Wagner's music with aestheticism, the celebration of as well as turning away from life. In *Buddenbrooks* this connection is illustrated by Hanno's retreat into his lonely, musical world where he improvises on Wagner's themes, especially those from the *Ring* cycle, to create the illusion that he participates in life: "What was he feeling? Was this his way of overcoming dreadful obstacles? Was he slaying dragons, scaling mountains, swimming great rivers, walking through fire?" (*B* 640) Wagner's music provides Hanno with the desired deliverance from his existence by leading him away from a practical, productive life. It seduces him to aestheticism, decadence, illness, it deprives him of the will to live, and it ultimately brings about his death. In reality, Hanno dies from typhoid. Symbolically, it is his renunciation of the bourgeois world and his escapism into aestheticism that brings an end to the male offspring of the Buddenbrooks.

Wagner's *Ring* cycle is not the only significant influence on Mann's depiction of the steady erosion of existential security and the turn toward nihilism in

Buddenbrooks. Of similar importance is the philosophy of Arthur Schopenhauer. In *Reflections of a Nonpolitical Man* (hereafter referred to as *Reflections*), Mann remembered that his reading of Schopenhauer's *The World as Will and Representation* had a profound impact upon him while writing *Buddenbrooks*: "One only reads this way once. Never again. . . . Two steps from my couch the manuscript lay open that was swelling in an impossible and impractical way . . . that had just grown to the point where it was time to have Thomas Buddenbrook die" *R* 49). Like his author, Thomas Buddenbrook also reads passages from Schopenhauer's book, and is both deeply engrossed and intoxicated by them. While Mann neither mentions Schopenhauer nor the title of his book, readers will recognize the source, as the Schopenhauer chapter read by Thomas Buddenbrook is explicitly identified as "Concerning Death and Its Relation to the Indestructibility of Our Essential Nature" (*B* 565). His "poor average brain" cannot comprehend all he reads, "he felt overwhelmed by this heavy, dark, unthinking intoxication" (*B* 566). He nevertheless concludes that Schopenhauer's philosophical treatise proposes that life is wretched and death a blessing: "Was not every human being a mistake, a blunder? Did we not, at the very moment of birth, stumble into agonizing captivity? A prison, a prison with bars and chains everywhere. And, staring out hopelessly from between the bars of his individuality, a man sees only the surrounding walls of external circumstance, until death comes and calls him home to freedom" (*B* 567). Through Thomas Buddenbrook, Mann introduces Schopenhauer's thought that the individual suffers throughout life by being subjected to and imprisoned by the will, and that death alone is the release from this suffering. Thomas Buddenbrook yearns for the erasure of his individual existence, the liberation from his role as a burgher leading a socially respectable life, a seemingly upright citizen who, for the sake of his family, has taken on an identity that alienates him from himself, that stifles talents and yearnings that are irreconcilable with his duties. Thomas Buddenbrook's infatuation with Schopenhauer's life-negating, nihilistic philosophy is, however, short-lived; his encounter with philosophy a brief, inconsequential one. The day after his Schopenhauer experience, he feels embarrassed to have indulged in such extravagant ideas, and his "middle-class instincts" return him to a life controlled by "five hundred pointless, workaday trifles" (*B* 569). He lacks both the will and energy to revisit the philosopher's writings and, instead, asks the maid to put the Schopenhauer volume back on the bookshelf where it can resume its half-surreptitious, forgotten existence. Thomas Buddenbrook's discarding of the book can be regarded as Mann's symbolic gesture that he wants to distance himself from the nihilistic thinker—and that he does not consider a pessimistic assessment of life to be a central aspect of *Buddenbrooks*.

In his search for "high and final truths" (*B* 569), Thomas Buddenbrook ponders for a few moments the Christian religion he has been introduced to as a child. But can he find consolation in the biblical account that the God of Christianity sent part of himself, Jesus Christ, to earth so that he could suffer for us, and bring about our redemption? Thomas Buddenbrook thinks it to be a "rather vague and rather absurd story" (*B* 569). In the end he becomes indifferent to finding answers to his existential questions. A stroke finally saves him from the necessity of continuing an empty life. He is struck down in the street and falls to the wet, dirty pavement. Within hours he dies, his eyes glazed, gurgling sounds escaping his lips, disheveled and with his clothes soiled and wet, the antithesis of the man he had all his life striven to be. In the final analysis, his life, with its high-principled commitment to civic duty and furthering the family business, and with its grandiose pretensions of style and form, is exposed as nothing but a lie, void of idealism, self-fulfillment, and love.

The presence in *Buddenbrooks* of Schopenhauer, the voice of pessimism and nihilism, and Nietzsche, the "psychologist of decadence" (*R* 54) has led many critics to interpret Mann's novel as a statement that reflects his pessimistic assessment of life.[8] Granted, *Buddenbrooks* is permeated by biological and psychological degeneration, suffering, and death. The narrator often views events with a merciless detachment, describing them without noticeable sympathy in short, staccato-style sentences. Thus, when Thomas Buddenbrook falls, never to regain consciousness, the narrator remarks: "His hat rolled off down the street a little way. His fur coat was splattered with muck and slush. His outstretched hands in their white kid gloves had come to rest in a puddle. There he lay" (*B* 585). Mann describes death here as a banal event; the novel leaves the impression, ostensibly a Schopenhauerian touch, that life is not worth living and that death is not a grand event. But despite the fact that the narrative blend of nihilism, decadence, determinism, and fate invests *Buddenbrooks* with all the ingredients for a gloomy, disillusioned, and anti-idealistic work, it is in its end result not one. As noted earlier in this chapter, Mann continually counterbalances the novel's darker sides with his humorous, detailed portrayal of this world.

The principal challenge that *Buddenbrooks* continues to present to its readers is that of understanding its ambiguities and inner tensions. Mann's early stories have shown that we should never trust the all too obvious. Underneath the skillful weaving of trendy, antibourgeois philosophies into the text lies Mann's attachment to life and an ambiguity that should prevent us from adopting a one-sided interpretation of the novel. The decline of the male members of the Buddenbrooks provides a focus that proves to be a distraction from other, equally central aspects of the novel and other literary influences, in particular those that evolve around the character of Tony Buddenbrook. Mann devotes approximately one-third of the novel to her, more than to any other character. Her importance is underscored by her appearance at both the very beginning and very end of the novel. Mann's aunt Elisabeth is the direct model for Tony Buddenbrook; equally important in shaping her character are novels about women at that time, in particular the 1895 novel *Aus guter Familie* (*From a Good Family*) by Gabriele Reuter,[9] one with which Mann was certainly familiar when he jotted down notes on Tony (*NB 1–6* 102–3).

Agathe Heidling, the protagonist of *From a Good Family*, promises at the age of fifteen to lead the submissive life of a dutiful daughter in the hope of being rewarded with marriage and motherhood.[10] Her self-renunciation, however, is in vain. When her father spends her dowry, her economic value is lost, condemning her to becoming a frustrated spinster. The novel suggests that the pursuit of a sexually emancipated existence comes with a high price: social ostracism. Agathe Heidling chooses conformity over freedom, presented in the novel as an anarchic, miserable existence. Reuter's novel is a critical commentary on bourgeois, patriarchal society that causes women's sufferings and self-effacing sacrifices. It is furthermore a novel that asks us to evaluate the pros and cons of conformity.[11]

Like Agathe Heidling, Tony Buddenbrook learns compliance and self-renunciation in the service of bourgeois ideology from childhood. She recites the catechism with its list of God's creations that includes shoes and clothing, "wife and child, fields and cattle" (*B* 6). The inclusion of women and children on the same level as cattle reveals the objectified status of women in the bourgeois-Christian world of *Buddenbrooks*. Ten years later, in need of money and anticipating an expanding business through marriage, Johann Buddenbrook Jr. treats Tony as a useful commodity, a potential investment. He appeals to her as a loyal daughter, whose duty it is to put the interest of the family above selfish happiness by encouraging her to marry the repulsive businessman, Bendix Grünlich. Tony feels morally obligated to serve her family. The family itself becomes a pseudodeity to whom sacrifices must be made if condemnation and retribution are not to follow. Her father leaves no doubt that a defiant Tony would face the wrath of her family were she to pursue her "stubbornness and frivolity" and "follow an aberrant path" (*B* 131). Tony complies with her father's request, choosing to become an esteemed and constructive part in the family's history, thereby fulfilling what she had set as a goal in young age: "I'll marry a merchant, of course. . . . He'll have to have lots of money, so that we can furnish the house elegantly. I owe that much to my family and the firm" (*B* 78). The marriage partner is not important, neither is love. What counts are social and economic standing.

For many years, discussions on *Buddenbrooks* have either largely ignored Tony Buddenbrook or dismissed her as a one-dimensional character. The novel does not justify this neglect. While Tony submits herself to the expectations and pressures of her bourgeois world, she nevertheless retains some of her audacity, insolence, and jocularity, as well as her disrespect for an authoritarian, oppressive world that she had displayed during her youth. Her mocking appraisal of Grünlich and her intuitive understanding of his true intentions set her apart from the paternal, calculating, mercantile world. It is a world that she agrees to embrace, driven by a sense of duty and destination. But the narrator mentions that "her pronounced sense of family-identity nearly alienated her from the concepts of free will and self-determination." The word "nearly,"[12] so easily overlooked, reveals that the author wants her to preserve some sense of independence and self-determination. When she marries Grünlich, she is not simply a passive, ignorant victim coerced into leading an emotionally and sexually crippling life. Rather, Tony renounces her sexual and emotional desires for her privileged social and economic status. That she has self-determination, that there are indeed limitations to how far her sense of duty goes, becomes apparent when she takes the unusual step of initiating a divorce from her second husband, aware that her family's honor and bourgeois respectability are at stake.

With Tony's predicament, Mann throws a negative light upon bourgeois society. Yet Mann does not want us to see Tony as a victim. Despite two disastrous marriages and the family's decline she maintains an unabiding, resolute spirit. This world that has hurt her, that has suffocated her self and denied her sexual fulfillment, is nonetheless still worthy of her love and compassion. By imbuing Tony with an unfaltering sympathy for the bourgeois world, Mann brings us closer to it; simultaneously, her fate makes us critical and detached. Her perseverance is testimony to her love for life. Thus, with Tony, Mann presents a counterpoint to decadence, and the morbid, nihilistic thoughts and yearning for death that have afflicted Thomas and Hanno Buddenbrook. However, like other characters, Tony, the survivor, presents us with ambiguities. She has a stomach affected by nervous stress, and, together with the remainder of the family, declines socially.

From today's perspective, it might seem puzzling that critical, intelligent women like Tony do not leave their repressive environment. Neither higher education nor any active participation in this bourgeois mercantile world of the mid–nineteenth century was an option. Madame Buddenbrook's crocheting, cited earlier, illustrates that upper-class women had to keep themselves busy to mask their unproductive lives. The novel suggests that these women, being afraid to lose their social position and identity and having limited control over their own destinies, have no choice but to embrace the only space that patriarchy provides for them, namely the domestic sphere of the family. Tony's identity is tied to the name of her family. She therefore clings to its former reputation and prestige even after the deaths of her brother Thomas and her nephew Hanno, and the subsequent liquidation of the family firm. In weekly meetings with the rest of the family, all divorced or unmarried women, and Tony's old teacher Sesemi Weichbrodt, Tony looks with nostalgia at the old family papers. None of these women have a promising future without their patriarchal family. Neither, as the novel has illustrated all along, did they ever have one when the patriarchs were alive.

With Tony's fate, Mann launches an accusation against the misogynist practices of bourgeois-patriarchal society. Furthermore, he underscores one central aspect of the novel: the renunciation of love for money. The course of Tony's life is by no means unique in *Buddenbrooks*. At the same time that she renounces her love for Morten, her brother Thomas bids farewell to his secret lover, the flowergirl Anna, and marries the rich, beautiful, yet emotionally and physically cold Gerda Arnoldsen. Like his sister, he understands his duty, that it is his destiny and obligation to take over the firm and to make a good match (*B* 150). The desire for a socially and financially privileged existence dissuades both status-oriented burghers from pursuing their individual happiness. *Buddenbrooks* gradually unmasks this pursuit of material gain and status as self-destructive.

Noticeably, from one generation to the next, love disappears more and more from the Buddenbrooks' marriages. The increasing absence of love is accompanied by the family's decline. Perhaps the most tragic aspect of *Buddenbrooks* lies in the futility of all the self-sacrifices the members of the patrician clan make to keep their bourgeois world intact. The presence of Tony Buddenbrook throughout the novel is a steady reminder of this futility. But why does Mann focus so much on the absence of love? The answer to this question leads us back to the autobiographical dimension of *Buddenbrooks*. When Mann wrote his novel, he saw himself both as a social and sexual outsider. Tony, while not the author's alter ego, functions as yet another mask for the author's own repressed sexuality, his sexual frustrations and disappointment. Through her, he launches an accusation against a cold-hearted, materialistic world that denies love, companionship, and self-realization, and punishes deviation from strict, impersonal norms and conventions. Implicitly, Mann pleas for a more humane world.

When Mann wrote *Buddenbrooks*, he was torn between being part of the bourgeois, mercantile world, its respectability and social privileges, and his emancipation from it. *Buddenbrooks* suggests that it is not worth making sacrifices to remain part of this world. Tony Buddenbrook's renunciation of love and freedom in the service of the bourgeois-Christian work ethic, social respectability, and recognition cannot impede the family's decline. In addition, Thomas Buddenbrook's empty existence, which in the end reduces bourgeois respectability to a facade, is another indictment of this world. Unlike his character, the alienated burgher, who feels obliged to maintain the firm and to spend the rest of his life with mercantile duties, Mann was able to leave without making any painstaking choices his father had ordered the liquidation of the family business.

Buddenbrooks, with all its poignant scenes about unfulfilled lives, can be read as Mann's secret justification for leaving the repressive bourgeois world behind. However, writing his epic family saga with all its myriad details, permeated by love and hate, sympathy and cynicism, attests to the fact that, rather than severing his connections to this world, he took elements of it with him. His detached artistic existence, an escape from home, always kept him, ironically, close to home. At the end of the novel, Mann addresses his own ambivalent relationship as an artist to bourgeois society in the figures of Hanno Buddenbrook and his friend Kai Mölln.

Hanno, upon whom Mann projects his own experiences in a boring, stifling, and authoritarian school in Lübeck, lacks vitality, hope, and the will to create art. Lacking any discipline, he merely uses his musical talents to improvise on Wagner's music in order to find a sanctuary from reality in a make-believe world of life, death, and sexuality. Hanno represents the dangerous side of antibourgeois, aesthetic life. With Hanno's death, Mann distances himself from asocial, life-negating aestheticism. Adopting Wagner's contrapuntal technique for his own writing style, Mann contrasts Hanno's decadent, self-destructive art with that of his friend Kai Mölln. Kai Mölln stands out in *Buddenbrooks* because his future is not overshadowed by signs of decadence, suffering, or a passive acceptance of fate. Ironically, he is the son of a decadent, aristocratic family. His father, an impoverished, rather strange man, lives in an old farmhouse and occupies his time raising chickens and vegetables. He allows his only son to grow up "like a wild animal among the chickens and dogs" (*B* 451). Kai Mölln is the counter image of the bourgeois conformist; his appearance is totally scruffy and stands in stark contrast to Thomas Buddenbrook's, yet his features display "the marks of a fine and noble pedigree" (*B* 450). He stands out in the novel because, despite a decadent background, he is strong, not afraid of authority, and full of humor and irony. Unlike Hanno and the sons of other upper-middle-class families in *Buddenbrooks*, Kai Mölln is not burdened by paternal expectations and pressures. He wants to become a storyteller and write narratives like Edgar Allen Poe's *The Fall of the House of Usher*, the story of a family's decline. His first stories, presented orally, fascinate Hanno, "because they were not pure fabrications but had some basis in reality, but a reality bathed in a strange and mysterious light" (*B* 453). What Mann describes here is his own novel that hovers between realism and a symbolic, mysterious world.

To identify Kai Mölln with Mann is tempting, yet Mann gave Kai Mölln an aristocratic, not a bourgeois background. He can be considered a projection of the artist Mann imagines he could become, one whose art reaches out to life and transforms it. In contrast to Hanno, Kai can combine his outsiderness with love and compassion. But is he the ideal artist? The nature and object of his compassion raise doubts. Kai Mölln aggressively woos Hanno for his friendship. Hand in hand he walks with Hanno on the schoolyard, and, before the latter's death, kisses his hands incessantly. There is more than a homoerotic subtext to this friendship. We are to understand Kai Mölln's love for the decadent Hanno Buddenbrook not as one for life, but as the healthy, life-oriented artist's love for the realm of life-negating art. We cannot discard the possibility that through Kai Mölln Mann is confessing his own love for aestheticism.

The temptation of the nonconformist artist-outsider, whose sexuality and creativity distance him from society, is to lean towards the forces of decadence and death. With Kai Mölln, Mann addresses the dangers—with Hanno, the self-destructive aspects—of outsiderness. Equally self-destructive can be conformity, which leads to self-effacement, as *Buddenbrooks* shows. The novel does not resolve its underlying central issue, namely that of how to balance a life torn between conformity and individual desires and, on a more autobiographical level, Mann's personal dilemma, the need for bourgeois respectability on the one hand, and artistic and sexual freedom and contempt for a mediocre, banal existence on the other. This quandary is not restricted to nineteenth-century German burghers and artists, but occurs wherever the fetters of conventions and anti-individualistic norms clash with individual aspirations. *Buddenbrooks* is thus a novel not only of a bygone German bourgeois world, but also of our own times.

CHAPTER 4

Narratives after *Buddenbrooks*

Mann's second volume of short stories, *Tristan: Six Novellas*, appeared in 1903. Some of the stories were written either before or during Mann's work on *Buddenbrooks*. The earliest one is "Luischen" ("Little Lizzy"), written in 1897 and first published in January 1900 in the magazine *Die Gesellschaft*. Influenced by Turgenjev's *Torrents of Spring* from 1872, Mann's story about misdirected desire is pseudotragic, hilarious, and grotesque; it shows a world that is, in Mann's own words, "strange and ugly."[1] Its main characters are the beautiful and cunning Amra and her repulsively fat and impotent husband Christian Jacoby, whom Amra betrays with Alfred Läutner, a young composer of dubious talent. When Amra asks Christian Jacoby to dance in a ballerina's pink tutu at a party to a tune she and the composer will perform, her monstrous husband agrees out of love for his wife. On stage, at the moment of utmost humiliation, full of despair and self-disgust, he recognizes that his wife has been committing adultery and, as the narrator comments laconically and sardonically, "the fat man collapsed so heavily that the boards groaned" (*Tales* 81). In an instant, he is dead.

In this story, Mann addresses, in a grotesque way, the outsider's yearning to participate in life and his punishment for it. Life, represented by Amra, is banal, cruel, and obtuse. Christian's miserable suffering from his outsiderness, his animal-like body, and his submission to his wife's demands do not warrant pity from the perspective of a cruel, amoral world—a perspective readers are tempted to adopt, yet also to question. Without doubt, Christian is a repulsive outsider, but his immense suffering, his ability to love, and his, albeit false, clinging to the sanctity of bourgeois marriage and mores also draw our sympathy. By choosing the name Christian for his protagonist, Mann points at his character's belief in bourgeois-Christian morality and his sacrifice for his marriage. Ironically, this sacrifice takes the form of the singing and performing of the popular song "Luischen," a song about a prostitute. Christian dismantles his own world and, initially unknowingly, affirms a cruel, treacherous world bereft of moral values. The story, which Mann narrates in five segments thereby perhaps mocking the classical structure of tragedy, evolves toward a nihilistic undertone. Christian's repellent body and his humiliating, ridiculous behavior are insufficient reasons to perceive his death as tragic. At the end, a young doctor curtly comments on Jacoby's death with the words "It's over" (*Tales* 82). Death becomes a trite event, reminiscent of Mann's earlier story "Death."

When Mann wrote "Little Lizzy," he saw himself as an outsider, apprehensive toward his stigmatized desires and alienated from what he perceived to be a banal and boring bourgeois world. In "Little Lizzy," he presents not only his sexual frustrations, his resentments against his otherness and his self-pity, and, moreover, his loathing of the world, but also an ambiguous view of the artist's relationship to society. Läutner, who embraces life through his love affair with a married woman, is a naive snob, "consciously childlike, immoral, unscrupulous, . . . smug, cheerful" (*Tales* 69). Cheerful also are his compositions, which are geared toward his audience's taste for unsophisticated, light-hearted entertainment; he composes pretty waltzes and tunes to gain popularity. Läutner is not without artistic talents. Mann points out that Läutner's musical pieces contain ingenious elements, such as an original disharmony, an unexpected modulation, "some kind of small nervous effect revealing wit and deftness, for the sake of which they seemed to have been composed in the first place" (*Tales* 69). Fleetingly they capture life's melancholy, before falling back into triviality. By implicitly criticizing Läutner for prostituting himself and his talents rather than pursuing originality and artistic integrity, Mann suggests that art should not be subordinated to banal life, that the artist, in order to capture life, must remain above it.

"Der Kleiderschrank: Eine Geschichte voller Rätsel" ("The Wardrobe: A Story Full of Riddles"), written in November 1898 and first published in the magazine *Neue Deutsche Rundschau* in June 1899, takes a different approach to the relationship between art and life.[2] The protagonist of the story, the terminally ill Albrecht van der Qualen (*Qual* is the German word for suffering, pain), impulsively gets off a train that is to take him south, and rents an apartment in an unknown city.[3] The story then takes a surreal turn. In the wardrobe of the apartment a young, beautiful woman appears who, night after night, tells van der Qualen sad stories about love. She does not resist his sexual advances, yet after every sexual union she disappears for a few nights, only to reappear subsequently and remain silent. Gradually she resumes her story telling until van der Qualen approaches her again. Mann's narrator leaves open whether the encounter between van der Qualen and the woman ever really took place.

"The Wardrobe" evokes the irrational, occult world of Romantic tales in which the laws of time and place and the boundaries between hallucination and reality are suspended. The story also takes on a mythological dimension when van der Qualen encounters a boatman on a decrepit boat, an allusion to Charon and the river Styx. With van der Qualen's illness and his decision to step off the train, that is, to turn away from reality, Mann signals outsider existence. The themes of death, yearning for love and beauty, and the exclusion of life from art are intertwined. "The Wardrobe" is a symbolic admission that art necessitates a detachment from life and that life silences art.

"Der Weg zum Friedhof" ("The Road to the Churchyard"), a "short grotesque story" (*GW 11* 620), was written shortly before the completion of *Buddenbrooks* in July 1900, and first published the same year in *Simplicissimus*. With this story, Mann first embarked on his career as a public reader of his own works, and, according to press reports, his performance was a complete success.[4] The story can be read as an allegory of life, reminiscent of medieval mystery plays. Lobgott Piepsam, who has lost his wife, his three children, and his job due to his drinking, is walking on the road to the cemetery. A cyclist, referred to as Life—thus a realistic character as well as an allegorical embodiment of life—crosses the path of the self-destructive Piepsam. Life—blond and blue-eyed, bold and strong—annoys Piepsam, who insists that he should take another path. Life ignores the wretched man; an ambivalent chase follows. On the one hand, Piepsam wants Life out of his way, while on the other, he chases Life expressing his yearning to participate in it: "Anyone who had seen [Piepsam] might have wondered whether he maliciously intended to prevent the young man from riding on, or whether the fancy had suddenly taken him to be towed in the rider's wake" (*Stories* 68). Life escapes, and Piepsam's diatribe against the cyclist ends when he suddenly drops dead. His corpse is unceremoniously shoved into an ambulance "like a loaf into an oven" (*Stories* 71).

Notebook entries and letters of this period suggest that Mann projected his sense of alienation and outsiderness, as well as his yearning for life, upon grotesque characters like Christian Jacoby and Gotthold Piepsam, both of whom are unlikable yet stir our empathy because life treats them so cruelly. Often, a satirical acrimony accompanies Mann's presentation of the outsider's existence, but his presentation of life does not fare much better. In both "Little Lizzy" and "The Road to the Churchyard," life, while desirable, is cruel. Life is nothing but a "pantomime" (*Stories* 71), as the narrator suggests at the end of "The Road to the Churchyard." Death provides an easy fictional solution to his characters' problems. Not so in real life, where Mann found the strength to cope with his problems by writing about outsiderness, by killing it off in his fiction, and by taking an ironic view of life and asking us to laugh about it with him, like the people surrounding the yelling Piepsam, joined by a small dog who "wedged its tail between its hindquarters and howled up into his face" (*Stories* 70).

With "Gladius Dei" (Latin for "God's Sword"), written in 1901 and published in 1902, Mann takes his readers to fin-de-siècle Munich, at the time an important center of the arts and culture in Germany. The city is introduced as radiant, emanating a carefree, light-hearted ambiance. Among a cheerful, curious crowd gathered in front of an art gallery admiring a photograph of a beautiful woman in the pose of a half-naked Madonna with Jesus at her breast, stands a frowning monkish figure. It is Hieronymus, whom Mann modeled after Fra Bartolomeos's famous renaissance painting of Girolamo Savonarola (1452–1498). Mann's character, who shares with his model a contempt for pagan, sensuous art, unsuccessfully attempts to convince the owner of the gallery, Herr Blüthenzweig, to destroy this photograph as well as all his other art. When Blütenzweig's servant throws the adamant ascetic out of the gallery, Mann again allows brutal life to win over an outsider.

"Gladius Dei" marks a shift from Mann's focus on the problematic existence of the outsider to questions about the function and responsibility of art, questions that are as pertinent today as they were in the late 1890s. Hieronymus is an opponent of aestheticism and what he perceives to be immoral art—art that caters to sensuality and stimulates the sexual imagination. Furthermore, he is a proponent of art that brings knowledge and liberation from suffering: "Art is not a cynical deception, a seductive stimulus to confirm and strengthen the lusts of the flesh! Art is the sacred torch that must shed its merciful light into all life's terrible depths, into every shameful and sorrowful abyss; art is the divine flame that must set fire to the world, until the world with all its infamy and anguish burns and melts way in redeeming compassion!" (*Stories* 87). Mann's portrayal of Hieronymus as an advocate to be ridiculed, his face contorted into an expression of derangement, encourages us to question the validity of his perspective on art. Hieronymus's apocalyptic demand at the end, "Gladius Dei super terram . . . cito et velociter" ["May God's sword come upon earth . . . swiftly and soon"],[5] cannot be taken seriously. But does aestheticism win when he gets thrown out of the art gallery with its immoral art? "Gladius Dei" is open-ended and challenges us to ask ourselves whether art should be free, thereby potentially irresponsible and immoral, or in the service of morality, and thereby dogmatic and biased.

Written over a hundred years ago, *Tristan*, from 1903, remains one of Mann's most popular novellas, largely due to the fact that Mann employs a narrator who tells his story about patients in a sanatorium with a rich clientele from a humorous, ironic viewpoint. Among the bourgeois patients are a group of men with lean, shriveled faces, always throwing their legs in the air, symptomatic of syphilis, and a pastor's wife with the curious last name Höhlenrauch (cave smoke), who has allegedly gone insane due to having borne nineteen children. Of particular interest to the narrator is an odd figure, the artist Detlev Spinell, whose profession he labels a "dubious activity" (*Stories* 112). Throughout the novella, Mann voices reservations about this artist figure who is referred to as being "only" from Lemberg (a town now in the eastern part of Poland that was home to a large Jewish population), and thus obviously of Jewish ancestry, as further alluded to by his name, Detlev Spinell. That Mann stigmatizes people of Jewish descent by identifying them with outsiders indicates that, though skeptical of customary values and prejudices, he himself was not immune to the type of anti-Semitic views that have long pervaded German and other European literatures and societies. Spinell is an unattractive figure, with his decaying teeth and exceptionally large feet. His lack of facial hair and his resentment of everything associated with life suggest sexual impotence, an impotence for which Mann has him compensate with his artistic creativity. Ironically, this compensation yields minimal results: as a writer of one unsuccessful novel, his talent is questionable.

As in many of his earlier stories, in *Tristan* Mann juxtaposes art and life. Spinell is an aesthete who hates the banality of life. He likes to gain only fleeting impressions of reality and attempts to turn these into images of captivating beauty. Mann illustrates the artist's disposition to convert transitory, ordinary life into beauty and permanent art with the arrival of a new patient, Gabriele Klöterjahn, the wife of an unrefined yet compassionate businessman, and mother of a fat, healthy infant. When Gabriele Klöterjahn tells Spinell, who is smitten by the beautiful young woman, about her youth and her gossiping and crocheting with her girlfriends, he lifts this ordinary event out of its banality. His creative powers turn Gabriele into a singing princess wearing a crown; he thus aesthetically removes her from a mundane bourgeois marriage, life-sapping motherhood, and sexuality. Mann contrasts the artist's attempt to detach her from life with Gabriele Klöterjahn's repeated insistence that it had been her "will," the will of nature to marry and to procreate.[6] As Mann so conspicuously excludes love as a reason for Gabriele's marriage, he contrasts Schopenhauer's concept of the will to life, expressed through sexuality, with Spinell's flight from life into aestheticism as a substitute for life and sexuality. The decadent, sickly Spinell, whose sexual prowess is dubious, transforms Gabriele Klöterjahn into a lifeless artifact. Only as such can he admire her.

Mann pokes fun at Spinell, as he accompanies his vision with his comment "What beauty! . . . how beautiful" and a description of Spinell's "quite contorted" face (*Stories* 108). Despite the fact that doubts are cast on the life-negating artist, we are not to dismiss Spinell's "vision" of Gabriele as an extraordinary woman. Her illness identifies her as just another patient; in contrast, her light-blue veins, reminiscent of Gerda Buddenbrook, and her artistic inclinations identify her as an outsider. When Spinell asks her to play the piano, she acquiesces, even though she is under strict orders to refrain from doing so. His request serves to reactivate her artistic side, repressed by her bourgeois marriage. Through Spinell, Gabriele experiences "a strange curiosity about her own nature" (*Stories* 106). Playing Chopin's *Nocturnes*, followed by excerpts from Wagner's *Tristan and Isolde* that center on passionate love, lifts her above bourgeois normalcy into the realm of life-transcending art. But it also leads to a violent eruption of her disease and a swift death, leaving a husband and infant behind. Mann sends an ambivalent message. Art liberates and elevates; but it leads to a destructive renunciation of reality and belongs to the realm of death.

The transference of Wagner's *Tristan and Isolde* into a bourgeois setting sheds additional light upon Mann's ambivalent stance toward aestheticism. In Wagner's opera, the figures of Tristan and Isolde, having taken a love potion, experience a sexual love so powerful that they break with moral and social conventions. Sexuality in *Tristan and Isolde* is explicitly related to Schopenhauer's will to life and the deliverance from the *principium individuationis* to become part of the vast cosmos of the ever striving will. Wagner's star-crossed lovers yearn for transcendental, eternal unity. Their longing is fulfilled with the *Liebestod* (death-in-love). Mann asks us to associate Spinell and the married Gabriele Klöterjahn with Wagner's characters when Gabriele plays Wagner's *Sehnsuchtsmotiv* (motif of yearning) and the *Liebestod*. But the impotent Spinell is a mere caricature of Wagner's knight and lover; Gabriele, even though attracted to Spinell's artistic world, does not desire him sexually. While Wagner's *Tristan and Isolde* glorifies the power of life, love, and passion, as well as death, in Mann's narrative Spinell experiences music as an aesthetic substitute for life and sexuality, and Gabriele finds brief deliverance from bourgeois life. Their musical escapade is thus to be understood as an ironic reversal of Schopenhauer's will to life and of Wagner's celebration of sexual union and transcendental redemption.

Mann's irony does not stop there. Against *Tristan and Isolde*, the quintessential work of German bourgeois art and culture celebrating sexuality at the time, Mann sets the unglamorous hardship of life associated with sexuality. Frau Höhlenrauch's sexuality has generated nineteen pregnancies and insanity. Then there are the syphilitic gentlemen's ailments. Less bizarre, and not subjected to Mann's mocking tone, is the fate of Gabriele Klöterjahn. Her pregnancy has weakened her enough to exacerbate deadly tuberculosis. All these examples insinuate that art, in glorifying Eros and Thanatos, does not do justice to real life; they also support Spinell's contempt for life.

In the conversation between Spinell and Klöterjahn that follows the piano-playing episode that leads to Gabriele's death, Mann confronts life-negating aestheticism with life-affirming bourgeois orientation. Spinell's lack of virility, his aesthetic interests, and his renunciation of vulgar, banal life are juxtaposed with the compassionate, somewhat hedonistic attitudes of Klöterjahn, who displays a "warm, kindly, honest, human emotion" (*Stories* 130) and does not need art as substitute for real life. Mann leaves open the question of who is right: Spinell, who attributes Gabriele's death to "crude existence" (*Stories* 125), leading her to lose vitality and resulting in her degradation, or Klöterjahn, who blames Spinell and art for her demise? The story ends with Spinell's encounter with Gabriele's strong, perversely healthy, flourishing son. The infant, a symbol of the future, represents in its primordial desires Schopenhauer's will to life. Spinell is overcome by this monstrous display of life and runs away. The artist's flight implies the victory of life over aestheticism, an aestheticism that in *Tristan* turns away from life and caters to the transfiguration of death. In "Bilse und Ich" ("Bilse and I"), from 1906, Mann stats that in his novella *Tristan* he put a questionable part of himself—his aestheticism—on trial and that he castigated himself with the satirized figure of the modern artist (*E 1* 43). The exploration of a different art, one that is not founded in renunciation of life, not aimed at celebrating lifeless beauty and death, takes on a central role in *Tonio Kröger*, from 1903.

The contrast between the artist's extraordinary and the burgher's ordinary existence, and the artist's distance from life form the basis of *Tonio Kröger*, a novella that covers in a few episodes approximately twenty-five years of the protagonist's life. It belongs in the tradition of the German artist novellas of the nineteenth century but goes far beyond this genre, made evident by its worldwide popularity. Prior to Mann's death in 1955, over fifty translations existed. Its universal appeal lies to a large extent in Mann's perceptive presentation of a collective human experience: understanding and coming to terms with one's self.

Tonio Kröger starts out as a narrative about a teenager in search of an identity and hoping for acceptance and recognition. The fourteen-year-old Tonio Kröger grows up as the son of a reputable north German merchant and an artistically inclined mother of Latin origins in a town on the Baltic Sea, obviously modeled after Lübeck. Tonio Kröger admires his father's work ethic and shares his pride in living a respected, orderly existence, values Mann encapsulates in a reoccurring sentence in *Tonio Kröger*: "We're not gypsies in a green caravan, but respectable people" (*Stories* 138). Yet, Mann's pensive adolescent cannot follow in the footsteps of his father and the conventional lifestyle of his peers, oriented toward integration and success in a commercial world. Nor does he feel comfortable in his mother's world. Consuelo Kröger plays music and is not bothered by her son's poor performance in school. Tonio finds "his mother's blithe unconcern slightly disreputable" (*Stories* 138). Thus he spends his young life torn between a bourgeois and an artistic orientation, between a stable world, symbolized in the novella by a fountain and an old walnut tree, and the infinite, nonconformist, and chaotic world, symbolized by the sea and caravan-dwelling gypsies.

Tonio Kröger's quest to find himself and to be accepted is particularly agonizing since Mann shows him to be different in two unusual ways from his peers. First, he is a creative adolescent who writes poetry, plays the violin, and spends his life lounging about, while his friend, the blonde, blue-eyed Hans Hansen, a well-adjusted, admired young man, loves books about horses and enjoys an active lifestyle. Often Hans disappoints the sensitive Tonio Kröger, with whom we sympathize because he is only fully accepted by those who also feel marginalized, like the unattractive Magdalena Vermehren. At dance lessons she inevitably falls down, a symbol that she too does not fit in. Second, with Tonio Kröger's love for Hans Hansen, Mann includes a homosexual subtext. Hans Hansen is undoubtedly based on Mann's school friend Armin Martens. Just a few months before his death Mann confessed, "This one I have loved—he was truly my first love, and a more tender, blissfully more painful one was never again granted me" (*Br 3* 387). Mann transfers his pain to his character. Tonio Kröger suffers immensely and learns a lesson that Mann phrases in universal terms: "Whoever loves the more is at a disadvantage and must suffer" (*Stories* 137).

How does a person who is different and suffers from this difference survive in this world? In Mann's novella, the lonely outsider turns away from life. We meet Tonio Kröger again, when he is thirty years old, apparently living alone. After his father's death, preceded by the family's decline (a theme from *Buddenbrooks*), Tonio Kröger has left his provincial hometown, become an artist, contemptuous of mocking "the crude and primitive way of life," and devoted his life to "the power of intellect and words" (*Stories* 151). In his delineation of Tonio Kröger's artistic psyche and aesthetics, Mann's novella again embeds Schopenhauer's idea that art provides distance from the world and thereby provides a release from suffering. Tonio Kröger's writing "showed him life from the inside and revealed to him the fundamental motives behind what men say and do. But what did he see? Absurdity and wretchedness—absurdity and wretchedness" (*Stories* 151). With this repetition Mann underscores Tonio Kröger's propensity to accept Schopenhauer's pessimism and the idea that life is suffering. That knowledge is a curse rather than a blessing is a notion also offered by Nietzsche in *The Birth of Tragedy* (1872): "Once truth has been seen, the consciousness of it prompts man to see only what is terrible or absurd in existence wherever he looks."[7] Attaching ideas from Schopenhauer and Nietzsche to Tonio Kröger's perspective allows Mann to identify his character as an antibourgeois, disillusioned, even nihilistic outsider, but not necessarily as a proponent of both philosophers. In fact, while Tonio Kröger has lost his earlier ability to love, and now hates life, he yearns to escape his repugnance of it. He "fell into carnal adventures, far into the hot guilty depths of sensuality, although such experiences cost him intense suffering" (*Stories* 151). Whether these adventures are of a hetero- or a homosexual nature, is left open in the novella. Tonio Kröger's sufferings are twofold. First, being "intolerant of the banalities" (*Stories* 152) of life, as the artist-outsider he cannot take pleasure in the daily joys of existence. Second, his bourgeois conscience forbids him an unsteady and promiscuous life. Mann has his character constantly reminding himself of the indecent life of "a gypsy in a green caravan." Tonio Kröger chooses the life of an artist whose growing success as a writer is accompanied by exclusion from life and declining health. Thus Mann accentuates the incompatibility of art and life, outsiderness and integrated existence. However, one aspect of bourgeois life that Tonio Kröger shares with his author carries over into artistic existence, namely a bourgeois work ethic, a relentless striving for aesthetic excellence to produce the "good work" (*Stories* 152).

Again, the novella moves forward in time. The next segment shows the artist in his forties in Munich, impeccably dressed—a testimony to his bourgeois conscience—and visiting a Russian friend, Lisaveta Ivanovna. She is an intelligent, emancipated, and independent woman in her early forties with a very charming face, who appears to be an abstract, modern painter living a single, bohemian lifestyle. Tonio Kröger confesses to her his belief that a respectable, decent human being is not an artist, and that literature is a curse, because the artist always suffers from a consequential, necessary exclusion from life.[8] While sensitive and empathetic, Lisaveta opposes Tonio Kröger's pang of conscience with the argument that the true artist, aloof from society, destroys passions by transforming them into art and disinterested knowledge. Hers is a Schopenhauerian stance: art brings deliverance from suffering. Tonio Kröger argues conversely that the insights gained through art result in "nausea of knowledge" (*Stories* 160). Literature does not bring liberation from passions and suffering; words "refrigerate them and put them in cold storage" (*Stories* 160). To the utmost surprise of Lisaveta, Tonio confesses that he loves life, not the demonic, wild, strong life glorified by Nietzsche, but "life in its seductive banality! . . . normality, respectability, decency—these are our heart's desire." Tonio's yearning for "innocence, simplicity, and living warmth" (*Stories* 161) is a longing for human communication, for social and erotic interaction. Both are part and parcel of bourgeois, but not artistic, existence as Mann underscores with Lisaveta's response. She calls Tonio a "bourgeois who has taken the wrong turning;" Tonio replies: *"I have been eliminated"* (*Stories* 164). Having exposed his feelings, he is afraid that he will no longer be recognized as an artist by other artists, and that, after having been marginalized by the bourgeois world, he will now be also excluded from the world of outsiders.

What follows in *Tonio Kröger* are examples of the creative individual's alienated existence. After a thirteen-year absence, Tonio Kröger returns to his hometown. His outward identity as a burgher cannot mask the fact that he does not belong to the world that once had been his home. Mann even has his artist be mistaken for a criminal to underscore the artist's dissociation from bourgeois respectability. This tenuous connection of the artist with the criminal also implies a criticism of art as being deceptive and morally questionable. That Tonio Kröger does not belong to the world of normalcy is reiterated by Mann toward the end of the novella. At the Danish seaside resort of Aalsgaard, where Mann himself had spent some time in 1900, Tonio Kröger sees from afar two people that he mistakenly thinks to be Hans Hansen and another former student, Ingeborg Holm. From his peripheral viewpoint, he is not noticed by them, but is seen by a young woman, a girl who falls down, reminiscent of Magdalena Vermehren. Mann repeats an earlier sentence to indicate that Tonio Kröger will remain excluded from the world of the blonde and blue-eyed: "For they did not speak the same language" (*Stories* 188). What Tonio Kröger can only hope for is that his art will be read by people like Magdalena Vermehren. Mann ends his novella with Tonio Kröger's letter to Lisaveta Ivanovna, acknowledging that he stands between two worlds as an artist who is detached from, yet loves, life: "For if there is anything that can turn a *littérateur* into a true writer, then it is this bourgeois love of mine for the human and the living and the ordinary. It is the source of all warmth, of all kindheartedness, and of all humor" (*Stories* 191). With Tonio Kröger's turning toward life, Mann takes a decisive step away from the artist's aestheticism and contempt for life in *Tristan*. Arrogant hostility and mockery are replaced by an emotional engagement in life and the desire not to produce art for art's sake, but to communicate.

Are Tonio Kröger's confession and artistic credo to be taken seriously?[9] Are they, given the many parallels between Mann's and his character's life, Mann's own? Although Tonio Kröger declares his love for happy, ordinary people, he makes the comment: "The bourgeois are fools" (*Stories* 191). Tonio Kröger's compassion is questionable; he remains detached and loves people from a distance. The aloofness from the world that he displays is an aloofness shared by his author. Noticeably, the bourgeois world exists only marginally in the novella. A brief episode, in which Tonio Kröger encounters a sentimental businessman from northern Germany on his journey to Denmark, underscores the distance. While Tonio Kröger listens with "a certain secret sympathy" to the businessman's account about indigestible food, he identifies it as "foolish familiar overtures"

(*Stories* 176). In the fictional world of *Tonio Kröger*, Mann, like his protagonist, exhibits a striking detachment from ordinary human beings despite the declaration of a deeply-felt "bourgeois love . . . for the human and the living and the ordinary." The artist needs this love, "without which, as we are told, one may speak with the tongues of men and of angels and yet be a sounding brass and a tinkling cymbal" (*Stories* 191). These are neither Mann's words nor Tonio Kröger's, although he expresses them; they are quoted from the Bible (1 Cor. 13.1). How are we to interpret that Tonio Kröger, who throughout the novella has not been associated with biblical and Christian texts, suddenly uses a biblical passage to accentuate his love and the artist's desire to communicate?[10] Perhaps, on the one hand, Mann is avowing the value of artistic communication and the rejection of an art that is nothing more than "sounding brass." On the other, Tonio Kröger's acknowledgment for the artist's need for love and communication is presented in the form of a quotation; it is not his own voice that speaks here. In distancing Tonio Kröger from his commitment to the world of the ordinary and banal existence, Mann sustains the artist's detachment from reality, without unequivocally affirming it.[11]

From the early 1900s on, Mann's notebooks reveal his plans for a society novel, tentatively entitled *The Loved Ones*, featuring a woman, Adelaide, as the central figure and Mann's fictional alter ego.[12] In this planned novel, Mann returns to the masks of his story "Little Herr Friedemann" that allowed him to write about his stigmatized desires. The married Adelaide loves a violinist who resembles Mann's secret love-interest, Paul Ehrenberg. The notebook entries justify Adelaide's adultery and her defiance of moral conventions, but nonetheless throw a dubious light on her passion. Adelaide spends her time in painful longing for the object of her love. But the violinist does not need her. He leads a fully integrated existence, one that does not include a special place for her. Ultimately, he betrays her. Her passive suffering, loathing of her beloved, and self-detestation for enduring humiliation control her life (*NB 7–14* 47). Adelaide is struck by a "suffering of the yearning for unity on those days when she does not see him" (*NB 7–14* 72)—an obvious reference to Wagner's opera of forbidden love, *Tristan and Isolde*.

With this novel Mann intended to express what he felt had to be repressed in public. Yet writing could not free him entirely from the fetters of heterosexual and bourgeois norms, because even in the realm of creativity Mann masks his homosexual inclinations. His internalization of these norms also becomes evident when he mentions in his notebook "the moral superiority over the abominable invention of existence!" (*NB 7–14* 48). This sentence indicates Mann's submission to bourgeois mores, which he certainly must have interpreted as "slave morality" in light of his readings of Nietzsche and his own resentment towards his physical needs. Despite this resentment, Mann continued to cling emotionally to his unfulfilled homosexual desires. His writing served as an instrument to look upon these sufferings with ambivalence.

Through his fiction Mann broke his silence about his carefully hidden homosexual desires while at the same time very deliberately censoring himself. This paradox becomes an omnipresent aspect of his short stories written between 1903 and 1904. "Die Hungernden: Studie" ("The Starvelings: A Study"), written between *Tristan* and *Tonio Kröger*, describes an evening in the life of the artist Detlef, who feels superfluous at a party that is apparently being held at the opera in Munich. While listening to the music of Wagner's *Tristan and Isolde*, he is painfully reminded of his unrequited love for an "ordinary creature" (*Tales* 154), the beautiful Lilli. But Lilli only has eyes for a young painter. Detlef reflects upon his loneliness, his yearning for some intimacy and human happiness, but knows that, as an artist, he is condemned to loneliness, to the "world of petrifaction, of ice, bleakness, intellect, and art!" (*Tales* 157) Upon leaving the opera, Detlef encounters a haggard vagrant who stares at him with an expression of anger and envy. The story suggests that both men yearn for life, Detlef for love, the destitute outcast for a better life. Detlef identifies himself with this vagrant, "We are brothers, after all!" (*Tales* 159). This comment certainly does not indicate social awareness. Neither the plight of the working class poor, excluded from the warm, luxurious bourgeois world, nor the revolutionary thoughts of breaking down class barriers or creating an egalitarian society occupy Detlef's mind. The one and only affinity between the characters is their recognition that both are condemned to be voyeurs of life.

What on the surface level appears to be a story about the artist's ambivalent stance toward life, is a secret confession of Mann's agony that he, the homosexually inclined outsider, remains marginalized and excluded from happiness. From a notebook entry we know that Detlef serves as Mann's alter ego (*NB 7–14* 97). Lilli, who ignores Detlef and loves somebody else, is a fictional rendering of Paul Ehrenberg who at that time was engaged, thereby exacerbating Mann's feelings of exclusion. The artist's love for Lilli, the embodiment of banal and ordinary life, simultaneously expresses and conceals Mann's stigmatized desires. The reference within the story to Wagner's *Tristan and Isolde* sends a clear signal about illicit love. Wagner's sublime and erotic music, meant to express "the passionate yearning for unity" (*Tales* 154), induces in Detlef an increased longing for Lilly. But the music is distorted and badly played on poorly tuned instruments by musicians dressed in peasant costumes in Mann's story, indicating a resistance to and resentment of illicit love.

When Detlef leaves the opera with mixed feelings of despair and defiance, Mann sends ambivalent signals about his character: on the one hand he feels relief at having escaped a banal existence and having fought his erotic desires successfully, at having kept his dignity, on the other hand he also suffers from being excluded from life and love. The vagrant brings back the world Detlef had tried to escape. Detlef recognizes himself in the vagrant's posture; his piercing gaze at Detlef, associated with a "lecherous and greedy probing" (*Tales* 158) is reminiscent of the way Detlef had stared at Lilli and the painter. Both men's eyes are inflamed; they are brothers in their marginalized existences as well as in their longings and jealousies. A step toward the vagrant would mean identification. But Detlef remains silent, moves away, and is unable "of clearing things up." The connection between both, "an awful, alien world" (*Tales* 159), remains a tacit understanding.

In "The Starvelings" erotic yearnings are associated with filth, the world of the vulgar, the detestable, and a loss of dignity. It is a story in which Mann voices his self-contempt for having feelings for a "disgraceful love" (*Tales* 159). With the wish for a "a different love, a different love" (*Tales* 160) at the end of this short story, Mann expresses his need to free himself from desires that he could not and should not pursue. The wish "Children, love one another . . ." (*Tales* 160) desexualizes men and women, conjures up the carefree, nonsexual world of childhood.

"Ein Glück" (Bliss), from 1904, is a complementary story to "The Starvelings" and an adaptation of notes on "The Loved Ones."[13] It takes place at a party in an officers' club where the guests include members of the aristocracy, a cadet and a writer of bourgeois origins, and members of a female song and dance ensemble of working class background. The female protagonist, Baroness Anna, a variation of Mann/Adelaide, witnesses the infidelity of her husband, Baron Harry, who flirts with one of the singers, Emmy, even going so far as to give her his wedding band. Mann contrasts a masculine, active, insensitive world with Anna's passive, tormented existence. Although the narrator's identification with the humiliated, silently suffering Anna promotes a critical stance toward a sordid heterosexual world of vulgar cheerfulness, the story also casts Anna in a questionable light. Her love is latently masochistic, characterized by jealousy, yearning, hate, and self-contempt, similar to Mann's secret love for Paul Ehrenberg. "Ein Glück" thus again reflects Mann's anger and pain for being different.

Besides being a coded story about Mann's frustrated homosexual desires, "Ein Glück" is also a story about the sensitive artist-outsider who must remain alienated from the world and is condemned to be a voyeur of life. Anna, watching others dance while yearning to be part of life, reiterates Tonio Kröger's fate: "Indeed, it is difficult not to feel at home in one world or another,—we know it! But there is no conciliation" (*GW* 8 358). Yet there is a moment of accord in an unexpected turn of events. Anna discovers her erotic desire for Emmy, a longing that is "hotter" and "deeper" than the one for Harry (*GW* 8 359). When Emmy returns Harry's wedding ring to Anna and kisses her hand, Mann presents not only a momentary reconciliation between life and art, but also an erotic exchange hinting at lesbian and stigmatized love. Their momentary touch brings "a sweet, hot, and clandestine happiness" (*GW* 8 354). A fleeting moment of happiness must suffice. Even in the escapist world of make-believe, Mann refrains from further developing what bourgeois heterosexual mores condemn. Internalized self-censorship, submission to anti-individualistic norms are necessary in his striving for fame and recognition.

Fame and recognition are themes of "Das Wunderkind" ("The Wunderkind"), from 1903, a brief, humorous sketch about the artist's psyche and the impact of his art, inspired by the performance of a child prodigy that Mann attended in Munich in 1903. In Mann's sketch the extraordinarily talented musician is a presumably eight-year-old, narcissistic pianist with the Greek name Bibi Saccellaphylaccas. Mann's reduction of the artist to a child suggests an ironic treatment of artistic existence. Yet, he positions a critic in the audience who comments that the child prodigy displays all the features of a grown up artist: "He has the artist's grandeur and his lack of dignity, his charlatanry, and his holy spark, his scorn and his secret rapture" (*Tales* 237). The words "secret rapture" are particularly noteworthy, as the eroticized relationship between the artist and his audience develops into the most prominent theme in the sketch. Bibi feels superior to his audience yet loves to be admired and, consequently, even makes artistic compromises in order to be loved. After the performance, in a scene that would have been impossible with an older artist, the impresario kisses the young artist on the lips, and "this kiss shoots through the hall like an electric shock, surges through the crowd like a nervous shudder" (*Tales* 238). Perhaps Mann wrote this story as an antidote to the previous ones that focus on the frustrations and self-hatred of the lonely, marginalized, and disregarded outsiders such as Detlef and Anna. In "The Wunderkind" outsiderness is rewarded and rewarding. On an autobiographical level, the sketch suggests that art can indeed become a substitute for stigmatized love and that it might be best for the artist, in order to escape suffering, to remain aloof, cold-hearted, and narcissistic like the young prodigy.

A performance based on Mann's personal experiences is also at the center of "Beim Propheten" (At the prophet's), from 1904.[14] In a small apartment the proclamations of a prophet, Daniel, are read aloud "with reluctance" (*GW 8* 368) by one of his disciples. The absence of the prophet himself signals the artist's lack of interest in communicating with his audience. Among the audience is a writer, a self-portrait of Mann, who takes a critical stance toward the prophet's provocative ideas because they call for an aggressive, destructive, even self-destructive world. Mann's short story poses the question: How far should creativity go? The prophet is a dangerous demagogue; his visions are irresponsible, indifferent to life and exemplify a creativity run amuck. Mann's writer wonders whether the prophet lacks humanity, "a little sensitivity, yearning, love?" (*GW 8* 370) "Beim Propheten" thus reiterates the notion of *Tonio Kröger* that art should communicate with and include life and love, rather than self-servingly and with contempt for everything conjure up violence and defamations.

Mann includes a further autobiographical touch at the end of the story when his writer intends to send flowers to the absent and ill daughter of a rich woman who is also among the listeners at the apartment. She resembles Mann's future mother-in-law, Hedwig Pringsheim, who had actually been at the reading that served as a model for the story. The daughter is the ill Katia Pringsheim. The writer's kind, life-affirming attitude is questioned by the caveat: "He had *a certain* relationship to life" (*GW 8* 370; italics mine). Here it becomes evident that the narrative addresses the dilemma of artistic existence in general and Mann's personal situation at that time in particular. Can love for life and commitment to life coexist with artistic creativity, which is associated with loneliness, freedom, intellectual passion, even criminality and insanity? Debunking creativity as absolutely irresponsible in "Beim Propheten" similar to the way stigmatized desire had been debunked in previous stories as being contemptuous, is certainly a writer's tool to rid himself from that which haunts him, in Mann's case the fear of unbound aestheticism and of the loss of bourgeois respectability. "Beim Propheten" disapproves overtly of unrestricted creativity, gravitating instead towards life-affirming art and existence, a perspective that led Mann to the decision to marry despite skepticism about a banal, restrictive, bourgeois existence.

"Schwere Stunde" ("Harsh Hour"), from 1905, Mann's first fictional text after his marriage to Katia Pringsheim in February 1905, is a study commemorating the one hundredth anniversary of Friedrich Schiller's death. The sketch is a interior monologue in which an unnamed writer, living in Jena, ponders his artistic capabilities. We can identify the writer as Friedrich Schiller (1759–1805), an identity that Mann does not conceal. Mann incorporates sentences and ideas from Schiller's letters and writings into his character's thoughts about his doubts about completing a drama (*Wallenstein*, 1798–99). Furthermore, Mann's Schiller compares himself to "the other man" (*Tales* 244) in Weimar, a reference to

Goethe, who approaches his art with wisdom and peaceful contemplation while he suffers from weakness, hesitation, and self-doubts. That Mann does not mention Schiller's name despite his known identity allows us to understand Mann's Schiller as a representative artist as well as an individual. When writing this story, Mann probably also had his own writing difficulties in mind and, in particular, his failed drama *Fiorenza*. Later he admitted to the "very subjective" (*GW 11* 106) nature of the sketch.

Another affinity between Mann and Schiller is that, prior to the events of the text, Schiller had recently married, and had thereby gained "a bit of legitimacy and middle-class solidity, . . . status, and honor" (*Tales* 246). But life and human happiness, "that silken fetter, that soft, sweet bond" (*Tales* 250), sap his creative powers; he is haunted by failure and despair. Thus Mann establishes a connection between his entree into a respectable bourgeois life and his writer's block, and insinuates that artistic creativity and a comfortable, conventional life are at odds, that suffering is the source of creativity. Mann's Schiller confesses to his sleeping wife how much he loves her, but that he cannot find complete happiness with her as he is bound to his artistic mission. He kisses her just before he returns to the next room to complete "the work of his suffering" (*Tales* 251). Schiller's confession to his wife is also Mann's fictionalized confession to his new wife, Katia.

The last paragraph of "Harsh Hour" is a celebration of artistic creativity. Mann mentions Schiller's successful completion of this work: "And when it was completed, lo and behold, it was good" (*Tales* 251). Mann plays with biblical language from the Book of Genesis, a reference that art functions as substitute religion for the German burgher. It also underscores that the artist's sacrifices are not in vain, and that, despite his embrace of life through marriage, the urge to create has not faltered. More works will follow, "resonant and shimmering creations" (*Tales* 251). Before his marriage to Katia Pringsheim, Mann confessed in December 1904 to his brother Heinrich, who had accused his younger brother Thomas of "selling out," that his new bliss, his life as husband and burgher, will not end his artistic endeavors: "Bliss, *my* bliss is to too great an extent experience, movement, realization, torment, is too little related to peace and too much to suffering for it to become a constant threat to my art" (*HM/TM* 68). "Harsh Hour" is Mann's fictional affirmation, directed at Katia as well as at Heinrich, that he had not betrayed his creativity.

Indeed Mann's bourgeois marriage did not stop him from writing, although he scrutinized it in his subsequent story from 1905, "Wälsungenblut" ("The Blood of the Walsungs"). The title refers to the second part of Wagner's *Ring* cycle, *The Valkyrie*: "Bride and sister you are to your brother, / So flourish then the Walsung blood."[15] Mann transfers Wagner's story about incestuous love to a nouveau riche Jewish family living in Berlin at the turn of the century. Rumors of an alleged anti-Semitic tenor, coupled with Mann's awareness of his in-laws' Jewish ancestry, led him to withdraw the narrative prior to its publication in the *Neue Rundschau* in January 1906.[16] To his brother Heinrich he justified its necessary withdrawal by pointing out that he was no longer "free individually and socially." That Thomas Mann was burdened by the conflict between unbound artistic creativity and his need to be an integrated, respected artist and husband, becomes evident in the same letter: "To be sure, I've not been free since of a feeling of constraint, which in moments of hypochondria becomes very oppressive, and you will no doubt call me a cowardly bourgeois. But it's easy for you to talk. You are absolute. I, in contrast, have deigned to submit to my situation" (*HM/TM* 77).

To what extent Mann's amalgamation of Germanic mythological figures with Jewish parvenus testifies to his anti-Semitism, or to some unpleasant encounters with the Pringsheims, or to his jealousy of the close relationship between the twins Katia and Klaus Pringsheim, must remain open.[17] What is certain is that Mann uses Jewishness in "The Blood of the Walsungs"—as in *Tristan*—as a symbol for outsider existence; concomitantly, whether unintentionally or not, he stigmatizes Jews, as his story about the twins Siegmund and Sieglinde Aarenhold attests. The twins, strikingly arrogant and self-centered, brassy yet witty, resent their outsider status. Their closeness, symbolized throughout the story by their holding hands, and their self-absorbed existence is about to end with Sieglinde's forthcoming marriage to the dull civil servant and German Protestant, von Beckerath. This union, certainly not based on mutual love, will bring money to von Beckerath and social integration and prestige to Sieglinde.

In the story, the Aarenhold twins attend a performance of Wagner's *The Valkyrie*. Mann outlines the events of the first act of the opera and uses them as a foil to shed light upon his two outsider figures. Wagner's Siegmund has always been spurned because of his foreign origins. Wherever he goes, he encounters "scorn and hatred and contempt" despite the fact that he "courted friendship and love" (*Tales* 274). His twin sister Sieglinde has been forced into marrying Hunding, a coarse man of unattractive physique. Hunding represents the world of convention. With their incest, Siegmund and Sieglinde intend vengeance against those who stigmatized and disgraced them. Wagner's opera withholds moral judgment. Stigmatized desire implies the victory of nature and love over a conventional world without love.

In contrast, Mann's twins Siegmund and Sieglinde Aarenhold are negatively portrayed. Siegmund is explicitly not Wagner's Siegmund: "He was no hero, he had no vast powers" (*Tales* 267). He has a hirsute body, sweaty hands, and a crooked nose. He is cynical toward the world, without love, save for that toward his sister. Mann's Sieglinde is an equally dubious character. We can sympathize with her aversion of von Beckerath, but not with her betrayal. Beckerath resembles Hunding who, in Mann's characterization of Wagner's figure, prides himself on leading a "simple and orderly existence" (*Tales* 273). Pedantic, philistine, lacking intelligence and sympathy for the plight of the outsider, he represents ordinary life. The Aarenhold twins' incest after their return from the opera is the outsider's revenge for being shut out from normal life. At the same time, it affirms their outsider status. Originally, Mann had ended the story with a phrase that included Yiddish words: "Beganeft haben wir ihn—den Goy" [We have betrayed him—the Goy].[18] However, as the story otherwise does not contain Yiddish, he changed the last sentence to "He will lead a less trivial existence from now on" (*Tales* 284).

Mann's presentation of the outcast twins lacks the heroic, tragic dimension of Wagner's world. Their sexual encounter is that of "self-absorbed invalids, drugging themselves like people without hope" (*Tales* 284). "The Blood of the Walsungs" is a sardonic presentation of outsider existence and of stigmatized desire. Yet the alternative is equally loathsome. Sieglinde's entrance into bourgeois respectability and normalcy, into a world embodied by the dull and uncreative von Beckerath where money rules over love, is far from desirable. With von Beckerath, Mann, who himself married into the wealthy Pringsheim family, added a facet of self-irony to the narrative.

Autobiographical concerns that go beyond the renunciation of stigmatized desires and of outsiderness after his marriage to Katia Pringsheim, can also be traced in Mann's text. Mann has Siegmund, a descendant of earlier decadent artist figures, reflect critically and mockingly upon his luxurious, secure life. It is a life of utmost leisure, bereft of passion and suffering, and therefore not a good breeding ground for art: "He was too astute not to realize that the circumstances of his existence were not exactly the most conductive for developing a creative gift" (*Tales* 266). With this thought, Mann's skepticism as to whether his new extravagant life style can keep his artistic creativity alive resonates throughout "The Blood of the Walsungs."

CHAPTER 5

Royal Highness

When Mann started writing *Royal Highness*, he intended it to be a novella. The final product, a novel and a much longer project than anticipated, was completed by mid-February 1909, and is, undeservedly, one of Mann's most neglected works.[1] Overshadowed by later masterworks, *Royal Highness* is known as Mann's lightest work, a highly entertaining novel with a happy ending, reminiscent of romance novels. Yet underneath its surface looms a complex, multifaceted work that tells us, with humor and irony, about human nature and the lonely individual's need for love and compassion, as well as about social responsibility and, on a symbolic level, about the artist and his art—in other words, about Mann himself.

Royal Highness is a departure from the bourgeois world of *Buddenbrooks* and Mann's preceding stories. It is set in a small, poor principality in a nameless part of Germany at an unspecified time during the reign of the house of Grimmburg. A son with a deformed hand, Klaus Heinrich, is born to the Grand Duke, Johann Albrecht III and his wife Dorothea. The Grand Duke, disappointed by his son's disfiguration, is reminded of a gypsy's prophecy that a one-handed prince will save the country. Mann guides his readers through various stages of Klaus Heinrich's education, which is preparing him to perform his role as "Royal Highness." This education serves him well when the successor to the throne, Klaus Heinrich's weak and sickly brother Albrecht II, asks him to represent him at public appearances. Klaus Heinrich, having experienced a few disappointing, close encounters with life, fully commits himself to a representative, detached, and dispassionate existence. All this changes with the arrival of the American millionaire Spoelmann and his beautiful daughter Imma. Klaus Heinrich falls madly in love with her and thus opens up to life. Mann's novel ends with an elaborate royal wedding. Not only has Klaus Heinrich found happiness through love but so has his principality. It receives financial support from his father-in-law to rejuvenate the economy. The prophecy has been fulfilled and everyone in the principality can rejoice.

In his comments on *Royal Highness*, written in 1910, Mann emphasizes that the novel presents a "didactic allegory," an analysis of royal existence as a "formal, composed, super-composed, in a word artistic existence and the deliverance of highness through love" (*GW 11* 570). Mann had already established an affinity between artistic and royal existence in *Tonio Kröger*. Both Tonio Kröger and Klaus Heinrich practice aloofness, and are excluded from ordinary life and love. Another reference to this affinity can be found in a notebook entry where Mann wrote that the artist renders his life in art: "He leads a symbolic, representative existence,—like a royal highness" (*NB 7–14* 96). Mann identified himself with such a cold, dispassionate existence, as a letter to Katia Pringsheim in June 1904 attests: "Only one thing can cure me of the disease of representation and art that clings to me, of my lack of trust in my personal and human side. Only happiness can cure me; only *you*, my clever, sweet, kind, beloved little queen!" (*Letters* 35) The "cure" came in the form of their marriage in February 1905, and allowed Mann to enter an existence of bourgeois normalcy and respectability. It was not only a way to shed his lonely artist-outsider existence, but also to detach himself from his homosexual desires. But did his new status as husband and father reconcile him with life? Did it bring happiness and provide deliverance from the representative life? Answers to these questions are to be found in *Royal Highness*. This is not to suggest that *Royal Highness*, shaped by Mann's marriage to his "queen," is primarily an autobiographical piece. While being a humorous, self-critical exploration of his own life, it is at the same time reflective of universal human experiences in which social and individual expectations clash.

With *Royal Highness*, Mann introduces us to a world populated by celebrities, to use a present-day expression. Mann's royalty is admired, their every move observed and worthy of comment by the local press. Their detachment from ordinary life is a fundamental part of an extraordinary existence. Among those whom Mann introduces as loyal subjects and admirers of their royal masters is Dr. Sammet, a young physician. We meet him in the first chapter of the novel, when he is consulted by the Grand Duke about the birth defect of the newborn Klaus Heinrich. Dr. Sammet identifies himself as an outsider whose Jewish background has resulted in professional disadvantages. Nonetheless, he argues that to be exceptional is better than to be part of the "common herd" and the "complacent majority" (*RH* 28). Mann makes Sammet an outspoken as well as comical advocate of extraordinary existence. He talks with an awkward and all-too-eager voice, constantly saying "yes" between sentences, while clumsily thrusting one of his elbows about like a short wing. By ridiculing him, Mann throws a dubious light upon the outsider and his words.

Another tragicomic character in the novel who defends individualism and elitism yet whose authority is questionable, is Klaus Heinrich's tutor Überbein. Like Sammet, he is an outsider by birth. The illegitimate son of an actress,

Überbein considers "his very birth a misfortune" (*RH* 73). His physical defor-mities include a greenish face with a red beard and "exceedingly ugly, protruding, pointed ears" (*RH* 71). Discipline and hard work have earned him a doctorate. His renunciation of life and complete submission to an ascetic existence devoted to the attainment of the highest achievements are ideals he wants to instill in his student, Klaus Heinrich. "Formality and intimacy," according to Überbein, "are mutually exclusive" (*RH* 75). Überbein insists on differentiating between the world of ordinary people, their "humanitarianism and familiarity" (*RH* 76–77), and the world of royalty, the world of the select few who have to exercise dis-tance and dignity, subscribe their lives to duty, formality, and a rigid demeanor.

Later in the novel, Überbein reacts negatively when Klaus Heinrich falls in love with Imma Spoelmann. He himself had renounced his human nature, pas-sion, love, and happiness when, earlier in his life, he refrained from engaging in a love affair with a married woman, a "forbidden" relationship. Is this a victory of discipline and morality as he suggests?[2] His ambivalent comment that he chose success, "because he could and would not win her" (*RH* 237) inadver-tently raises more questions than it provides answers. Is there a hidden homo-sexual subtext? Mann mentions Überbein's empathetic interest in some of the boys in his charge, which contradicts his overall distance from life.[3] This contra-diction opens up the possibility that Überbein's excessive self-discipline, his striving for success, and his need for recognition are substitutes for his stigma-tized desire. In all probability, Mann addresses through Überbein his own homo-sexual frustrations that led him to self-doubts, as we know from his earlier stories, and which he countered by escaping into the impassioned realm of art. Überbein's fate also attests to the author's skepticism of the world of artistic exis-tence that cannot communicate because it lacks love. Überbein's unremitting, hard work goes unrewarded, and subsequently the ascetic pedagogue commits suicide.

In presenting both characters as peculiar and eccentric, Mann voices his reservations about outsider existence, elitism, and egocentric individualism, and, on the symbolic level of *Royal Highness*, about the aloofness of artistic exis-tence. However, neither Sammet's comments nor Überbein's teachings should be treated lightly and dismissed. They provide a counterbalance to the deprecation of an exalted, detached existence. This deprecation underlies Mann's presentation of the members of the royal family, whose lives, remote from ordinary existence, have an overwhelmingly negative impact on others as well as on themselves. Under their rule, the deterioration of their principality has reached dire propor-tions: the buildings are decrepit, the economy is collapsing, the forests are dying due to the overuse of natural resources, the people are poor, the working-class children suffer. The deficient state of the principality mirrors that of its ruling family. The aristocrats themselves are decadent. Similar to the Buddenbrook family, the House of Grimmburg is in decline. Johann wishes to die, his wife Dorothea suffers from bouts of insanity once her beauty is gone, Albrecht is sick, Klaus Heinrich has a disfigured arm and hand. What appears to be so grand and admirable on the outside, the life of royal celebrities, is unmasked by Mann as arduous, and frequently ridiculously petty and trite. We are to understand that the psychological and physiological deformities of the royals result from their elevated status. All of them resent, to a greater or lesser degree, their "chosen and isolated, melancholy forms of existence" (*RH* 77). This resentment hovers over the novel from the very beginning. In the novel's prelude, Klaus Heinrich, while moving through a deferential crowd, feels "the burden of his royal station" (*RH* 9).

The Grand Duke, Johann Albrecht III, whose face reveals weariness and boredom with his formal existence, is, like Thomas Buddenbrook, alienated from the world he is supposed to represent and identify with. Suffering from a blood disease, he wants to die, as he is sick to death of his "whole exalted life in the glare of publicity" (*RH* 107). Even in death, however, he cannot escape it: his funeral becomes a state affair at which he is the center of attraction. His son Albrecht II, whose outsider existence Mann emphasizes with his nervous condition and general weak health, formally resigns from all his duties as Grand Duke because he finds the princely existence ridiculous and self-alienating. Albrecht is all too aware that his public life is an illusionary existence of pseudoimportance and authority, because his ministers make all the decisions. To illustrate his lack of power and senseless existence, Mann has Albrecht tell Klaus Heinrich and their sister Ditlinde the story of the pensioner Dotty Gottlieb who needs to feel useful and important. Gottlieb fulfills his need by going to the train station a few times a day, where he inspects the passengers' luggage and the wheels of departing trains. When the stationmaster signals to the locomotive engineer to start the train, Dotty Gottlieb signals too. Albrecht points out that he is in the same position as the old retired man, even identifies with him: "That's like me. I wave, and the train starts off. But it would start off without me just the same, and my waving makes no difference, it's a farce. I'm sick of it" (*RH* 126).

Is the escape from royal representation, from an elevated existence, a viable antidote to an unfulfilled life? *Royal Highness* presents various perspectives on this theme. When Albrecht withdraws from the masquerade of his empty life at court, he enters an equally unproductive existence without any goals or direction. Another member of the royal family, the old Grand Duke's brother, Prince Lambert, marries below his station (analogously to Christian Buddenbrook) and is treated coldly by his family. Lambert's wife is an ex-ballerina; his household is well known for its slovenly indigence. Lambert desires only to be a private citizen, without obligations to representative duties determined by royal protocol, so that he can pursue his ardent interests in the theater and the ballet. Noticeable in both Albrecht and Lambert is a withdrawal from social engagement and a sense of lack of self-realization.

The third member of the family who turns away from a royal life is Albrecht's and Klaus Heinrich's sister, Ditlinde. Her choice to marry an ordinary nobleman who had become a businessman and thus entered the bourgeois world is very much influenced by the warmth and friendliness of that world, standing diametrically opposed to the desolation and sadness of the royal world. An expression of sadness appears in Klaus Heinrich's eyes when he hears about his brother-in-law's self-respect, his self-fulfillment, and the pleasure that his work engenders. It is a very bright, healthy, and productive world, unlike the bourgeois worlds of Mann's previous stories and *Buddenbrooks*. Ditlinde's husband is a successful producer of peat, while she is involved in the economic aspects of her household even though pregnant. The world around them is described as being full of blooming, fragrant flowers. In contrast, the royal world, with its economical and political incompetence and its self-alienating, self-negating practices, serves neither the public nor its individual members. It is drab and unnatural, cursed with decline; the formal lifestyle, with its regulated phrases and practiced movements, is hardly productive, and, to emphasize the disparity between the bourgeois and the royal world, there is a foul-smelling but beautiful rosebush in the old castle, a symbol of the rotten state of aesthetic existence. We are meant to question this artificial, cold world. Yet Mann's narrator, who is aware of this world's shortcomings, nevertheless identifies himself by his use of pronouns like "we" and "our" as a supporter of it. Mann positions the reader in such as way that they cannot simply reject this world and its representatives, while inviting them to look with critical sympathy upon it all. This is particularly the case when it comes to Klaus Heinrich.

With the young prince Klaus Heinrich, Mann creates a character comparable to Tonio Kröger, and suggests that, similarly, we ought to understand Klaus Heinrich's existence as symbolic of artistic existence. On the one hand, by virtue of his birth and his deformed arm and hand he belongs to the world of outsiders. On the other, his high cheekbones are a typical physical characteristic of the common people of the principality, thus identifying him as also being close to them. This duality sets him apart from the rest of the family. Likewise, his sensitivity, his tendency to cry easily, his moments of sadness concerning his exclusive life, and his inquisitive nature, which stirs his desire "to feel some contact with what lay outside the charmed circle" (*RH* 48), make him different from others in his family, who do not let the world intrude upon them.

Royal Highness can be understood as a bildungsroman (novel of education), as Mann takes us through the various stages of Klaus Heinrich's development as a prince and of his relationship to life. On the symbolic level, the novel shows an artist's exclusion from bourgeois life and his attempt to get closer to it. In this regard, *Royal Highness* continues the idea of the artist's problematic existence Mann explored in *Tonio Kröger*. Klaus Heinrich grows up imprisoned in a world of empty decorum and formal yet pointless, self-sufficient symmetry. In this world feelings are not permitted. Everything is cold, even the hearts of his family, with the exception of his younger sister, Ditlinde. Like Hans Christian Andersen's Snow Queen, his mother is as cold as the castle's great room: "And it was cold in the Silver Hall, cold as in the palace of the Snow Queen where the children's hearts turn to ice" (*RH* 51). In Andersen's fairy tale, the queen banishes a little boy to the grand room; in *Royal Highness* Dorothea coerces her young son into a world of performance, a world dominated by incessant discipline, self-alienating countenance, and public dignity. She teaches him to deny what she denies herself: kindness, compassion, individuality, and spontaneity. In accordance with his exalted calling, Klaus Heinrich learns to take on a royal demeanor. His dignity and the skills needed to play his role become more refined. Simultaneously, his inquisitiveness and longing to experience the "other" world grow.

The Prince experiences a lesson of a different kind quite accidentally when he and his sister Ditlinde are engaged in one of their explorations of the old castle. They meet the royal shoemaker Hinnerke who, before being given leave to do so, addresses the prince. With this encounter Mann presents the Prince's first immediate contact with life outside his formal world. Intrigued by the shoemaker's inappropriate, yet revealing talk, his pleasant and honest personality, Klaus Heinrich does not persist with his detached, ceremonial mannerisms, but rather uses the opportunity to satisfy his curiosity about aspects of life foreign to him from the garrulous man. Thus he learns that many newborns in the principality are named after him, and, more importantly, that the servants and lackeys are wicked and corruptible. Ironically, in bringing the world closer to him, Hinnerke makes Klaus Heinrich more distant. He now doubts the integrity of the people who look upon him with such apparent devotion and respectfulness. What might they think when they see him? With Hinnerke's account Mann justifies detachment from a less-than-honest world. But while the Prince now has good reason to remain aloof, Hinnerke also raises his awareness that beyond the walls of the castle exists a world outside formalities and pointless symbolism, a world full of "bold, unruly things" (*RH* 66), a world that makes his heart beat faster and from which his royal existence is excluded.

Should the exalted individual give in to his yearning for life or should he remain aloof? This question underlies Mann's presentation of Klaus Heinrich's education. His narrator, in taking a critical stance toward a detached existence, suggests that the elitist views of Klaus Heinrich's tutor Überbein might have influenced his student's thinking and self-perception more than necessary while attending the private aristocratic seminary specially established for him at the hunting castle Fasanerie. But the narrator, we are to understand, underestimates the Prince's desire to participate in life. Spending his last school year at a public school, a popular formal measure ostensibly intended to bridge the gap between royal highness and royal subjects, Klaus Heinrich wants to participate in what he perceives to be magnificent humanity. Like Mann's artist figure Tonio Kröger, he experiences "something like jealousy, a small, burning twinge of regret" (*RH* 83) because he is set apart. As in *Tonio Kröger*, Thomas Mann resorts to a citizen's ball to create an encounter between the outsider and ordinary people. Dressed in citizen's clothes, Klaus Heinrich ventures into the bourgeois world with its "warm human throng" (*RH* 84) and dances with Fräulein Unschlitt, identified as a soap-maker's daughter. Klaus Heinrich, eager to fit into this world, imitates the bour-geois adolescents, maladroitly dancing with his partner who pushes him around. His clumsiness further reminds us of Tonio Kröger. In his vain attempt to fit in, he lets his dance partner bite off half of his sandwich before eating the rest himself, a violation of protocol. Repeatedly he uses the term "we" to refer to the attendees at the ball, as if he belonged to this group. Klaus Heinrich does not realize that he has fallen prey to an illusion of commonality. The commoners poke fun at the royal outsider, intending to humiliate him and bring him down to their level. They laugh at him and intentionally push him to the floor where he finds himself amidst a pile of fallen dancers. Covered with flowers and a punch-bowl lid on his head, he becomes a laughing stock. The attempt to reduce the dis-tance between the outsider and the world, his yearning to participate in life, has failed.

In this episode, *Royal Highness* criticizes the ordinary, mean-spirited world, suggesting that longing for it is not worthwhile. We cannot fail to recognize Mann's ironic and elitist perspective here: after all, the world Klaus Heinrich yearns for, is, among other things, busy manufacturing soap! More importantly, the novel criticizes the exalted individual who prostitutes himself to life, thereby affirming Sammet's and Überbein's perspectives. Concomitantly, Mann addresses the danger of the artist who, in order to be popular, becomes ordinary and thus loses his significance. The requirement of a formal existence to maintain distance is underscored at the end of the same chapter of *Royal Highness* by events at another festivity.

On his eighteenth birthday, Klaus Heinrich officially becomes a representative of the principality. A celebration exclusively for the Court and royal representatives of other countries takes place in the old, decrepit castle. The aristocrats create an illusion of grandeur, glamour, and importance. Mann dismantles this illusion with detailed descriptions of dilapidated decorations and worn-out furniture. It is a world of pompous cult and rituals where even sunlight fails to penetrate through the windows to brighten things up. On the symbolic level, the episode comments critically on the illusionary character of art and its severance from compassion and love. An explicit reference to art follows with Klaus Heinrich's subsequent public appearance. His appointment as officer in chief of a royal regiment at a public ceremony and parade, witnessed by journalists and the general public, carries no political or "practical significance; its effect began and ended there" (*RH* 99). It is merely a show, like a self-sufficient work of art.

Although *Royal Highness* pokes fun at a vain, self-serving royal (and symbolically artistic) world, it simultaneously draws attention to that world's important communal service. In the chapter titled "The Lofty Calling" Mann points out that Klaus Heinrich's public appearances are invaluable: "The people glorified themselves in the person of their sovereign, the humdrum of existence became transfigured by an element of poetry" (*RH* 139). Klaus Heinrich is both proud and pleased to read in newspapers that with his grace and dignity he has "lifted the people's minds above the rut of everyday existence, and moved them to loyalty and gladness" (*RH* 146). Mann does not debunk the power of representation, and thus art, as a tool to transcend banal reality, because this power raises the ordinary people, albeit temporarily, above their lackluster lives. It promotes the transitory illusion of celebrity status. However, this scene also suggests how the powerlessness of the principality's sovereign parallels that of the artist. Both can cover up misery, but neither can eradicate it.

Mann's ambivalent stance toward art and the artist continues when his prince grants the writer Axel Martini an audience. To create the illusion of industriousness and importance, Klaus Heinrich lets Martini wait in the anteroom for a few minutes. But Klaus Heinrich is neither busy nor is he very good at maintaining his formal demeanor. When he dismisses Martini, he does so with a "certain genial, somewhat theatrical wave of the hand which did not always succeed equally well" (*RH* 157). With this portrayal of a dilettantish, idle prince, and furthermore, with the poet Martini, Mann questions whether creating art is a real, serious profession—thereby simultaneously poking fun at his own existence. This element of self-irony in *Royal Highness* is further magnified when Mann imbues

Alex Martini with certain autobiographical facets, such as an incomplete educational career and a bourgeois father who does not support his son's artistic calling. To further ridicule the artist—and himself—Mann makes Martini unattractive, physically weak, and repulsive. Martini is unable to participate fully in life. But Mann also distances himself from Martini, and in doing so thus discredits and affirms his own artistic existence at the same time. Martini's artistic creativity is limited; periods of ennui and idleness and a lack of work ethic result in meager productivity. He compensates for his detachment from life with poetry that is full of Dionysian elements and that reflects a Nietzschean cult of life.[4] Yet he goes to bed at ten o'clock at night to avoid contact with life.

Both Klaus Heinrich's skeptical reaction to the unattractive poet and Mann's unflattering depiction of him are meant to diminish our sympathy for him. Yet, as is the case with Sammet and Überbein, there is some merit to Mann's ugly outsider Martini. While coughing and hunching his shoulders, tears filling his eyes, Martini makes the following comment about the artist's necessary detachment from life: "Renunciation . . . is our pact with the muse, our strength depends on it, our dignity, and life for us is the forbidden fruit, our great temptation, to which we sometimes submit, but never to our own good" (*RH* 155). By focusing on Martini's physical mannerisms, Mann diverts us from the fact that his statement contains a certain truth. With the Prince's marriage providing a seemingly harmonious conclusion, *Royal Highness* avoids and conceals the unresolved tension between aloof artistic existence and integration in life.

The sphere of life and love enters halfway through the narrative with the appearance of the quick-witted, intelligent Imma Spoelmann, for whom Mann's wife Katia served as the model. Imma, the motherless, nineteen-year-old sole heir to Samuel Spoelmann's immense fortune, disregards order and ritual. She is bold and outspoken, and has the aura of an exotic woman, symbolized by her riding a white Arabian horse. She owns an unruly dog, and, furthermore, employs a strange governess, Countess Löwenjoul, who talks to herself while walking through town. Upon first glance, Imma's world seems to be the opposite of Klaus Heinrich's disciplined, restricted world where every movement is calculated.

Yet, like Klaus Heinrich, Imma is an outsider figure. First, because of her father's wealth, she is exceptional purely by means of her birth. Furthermore, her multiethnic background, which includes American Indian ancestors, puts her at odds with the majority.[5] She grew up lonely and separated from others. Klaus Heinrich recognizes the affinities between them, and calls her a "Princess" (*RH* 235). As a rich man's daughter she holds celebrity status, like Klaus Heinrich. Mann draws various further parallels between both. She represents her father at parties and other social events, thus she "performs" just like the Prince whom she constantly mocks. Because she understands that he plays a role, she is critical of his calculated, rehearsed demeanor, although she herself hides behind stock phrases. While Klaus Heinrich shields himself from life by playing "Royal Highness," she does so by studying mathematics. Both escape into an abstract and lifeless world. Despite her distance from life and her nonconformist and noncommittal tendencies, both attributes that Klaus Heinrich shares with her, she also has an ability to care and show compassion for others.

Through Imma, Mann brings about a change in Klaus Heinrich. We can assume that Mann had Katia Pringsheim's impact upon himself in mind. Until her appearance, Klaus Heinrich lives the empty, aimless life of a member of the royal family, whose every movement and gesture is calculated. His carefully constructed life is shattered, all self-restraint gone, when he appears at the Spoelmann's residence "devoid of a will of his own and driven by fate" (*RH* 229). He acts "blindly, without regard for the outside world and in obedience only to an inner impulse" (*RH* 251). The encounter with love, which led in Mann's earlier stories to death, self-destruction, or frustration, leads contrastingly in *Royal Highness* to a world of compassion, leniency, and kindness. Imma takes on the function of the healer and savior from his disciplined, cold, and meaningless existence. Klaus Heinrich claims that she alone can cure him from his stern, loveless life (*RH* 263), a claim Mann had once made in a letter to Katia. Through Imma Spoelmann's relationship to the Countess Löwenjoul, Mann adds a further element to the Prince's education. A devastating marriage to an abusive, exploitative husband left the Countess penniless and drove her insane. Although Löwenjoul's self-destructive love raises suspicions about love, these are, unlike in Mann's earlier stories, quickly dispelled. Löwenjoul's love finds the respect and understanding of the kind, altruistic Imma, who saves her from a vagrant's existence. Löwenjoul's frequent lack of composure and bewildering bouts of insanity contradict the Prince's sense of dignity and self-restraint. When Klaus Heinrich frowns upon the Countess's uninhibited, improper behavior, Imma asks him to be compassionate and forgiving. Confronted with Löwenjoul's tragic life and eager to gain Imma's affection, the Prince sheds his public self and steps out of his world of indifference, of trite, mechanical phrases and calculated effects. He moves from the lofty heights of formal existence to a world that contains compassion and social orientation.

Mann then takes his tale of the outsider who has learned to embrace life one step further. The Prince soon becomes engaged in the economic and political spheres. When Imma introduces the Prince to books about economics, she promotes his transition to an active life. Klaus Heinrich literally comes alive at the prospect of participating in the well-being of his principality: "He felt his cheeks grow hot with zeal, like his brother-in-law zu Ried-Hohenried's over his peat" (*RH* 276). On the realistic level of the novel, Mann describes the Prince's study of economics that will allow him to obtain a closer understanding of life and to serve his people in a responsible, caring manner. On the symbolic level, Mann insinuates that the artist should study life so that it becomes a solid foundation for his art, instead of shunning it and merely relying on his imagination.

The reconciliation of the rich nature of real life with its representation, whether depicted through art or through stilted, formalized behavior, appears as the dominant theme at the conclusion of *Royal Highness*. Before his marriage to Imma, Klaus Heinrich states that he can only be united with her under the condition "that we don't think of our happiness in a selfish, frivolous way, but regard it all from the standpoint of the general good of the whole. For the general good and our happiness, you see, are interdependent" (*RH* 286). *Royal Highness* ends with the Prince's proclamation: "That shall from now on be our task—a twofold one: To do our royal duty and to love: an austere happiness" (*RH* 308). Readers and critics alike have focused on the positive note at the end of the novel. The marriage symbolizes the "synthesis of royal highness and social usefulness."[6] Undoubtedly, both characters descend, as part of their marriage pact, from the lofty heights of their formal existence to a world that includes compassion and social engagement. After their wedding, suggestive of the conventional ending of fairy tales, both look down upon the cheering crowd gathered in the illuminated square in front of the Old Castle. The newlyweds are "watching the crowd and at the same time offered themselves to the general curiosity" (*RH* 308). They are, after all, royalty, and, as objects of admiration, they have to represent the royal ethos and stand above. But they are also looking at—and not past—the crowd, as Klaus Heinrich had done at the beginning of the novel when he walked through the town: "People look at him but he looks at no one" (*RH* 8). This direct gaze at the end of the novel indicates social commitment.

But is all well that ends well? In contrast to earlier parts of the novel, in which Mann presents the Prince's inner conflict between his calling and life, Mann avoids insights into his inner thoughts at the end of the novel. Readers also notice that the "austere happiness" is not the "blissful happiness" (*RH* 235) Klaus Heinrich had hoped for earlier. This is not the only signal that underneath the fairy tale–like conclusion of *Royal Highness* lies another story, one that dismantles what is being constructed. In the last chapter, the narrative ostensibly moves away from the couple, and is instead occupied with the formal marriage arrangements and the wedding ceremony. With ironic detachment, the narrator mentions that a murderer, released from prison as part of the wedding celebrations, has returned to his old criminal ways and has to be incarcerated again.

During the ceremony, the fact that the guns fail to fire on time is not only comical, it also hints that this happy world is far from perfect. The narrator comments on the uncharacteristic behavior of Imma's dog, Percival, who usually behaves wildly with no sense of discipline. During the wedding he is tame, subdued, and well-behaved; in other words, he is not himself. Neither is his owner. Throughout the narrative, Imma wears unusual outfits in bright, striking colors. Now, in her white bridal gown, she has become colorless. The gown, which shines like snow in the sun, the white flowers, and her pale, "alien childlike little face" (*GW 2* 360)[7] complete a portrayal of Imma as a woman who has lost part of her former, radiant self. Still another symbol serves to undermine the seemingly ubiquitous images of happiness and harmony, namely the rose bush that will be transplanted from the old castle to the couple's permanent residence, "Hermitage," with its foul-smelling flowers. Conspicuously, Mann leaves open the question of whether the rosebush will manage to bring forth fragrant flowers.

The fairy-tale structure at the conclusion of *Royal Highness* with its obligatory happy ending—the heterosexual marriage—appears to affirm the author's marriage, and, at the same time, the artist-outsider's allegiance to the bourgeois world of patriarchal norms and expectations, and his renunciation of asocial aestheticism. However, as the examples above illustrate, Mann also uses this structure as a vehicle to tell a different tale, one which voices the author's resistance to the conventional, bourgeois-patriarchal world, a resistance underscored by the inclusion of, albeit comical, staunch advocates of aloof, individualistic existence throughout the novel, the artist Martini, Überbein, and Sammet. That the novel hovers between a social and individualistic orientation and defies a one-sided reading, Mann later emphasized in his 1918 *Reflections*. There Mann made the point that while on the one hand *Royal* Highness shows how a lonely, detached prince undergoes an educational transition to become a "political economist" and an "active humanitarian," it also "presents a true orgy of individualism" (*R* 68).

The political dimension of *Royal Highness* has thus far remained unmentioned. When the novel was first published in 1909, many contemporary readers understood it as a political allegory. In 1910, in response to the critics, Mann called the interpretation of the novel as a "court novel" a mistake (*GW 11* 570), although he himself had certainly provoked such an understanding. The deformed arm and hand of his fictional prince evoked a comparison with Germany's ruler, Kaiser Wilhelm II. The novel's brief prelude, in which Mann describes an encounter between the young prince Klaus Heinrich and a military officer, makes light of the Prussian-militaristic tradition. Arguing against the interpretation of the novel as a political allegory is the fact that the backward-oriented principality does not correspond to the economic and political landscape of Wilhelmian

Germany. The size and population of the principality (one million inhabitants on 3,100 square miles) and, most strikingly, the submissive attitude of the common people, all indicate a bygone world, that of eighteenth-century German principalities. That *Royal Highness* is also situated in the early twentieth century is indicated by the presence of the nouveau riche Spoelmanns, electricity, and automobiles. Does Mann, in merging both past and present, therefore imply that Germany, whose political structure has feudal remnants and whose population largely adores their royals, is provincial and backward-oriented?

While *Royal Highness* can be regarded as a humorous, light-hearted novel that pokes fun at Germany's aristocracy, it nonetheless highlights contemporary social and political issues. Critics have raised the question whether the novel contains a political message and utopian dimension, embodied in the rich American, Samuel Spoelmann, whose financial underwritings avert the bankruptcy of the principality.[8] With his appearance, the democratic New World, epitomized by the United States in the early twentieth century, strikes a deal with the Old World aristocracy. That democracy as a potential historical-political force in Germany is not on Mann's mind is apparent in the novel. Spoelmann, although a representative of the bourgeoisie, is not a representative of democracy.[9] Ill and decadent, he lives with his daughter in an elitist-aristocratic ambiance; and while providing credit to the principality and giving money to its welfare organizations, they remain politically separate. With Spoelmann's monetary support, the principality changes from a feudalistic to an open, nonfeudalistic economic structure. The marriage between the aristocrat and the bourgeois breaks down traditional social barriers in the union of commoner and royalty. However, Mann blurs these barriers. The bourgeois Imma ranks financially above the poor Prince. Thus Mann does not really present a social mésalliance. Evidently, then, *Royal Highness* does not challenge existing feudal structures; egalitarian politics are never envisioned. What however has changed in *Royal Highness* is the attitude of the main character, the royal Klaus Heinrich, toward life. If there is an underlying political message in the novel, it must be found in this change.

With the Prince's turning toward the social sphere, Mann's novel itself turns toward the political, though in an intangible way. Mann suggested in his comments on *Royal Highness* in 1910 that, besides writing a novel about artistic existence, he also attempted a symbolic rendering of "the crisis of individualism," the "intellectual turning toward the democratic, toward communality, connection, toward love" (*GW 12* 571). What the novel scrutinizes, arguably unintentionally when Mann began writing it, is the elitist consciousness of the upper echelon of bourgeois society, the social indifference of the educated upper middle class. Subtly, *Royal Highness* raises the issue of whether its members should leave their individualistic, aristocratic realm, and become socially engaged. Read from this perspective, *Royal Highness* attests to Mann's understanding, still in its nascent stage and later fully explored in his last completed novel, *Doctor Faustus*, of German inwardness and apolitical attitude. In *Royal Highness*, this inwardness is questioned and transformed to social consciousness in a utopian, fairy-tale resolution. The descent from the lofty heights of representation and art, and of bourgeois individualism to embrace democracy might be reasonable and in tune with the progressive political and social currents of 1909, but is it desirable? Mann admitted that "a deep hesitation accompanies that turn to democracy, to community, and to humanity, yes, that this turn is actually completed only humorously, only *ironice*" (*R* 68).

CHAPTER 6

Death in Venice

From 26 May to 2 June 1911 Mann stayed in Venice with his wife Katia and his brother Heinrich. There he wrote "Auseinandersetzung mit Wagner" (Taking issue with Wagner) in 1911, a short essay based on parts of the unfinished manuscript of "Intellect and Art," which he composed between 1909 and 1911. Although voicing his admiration for Wagner's art, Mann casts it off as outdated and belonging to the nineteenth century. He predicts that the twentieth century will bring forth masterpieces that will be fundamentally different from Wagner's œuvre: works that emphasize logic and form, austerity and serenity. He envisions a new art "that does not search for its greatness in the baroque-colossal and for its beauty in intoxication,—a new classicism, it seems to me, must come" (*GW 10* 842). Striving for a new classicism implies looking back at the "old" classicism embodied in Germany's greatest writer, Johann Wolfgang von Goethe (1749–1832). Was Mann thinking of following in his footsteps, thus aiming at becoming Germany's major writer of the twentieth century? Was the pursuit of his own ambitions the underlying motive for criticizing Wagner in the essay, despite continuing regularly to attend Wagner's operas for the rest of his life?

Goethe and assuming the mantle of his legacy were certainly on Mann's mind. We find the first indication of Mann's interest in Goethe and classical narratives in 1905. A notebook entry mentions a syphilitic artist who creates genial works while intoxicated and who, like Goethe's Faust, enters into a pact with the devil. This story about the Faustian artist did not emerge until 1943 when Mann began his novel, *Doctor Faustus*. Another potential story, about Goethe's passionate, unrequited love for a seventeen-year-old girl in Marienbad when he was seventy, also held his interest. In his comments on the genesis of *Death in Venice*, Mann repeatedly refers to this incident, which he had considered turning into a story about "the degradation of an ambitious intellect by his passion for a lovely, innocent piece of life" (*GW 13* 148). But "Goethe in Marienbad" was never written. Instead, Mann turned toward writing *Death in Venice*, his most famous novella. Whether he began it with Goethe's late love in mind or whether it is the outcome of other, older plans that go back to 1905 (*NB 7–14* 120) about an artist's ambitions and his downfall, remains unknown. What remains certain, however, is Mann's repeated and continual interest in Goethe, in the artist's dignity and the questionable sides of artistic ambitions. These aspects decisively shape *Death in Venice*. But the novella is far more than the story of an artist. It is about anti-individualistic mores and conventions, social expectations and personal choices, the liberating as well as destructive impact of chaotic, irrational forces upon one's life. Last but by no means least, it is also a timeless love story. It is this multidimensionality that has endeared the story to readers since its publication and made it into one of the classics of twentieth-century world literature, bringing German literature to the new level Mann had ambitiously hoped for.

The protagonist of *Death in Venice* is the fifty-three-year-old, reputable writer Gustav Aschenbach who, troubled by a lack of creativity, interrupts his daily duties. While walking by the cemetery in the north of Munich, he decides to travel south. His journey takes him to Venice, where he encounters the beautiful Polish boy, Tadzio. His infatuation with the fourteen-year-old boy leads him to abandon all discipline and reason. He submits more and more to his passion and, despite an outbreak of cholera, stays on in Venice to catch glimpses of his beloved. His love for the boy, which never leads to physical involvement, is like an intoxication. Aschenbach follows him everywhere. While watching Tadzio at the beach, Aschenbach loses consciousness and dies, apparently from cholera. The world reacts to his death with shock and mourning.

Before discussing the narrative themes and strands of *Death in Venice*, the name of Mann's protagonist warrants some clarification. Gustav Aschenbach is a composite, based in part on the composer Gustav Mahler who had died on 18 May 1911 while the Manns were in Venice. Mahler's art and life do not play a role in *Death in Venice*. Choosing his first name is Mann's tribute to the composer and German high art in general. Aschenbach is the last name of the painter Andreas Aschenbach (1815–1910), who broke with the romantic tradition of painting landscapes. Perhaps the choice of this last name signals Mann's desire to break with Wagner's influence. Aschenbach, which can be roughly translated as "ash creek," is also a reference to death. "Gustav Aschenbach or von Aschenbach" (*Stories* 195) indicates that nobility was conferred upon Aschenbach due to his outstanding literary achievements, and that he leads a dignified, respected existence that is based on a strict work ethic. Truly, *nomen est omen* in *Death in Venice*. In his name the artist's commitment to the world of order and dignity is intertwined with the realm of death as a counterforce to this world.

Death in Venice, formally divided into five chapters, introduces Aschenbach as being overstimulated by his writing and therefore in danger of becoming careless and undisciplined in his work. The contrast between the will to create a perfectly composed piece of art and the inability to do so is one of many contrasts at the beginning of the narrative. It is spring, yet the temperatures belong to a late, hot summer day. The time is vague and, paradoxically, precise. It is a time of crisis, spring in "19—" (*Stories* 195), when Europe's peace is threatened. This is a reference to the second Morocco crisis of 1911 in which political unrest in Morocco had brought about a conflict between Germany and France. Mann's refusal to give a precise date places the narrative in the realm of a mythical, timeless world, while simultaneously allowing for a specific time identification. Aschenbach's crisis as a writer parallels the historical-political crisis, which the narrative explores no further. That Aschenbach's artistic stagnation is more than a momentary one becomes apparent when the narrator points out that Aschenbach is "increasingly subject to fatigue" (*Stories* 195). Fatigue and nervous overstimulation are attributes of the decadent artist. Mann's earlier works presented decadence ambiguously. On the one hand, it was linked to asocial aestheticism, irresponsibility toward life, and the embrace of death. On the other, it was associated with liberation, a justified rebellion against and withdrawal from a stifling, banal bourgeois world, a dissolution of rigid bourgeois morality. Furthermore, decadence was presented as an artistic force that could produce art that transcends bourgeois norms and conventions. This ambivalence, bestowing both negative and positive meanings upon decadence, is a central key to our understanding of Aschenbach's departure from his bourgeois existence.

A world full of ambiguities and paradoxes characterizes *Death of Venice.* Beginning in the first chapter, Mann describes an atmosphere of death, decadence, and chaos, thereby setting the tone for the rest of the novella. When Mann takes his protagonist on a walk by the north-Munich cemetery, Aschenbach's attention is drawn to passages from the New Testament written on the facade of the mortuary chapel. These passages hold the promise of eternal life, but this promise is undermined when Aschenbach notices two "apocalyptic beasts" (*Stories* 196) and a strange figure just above them. It is a man who has a snub nose and thin, withdrawn lips that expose his teeth. As a medieval figure of death, he signifies the transitoriness of life. With his straw hat and iron-tipped cane the stranger reminds us of the Greek god Hermes who guides souls into the Underworld.[1] His strange appearance identifies him as someone who has come from far away, and thus links him to the cult of life and its god of Asian origin, Dionysus, as Mann had learned from Nietzsche's *The Birth of Tragedy.* Ambivalently, the stranger is a representative of life as well as death. Since he wears local, Bavarian clothes, timelessness and time, myth, and reality again enter into a paradoxical unity.[2] This messenger of death, alluding to Aschenbach's death, reappears in subsequent episodes in different manifestations. Foreshadowing Aschenbach's fate is also his vision of a jungle, "a primeval wilderness" (*Stories* 197) with luscious plants and a crouching tiger, an allusion to Nietzsche's Dionysian realm of chaos, irrationality, intoxication, sexuality, and decadence. With Aschenbach's ambivalent reaction to his vision—he simultaneously feels terror of and longing for this exotic world of chaos and disorder—Mann opens up the possibility for his character to enter a world that stands in contrast to his classicist, artistic program and his disciplined, ascetic life.

With the second chapter of *Death in Venice*, Mann takes his readers back in time, focusing on Aschenbach's biography and achievements. Aschenbach is the son of a civil servant whose ancestors had lived a "disciplined, decently austere life" (*Stories* 200), and a mother who comes from a family with musical gifts; this parental combination has autobiographical roots and is familiar in Mann's work by now. From his early life on, Aschenbach is an outsider who feels that he can achieve fame by submitting his artistic talent to self-control. Ascetic existence, denial, and perseverance characterize his lonely existence, interrupted only by a brief marriage. It is significant that Mann's narrator chooses not to provide information about Aschenbach's heterosexual life, an indication that he wants to exclude the creative artist from conventional relationships. The narrator merely mentions that the marriage, which results in the birth of a daughter, ends with the early death of his wife. His casual remark that Aschenbach never had a son is a narrative strategy to induce readers to perceive Aschenbach's subsequent feelings for Tadzio as a sign of paternal love, and thus as conventional. The narrator's double standard in expecting Aschenbach to live outside sexual conventions yet adhere to bourgeois morality with its homophobia, reflects the ambivalence of the narrative.

Through discipline, a strong work ethic, and his devotion to a style characterized by "noble purity, simplicity, and symmetry" (*Stories* 204), Aschenbach had become a highly praised artist whose moral and intellectual leadership the narrator admires. He emphasizes that Aschenbach's work, due to its formalism and neoclassical style, has found its way into the public school curriculum, and has thus brought him recognition and ennoblement. The cost of, renunciation of, and alienation from life, is a consequence of artistic existence that Mann's narrator not only accepts but also expects. When he describes Aschenbach's life as a "heightened existence,"[3] and one of "cloistral tranquility" (*Stories* 206), Mann's narrator reveals that he sees art as a substitute for religion. Mann questions this ascetic artistry when he has his narrator wonder whether Aschenbach's devotion to form and moral firmness might be problematic: "Does this not . . . signify a simplification, a morally simplistic view of the world and of human psychology, and thus also a resurgence of energies that are evil, forbidden, morally impossible?

And is form not two-faced? Is it not at one and the same time moral and immoral?" Mann leaves open whether his narrator knows the answer to his questions, or whether he simply chooses not to answer: "Be that as it may!" (*Stories* 205), he says. What the narrator cannot or does not want to concede is that an art dedicated to moral standards, to the exclusion of life and sexuality, can subvert what it imparts.

Aschenbach's departure from a life-negating, disciplined life is described in the third chapter. In the hope of experiencing "something strange and random" (*Stories* 206), and of finding "a fantastic mutation of normal reality" (*Stories* 207), Aschenbach travels first to an island in the Adriatic Sea, then to Venice. Reminiscent of the stranger at the beginning of *Death in Venice*, a Charon-like figure appears on the ship to Venice, as does an aging dandy who tries to camouflage his deteriorating physical appearance with makeup. He is a revolting character, with dyed hair and false teeth, and perpetually drunk. His presence foreshadows Aschenbach's cosmetic changes and his own loss of dignity and deportment. The coffin-like gondola that takes Aschenbach through Venice is a symbol of Aschenbach's journey towards death. These messengers and symbols of death hint at Aschenbach's fate while simultaneously suggesting the ugliness, decadence, and transitoriness of life.

The beautiful fourteen-year-old Tadzio, the effeminate, spoiled son of an aristocratic Polish family, is not excluded from this transitoriness. Initially Aschenbach sees him as the embodiment of classical beauty as portrayed in Greek statues of androgynous boys and thus takes an aesthetic-contemplative delight in Tadzio's physical appearance. That Tadzio's beauty is tainted because he has bad teeth, indicative of his own mortality, pleases Aschenbach, as he himself associates art not only with beauty and timelessness, but also with death. Being subjected to the physical world, with its deterioration and decadence, Tadzio resides in that part of life to which Aschenbach starts to feel irrevocably drawn. Mann makes it clear that Aschenbach's attempt to leave the city, prompted by the intolerably stale, sultry climate, does not fail because his luggage had been sent to the wrong place, but because he does not want to leave Tadzio. That Tadzio has become an erotic object for Aschenbach is indicated by his consuming ripe strawberries, suggesting erotic desire and promise. On the realistic level, this causes his infection with cholera; symbolically, it unmasks his forbidden desires. At the end of the chapter Mann implies that his character has reached a point of no return. Aschenbach, sitting in a chair in his hotel room, opens his arms in a welcoming gesture embracing his departure from the world of respectability, from his disciplined life and literary ambitions, submitting to his love for Tadzio.

In the fourth chapter, Mann further reveals Aschenbach's sexual desires. Aschenbach feels a "delicate delight of his senses" (*Stories* 233), while simultaneously turning Tadzio into an artifact by thinking of him in terms of a chiseled body. In order to justify his infatuation, Aschenbach draws from the Platonic idea, expressed in the Socrates/Phaidros relationship in *Symposium*, that "Beauty is in the lover's path to the spirit" (*Stories* 235), in other words, that physical attraction leads to spiritual knowledge. This comparison can hardly divert us from the fact that Aschenbach's attraction to Tadzio is physical, not metaphysical. To escape from life, he seeks refuge in the world of bourgeois discipline and work and writes a short essay that is later recognized and admired for its "exquisite prose." This essay is inspired by life, not merely by the artist's imagination; it is created in the presence of Tadzio, which allows Aschenbach "to take the boy's physique for a model as he wrote, to let his style follow the lineaments of his body." Mann reiterates here a point made earlier in *Tonio Kröger* and *Royal Highness*: great art that communicates necessitates the artist's knowledge of and interest in life. Interestingly, in this brief scene in which Aschenbach writes while watching Tadzio, life is brought closer to art, while art simultaneously becomes a substitute for life. The narrator comments about Aschenbach's writing, inspired by his forbidden love: "How strangely exhausting that labor! How mysterious this act of intercourse and begetting between a mind and a body!" (*Stories* 236). Writing assumes the function of sexuality, channeling Aschenbach's stigmatized desire into a respected activity.

With growing distance, the narrator begins to observe that Aschenbach's infatuation with Tadzio takes on the quality of irrationality and uncontainable rapture, and that it has become a pathological obsession. Due to his increasing "dissoluteness," his lack of discipline and self-criticism, and unwillingness to achieve "wholesome disenchantment" (*Stories* 237), Aschenbach becomes subject to the narrator's criticism. But does the narrator side with conventional morality? At first sight, this seems to be the case. When he senses that Aschenbach is afflicted by emotions frowned upon by conventional morality, he welcomes Aschenbach's taking refuge in Platonic ideas. Furthermore, he does not name what is taboo in bourgeois society, namely homosexuality. However, we realize that the narrator is not an advocate of rigid morality, because he reacts towards Aschenbach's confession of love with ambivalence. Aschenbach "whispered the standing formula of the heart's desire—impossible here, absurd, depraved, ludicrous, and sacred nevertheless, still worthy of honor even here: 'I love you!'" (*Stories* 241). The "sacred nevertheless" reveals that it is not the love for the boy that the narrator categorically condemns but what this love does to Aschenbach. It takes him away from his detached stance toward life. Here it becomes most

apparent in *Death in Venice* that the narrator's voice is not simply one of conventional bourgeois morality, but the voice of somebody who clings to the idea
of the aloof bourgeois artist.[4]

This aloofness disappears completely in the fifth and final chapter, when
Aschenbach, by now a beguiled lover and completely beleaguered by his emotions, welcomes the deadly Asian cholera as an adventure and a counterforce to
order: "For to passion, as to crime, the assured everyday order and stability of
things is not opportune, and any weakening of the civil structure, any chaos and
disaster afflicting the world, must be welcome to it" (*Stories* 243). While we can
sympathize with Aschenbach's love and his desire to be liberated from a world
of stifling order, a world that has imposed upon him a loveless, life-negating
existence, Mann also wants us to take a critical stance. Aschenbach's love is controlled by asocial, selfish emotions and nourishes anarchic-nihilistic thoughts.
Not only is he willing to destroy himself and to see the obliteration of social and
cultural institutions, but he also risks the life of his beloved. As he withholds his
knowledge about the cholera epidemic from Tadzio and his family, he exposes
them to the possibility of infection and death. Mann presents the paradox that
Aschenbach's turning toward life is accompanied by an increasing readiness to
embrace destruction and death.

Mann's allusions to Nietzsche's *Birth of Tragedy* in Aschenbach's vision in
the first chapter set the stage for Aschenbach's departure from the realm of reason, knowledge, and sobriety, to the realm of chaos and intoxication—from the
Apollonian to the Dionysian. References to the latter resurface toward the end of
Death in Venice. First, the narrator points out that Aschenbach's thoughts and
actions are controlled by "that dark god whose pleasure it is to trample man's
reason and dignity underfoot" (*Stories* 244). This god is Dionysus, the god of
intoxication, rapture, and chaos. Second, Aschenbach's move away from his ascetic, respectable, Apollonian existence to a Dionysian, intoxicated state of mind is
reflected in his dream which abounds with visions of "leaving his whole being,
the culture of a lifetime, devastated and destroyed" (*Stories* 256). In a mountain
landscape populated by tree trunks and mossy boulders, and men with horns
growing out of their heads reminiscent of Wagner's Nordic-Germanic mythological world, an "orgy of limitless coupling" (*Stories* 257) takes place.[5] It is the
world of "the stranger-god" (*Stories* 256), of Dionysus, whose central symbol is
a huge wooden phallus. It is a barbaric world in which sexuality, debauchery, and
promiscuity reign, where life is celebrated unconditionally. This dream gives testimony to Aschenbach's final, irreversible departure from his former disciplined
existence as artist to a realm of chaos and self-negation: "And his very soul
savored the lascivious delirium of annihilation" (*Stories* 257). It is quite possible

that bourgeois morality and sensitivity toward his readers restrained Mann from turning Aschenbach's dream into physical reality. Aschenbach never touches Tadzio. In challenging this morality by evoking images that stand in contrast to bourgeois-Christian mores and restrictions, and by denying them realization in the life of his character, *Death in Venice* contains both an affirmation and a resistance to the world of antibourgeois values, anarchic chaos, and nihilism.

Aschenbach's shedding of his bourgeois identity, envisioned in his dream, takes on concrete form when, disgusted with his aging body, he has his hair dyed and his face covered with makeup. The separation from his previous existence becomes complete when, before his death, he both negates his life's work and rejects the artist's role as quasireligious guide and educator: "The magisterial poise of our style is a lie and a farce, our fame and social position are an absurdity, the public's faith in us is altogether ridiculous, the use of art to educate the nation and its youth is a reprehensible undertaking which should be forbidden by law" (*Stories* 261). Aschenbach's criticisms are twofold. First, the artist who wants recognition and dignity must stay away from life, even though distance leads to stagnation of the imagination. Second, the bourgeois notion of artist as guide is flawed, as his imagination ignores and transgresses the norms and binding rules of society. Imagination by definition goes beyond what is and what should be. Thus the insights and knowledge that art conveys are antibourgeois, destructive forces, leading to a sympathy with the abyss. Art is thus a questionable authority. An antibourgeois dimension is inherent in art even when Mann's artist suggests an art striving for "Beauty which is simplicity, which is grandeur and a new kind of rigor and a second naiveté, of Beauty which is Form. But form and naiveté . . . lead to intoxication and lust" (*Stories* 261). Mann's own, later comments that Aschenbach's critical assessment of the artist and his art lies at the heart of the narrative imply his own skepticism toward an existence that embodies nothing but artistic ideals and endeavors (*DüD 1* 406, 411). Yet it cannot be ignored that Mann has Aschenbach deliver his critique with his brain half-asleep resulting in his "strange dream-logic" (*Stories* 260).

Should Aschenbach's critical stance toward the position of the bourgeois artist and his art be taken seriously or be discarded as irrational? *Death in Venice* refuses to resolve this ambiguity, and the novella's underlying question remains unanswered at the end: can and should the bourgeois artist be a representative and guide of the nation despite the fact that the artist has to live a life of self-alienating discipline, and that art contains an immoral dimension? This is also a very personal question, underscored especially by the affinities between Aschenbach and Mann himself. There are striking parallels between Mann's writing and Aschenbach's. Both write in the mornings. Aschenbach's works "had been built up to their impressive size from layer upon layer of daily opuscula, from a hundred or a thousand separate inspirations" (*Stories* 202). The same can be said about Mann's novella, which draws heavily from mythology, Greek and German philosophy, Wagner's and Goethe's œuvres, poems on Venice by August von Platen (1796–1835), and his own works and life. Aschenbach's fame rests on works that Mann did not finish, the novel on Frederick the Great, the essay "Geist und Kunst," and the narrative "Ein Elender" (A miserable one). In allowing Aschenbach to be the author of unfinished manuscripts, Mann frees himself from "ballast"[6] and makes way for works like *Death in Venice*. Aschenbach is the artist Mann both wants and does not want to be. He projects upon Aschenbach the fulfillment of his own ambition to become an honored, nationally recognized writer. He allows Aschenbach initially to play this role before subsequently rejecting it, after he has lost his belief in bourgeois morality and values, has become nihilistic in his yearning for social destruction and "nothingness" (*Stories* 221), and gives in to his intoxication and love. Does Mann therefore reject this role for himself? The final lines of *Death in Venice*, which tell of the shock and mourning of Aschenbach's readers, hover between irony and respect for the author's reputation. Undoubtedly, *Death in Venice* resists what it espouses.

Another question the narrative raises is whether Mann condemns or redeems his artist, a man who can no longer distance himself from life. In *Death in Venice*, turning toward life is as questionable as keeping away from it, but notably not only on moral grounds. Life, although beautiful, enticing and holding the promise of sexual fulfillment, is also the sphere where ugliness, banality, and transitoriness reign. Aschenbach cannot sustain his artistic discipline to capture the beauty of life and to transcend it, as he was once able to do in the outstanding prose written at the beach. In betraying his artistic calling, he becomes a victim of reality. At the same time, Mann redeems his lovesick artist. Just before Tadzio's departure, Aschenbach, terminally ill, observes him at the beach and, while glancing at his beloved, dies. His death, which on the realistic level of the novella results from cholera, is symbolically a *Liebestod*—a sign of Mann's continual fascination with Wagner. Aschenbach dies, "his eyes stared up from below, while his face wore the inert, deep-sunken expression of profound slumber. But to him it was, as if the pale and lovely soul-summoner out there were smiling to him, beckoning to him; as if he loosed his hand from his hip and pointed outward, hovering ahead and onward, into an immensity rich with unutterable expectation. And as so often, he set out to follow him" (*Stories* 263). Mann casts Tadzio in the role of Hermes, leading Aschenbach into the underworld. The word "hovering," and Aschenbach's glance upwards, hint at Mann's redemption of the artist who has fallen prey to intoxication and who, at the final reckoning, is elevated to the mythological-religious realm. By evoking Faust being lifted up into higher spheres in Goethe's *Faust* drama,[7] Mann indicates that the artist, whose yearning for life and love overthrows a disciplined, repressed existence, deserves some mercy.

It is not only the end of *Death in Venice* that alludes to Goethe. Mann's extensive use of motifs and elements from Goethe's *Faust*, such as the Walpurgis Night elements in Aschenbach's dream, Faust's rejuvenation and the form of classical tragedy (five chapters paralleling five acts) testify to Mann's respect for classicism,[8] and reflect his attempt to reject nineteenth-century romanticism and decadence. Yet the counterforces to classicism, associated with humanism and rationality, are the voices of decadence and nihilism, manifested both by Aschenbach's fate and the allusions to Wagner and Nietzsche. These voices are by no means absent from *Death in Venice*, their presence underscored by a transparent reference to Schopenhauer. In *Buddenbrooks* Mann presented, through Thomas Buddenbrook's perspective, the sea as a world in which time and place are suspended, notions of individuality and suffering erased. Aschenbach too is mesmerized by the sea. It fulfills his "longing for the unarticulated and immeasurable, for eternity, for nothingness" (*Stories* 221). Schopenhauer's dissolution of the *principium individuationis*, Wagner's celebration of love and death, and Nietzsche's concept of Dionysian intoxication, together with his questioning of bourgeois morality permeate the narrative.

Is *Death in Venice* the "story of a failed overcoming of decadence"?[9] Mann himself suggests this in *Reflections*: "Intellectually, I belong to that race of writers throughout Europe who, coming from *décadence*, appointed to be chroniclers and analysts of *décadence*, at the same time have the emancipatory desire to reject it—let us say pessimistically: they bear the velleity of this rejection in their hearts and at least *experiment* with overcoming *décadence* and nihilism" (*R* 144). In contrast, in a letter to his publisher Samuel Fischer, Mann left no doubt that "German culture and discipline" were victorious in *Death in Venice* (*DüD 1* 404). Such self-interpretations, although not necessarily reliable sources on Mann's writing, can enhance and confirm our understanding of the complex, ambivalent nature of *Death in Venice*. On the one hand, the novella takes us on a journey into decadence and nihilism during which Aschenbach loses his discipline and, eventually, control over his life. On the other, it resists this journey through the narrator's critical stance and through narrative hints that Aschenbach's path to intoxication and death is not tragic and unavoidable. The forces of life destroy Aschenbach because the artist succumbs to his emotions. *Death in Venice* makes the point that Aschenbach, a pathetic voyeur and solitary man, and repeatedly identified as a "lonely man" in the last chapter, fails to take the opportunity to communicate with Tadzio and to channel his infatuation into artistic productivity. Subsequently, *Death in Venice* can be understood as a counterstory to *Tonio Kröger* in which the voyeuristic artist turns his impressions and love for life into art.

The narrative's resistance to decadence, death, and nihilism becomes further evident when we consider Mann's homosexual inclinations. Until the publication of his diaries, beginning in the late 1970s, the themes of pederasty and homosexuality in *Death in Venice* were predominantly discussed in terms of classical Greek culture, not as an expression of the author's homosexual desires.[10] Who would have suspected that Mann, husband and father of four children when he wrote the novella and a writer of national reputation, could have been so daring as to write about what German society and culture at that time openly condemned and harshly punished? In contrast to previous narratives that had used female characters to mask his homosexual desires, *Death in Venice* drops this mask. In writing openly about his stigmatized desires and secret identity, Thomas Mann found—paradoxically—another, perfect mask,[11] and a way to defy bourgeois morality.

However, the narrative is not a "celebration"[12] of homosexuality; its sympathies lie with the infatuated Aschenbach and bourgeois-moral judgment is suspended only as long as he retains his dignity. With Aschenbach's pathological behavior, when he shamelessly follows Tadzio through Venice, and with his loss of self-respect, which relegates him to the level of the Venetian dandy and prostitute, the narrative corroborates the generally negative image of homosexuals in the 1910s. Consequently, *Death in Venice* is both an affirmation of forbidden desires and a renunciation of them; it is a rebellion against a homophobic culture and at the same time a submission to this culture and its bourgeois-Christian morality. Mann's confession that *Death in Venice* contains his "moral self-chastisement" (*GW 13* 149) reflects an acknowledgment of the necessity to renounce a life that can destroy bourgeois respectability and the national reputation he deeply wanted to preserve. This acknowledgment also implies an affirmation of his bourgeois marriage.

While *Death in Venice* is a very personal narrative, at the same time it addresses broader social and political issues by intertwining the private and the public. The representative function of the individual, in particular the artist, is made explicit in *Death in Venice* by the following sentence: "For a significant intellectual product to make a broad and deep immediate appeal, there must be a hidden affinity, indeed a congruence, between the personal destiny of the author and the wider destiny of his generation" (*Stories* 202). Aschenbach's self-destructive path, accompanied by his embrace of a world where order is suspended, is analogous to the self-destructive trends in Europe in the early 1910s.[13] Mann could not know that Aschenbach's failure to communicate, his indifference to human life, and his willingness to relinquish a rational, dignified existence for aestheticism and intoxication anticipates the irrational enthusiasm for war in 1914 and Germany's self-destructive path, culminating in the barbarism of Nazi Germany. With its depiction of the deadly consequences of asocial aestheticism and the unleashing of the archaic-primitive and chaotic, antihumanistic forces, *Death in Venice* certainly has visionary qualities. The narrative raises concerns that will occupy Mann after 1933 and result in two of his most famous essays, "Brother Hitler" and "Nietzsche's Philosophy in the Light of Contemporary Events."

Death in Venice does not proclaim the end of bourgeois humanism, the victory of decadence and nihilism over order and form. After all, the voice of rationality, represented by the narrator, provides a counterbalance to Aschenbach's self-destruction. Another counterforce is the rigid form of the novella—the classical tragedy structure, the recurring motifs such as the nemesis figures and the eating of strawberries—which stand in contrast to the chaos to which Aschenbach gradually surrenders.[14] Rather, *Death in Venice* expresses a warning against destructive forces and against the irresponsibility of art. Art can conjure up these destructive forces, but it can also side with reason and dignity. In a 1920 letter to the critic and essayist Carl Maria Weber, Mann reminded him that with *Death in Venice* he was striving for "an equilibrium of sensuality and morality" (*Letters* 103). Again, *Death in Venice* is both Dionysian and Apollonian, "irresponsible and individualistic," and "morally and socially responsible" (*Letters* 102–3). Consequently, the novella is not only about the "loss of Künstlerwürde;"[15] it is also about the need to sustain and use the artist's dignity productively. Mann's often cited words that he wrote *Death in Venice* in order "to revoke his sympathy with the abyss" (*DüD 1* 405) is thus a half-truth.

CHAPTER 7

Political Essays, 1914–1925

Until the beginning of the First World War on 1 August 1914, Germany's social and political conflicts played at best a minor role in Mann's work. In *Buddenbrooks* merchants and their workers interact in an affable, respectful way. When he criticizes authority in the school episode of the novel, Mann does not challenge the underlying undemocratic fabric of German society under Bismarck and the Emperor Wilhelm II. He was interested in the autonomy of the creative mind, not social freedom and political turmoil. This is also evident in Mann's subsequent fiction. Despite the ironic view of aristocratic rule it presents, *Royal Highness* does not suggest its demise. *Death in Venice* alludes to the political crisis of 1911 primarily to shed light upon the protagonist and to situate his self-destructive behavior in the gloomy intellectual atmosphere of the time. Mann had good reasons to brush politics aside. The authorities honored artistic creativity and freedom as long as they posed no threat to political stability. Mann's fiction, critical yet undogmatic, and without an underlying political agenda, posed no such threat. The antagonist of his fictional world was not the political system, but life itself. It had shattered the bourgeois, regimented existence of many of his characters, the latest of whom had been Gustav Aschenbach. Whenever Mann cast doubt upon the bourgeois world, his focus was on its sexual and moral politics.

This is not to say that Mann ignored or was indifferent to political and historical developments. On 30 July 1914 he wrote to his brother Heinrich from his summer residence in Bad Tölz: "Who knows what insanity can seize Europe once it has been pulled into the fray!" (*HM/TM* 121). Two days later, the First World War broke out. Mann was concerned that this "catastrophe" and "visitation" (*HM/TM* 121) would throw Europe into political pandemonium and have an adverse financial and psychological impact upon his family and himself. He resented, yet also approved of war as a blessing, a sort of "cleansing, elevation, liberation,"[1] welcoming it because it created opportunities to experience great, unexpected things and because it offered a break from the drudgery of daily routine. These contradictory reactions reflect his acceptance of and allegiance to a world that, on the one hand, gave him creative freedom, economic success, and social privileges, while on the other included conventions and restrictions that he felt compelled to reject, an ambivalence summed up in what he identified as his "deepest sympathy for the execrated, indecipherable, fateful Germany" (*HM/TM* 121).

This sympathy is reflected in the 1914 essay "Gedanken im Krieg" ("Thoughts in War"), Mann's very first public commentary on contemporary German politics. Mann interrupted his work on *The Magic Mountain*, started in 1913, to write the essay, completing it by 12 September 1914. In the opening of the essay Mann juxtaposes civilization with culture. Civilization is "rationality, enlightenment, appeasement, skepticism, dissolution,—intellect" (*E 1* 188) and is represented by the democratic world of England and France. Germany, on the other hand, is the land of culture and characterized by "unity, style, form, dignity, taste, . . . some certain intellectual organization of the world" (*E 1* 188). From Mann's point of view, the First World War was a war of opposing intellectual principles, of culture against civilization, a war of a morally oriented Germany against politically oriented nations, for him primarily epitomized by France. What he sought from this war was not liberation from Germany's authoritarian political structure and Germany's way into "civilization," but Germany's cultural reorientation toward form, structure, and dignity, in other words, a deliverance from an irrational, irresponsible world of (self-)destructive decadence, the very same to which Aschenbach in *Death in Venice* had submitted himself.[2]

Art that, as part of culture, "is a preserving and form-giving, not a disintegrating power" (*E 1* 190) could assist in this liberation. The notion of art as moral guide, previously suggested in *Death in Venice* with Aschenbach's neoclassical art, is set into a larger political context in "Thoughts in War." The essay proposes that the humanism and the morality of art is independent from political and social structures and does not take political sides. It suggests that, unlike democracy, with its instrumental humanism, art propagates the elementary powers of life that civilization suppresses and supports a humanism that addresses human needs, not ideological demands, regarded by Mann as self-alienating. Mann chooses to compare the life of the artist with that of the soldier, in order to express his sympathy with Germany's war efforts, to reduce the gap between artistic and common existence, and to advocate German culture and its art. Both artist and soldier display enthusiasm coupled with order and organization, perseverance, utmost devotion, renunciation of bourgeois security, and weariness of a world of peace and its lulling comforts. Their mutual goal is not to establish a politically new Germany, "lawyer-parliamentarianism" (*E 1* 197), but to defend a revitalization and strengthening of Germany as a cultural nation.

Mann ends the essay with the hope that German culture will not disappear in favor of French-style "*humanité*" and "*raison*" and "*cant*" (*E 1* 205),[3] and that the German spirit will prevail, even though it also contains irrational dimensions and a tendency toward the demonic and the heroic. That this spirit includes questionable elements, even Mann admits, but, being an essential part of Germany, it cannot be erased. He concludes that it would be sheer folly for Germany's enemies to intentionally negate "the mission-filled and indispensable peculiarity of this nation" (*E 1* 205).

The overt enthusiasm for a cause, and the lack of ambivalence and ironic detachment in the essay are certainly not typical of Mann. We must therefore wonder about the essay's underlying intentions. Public engagement meant accepting the artist's cultural and intellectual leadership, a role resented in *Death in Venice* but one that Mann displays here for various reasons. First, brotherly rivalry plays a central role. The essay was meant as a direct attack against his brother Heinrich, who favored French democracy and had taken a stand for a democratic, anticonservative Germany. Second, Mann's unusual celebration of a cause discloses his need to counterbalance his outsider position as artist and his tendency toward nihilism, a philosophy that his writings frequently both affirm and reject. And third, by writing the essay Mann tried to provide some resistance to the apocalyptic visions of expressionists such as Georg Heym (1887–1912), Georg Trakl (1887–1914), and Gottfried Benn (1886–1956) who were calling for the demise of the bourgeois world. When Mann wrote his essay, he was well aware that the old bourgeois world, despite its stifling conventions, provided a haven for the creative artist, and that the future might not necessarily guarantee the artistic freedom that the old Germany tolerated.

After he had finished "Thoughts in War," Mann planned to resume his work on *The Magic Mountain*. But the events surrounding the First World War were on his mind, not fiction. Between the end of September and mid-December 1914 he wrote "Friedrich und die Große Koalition" ("Frederick and the Grand Coalition"), based on his notes for the novel he had planned to write about Frederick the Great nearly a decade before, the completion of which he would leave to his fictional character, Gustav Aschenbach. This essay looks back at Germany's politics in the mid–eighteenth century and revisits the life and deeds of the king of Prussia, while at the same time shedding light upon contemporary historical events. Mann draws parallels between Frederick's occupation of Saxony, resulting in his long fight against enemies from all sides in the Seven Years War (1756–63), and Germany's occupation of Belgium and battles against the Western enemies. In pointing out that Frederick acted in "most bitter self-defense" (*E 1* 250), Mann seems to take sides with Germany's aggressive war politics in 1914. But "Frederick and the Grand Coalition" evolves differently, thereby presenting a counterpoise to the patriotic "Thoughts in War."

Throughout the essay, Mann portrays Frederick as a highly ambivalent character. The king loves Voltaire, humanism, and enlightenment, yet he displays something "inhuman and antagonistic to life" (*E 1* 223). Repeatedly Mann describes Frederick as malicious, spiteful, radical, and dangerous, and presents him as a misogynist and misanthrope.[4] With his contempt for the world, Frederick belongs to and continues the long line of Mann's decadent characters. Yet, unlike those encountered earlier, Frederick has "fought and suffered superhumanly" and exhibits the "nihilistic fanaticism of his achievement" (*E 1* 266–67). In other words, Mann's Frederick is a model of how decadence and nihilism can be overcome with perseverance, resourcefulness, and patient determination.

With this ambivalent portrayal Mann moves away from the standard, contemporary view of Frederick as an indisputable hero of German history. Mann himself made the comment that his essay is infused with a "perfidious enthusiasm" (*GW 10* 568) for the Prussian king.[5] The same holds true for Mann's attitude toward Germany. By leaving open the question of whether the Prussian king was fighting an aggressive or a defensive war when he marched into a peaceful Saxony and by casting doubts upon Frederick's motifs and belligerent actions, Mann indirectly voices his skepticism about German war politics of his own time.

As in most of Mann's fiction, autobiographical elements can also be detected in his essays. Mann unfolds a psychological profile of Frederick as a man who had been forced by his father to live a life he resented, and whose sexuality was highly ambiguous. Connections can be drawn to Mann's self-denial, his immersion in a heterosexual life to meet bourgeois expectations and achieve recognition. What stands out as a further affinity between Frederick and Mann is their "radical skepticism." According to Mann, Frederick was hovering between antagonistic forces, "thought and deed, freedom and fate, rationality and the demonic" resulting in "irony toward both sides" (*E 1* 267). The question as to what extent Mann's psychological portrayal of Frederick is a projection of himself must remain open. What can be ascertained is that out of the essay emerges the image of Mann as a noncommitted, ironic artist who chooses not to seek allegiance with any camp.

As in "Thoughts in War," in "Frederick and the Grand Coalition" Mann voices criticism against democracy, whose "humanism, ideology, and phraseology"[6] he felt to be antithetical to intellectual and artistic freedom. Mann left no doubt about what he was against, often driven by the need to set himself apart from his brother (and his predilection for French democracy), and what he himself wished for: a world that would allow him to sustain a creative, artistic existence outside ideological frameworks. In a letter to Paul Amann in March 1915 he wrote, "The German love of reality is ironically melancholic, rather gloomy, and rather brutal." This paradoxical stance toward reality—a love which thrives on ironic, nihilistic detachment, even contempt—could not bring about the end of decadence and nihilism as Mann had hoped at the beginning of the war. Mann himself was aware that a different love would be necessary so that, as he admits in the same letter, Germany's "relationship to reality may take a more intimate and happy form."[7] That this reality could take the form of German democracy, Mann considered to be a possibility.

Mann's attempt to delineate his own position in "Frederick and the Grand Coalition" was followed by a broader exploration of the foundations of his own existence as an artist and burgher in that time of uncertainty. The result was *Reflections*, written between fall 1915 and spring 1918. The latter parts of the manuscript were completed after March 1917, when Germany's defeat and an upheaval of existing social and political structures were expected. The work, nearly six hundred pages long and "something intermediate between work and effusion, composition, and hackwork" (*R* 2), presents a challenge to its reader. Numerous historical, philosophical, and literary references, direct and indirect quotations, mainly from Nietzsche, Wagner, Schopenhauer, and Goethe, as well as the Russian writers Dostoevsky and Tolstoy, together with many unidentified quotations from and references to his brother Heinrich's work, turn *Reflections* into an often seemingly disorganized and confusing text. In resorting extensively to the opinions of others, and in bestowing upon them a voice of authority, Mann not only seeks verification for his own reflections, but also creates ambiguity in the reader's mind as to whose opinions are being expressed. This narrative technique also indicates the author's detachment from his subject, which is often presented in a polemical, aggressive tone.

Reflections has earned Mann the reputation of being a conservative writer, an apolitical aesthete who clings to a bygone world. Sweeping statements, for example that democracy and politics are alien, even "poisonous" (*R* 16) to the German being, that Germany needs an authoritarian government, and that German tradition is "culture, soul, freedom, art, and *not* civilization, society, voting rights, and literature" (*R* 17), raised the eyebrows of many of his contemporaries, yet also found supporters among the members of the Conservative Revolution, who were eager to extract a single voice and meaning from the essay. That they co-opted it for their right-wing ideological purposes, albeit only briefly,[8] enhanced Mann's reputation as a conservative, and, to this day, has distracted readers from its ambiguities.

First and foremost, the essay is a rhetorical, polemical attack against his brother Heinrich, despite the fact that his name is not mentioned once. In his essay

"Zola," from 1915, Heinrich had, indirectly yet quite recognizably, criticized his younger brother Thomas for striving to become a "national poet," an "entertaining parasite" who clings to the old world, even belongs to its "intellectual followers."[9] This accusation must have hurt Thomas who, although eager for recognition and literary success, had over the years displayed in his works up to and including "Frederick and the Grand Coalition" an ironic detachment from German society. In *Reflections*, the chapters titled "Civilization's Literary Man" and "Against Justice and Truth" turn the tables on Heinrich. In criticizing "civilization's literary man," who puts his talent in the service of political interests and ideology, specifically in political ideas disseminated by the French Revolution, Thomas Mann denounces his brother's prose. He bluntly makes the point that creativity, used in the service of dogma, is no longer art.

Against his brother's Francophile orientation Mann sets his own ideological openness in the chapter titled "Soul-Searching." He confesses to having been influenced by Wagner's romantic fascination for death, Schopenhauer's pessimism and nihilism, and, above all, Nietzsche's unmasking and radical questioning of bourgeois morality and life, and his criticism of the bourgeois work ethic and pursuit of success. When quoting Nietzsche—"The great human being is necessarily a skeptic" (*R* 374)—Mann implies that he not only appropriates the skepticism of the three nineteenth-century thinkers, but that he also doubts those who have initiated him into skepticism. Mann's resistance to the life-negating tendencies of the "three-star-constellation" (*R* 231) is most apparent in his novella *Tonio Kröger*, which, besides recognizing the artist's necessary detachment and rejection of life, reveals the author's love for the mediocre, everyday world of bourgeois existence, not for the strong life of Nietzsche's Dionysian world. This ambiguity toward life and art is presented in *Reflections* as a demonstration of his irony toward both sides. To show that he resents being associated with a single perspective, Mann also refers to *Royal Highness* as a work that oscillates between individualism and social orientation. He even adds ironically, in what is almost certainly a passing shot at his brother, that the novel is "to the highest degree in the spirit of civilization's literary man" (*R* 68), implying that social engagement is possible without subscribing to ideological constructions of life, and that ideologically independent creativity and humanism result in superior art.

The character of German humanism is a central subject of the chapter titled "Burgherly Nature." For Mann, humanism and democratic civil rights are not identical. In contrast to the humanism of democracies, a product of politics and reflection, German humanism is a "legitimate intellectual way of life." Its exponents are the German *Bildungsbürger*, the educated middle class, with their "humanity, freedom, and culture" (*R* 97). These *Bildungsbürger* represent

Germany: "The *German* spirit is burgherly in a special way, German *culture* is burgherly, the German burgherly nature is *human*" (*R* 75). The original German *Geist*, translated as "spirit" and occasionally as "intellect," suggests in the German text a combination of critical intellect and creativity, a nonconformist, cultural force unique to Germany and worth defending against "civilized" influences.

In the longest chapter of *Reflections*, titled "Politics," Mann presents Germany as a nation that is defined by its culture, not by its social and political structures or its orientations. This definition has historical roots. Before German unification under Bismarck in 1871, the term "German nation" referred to many separate political entities, its people linked by a common language and culture. The idea of nation for the Germans was not a sociopolitical body but a "metaphysical being" (*R* 179) in which culture and intellect were separated from power, and in which the "blossoming of the state and blossoming of culture" took place independently (*R* 183). While the idea of a German nation took on a decisively sociopolitical meaning by 1871, Mann's view of Germany as a cultural nation is not completely anachronistic. The German *Bildungsbürger* were traditionally excluded from high political offices and power and were thus largely indifferent to politics. They therefore continued to see their culture as Germany's unifying principle and remained detached from Wilhelmian Germany which experienced a drastic turn toward industrialization, mercantilism, social Darwinism, and bureaucracy while leaving the class society intact, and which continued to look upon art as authority and guide. Mann feared that democracy, a nationalizing force aimed at building a homogeneous civilization, would result in the erasure of the cultural uniqueness of Germany as well as in the demise of an independent cultural sphere. Polemically, he argues in *Reflections* that a politicization of Germany would lead to "the stultification of the German into a social and political animal, it would be de-Germanization" (*R* 197). In Mann's opinion, Germany's national spirit is inseparable from its intellectual life. Those who demand the democratization of Germany, forget "that the German concept of freedom will always be of a spiritual nature" (*R* 201). In underscoring his understanding of freedom as a state of mind, an inner, and thus, private freedom, Mann invokes the authority of Martin Luther, whose Reformation he deems to have been a democratic event. Luther "perfected the freedom and self-authority of the German human being by internalizing them and thus removing them forever from the sphere of the political argument" (*R* 202). The value of inner freedom continued to rank above social and political emancipation in German culture. Kant, Goethe, and Nietzsche are among the most famous proponents of this concept. Only freedom from politics and ideology nourishes free thinking. "Evolution, development, originality, manifoldness, and richness of individuality have always been the basic law of German life" (*R* 202). In other words, Mann understands Germany as a pluralistic, modern, and nonpolitical world.

Mann places this modern world in an aristocratic, politically conservative setting. Following in the footsteps of such thinkers as Edmund Burke who, particularly in his 1790 work, *Reflections on the Revolution in France*, understands a hierarchical, traditional world as an organic, natural state of being and not as a manifestation of ideological interests which favor the few,[10] Mann makes the point that all conservatism is nonpolitical, and that only progressive, liberal thinkers believe in politics. Consequently, Mann's nondogmatic, free conservativism is not identical with Germany's conservative political powers. It is "erotic irony of the intellect" (*R* 420). This phrase contains a paradox: the intellect desires and rejects life simultaneously. Love for life is counterbalanced by intellectual detachment from life as, for example, *Tonio Kröger* and *Royal Highness* exhibit.

Although *Reflections* is a plea for political noncommitment, Mann does not always remain aloof in his neutral zone of irony. He favors a "strong monarchical government" (*R* 188), which he expects to practice a democracy "from above."[11] In consideration of Germany's progressive social security system that had been established under the monarchy, he believes in an open, morally oriented, ruling upper class that treats all citizens with "goodness" (*R* 357). Aware of social inequalities in Wilhelmian Germany, he critically assesses the educational privileges of the upper classes and demands educational opportunities for the lower classes. He agrees with Nietzsche that "the duller, less intellectual families" of the upper classes should be demoted, while the intelligent, free thinkers of the lower classes should be promoted to a higher social ranking. The goal of this "democratization of the means of education" (*R* 186–87), which defies traditional class boundaries, is not to dismantle traditional class structures with their social and economic inequalities. Mann demands social mobility and the promotion of extraordinary human beings, no matter what their social background, so that they can fulfill the potential of their individual talents and creativity, and thereby can contribute to the intellectual and cultural growth of Germany.

Mann's advocacy of the creative, autonomous individual is commendable yet problematic, because he presents the realm of the intellect as antithetical to the realm of power and politics throughout *Reflections*. Striving for freedom outside the rules of ideology, for a private sanctuary of free thinking, induces political irresponsibility and indifference. Mann addresses the dangers of this German inwardness later in *Doctor Faustus*. When he wrote *Reflections*, he was concerned about the loss of creative freedom. This concern explains his frequent rhetorical diatribes against democracy and active engagement in politics. Mann defends a free art, "*l'art pour l'art* is truly my ideal of art" (*R* 232). It is an art without fanatism, without an ideological agenda. Nonetheless it offers a valuable service to mankind. "Art as life, art as the mastered, liberated, and liberating knowledge of life through form" (*R* 225) allows exploration of the human condition without a dogmatic perspective, leading to a critique of reality and a deeper understanding of life. Art should not ideologize readers and reduce them to political beings, but should address the richness of life and bring about a "seduction to life." But Mann knows all too well that art that turns toward life also criticizes it. Because of its connection to the intellect, "the critical, negative, and destructive principle," art subscribes to "creative affirmation of life with the finally nihilistic emotional appeal of radical criticism" (*R* 420) and is thus susceptible to romantic "sympathy with death" (*R* 24) and decadence. The fictional rendering of this duality will be the novel Mann did not finish until 1924, *The Magic Mountain.*

The passion with which *Reflections* speaks out against democracy and its artistic advocates is uncharacteristic of Mann, who otherwise was ironic and detached. Provocation by his brother Heinrich can explain this passion and the often highly disputatious tone. But Mann is not against a democratic system in principle, as the following thoughts in *Reflections* attest: "What galls me and what I struggle against is the secure virtue, the self-righteous and tyrannical thick-headedness of civilization's literary man who has found the bottom that eternally holds his anchor, and who announces that every talent must wither that does not quickly politicize itself democratically—his bold enterprise, that is, to commit intellect and art to a democratic doctrine of salvation" (*R* 240).[12] This passage reveals Mann's strong opposition to ideological commitment and is indicative of his fear of losing his world, the world of the creative, independent artist. Doubtless he was well aware that a new world would arrive when he made the following prediction: "The advance of democracy is victorious and unstoppable" (*R* 180). But he voices skepticism that a democratic system brings a humanistic society, and he is apprehensive that, in the name of the principles of humanity, fanaticism, despotism, and radical dogmatism can reign, as the bloodshed of the French Revolution attests (*R* 282). What becomes evident here is that Mann's understanding of democracy, similar to his belief in a benign aristocratic leadership, is anchored in eighteenth-century European history. Is it thus anachronistic?[13] The economic and sociopolitical dynamics of the early twentieth century are different, but intolerance, the tyranny of the majority, and herd mentality are not merely eighteenth-century phenomena, as the history of the twentieth century confirms.

At the beginning of *Reflections*, Mann admits that literature is "democratic and civilizing from the ground up," that the essay is not a manifesto of a conservative German *Bildungsbürger*, but is instead the presentation of an "inner-personal discord and conflict." Like his ambivalent fiction, the essay is full of inconsistencies and ambiguities. Mann wants his readers to understand that *Reflections* is neither a lengthy essay nor fiction; it is "a story" full of contradictions and ironic toward all sides (*R* 24). The author avoids ideological commitment; neither the conservative nor the democratic wins in the end.[14] Beyond doubt is Mann's commitment to openness, to artistic freedom, and to unfettered creativity, and his fear, expressed through his polemical voice, that they will be lost.[15]

With the defeat of Germany in 1918 the future of bourgeois liberalism and humanism became uncertain. The abdication of Kaiser Wilhelm II, political and economic instability, and the dissolution of authority that in the nineteenth century had honored artistic, creative freedom in return for the artist's disengagement in politics, undermined Mann's self-consciousness. Although in August 1919 the University of Bonn would bestow an honorary doctorate upon him, this prestigious recognition could not divert Mann from the fact that the bourgeois world, with its respect for the artist, could no longer be taken for granted. In this time of political turmoil and social unrest, he escaped into the realm of fiction and wrote two idylls, *Herr und Hund* (*A Man and His Dog*) and *Gesang vom Kindchen* (*Song of a Child*), and emerged as one of Germany's most public and admired artistic figures during the Weimar Republic.

With his public speech "The German Republic," from 1922, Mann asserted the leadership role of the bourgeois artist in Germany. It is addressed to the famous writer Gerhart Hauptmann (1862–1946) who, as Mann points out, deserves his "present princely and representative position as the intellectual head" (*OD* 6) in German society. By expressing the view that this leadership could continue under the newly established democratic system, Mann signals his shift toward democracy. The confession "I want the monarchy" (*R* 188), made in *Reflections* because Mann deemed a monarchical state as a guarantor of political, economic, and, above all, intellectual freedom, is now replaced by his appeal to Germany's youth to embrace the new republic, a "name for the good fortune residing for the people in a union of State and culture!" (*OD* 21). The notion of "union" appears strikingly often. For example, Mann speaks of the "union of the intellectual-national life and the life of the State" (*OD* 27) and of the "union of freedom and equality" (*OD* 29). At first sight, it appears as if Mann has abandoned his previous insistence on the separation of culture from the state, of individual and intellectual from national and social interests, an insistence that had identified him as a staunch defender of autonomous creativity. Yet he emphasizes that he has not betrayed the ideas expressed in *Reflections*. The humanism that he calls for in "The German Republic" has not forsworn its ideologically free position. It hovers "between aesthetic isolation and undignified leveling of the individual to the general; between mysticism and ethics; between inwardness and the State; between a death-bound negation of ethical and civic values and a purely ethical philistine rationalism." This position is "the German mean, the Beautiful and Human," and the republic is its legal representation and embodiment (*OD* 45).

To emphasize that individualistic and social orientations not only coexist, but are even interdependent, Mann refers to the romantic poet Friedrich von Hardenberg (also known as Novalis, 1772–1801) and the American poet Walt Whitman (1819–1892). Both, according to Mann, are prophets of the idea that "the individual lives in the whole and the whole in the individual" (*OD* 31). However, Mann's choice of Novalis and Whitman to illustrate this interdependence is questionable. After all, Novalis's fame rests on his *Hymns to the Night*, a work that embraces death. Whitman, the poet who yearns for the dissolution of individuality, celebrates anarchic, radical individualism in *Leaves of Grass*. Mann's focus on a democratically oriented Whitman and a life-affirming Novalis covers up what the speech simultaneously, in its references to German inwardness and aesthetic individualism, unveils: Mann's continuing belief in the exceptional position of the artist who subscribes to a nonpolitical and asocial stance. In the last analysis, "The German Republic" defends the cultural life of the *Bildungsbürger*. Mann's affirmation of life and German politics must remain ambivalent because he continues to hover between polar opposites, the realms of individuality and community, romanticism and rationalism.[16] "The German Republic" does not reflect Mann's fundamental conversion to democratic principles; it reflects his endeavor to integrate his artistic existence, and bourgeois liberalism and humanism, into the new German political environment.

Mann's 1921 speech "Goethe und Tolstoy" ("Goethe and Tolstoy"), presented one year before "The German Republic" as an abbreviated lecture and published in 1925 as an essay based on the speech and existing notes of 1921, also strives for integration into a democratic world.[17] While *Reflections* centers on the contrast between Western democracies and German culture, the speech contrasts the anarchic individualism of the great Russian writer Leo Nikolaevich Tolstoy (1828–1910) with the European humanism of the German Goethe. For Mann, Tolstoy embodies the writer who disparages Western civilization and advocates absolute individual freedom, whereas Goethe does not subscribe to anarchic individualism. His humanism is shaped by European classical ideals of human dignity and respect for tradition and culture, and openness for the new. Notably here, Mann no longer sees France and its democracy as the antagonist of Germany. He now wishes for a Germany that is not "Asiatic" and "wild," but

European, "gifted with a sense for system, order, proportion." In "Goethe and Tolstoy" Germany is the nation in the middle, between Western dogmatic humanism and Eastern chaos, a nation of bourgeois culture full of "voices in artful freedom,"[18] which honors tradition and creativity. Thus the speech does not express Mann's "prophecy of the death of humanism,"[19] but the hope that German humanism survive in an age of upheaval and uncertainties.

The extended published essay of 1925 is not a "total reversal"[20] of the earlier speech, but, in adding both elements left out of the 1921 speech and a new ending, Mann expands upon the notion that the openness of German culture and humanism can be a guiding principle for Germany's middle class. In one of the additions, Mann identifies Goethe and Tolstoy, based on Schiller's essay *On Naïve and Sentimental Poetry* (1795–96), as naive writers whose "art is objective, creative contemplation, closely bound up with nature." They represent "nature" in contrast to sentimental writers such as Schiller and Dostoevsky, whose writings are led by a "moralizing, analyzing attitude toward life and nature" (*ETD* 113) and who represent "intellect" similarly to civilization's literary man in Mann's *Reflections*. Common to Goethe and Tolstoy is their rejection of ideological constructs. Both are presented as writers who understand freedom as a natural state of being, not as a constitutional right. But in contrast to Tolstoy, Goethe's individualism calls for dignity, order, and discipline. Goethe followed "a cultural and self-developing individualism" (*ETD* 99) that honors traditions while also meeting them with creative resistance. Standing between "Hellenism and pietism" (*ETD* 138), Goethe's humanistic ideas are embedded in the thoughts of classical antiquity and bourgeois-Christian traditions; therefore, they are both un-Christian and Christian, and, above all, characterized by tolerance. Mann's Goethe appears as a cosmopolitan world citizen receptive to all ideas and philosophies.

When Mann mentions Goethe despising Asia and its "primitive Russian, anti-civilization" (*ETD* 145), embodied, according to Mann, in Tolstoy, we should not identify Goethe's and Mann's perspectives as being uniform. After all, the motto of Mann's essay is: "I am still resolved not to pass judgment" (*ETD* 119). Despite Mann's criticism of Tolstoy's development from a naive to a sentimental writer who has turned away from nature and toward politics, he remains sympathetic toward the Russian and the "shapeless and savage human nature of Half-Asia" (*ETD* 146).[21] Mann does not want to decide whether the "sons of spirit" or the "sons of nature" best serve humanism and humanity. At the end of the essay he expresses his hopes that a "higher unity," a striving of the "sons of spirit" for nature, and a striving of the "sons of nature" for spirit, can be achieved (*ETD* 174). Goethe, who was able to strike a balance between nature and critical intellect, between a creative, subjective, and a critical understanding of humanity, approaches this ideal. This meshing of spheres does not mean a synthesis and a commitment to a new orientation, but results in "irony which glances at both sides" (*ETD* 173), a position of the middle, which does not take a firm, ideological position and is open and tolerant to all perspectives.

The essay itself displays this openness. Mann renounces a fixed notion of Goethe and Tolstoy. While both are characterized as naive writers, "children of nature" (*ETD* 113), their works also reveal traces attributed to the sentimental writer as defined by Schiller. Later in life, Tolstoy became an ideologically committed writer. Goethe, in contrast, remained ideologically independent, yet he too is not a pure "child of nature" because his works are influenced by the rational-humanistic philosophy of Immanuel Kant (1724–1804). Goethe's and Tolstoy's ambivalent natures are revealed most clearly by Mann's exploration of the auto-biographical dimensions of their works. To project one's self into one's art, to give one's individual life an important story worth telling, is not considered narcissistic by Mann. He identifies "love of the ego" with "love of the world" (*ETD* 103), assuming that whoever loves himself, loves life and the world. Egotism and altruism are not exclusive as both writers' lives can attest. Both were socially engaged men; Tolstoy was a judge and teacher, Goethe a privy councilor for Saxony-Weimar. Mann's emphasis on Goethe's and Tolstoy's social functions constitutes a decisive deviation of the essay from the earlier speech in 1921. This emphasis reflects his attempt to integrate himself as an artist into the new, democratic Germany. Yet Mann is far from depicting the "children of nature" as merely life-affirming, social beings full of happiness and kindness. The opposite also holds true: both Goethe and Tolstoy have a streak of nihilism; "the elemental, the sinister, the dark, neutral, negation- and confusion-loving devil" (*ETD* 136) is, paradoxically, present in both. Later, in his novel *Lotte in Weimar*, Mann will question Goethe's humanism.

The 1921 speech ended with the vision of a Germany that could serve as a "model of peoples,"[22] a pluralistic, artistic, and educated world. Its nationalistic tone was a reflection of Mann's patriotism resulting from Germany's defeat in 1918. Under the specter of rising dictatorships and terror in Germany and Europe, the essay of 1925 ends with Mann's rejection of radical nationalism and of rising antiliberal, conservative, fascist forces, instead offering a utopian vision of a humanistic world. Thus Mann now realized that democracy and parliamentary governments are needed to combat antihumanistic tendencies and, above all, to guarantee German bourgeois culture and its autonomy. While the comparison between the final pages of the speech and the later essay demonstrates Mann's shift from a conservative to a progressive, democratic argument, his loyalty to his bourgeois understanding of Germany as a cultural nation remains intact.[23]

Both the speech and the essay reveal his attempt to save the autonomy of the bourgeois artist in a new world.

Both versions of "Goethe and Tolstoy," as well as "Frederick and the Grand Coalition," *Reflections*, and "The German Republic" should not be judged by their historical and political content. Mann was not a scholar; his knowledge was fragmentary and originated mainly from secondary sources. Instead they must be judged by his intention both to support a world that allows creativity and a plurality of perspectives, and to warn against ideological dogma. Furthermore, they do not contain political directives for his audience, the German *Bildungs-bürger*, who are called upon to embrace humanism and tolerance. But Mann's rejection of ideological commitment has a problematic side. It justifies escape from political engagement into German inwardness. This becomes apparent when Mann identifies German nationalism as striving for freedom, self-understanding, and self-fulfillment, a striving also characteristic of artistic existence. This iden-tification implicitly advocates self-centeredness and artistic individualism. In addi-tion, his play with perspectives has a dark side as detachment from all beliefs fosters nihilism and a Nietzschean devaluation of all values that stands as a coun-terbalance to Mann's sympathy with life and humanistic appeals.

CHAPTER 8

The Magic Mountain

Nearly a quarter of a century after the publication of *Buddenbrooks* Mann finished his second great novel, a masterpiece of twentieth-century world literature, *Der Zauberberg* (*The Magic Mountain*). For decades, the novel has been part of the canon of "Great Books," due to its intellectual content. What has mesmerized and puzzled readers and scholars alike since its publication is its multifaceted lineament.[1] It is, as T. J. Reed commented, "spiritual autobiography, confession and apologia, an intricate allegory, a kind of historical novel, an analysis of Man and a declaration of principle for practical humanism. In appearance it is a parody of the German *Bildungsroman*."[2] These manifold layers are testimony to the openness of the novel, which, although embedded in its historical time, German literary tradition, and culture, has a universal, timeless quality, allowing each new generation of readers to approach *The Magic Mountain* with their own expectations and experiences. What makes the novel both remarkably contemporary and particularly alluring to today's readers is the central question that it poses: can we put our trust in ideologies and orientations in a modern, pluralistic world in light of all the terror, violence, and destruction they have engendered, even in the name of humanism?

Initially published in two separate volumes, *The Magic Mountain* presents the story of the twenty-three-year-old engineer, Hans Castorp, who visits his cousin Joachim Ziemssen at the sanatorium Berghof near Davos, Switzerland. The date is August 1907. The visit, initially planned to be three weeks, extends to seven years when Castorp is diagnosed with tuberculosis. During these seven years, Castorp falls in love with a Russian woman, Clavdia Chauchat, and spends one night with her. He has numerous conversations with the doctors of the sanatorium and various patients of international background, notably the Italian humanist, Ludovico Settembrini, the Jesuit and communist, Leo Naphta, and the Dutchman, Mynheer Peeperkorn. Life on "the magic mountain" offers variety with brief outings, festivities such as Mardi Gras, and other entertainment. Personal conflicts and tensions between the patients not only provide entertaining reading, but also insights into the human condition. The novel ends with Castorp's departure from the sanatorium, and a description of him walking over corpses on a World War I battlefield.

The Magic Mountain is, as is so often the case with Mann's work, loosely based on an autobiographical event. In 1912, Katia Mann spent a few months in a sanatorium in Davos. Her husband visited her from mid-May to mid-June, and thus had the opportunity to observe a world removed not only from social and professional obligations, but from time itself. At the outset Mann did not have a novel of nearly one thousand pages in mind, merely a short satyr play in which the fascination for death was to be presented with a comic twist. What was intended as a comical counterpoint to *Death in Venice* would become a serious depiction of decadence, death, and ideological choices, told with humor and irony. Among the more obvious affinities between *The Magic Mountain* and *Death in Venice* is the motif of a journey from a respectable and orderly bourgeois existence to a world of disease, death, and dissolution of bourgeois life and responsibilities. The cholera-stricken world of Venice is replaced with the tuberculosis-ridden world of a Swiss mountain resort. In both works, love keeps the protagonist away from his conventional life.[3] Analogous to *Death in Venice*, the second chapter of the novel, originally conceived as the first, goes back in time to provide biographical information about the protagonist. In changing the chronological sequence of the chapters, Mann again underscores the importance of the theme of the journey, associated in the first chapter with darkness and disorientation. Pivotal contrasts from *Death in Venice*, such as those between West and East, rationality and irrationality, order and chaos, Apollonian and Dionysian existence, as well as between life and death also return in *The Magic Mountain*.

In August 1914, while still in the early stages of writing, Mann was already certain that the novel would end with the outbreak of the First World War.[4] One year later, in an August 1915 letter to Paul Amann, he described *The Magic Mountain* as "a story with pedagogic and political overtones, in which a young man comes up against the most seductive of powers, death, and runs the gauntlet, in a comic-gruesome manner, of the intellectual polarities of Humanism and Romanticism, progress and reaction, health and disease; but not so much that he may be forced to decide, as for the sake of orientation and general enlightenment. The spirit of the whole is humoristically nihilistic, and the bias leans rather toward the side of sympathy with death."[5] Although Mann apparently knew exactly which direction and tone the novel was to take, work on the manuscript, which had reached the "Hippe" episode in chapter 4, came to a halt in October 1915. Probably affected by the war, Mann began to have doubts and reservations about the narrative objectives. It is also likely that he was motivated by his growing political awareness, displayed since "Thoughts in War," to turn toward cultural-political essays.[6] He was apprehensive about the fact that after the outbreak of the First World War and the subsequent transformation of Europe into a slaughterhouse, a fictional rendering of the polarities described in his letter to Amann might be unsuitable. Mann's own comment that he did not want to continue writing a novel which would be "unbearably overburdened intellectually,"[7] must, however, be taken with caution. In addressing similar polarities in his political-cultural essay *Reflections*, with which he had aspired to rise to the rank of national poet laureate, he saw an opportunity to surpass the fame of his older brother Heinrich.

Four years later, in the spring of 1919, when Mann resumed work on the manuscript, Germany was marked by defeat, the dismantling of its bourgeois-aristocratic world, and an uncertain political future. Mann wondered whether his manuscript had become historically outdated and whether the new, postwar world would not be better served by a literature characterized by "simplicity, kindness, health, humanity" (*TB 1918–1921* 195). Such elements Mann found in his reading of the Scandinavian author, Knut Hamsun (1859–1952); they are echoed in his own idyllic texts *A Man and His Dog* and *Song of a Child*. These thoughts indicate Mann's attempt to counterbalance his leaning toward decadence, something he had attempted earlier in both *Death in Venice* and *Reflections*, with ambiguous success. However, we know from his letters that his attraction to death, an expression of his lifelong denunciation of a conventional bourgeois existence, was a decisive factor in his resumption of *The Magic Mountain*. He found this morbid fascination, "more an uncanny magnetism than an arbitrary gravitation," repulsive yet inescapable, as he admitted to the writer Ida Boy-Ed in December 1919.[8] Since the publication of his diaries, we are also aware of a secret fascination that drew Mann to the manuscript not mentioned in letters, an irresistible attraction connected to the theme of "forbidden love" (*TB 1918–1921* 192, 201). Quite likely, this is an allusion to stigmatized desire and the "Hippe" episode with which Mann had put the manuscript aside in 1915. Decadence and forbidden love, as *Death in Venice* illustrates, are interrelated: in Mann's world, both are positioned against the healthy, conventional world, the world of conformity and repressive morality. Thus the old adversary in Mann's work prior to *The Magic Mountain*, a rigid bourgeois world with its stifling conventions and orientation, still exists. His defense of bourgeois culture and life in *Reflections* and the arrival of the new, postwar Germany have not changed this.

The Magic Mountain is set in a remote sanatorium far above and away from the north German flatlands. Despite the fact that its international clientele is preoccupied with disease and death, readers should not expect a somber or gloomy novel. Its mood is not so different from the German world of Mann's earlier stories and from *Buddenbrooks* as one might assume. *The Magic Mountain*, told by a detached yet empathetic narrator, teems with brief, humorous, ironic glimpses of the lives of ordinary people. We smile, amused by the patient Frau Stöhr, "this ridiculous woman" (*MM* 97) who continually misuses words. She is not the only one whose intellectual limitations Mann emphasizes and sporadically makes light of. An overwhelming majority of the patients are described as obtuse and peculiar. Most of them remain nameless, among them "[a young woman] with the face of a tapir; the gluttonous adolescent with the thick, circular glasses; another fifteen- or sixteen-year-old boy, who squinted through a monocle and at every cough put his little finger, its long nail shaped very much like a saltcellar spoon, to his lips—a first class ass, it would seem" (*MM* 109). These humorous, though often cruel, depictions of human shortcomings provide comic relief from this world of human suffering and a narrative counterbalance to the philosophical and ideological debates on life and death between Castorp, Settembrini, and Naphta. Hardly any character is immune from the narrator's humor and irony, including Castorp, whose clumsy attempts to hide his crush on Clavdia Chauchat amuse the sanatorium's patients and readers of the novel alike. Similar to those in *Buddenbrooks*, these descriptions reveal not only a vivid interest in life, combined with a love for detail, but also an irreverence toward this world ruled by medical examinations and repetitive daily schedules, that sometimes slides into misanthropic sarcasm. Because the narrator hovers between respect and disrespect for life, and pairs a sympathy for human weakness and frailty with an indifference toward life, the young and old patients' poor health and agonies rarely invite either his interest, sympathy, or compassion.

The lives and predicaments of most of these "extras" remain largely unknown. One of the few patients whose fate the narrator does briefly describe, is Frau von Mallinckrodt. Affection for a young man motivates her to escape from her boring husband and children. The affair, however, is short-lived due to the interference of the young man's relatives and her forbidding skin disease. Terminally ill, she spends the rest of her life forlorn at the Berghof. This tale of a woman's rebellion against a secure bourgeois existence, her stigmatized love and death, is a variation of Aschenbach's fate and will resurface three decades later in Mann's story, *Die Betrogene* (*The Black Swan*). In *The Magic Mountain* it provides not only a glimpse into a world of human disappointment and suffering, but is also an indictment of narrow-minded bourgeois morality.

Into the morbid world of the sanatorium enters the twenty-three-year-old, "ordinary young man," Hans Castorp from Hamburg (*MM* 3). The rationale for his visiting his cousin Joachim Ziemssen is a brief vacation on the mountain that is supposed to strengthen him for his imminent entrance into the productive world of bourgeois trade and manufacturing. Castorp even takes his book on ocean-going ships to prepare himself for his future professional tasks. However, once on the mountain, occasionally in the novel referred to as the world "above," Castorp forgoes the values and goals of the "flatlands," the bourgeois world in the Hanseatic city, and becomes fascinated by death. He takes an avid interest in diseases, dying people, and corpses. His observation that illness makes people wise and extraordinary, and enhances their existence, is at odds with Mann's patients, the descriptions of whom do not support the notion that illness has an ennobling quality. Consequently, the reader is distanced from Castorp's perspective. However, his veneration of illness and death is also warranted. With Castorp's fate Mann subsequently illustrates that disease, which removes the young man from everyday life, offers a glimpse of intellectual realms hitherto hidden by his "flatlands" existence. Life "above" uncovers the discrepancy between Castorp's unspoken desires to shed the identity that bourgeois life has imposed upon him and his pursuit of a world of activity and progress that he seemingly embraces with his intention to become an engineer.

Castorp's questioning of bourgeois life does not occur unexpectedly. Mann unfolds a childhood biography full of encounters with death. In early life, Castorp experienced the deaths of his mother, father, and grandfather within a short span of time, and subsequently developed a sympathy with death. In addition, during the brief period Castorp spends in his grandfather's house, the old man, an enemy of change with a deep interest in the past, draws him toward the world of "crypt and buried time" (*MM* 21). A portrait of his grandfather "in his official dress as a town councilor—the sober, even godly attire of citizens from a vanished century" (*MM* 24) makes a lasting impression upon the young Hans. In the picture his grandfather is all form and representation, with his pleated ruff collar and old-fashioned, broad-brimmed hat. With this outfit Mann conjures up the late Middle Ages in the Spanish Netherlands, a world of unbending authority, terror, and death, represented later in the novel by the Jesuit, Naphta. At the same time, this portrait alludes to the stifling atmosphere of the bourgeois world in which Castorp grew up. In an unconscious rebellion against this world and its present-day demands, Castorp sympathizes with the world of the past, assuming that life on earth is only an "interim stage" and that in death the individual finds his or her "appropriate form" (*MM* 25).

Mann underscores Castorp's tendency to lean toward death rather than life by giving him a weak physique. Castorp does not like to participate in school sports, is slightly anemic, and has teeth that, like Hanno Buddenbrook's, are already in the process of decay. Physical degeneration is accompanied by psychological degeneration. Bourgeois productivity and a strong work ethic do not give him a fulfilled life. Unlike his grandfather, "a most Christian gentleman" (*MM* 23), Castorp is without religious beliefs; to him ceremonies such as baptism are nothing but empty religious rituals. Subsequently, he asks himself "the question of why"; the answer is "hollow silence." Castorp lives in a time "with neither hopes nor prospects" (*MM* 31). Mann's narrator suggests that Castorp would not have stayed on the mountain "if only some sort of satisfactory answer about the meaning and purpose of life had been supplied to his prosaic soul out of the depths of time" (*MM* 226). In experiencing existential emptiness, Castorp is not as ordinary as we are led to believe by the very first sentence of *The Magic Mountain*. He has studied engineering and can follow the arguments of the Italian freemason and pedagogue, Settembrini. He is ordinary in the sense that he is not an artist-outsider like Tonio Kröger or Gustav Aschenbach. The choice of engineering as Castorp's profession reflects Mann's attempt to distance himself from the problems of the outsider of his previous works and to create a character with a collective experience. Mann succeeds in encompassing both the artist's troublesome existence as well as the state of mind of many members of his generation by having Castorp function as a representative of his times, an individual who lives "the lives of his epoch and contemporaries" (*MM* 31). Castorp is, like Mann's notion of the artist, one of "life's problem children" (*MM* 323)—the early-twentieth-century individual estranged from his world. His psychological profile not only mirrors the mood of a disillusioned generation in prewar Germany, it also represents the zeitgeist, the spirit of decadence and disorientation in prewar Europe, the desire to break out of an old world and, confronting an existential void, to embrace destruction and death with the arrival of war. With this theme Mann's novel becomes part of an illustrious group of European and American works of fiction—including Virginia Woolf's *Mrs. Dalloway*, Ernest Hemingway's *A Farewell to Arms*, and T. S. Eliot's *The Waste Land*. Undeniably, *The Magic Mountain* can be understood as "a very German book" (*GW 11* 610), as Mann himself suggested. Yet it is also Mann's most trans-German work.

It is not only Castorp who represents his time. In his Princeton lecture, "Introduction to the 'Magic Mountain,'" Mann commented that, although unique individuals, the other central characters of *The Magic Mountain*—the Western-style humanist, Ludovico Settembrini, the Russian, Clavdia Chauchat, with her anarchic freedom, the East European Jesuit, Leo Naphta, who reflects the prevailing political tendencies toward terror and destruction, and the Dutchman, Mynheer Peeperkorn, who celebrates a Dionysian life—are "exponents, representatives and messengers of intellectual realms and worlds" (*GW 11* 612) of the time.[9] Their function in the novel is to present to Castorp—and to the readers of *The Magic Mountain*—a range of perspectives and ideologies from prewar Europe.

Yet, these orientations are also universal in their opposing claims and goals, and thus accessible to the twenty-first-century reader, who is invited to draw parallels to current global ideological conflicts and fundamentalist tenets. Whether any of them qualify as valid orientations in the current or future era of ideological clashes, uncertainty and crisis is explored by Mann through Castorp's interaction with these "messengers" and his reactions to their positions.

The pedagogue and humanist, Ludovico Settembrini, was part of the original, pre–First World War plan for the novel. His main function is to defend the values of the flatlands, to offer Castorp ideological and existential security, and to warn Castorp not "to be lost to life" (*MM* 195). As Settembrini sides with rationality and a strong work ethic, he is an outspoken advocate of humanism, democracy, and progress, and the most severe critic in the novel of the world of the sanatorium. He uses mythological figures to facilitate his description of this world as Hades; the physicians of the Berghof, Behrens and Krokowski, are "Minos and Rhadamanthus" (*MM* 55), "those who reside in the nether world" (*MM* 349). However, Mann undermines Settembrini's authority as a life-affirming messenger. His first appearance alludes to the Hermes figure, reminiscent of the stranger in the cemetery in *Death in Venice*. He stands in front of Castorp, "propping himself on his cane and crossing his ankles" (*MM* 54). In introducing Castorp to the world of disease and death of the sanatorium and heightening Castorp's curiosity of this morbid world, Mann also gives Settembrini the function of a Charon figure. Notwithstanding this association with death, Settembrini is the unrelenting advocate of humanistic ideas and becomes the most critical voice against death in *The Magic Mountain*.

With his defense of democracy and progress, and his antiromanticism, Settembrini resembles civilization's literary man from *Reflections*. In *The Magic Mountain* Mann presents a more positive image of the ideologically engaged intellectual, reflecting his own changing perspectives that led to his defense of democratic principles in his essays and speeches of the early 1920s.[10] In his Princeton lecture Mann called Settembrini "a humoristic-sympathetic figure, occasionally also the mouthpiece of the author, but not at all identical with the author" (*GW 11* 613). Settembrini's life-affirming perspective, his wit, irony, and his humanism make him a congenial figure. But when he claims that illness is inhuman (*MM* 456), his judgment becomes suspect. His refusal to accept illness and death as part of the human condition is a blind spot in his arguments. After all, he is himself seriously ill, a man only in his thirties, and is therefore condemned to spend the rest of his brief life on the mountain. To distance readers from Settembrini's teaching, Mann also turns him into a figure of ridicule, given to exaggerated gestures: "Laying his head to one side and closing his eyes,

Settembrini held out a hand toward him in a very beautiful and gentle gesture of restraint, a plea to be heard further. He held his pose for several seconds, long after Hans Castorp had fallen silent to wait somewhat awkwardly for what was to come" (*MM* 197). Settembrini is shown to be as much devoted to his rhetorical skills and the effect he has upon his audience as he is to his humanistic appeals and beliefs.[11] Castorp listens to Settembrini and admits that his mentor introduces previously unknown issues to him. But he tires of Settembrini's predictable arguments and the sermon-like deliberations of the "organ-grinder" (*MM* 197). He remarks critically: "I always have the impression that what is really important to him is not the lecture itself—perhaps that's only secondary—but more especially the speaking of it, the way he lets his words roll and bounce, like little rubber balls" (*MM* 99). Mann sends clear signals that Settembrini's eloquence is often in the service of form rather than content. Also questionable is the absoluteness with which Settembrini defends, often to the point of absurdity, his humanistic principles. Because Mann displays the problematic nature of Settembrini's insistence upon his ideas, he reiterates his doubts about the despised, dogmatic writer in the service of civilization. Yet Settembrini's ideas should not be discarded; they are, as Mann notes in a diary entry from November 1919, "the morally only positive and the opposition to the vice of death" (*TB 1918–1921* 319).

About halfway through the novel, in the chapter titled "Walpurgis Night," Settembrini's humanistic deliberations are put to the test. It is Mardi Gras, and the patients are in costume. Quoting from Goethe's *Faust*, Settembrini associates the festivities with orgies of demons and witches. He identifies the Russian Clavdia Chauchat with one of the witches, a woman who embodies everything he rejects. He tries to warn Castorp against the seductions of love and the forces of chaos and dissolution. Castorp thanks Settembrini for his caring nature and pedagogical inclinations, but admits now that he has been a "poor student" (*MM* 323). When Castorp turns toward Clavdia Chauchat, Settembrini leaves the room, admitting defeat. This episode illustrates that anarchic love wins out over bourgeois liberalism, primeval desires over abstract principles.

Settembrini's defeat does not mean that Mann rejects his humanistic ideas. Castorp's expressed sympathy for Settembrini, while lost in the snow during an excursion into the countryside, echoes that of the novel—and Mann: "I like you. True, you're a windbag and organ-grinder, but you mean well, mean better than that caustic little Jesuit and terrorist, that Spanish torturer and flogger with his flashing glasses" (*MM* 468). Repeatedly in his arguments with the Jesuit Naphta, the defender of terror and oppression, Mann gives Settembrini the opportunity to make his case for humanism. Toward the end of the novel, in refusing to shoot at Naphta during a duel resulting from their irreconcilable differences, Settembrini is praised because he "had behaved very humanly" (*MM* 700), as the narrator comments. However, the life-negating side of Settembrini, alluded to when he first appears in the novel, is also reiterated. While he abhors committing violence himself, he supports fighting and bloodshed that serves "politics for the ideal of civilization's ultimate victory and dominion" (*MM* 700).[12]

In presenting Settembrini as a multifaceted figure, associated with both life and death, humanism, dispassionate dogma, and self-serving rhetoric, Mann sends a skeptical message that even a humanistic orientation contains an inhuman dimension. Notwithstanding the mixed signals *The Magic Mountain* sends about Settembrini and the ironic treatment that he receives, Mann allows him a kindly farewell from the novel. A fleeting emotional gesture characterizes Settembrini's last appearance. Bidding adieu to Castorp, who is leaving the mountain for the battlefields of Flanders, he waves with his right hand, "while with the tip of the ring finger of his left hand he gently brushed the corner of one eye" (*MM* 703). It is this human touch, void of any ideological considerations, that makes Settembrini likable in the end, especially since Mann provides this counterimage to that immediately following, one of Castorp walking over corpses on the battlefield in Flanders, insensitive and indifferent to life.[13]

Settembrini's major adversary in *The Magic Mountain* is Leo Naphta, whose arrival coincides with Clavdia Chauchat's departure. Unlike Settembrini, Naphta is not a character included in the original plan for the novel. His conception goes back to a diary entry of May 1919, in which Mann describes his resentment of communism and contemplates the figure of a Russian Jew, a mix of "Jewish intellectual radicalism and Slavic revelry for Christ" (*TB 1918–1921* 223). Naphta had been forced out of his homeland by a pogrom in which his father met an extremely cruel death; he was crucified at his door. In permanent exile, he finds ideological security in the teachings of communism and Jesuitism. He is, therefore, a living contradiction, subscribing to progressive and reactionary forces, preaching asceticism while leading an Epicurean life.

As a Jesuit, Naphta demands discipline and hierarchical structures; he favors oppression, inquisition, terror, war, and death as a means to establish a state of God. Mann derives the concurrent presence of piety and the desire for bloodshed in Naphta's character to his upbringing. His father, an orthodox Jew, was a butcher whose ritualistic slaughtering of animals combined religion with blood and violence. As a communist, Naphta rails against bourgeois morality and capitalism; he argues that the bourgeois-democratic movement, which goes back to the eighteenth century, is outdated, its humanism stale, the product of a spiritual ennui. His diatribes against bourgeois humanism do not stop him from leading a somewhat luxurious life style that undermines his credibility. In contrast to

Settembrini's positive assessment of human nature and his belief in rationality and progress stands Naphta's darker image of man, which includes irrationality and disease as part of the human condition. In light of the degenerative world of *The Magic Mountain* and Europe's political course, Naphta's perspective has merit. Nevertheless, the novel does not present Naphta in a sympathetic light. The Jesuit's totalitarian and anti-individualistic stance comes under attack when Castorp voices his resentment against intolerance and the enslavement of mankind: "Absolute authority! An ironclad bond! Coercion! Obedience! Terror! There might be something to it, but it showed very little consideration for the dignity of the individual and his critical faculties" (*MM* 458).[14] With Naphta's ugly physical appearance, Mann additionally underscores the unattractiveness of many of his beliefs.

At first glance the combination of established Christian and modern communist ideas in Naphta's thoughts and arguments might seem peculiar. However, this interweaving of religious and secular orientations becomes plausible because both oppose a decadent bourgeois world that distinguishes people by class. Naphta's growing anarchic nihilism and aggressiveness toward the end of the novel, his "mania for intellectual doubt, negation, and confusion" (*MM* 680), correspond to the antiprogressive, irrational demands of the extreme right in the Weimar Republic for the destruction of democratic structure and order.[15] With Naphta's reactionary, fanatical ideas, Mann warns his readers "against a right, eclectic, antihumanistic ideology."[16] But he does not do so to advocate an alternative political agenda. As in the case of Settembrini, Mann unmasks with Naphta the inherent danger of dogmatism. Dogmatism breeds intolerance; it is indifferent to human suffering because it lacks the one essential criterion for a humanistic world: love.

The unyielding dialogues between Settembrini and Naphta, which increasingly get lost in rhetorical mazes, come to an end with a duel demanded by Naphta. In this duel both sides can make their point. Settembrini, in refusing to shoot at Naphta, does not compromise his humanistic stance. Naphta feels defeated and commits suicide. Thus Mann has Naphta affirm his life-negating principles through self-destruction and violence. With Naphta's death, Mann lets the advocate of progress and humanism survive the spokesperson of totalitarian power, nihilism, and destruction, albeit for only a brief period, as Settembrini's health is deteriorating rapidly. Settembrini's survival can be seen as a symbolic yet fragile victory of democratic and humanistic over totalitarian forces. Analogous to his speeches of this period, Mann conveys here the notion that the survival of democracy is a political necessity. However, the writer of *The Magic Mountain* is far less optimistic than the writer of "The German Republic."

Because of their contradictory natures, Settembrini and Naphta are messengers of ideological paradigms as well as "anti-messengers," narrative figures employed to introduce and dismantle perspectives, to validate and invalidate them. Another ambivalent character who cannot be reduced to a fixed position is Clavdia Chauchat, the door-slamming, Kirghiz-eyed and enigmatic Russian woman. She is one of Mann's most remarkable female characters. Though married, she always travels without her husband, leading a sexually emancipated, even promiscuous existence, in defiance of bourgeois norms and morality. In the opinion of her most severe critic, the humanist Settembrini, Clavdia Chauchat is the personification of the uncivilized world, associated with the East, in particular with a barbaric Asia that stands for largesse, vice, formlessness, chaos, disease, and degeneration. She is for Castorp what Tadzio is for Aschenbach in *Death in Venice*. As Castorp's infatuation with Clavdia Chauchat influences his decision to remain in the sanatorium, thereby embroiling him further in the world of disease and death, irresponsibility and inertia, the novel tempts us to accept Settembrini's perspective that the persona of this enticing woman embodies all the dark, destructive, life-negating forces against which Mann is warning his readers.[17]

Castorp's conversation with Clavdia Chauchat during the Mardi Gras ball in the sanatorium parodies Wagner's *Tristan and Isolde* when he declares the unity of love, body, and death, and his yearning for a *Liebestod*. Love, however, is not only associated with death, and Clavdia Chauchat is not only the seductress of death, as Settembrini suggests. Upon Castorp's declaration of his love, she tenderly strokes his hair. Their sexual encounter that follows attests to her kindness as well as to her sexual emancipation. Later, in her relationship with Peeperkorn, she again displays a compassionate side and altruistic motives. Settembrini's humanistic diatribes and liberal homilies pale in comparison to her human touch. While Settembrini's humanism is theoretical, undermined by his arrogance and elitism, and only temporarily suspended by his emotional reaction to Castorp's departure, she performs a service to life. Mann wants us to understand that Clavdia Chauchat's compassionate, humanistic leaning results from her anarchic freedom, implying that real humanity is spontaneous and intuitive, not the rationalized, dispassionate humanity advocated by Settembrini.

Even though the novel carefully documents the nurturing side of Clavdia Chauchat's character, it does not diminish other aspects of her personality that are destructive. The impact of her sympathy and compassion for life is highly ambivalent. While her sexual generosity keeps Castorp away from a meaningless bourgeois life, she leads him toward an equally meaningless, self-indulgent, unproductive existence that will last for years. Her care for Peeperkorn is admirable;

but the Dutchman cannot cope with his impotence and physical failings along-side her sexual presence, and he commits suicide. The narrator points out that love, that is to say the sexual passion for an organic, decaying entity, is embracing life and death. This duality of love turns Castorp's encounter with Clavdia Chauchat into both an expression of sympathy with death as well as an "affirmation of life" (*MM* 590).

With Clavdia Chauchat, Mann employs a female character who is ideologically uncommitted and lives outside bourgeois-patriarchal mores, to play with and temporarily destabilize traditionally irreconcilable contrasts. She therefore functions as a site of convergence in which the novel's central principles and orientations overlap. Moreover, with her independence and display of caritas, Clavdia Chauchat approaches what is presented as the vision of an ideal human being, someone "whose head is a little clear and heart a little devout" (*MM* 486). Paradoxically, Mann establishes Clavdia Chauchat's affinity to this ideal not only to propose its possibility, but also to dismantle it. First, her influence upon others is not entirely beneficial. Second, her strikingly self-effacing attitude to Peeperkorn is characterized by self-imposed submission, very much in contrast to her earlier emancipated lifestyle. This relationship thus serves as the novel's testing ground for the compatibility of individualistic freedom and social compassion.

With this friction between individual freedom and social compassion Mann touches upon a very personal issue: his own vacillation between escape into aestheticism and his social responsibilities as a father and citizen. Clavdia Chauchat, the Russian outsider whose need for independence is counterbalanced by her social engagement and even her fear of being alone—a fear which compels her to become Peeperkorn's lover and to return to the Berghof and Castorp—becomes a narrative site for Mann to revisit his own problematic existence as a bourgeois artist. As is the case with Tony Buddenbrook, Mann projects his own hopes and fears onto a woman. There is another, hidden autobiographical dimension when we look at Clavdia Chauchat's uncertain sexual identity. This virile yet sensuous, childless woman displays remarkable character resemblances to the Slavic boy, Pribislav Hippe, on whom Castorp had a crush. Hippe is based on Mann's school friend Williram Timpe from the early 1890s.[18] Repeatedly, Clavdia Chauchat is identified as Hippe's reincarnation. It is likely that Mann had the constellation Hippe-Castorp-Chauchat in mind when he confided his fascination for the forbidden love in *The Magic Mountain* to his diary. Yet the sexual encounter between Castorp and Clavdia Chauchat is ambiguously hetero- as well as homosexual. Thus, in the realm of art Mann affirms and fulfills—again behind a mask—what bourgeois morality disavows. The fact that Castorp's emancipation from this morality is short-lived and that, upon Clavdia Chauchat's return with Peeperkorn, his relationship with her lacks its earlier erotic dimension, indicates Mann's ambivalence toward stigmatized sexuality, even to the extent of brushing it aside.

The theme of love and nurture, introduced through Chauchat in *The Magic Mountain*, returns in "Snow," the central chapter of *The Magic Mountain*. This was written in the early summer of 1923, after Mann's public advocacy for democracy in "The German Republic." Preceding this chapter is a rhetorically masterful, yet pointless debate between Settembrini and Naphta that leaves Castorp in "great confusion" (*MM* 459). He decides to venture alone into a dangerous mountain area. Before he can return he is caught in a snowstorm that reduces the visibility, restricting his ability to see clearly and causing him to lose track of time. His disoriented state is a reference to his loss of orientation in life. Like his initial journey to the sanatorium, Castorp's excursion into the snow is a "journey into death."[19] The wintry and white landscape, like the sea in *Buddenbrooks* and *Death in Venice*, symbolizes death, eternity, the dissolution of individuality, and nothingness. That Castorp undertakes this life-threatening excursion reiterates his fascination with death. He finds shelter behind a barn wall and, falling asleep, dreams about an Arcadian world. First the vision unfolds a Mediterranean landscape that simultaneously evokes Italy, Greece (as the cradle of Western civilization), Goethe, the Age of Classicism and Enlightenment, and the ideological and philosophical background from which the humanist Settembrini draws his ideas. A world of human kindness opens up in Castorp's mind. Young, healthy, beautiful men and women, "sunny people" (*MM* 483), interact in a friendly, courteous way. But Castorp's vision of this idyllic world of social harmony and life-affirming civility is short-lived as it takes him to a nearby archaic Doric temple. In the sanctuary of the temple, Castorp notices two ugly, half-naked, witch-like women tearing a child apart, devouring "it piece by piece, the brittle bones cracking in their mouths, blood dripping from their vile lips" (*MM* 485). Upon spotting him, the repulsive women curse Castorp in his hometown dialect. Here the vision ends.

In these dream images, humanism and barbarism, life and death clash. While still in a dreamlike state, Castorp wonders about the origins of this dream: "We don't form our dreams out of just our own souls. We dream anonymously and communally, though each in its own way. The great soul, of which we are just a little piece, dreams through us so to speak, dreams in our many different ways its own eternal, secret dream—about its youth, its hope, its joy, its peace, and its bloody feast" (*MM* 485). Castorp, the ordinary young man, establishes here an interrelationship between individual and universal experiences and senses that his dream is nothing less than a revelation of the human condition. The first part of the vision is mankind's yearning for a Golden Age, an idyllic world of peace and harmony; the second provides an understanding of the cruelty of life. Very likely, Mann was influenced by Nietzsche's *The Birth of Tragedy*, where Nietzsche points out that the Greeks had conjured up the illusion of the "Olympian magic mountain," an Apollonian world of beauty and dignity, as a counterforce to reality, "the terrors and horrors of existence."[20] This reality cannot be erased. That the "sunny people" do not stop barbarism and cruelty in Castorp's dream can be interpreted as an acknowledgment of the inevitable existence of death and horror, perhaps even as Mann's pessimism about the impotence of humanism against terror. Against this pessimism stands the "sunny people's" strength to embrace life despite their knowledge of death.

Castorp, still dreaming, draws from these visions the conclusion that both Settembrini and Naphta are "windbags," that neither the malicious Jesuit nor the philistine humanist are right when they contrast death with life, illness with health, and nature with spirit. Existence, "the *homo Dei's* state" (*MM* 486) is somewhere in the middle, "just as his condition is somewhere between mystical community and windy individualism." The dream brings Castorp to an affirmation of life. Clavdia Chauchat's love and compassion and a criticism of Settembrini's premeditated humanism resonate in Castorp's thought: "Love . . . not reason, is stronger than death. Only love, and not reason, yields kind thoughts." Castorp promises himself that, while he will remain devoted and faithful to death, and recognize its power, death from now on will not rule over him.[21] The lesson he learns is: "*For the sake of goodness and love, man shall grant death no dominion over his thoughts*" (*MM* 487). With this recognition the snowstorm passes and good weather returns. Castorp can again find his way—realistically as well as symbolically since the dream has enlightened him—and his life is no longer threatened by nature. While he forgets this lesson before the day is over after he returns to the Berghof, readers of the novel do not, because Mann emphasizes it by stating it in italics.

What Castorp does not forget is his negative judgment of Settembrini and Naphta as windbags and his rejection of their antithetical views; he sees himself now as the "master of contradictions" (*MM* 487). His newly found intellectual independence is put to the test when he meets Mynheer Pieter Peeperkorn. With Peeperkorn, a man of majestic stature, a lover of life and nature, resembling Goethe, Nietzsche, and Mann's contemporary, Gerhart Hauptmann,[22] Mann makes an allusion to the *Lebenskult* (cult of life) of the 1890s. Hauptmann was a follower of this life-affirming movement that had been inspired by some of Goethe's and Nietzsche's writings. In the chapter titled "Vingt et un," in which Peeperkorn hosts a feast, allusions to the Last Supper and the betrayal in Gethsemane are interwoven with images of a Bacchanalian feast. The novel sets up Peeperkorn as both a Christ figure and a Dionysus figure; the physical and the spiritual realm, the secular and the religious sphere enter into a temporary unity. With this character, as with his other central figures, Mann refuses to construct a monolithic personality.

Unlike the intellectuals Settembrini and Naphta, Peeperkorn is not "another instigator of intellectual and pedagogic confusion" (*MM* 539). When he speaks, he stutters and his sentences often go uncompleted. He does not measure up to the eloquence of Settembrini and Naphta, but he makes up for this deficit with his impressive physical presence. Peeperkorn radiates life, vitality, and exuberance. However, death in *The Magic Mountain* is omnipresent and permeates every aspect of existence. The messenger of *Lebenskult* is a terminally ill, impotent man; his vitality is a facade and his death by suicide is looming. Two incidents lead Peeperkorn to take his own life. First, Castorp confesses that he has been Chauchat's lover, thereby confronting Peeperkorn with his own inadequate sexual prowess and physical degeneration. Second, during a picnic the afternoon before his suicide, Peeperkorn raises his voice against a thundering waterfall in an attempt to compete with and dominate nature. Underscoring Peeperkorn's impotence, Mann has the waterfall drown out his voice. Peeperkorn's last words, as far as can be read from his lips, are "agreed" and "settled" (*MM* 612). Just as Settembrini's and Naphta's intellectual diatribes have lost their force, so, with his submission to death, has Peeperkorn's celebration of life.

The Peeperkorn episode is about both the vigor of life and the inescapable presence of death. Has Castorp drawn any consequences from his interactions with Peeperkorn? He follows Clavdia Chauchat's request to treat Peeperkorn kindly, and thus is given the opportunity to exercise the love and compassion his dream during the snowstorm had encouraged him to pursue. Most perplexing is his relationship to his former lover, whose return he had been awaiting, in the Peeperkorn episodes. Rather than being jealous, he befriends Peeperkorn and largely ignores Clavdia. Throughout the novel, and most explicitly in the chapter "Walpurgis Night," sexuality has been associated with death. Castorp's final, nonpassionate kiss on Cladvia Chauchat's forehead is a symbolic gesture both of his renunciation of sexual passions and of his sympathy with death. However, in light of Peeperkorn's explanation that life is symbolized by a "woman sprawled before us" challenging man's sexual vitality (*MM* 556), Castorp's kiss is also a turning away from the forces of life and, concomitantly, a leaning toward death.

That this kiss is an indication of his growing indifference toward life is accentuated in the chapters of *The Magic Mountain* that follow. After Peeperkorn's death and Clavdia Chauchat's departure, Castorp stays five more years on the mountain. These years, to which Mann devotes approximately ten percent of the novel, are characterized by "The Great Stupor," as the title of one chapter appropriately suggests. Around him Castorp observes "life without time, without care or hope, life as a stagnating hustle-bustle of depravity, dead life" (*MM* 619). Diversions like collecting stamps, drawing piglets, playing cards, and holding nightly spiritualist séances, one of which culminates in the apparition of Castorp's dead cousin Ziemssen in soldier's uniform and a helmet—a reference to the imminent war—can provide only temporary relief from a life of ennui and pointlessness. The result is an atmosphere of uncanniness, maliciousness, and aggression: "A love of quarrels. Acute petulance. Nameless impatience. A universal penchant for nasty verbal exchanges and outbursts of rage, even for fisticuffs" (*MM* 673). Frivolous conflicts erupt everywhere and, as is the case with Naphta and Settembrini, even end in death.

In this atmosphere of meaninglessness and indifference toward life, a lethargic Castorp takes charge of the new gramophone. Like *Buddenbrooks*, *The Magic Mountain* uses music as an intertextual device to comment upon the characters' state of mind and actions, and to expose their flight from reality.[23] References to Bizet's opera *Carmen*, in which love dominates over rationality and responsibility, emphasize that Castorp's love for Clavdia Chauchat has led him away from his life and duties in the flatlands. Music itself comes under scrutiny when Mann has Settembrini speak out against it because, like opiates, it creates "dullness, rigidity, stagnation, slavish inertia" (*MM* 112). Castorp's devotion to music allows him to escape into asocial aestheticism. When Mann calls the gramophone a "musical coffin" (*MM* 643), aestheticism and sympathy for death become mutually indistinguishable, and Castorp's life-negating attitude is underscored.

Music again manifests Castorp's state of mind when he sings a romantic folk song, Schubert's "Lindenbaum," on a battlefield in Flanders. Castorp leaves the Berghof not because of a budding social conscience, but out of sheer boredom and lack of sufficient diversions. His indifference to life, emphatically displayed when he steps on a dead soldier's hand, is further revealed by this popular song about lost love and death. The song is "something particularly, indeed exemplarily German" (*MM* 640), at the same time "an expression and exponent of a more universal spirit and intellect" (*MM* 641)—like Mann's novel. The narrator points out that whoever loves this song shares its central ideas that evolve around "sympathy with death" (*MM* 642). Ironically, Castorp's return to life in the flatlands leads him to another realm of death. The narrator proposes that in the midst of war's ghastly violence one could think of beautiful, idyllic scenes: "One might imagine such a lad spurring a horse on or swimming in a bay, strolling along the shore with a girlfriend, his lips pressed to his gentle beloved's ear, or in happy friendship instructing another lad to string a bow. And instead, there they all lie, noses in the fiery filth" (*MM* 705). These images, reminiscent of Castorp's life-affirming segment in his snow vision, are identified explicitly as images, as an aesthetic construct. The other segment of the snow vision, that of man's self-destructive nature, has, however, come true. At the end of the novel, Castorp becomes a symbol for his generation, which, with its romantic fascination for and transfiguration of death, marches forward euphorically to its doom.

Interpretations of *The Magic Mountain* have largely centered on those narrative strategies of the novel that align it with the genre of the bildungsroman, a characterization of the novel Mann welcomed as it placed him in the footsteps of Goethe.[24] The paradigm of the German bildungsroman is Goethe's 1795/96 work, *Wilhelm Meister*, in which the protagonist learns to shed his individualistic, aesthetic existence in order to become a productive member of bourgeois society. What has Castorp learned in seven years? From a dilettante's perspective, he has studied anatomy, biology, physiology. He has listened to the deliberations of Settembrini and Naphta and understood the anti-individualistic, inhuman dimensions of their dogmatic thinking, and realized that the "truly human or humane had to lie somewhere in the middle of this intolerant contentiousness, somewhere between rhetorical humanism and illiterate barbarism" (*MM* 513). Mann stressed this "presentiment of a new humanity" (*GW 11* 596) as the pivotal aspect of his protagonist's educational journey, a view many interpreters of *The Magic Mountain* have since shared. Castorp's acknowledgment of an "independent humanity,"[25] one that necessitates "the decision for individuality, the conviction that the individual must remain free from all seductions,"[26] implies a rejection of death, decadence, and nihilism, and entails a skepticism toward all ideologies. In an essay from 1922 titled "Das Problem der deutsch-französischen Beziehungen" (The problem of German-French relations), Mann coined the paradoxical phrase *Nihilismus der Menschenfreundlichkeit* ("nihilism of humanitarianism") (*E 2* 116) to describe this skepticism.[27] It is a nihilism that, while refusing to take refuge in ideological constructions and values, nonetheless is life-affirming. Its goal is not to escape into irresponsible, asocial freedom, but to find a world of "human order, civilization and dignified community" (*E 2* 116).

It is doubtful whether Castorp incorporates such a world in his thoughts and deeds. Although he gains ideological independence and a glimpse into a new humanity, he remains conspicuously silent, allowing the conflict between Settembrini and Naphta to culminate in the duel for which he provides the pistols. He falls prey to aestheticism, to a disrespect for life, and gives in to his fascination with death and nihilism. The lessons are forgotten; Castorp is indeed a "poor student." At the end of the novel, Mann's protagonist enters a life of adventure, a life in the service of death and violence—in contrast to Goethe's protagonist in *Wilhelm Meister*, who finds social integration and a dutiful life in the service of his community. Thus *The Magic Mountain* culminates in a parody of the German bildungsroman.

Even as a parody, *The Magic Mountain* still belongs to the tradition of the bildungsroman. It can be argued that the novel's pedagogical message does not hinge on the protagonist's message—hence the messenger's inability to live up to his insights and the humanistic appeal of the snow vision. What counts, and what lies at the heart of *The Magic Mountain* according to its author, is "the idea of man, the conception of a future humanity that has experienced the deepest knowledge about illness and death" (*GW 11* 617); the novel's "service is service to life, its volition health, its goal is the future" (*GW 11* 595). In an interview at the end of October 1925, Mann admitted that he might have committed a "compositional mistake" (*DüD 1* 509) by not placing the snowstorm chapter with its humanistic vision at the end of the novel, thus positioning it unequivocally as the most important and quintessential message of the text. Why, we must ask, was Mann so interested in convincing his readers of the life-affirming intentions of the novel, and, moreover, concerned that many of them had understood *The Magic Mountain* as a "heartless, cold, a nihilistic and diabolic book?"[28]

In defending democracy, Mann hoped that he could influence his audience, in particular the educated German burghers, to embrace Germany's new political world. In "The German Republic" he had stated: "No spiritual metamorphosis is more familiar to us than that where sympathy with death stands at the beginning and resolve to live and serve at the end. The history of European decadence and aestheticism is rich in examples of this thrust through to the positive, to the people, to the State" (*OD* 44). *The Magic Mountain* insinuates the possibility of this breakthrough with its central sentence "*For the sake of goodness and love, man shall grant death no dominion over his thoughts.*" The hope that love and social engagement will win over death is also expressed at the very end of the novel: "And out of this worldwide festival of death, this ugly rutting fever that inflames the rainy evening sky all round—will love someday rise up out of this, too?" (*MM* 706) Without doubt, Mann's novel expresses hope in humanity, and to call it cold and nihilistic is simplistic. On the other hand, as this hope is posed as a question, it is overshadowed by a doubt that permeates the whole novel. Again and again *The Magic Mountain* makes the point that human beings ought to be kind and loving, but with rare exceptions they opt not to be caring. Violence, aggression, and indifference to life reign toward the end of the novel, culminating in the destruction of humans by other humans. As a result, *The Magic Mountain* oscillates between optimistic and pessimistic assessments of human nature, between fascination with death and a resistance against it. Hope and pessimism, utopian dreams and nihilism are inseparably interwoven.

Still another dimension of *The Magic Mountain* raises doubts about Mann's own one-sided, optimistic statements. Mann probes and explores orientations in order to question and, ultimately, discredit them. *The Magic Mountain* points out the danger of pledging allegiance to ideologies because, unavoidably, they turn against human beings. In today's world, in which dogmatic and fundamentalist thinking, narrow-mindedness, and the clash of opposing views threaten the survival of humanity, Mann's skepticism against ideological tenets can raise our awareness of the consequences of intolerance on all sides. What remains in Mann's fictional world is "aesthetic idealism" (*E 3* 259), a nonideological concept of love and compassion as a guideline exemplified in the idyllic world of the "sunny people" remote from social and political realities of the twentieth century. Mann's well-intentioned moral appeal for compassion and nondogmatic humanism becomes problematic given that it endorses the continual alienation of the German *Bildungsbürger* from political processes. Mann's skepticism against ideologies invites his readers to remain detached, to renounce political engagement, and to take a critical, even nihilistic stance. With its theme of death, its pessimistic assessment of human nature, and its criticism and ironic treatment of the bourgeois world, *The Magic Mountain* is not a novel likely to engender readers to become socially active.

In a dispute with Naphta, Settembrini praises "the purifying, sanctifying effect of literature, the destruction of passions through knowledge and the Word; literature as the path to understanding, to forgiveness, and to love; the redemptive power of language, the literary spirit as the noblest manifestation of the human spirit per se" (*MM* 515). It is the "windbag" Settembrini who bestows a pedagogical, beneficial value upon literature. While Settembrini is not his author's mouthpiece, his aesthetic credo is partially validated by *The Magic Mountain*. With its many contradictions and ambivalence, *The Magic Mountain* assumes the position in the middle. It appeals to undogmatic humanism while simultaneously recognizing the power of aestheticism and death. This implies that the novel oscillates between Mann's advocacy for a humanistic, social orientation, expressed in various speeches since "The German Republic," and his embrace of German culture as characterized in *Reflections*, the world of the German *Bildungsbürger* and art, of aestheticism and romantic fascination for death. *The Magic Mountain* thus also reveals itself as a novel about affirmation of and resistance to Germany's bourgeois, aesthetic culture.

The coexistence of German culture and German democratic, life-embracing politics remains a utopian hope in *The Magic Mountain*. How difficult it is for the German *Bildungsbürger* to bridge this gap is a theme in Mann's story *Unordnung und frühes Leid* (*Disorder and Early Sorrow*) about a history professor, Abel Cornelius, and his family. The inflation of 1923 and the new social order in Germany have brought economic and ideological uncertainty into their household. While Cornelius's teenage children and their friends embrace the modern world, Cornelius clings to the past, the realm of timelessness and immortality, and thus the realm of death. He seeks escape in past history—Mann has made him a specialist on the conservative Spanish King Philip II to illustrate his backwards orientation—and in his love for his youngest daughter, the five-year-old Eleonorchen. Cornelius senses that this love is directed against life; it "has something to do with death."[29] With sympathy and understanding, Mann presents the difficulty this academic has in making the transition to a new world while retaining the old. We recognize Cornelius's willingness to make concessions to the changing times when he shaves off his pointed beard and opens up to progressive forces in history as he prepares a lecture on England during the Glorious Revolution. At a party at his house for his older children and their friends, he even disrupts his work to observe the new world, albeit with deep skepticism.

Mann indicates the arrival of a new era with references to music. Wagner's music, a nearly indispensable accessory of Mann's bourgeois world in earlier stories, has been replaced by the shimmy and the one-step; the German folk song "Lindenbaum" has made way for a French and a German folk song about the dismantling of traditional class differences. Mann portrays the new generation of young Germans, symbolic of contemporary, life-affirming Germany, who enjoy modern, international music and ignore bourgeois etiquette, morality, and elitist class-consciousness, with humor and sympathy. This new world breaks into the old bourgeois world when Eleonorchen falls in love with one of the guests, Herr Hergesell, while dancing with him, and cries bitterly when she has to leave the party. In agony over his daughter's heartache, Cornelius realizes that she will grow up and change, that he cannot escape the present time. Mann ends the story with Cornelius's hope that the next day he and Eleonorchen will return to their old games. Thus he caters to the illusion that time will stand still, an illusion the narrative does not confirm. Mann leaves open whether the young girl will still participate, thus drawing attention to the need for Cornelius, and the educated middle class, to be open to life and change.

Mann himself turned toward the present time. Instead of continuing to work steadily on his new fictional project begun in 1926, the biblical story of Joseph that was taking him into the past, he made public appearances in 1929 to warn against nationalistic and irrational forces in his "Rede über Lessing" ("Speech on Lessing") and "Die Stellung Freuds in der modernen Geistesgeschichte"

("Freud's Position in the History of Modern Thought"). Resentments against these same forces are also voiced in a novella written in the summer of the same year and published in 1930, *Mario und der Zauberer* (*Mario and the Magician*), based on Mann's encounter with a magician during a vacation in fascist Italy in 1926. The story, like some of Mann's earlier stories, tells about seduction, loss of dignity, and death. A first person German narrator and his family, vacationing in Italy, attend the performance of the magician, Cipolla. Cipolla, using his hypnotic powers, manipulates members of the audience to act against their wills. Among them is Mario, a waiter, who kisses the ugly, physically deformed magician in the false belief that he is kissing the girl he secretly loves. After the hypnotic spell is broken, an embarrassed and humiliated Mario shoots and kills Cipolla.

In the first part of the novella, Mann captures the aggressive, irrational, and highly nationalistic mood of a seaside resort in fascist Italy.[30] Mann later commented in a letter that he had not specifically intended a political allegory aimed at Germany and its growing National Socialist movement under Hitler, but that the novella is an "artwork," and thus ideologically disengaged. Yet in the same letter he also suggested that the novella definitely contained a "moral-political meaning" (*DüD 2* 371) and was directed against human degradation and the enslavement of human will. Mann's negative portrayal of the magician, whose talent lies in the "compulsion of volition"[31] and in causing self-surrender, shame, and humiliation in his victims from all social classes, is juxtaposed with the liberating effect it has upon them. Also ambiguous are the dynamics between victims and victimizer. Cipolla can seduce his audience because, despite their mixed feelings about him, they want to be seduced. It is the "voiceless common will which was in the air,"[32] a collective readiness for a loss of human dignity and of volition which provides the fertile grounds for Cipolla's success.

Mario and the Magician can be read on various levels. It is a story about the psychological dynamics between a leader and his people and about the rise of fascism. It is a European as well as a German story, aimed particularly at a criticism of Germany's educated middle class. Their representative in the novella, the narrator, responds to the Italians' xenophobia and degrading attitude with irony and wit. His criticism of antiliberal beliefs and morality is justified in the text. What puts him under scrutiny, however, is his inability to act. He asks himself why he has not left the seaside resort with his family; later he wonders why he stayed at Cipolla's show. The narrator's willpower and his claim that he can resist the magician's enthrallment are dubious. Having reluctantly admitted that he hovers between fascination and renunciation, he mentions toward the end of his story "that we had caught the general devil-may-careness of the hour. By that time it was all one."[33] With this inability to escape irrationality, with the fascination for evil and growing indifference, Mann indicates his skepticism toward middle-class, humanistic engagement in the Weimar Republic.

This skepticism also molds Mann's portrayal of the magician. With Cipolla, whose deformity and visible physical decline mark him as an outsider, *Mario and the Magician* exposes the artist as irresponsible and his power as highly suspect. Because Mann's public speeches at that time show him to be a determined promoter of the Weimar Republic,[34] an artist in favor of democracy and humanism, the fictional killing of the destructive, decadent artist can be understood as Mann's affirmation of his own democratic engagement as artist. However, it is also possible that Mann, called the "magician" by his family, questions his own artistic existence. Self-doubts about his own ability to fight off his fascination for the dark, destructive forces of German culture and doubts about his role as a public figure and a prominent voice of Germany hover over Mann's last narrative, written before forces indifferent to human dignity and life would come to power in Germany in 1933.

CHAPTER 9

Joseph and His Brothers

Mann had in mind to write a simple "historical novella" (*DüD* 2 92) when he began contemplating turning one of Western civilization's primary tales of fall and rise, love and hate, jealousy and forgiveness, betrayal and revenge—the story of Joseph from the Book of Genesis—into fiction.[1] As with *Royal Highness* and *The Magic Mountain*, the short project became longer than anticipated and turned into Mann's longest novel, written over a period of sixteen years. It was published in four installments: *Die Geschichten Jakobs* (*The Tales of Jacob*, 1933), *Der junge Joseph* (*Young Joseph*, 1934), *Joseph in Ägypten* (*Joseph in Egypt*, 1936), and *Joseph der Ernährer* (*Joseph the Provider*, 1943).[2] Repeatedly, Mann interrupted work on the manuscript to write essays and the fictional works *Mario and the Magician*, *Lotte in Weimar*, and *Die vertauschten Köpfe* (*The Transposed Heads*, 1940). Their central concerns—reflections upon the artist's powers and role in society, the isolated writer's withdrawal into his artistic realm, and the relationship between intellect and nature—echo those of the tetralogy and often present a counter perspective. For example, while the outsider-artist figure in *Joseph and His Brothers* becomes a socially engaged leader, in *Lotte in Weimar* he remains aloof. Other projects might have distracted Mann from pursuing the tetralogy relentlessly; they could not stop him from completing it, however. Neither did German politics and a rather restless, unsettled life. Mann finished the first two volumes in Germany amidst the political, ideological, and economic instability of the Weimar Republic. The third volume, begun in Germany, was written in exile, in southern France and Switzerland. Mann now shared with his Joseph figure a life away from his home, his culture, and his native audience. The final volume, *Joseph as Provider*, was completely written in the United States. Despite devastating historical events—the breakdown of the Weimar Republic, the rise of National Socialism, and the Second World War—and despite the personal and emotional hardships the Manns endured over these sixteen years, Mann never wavered in his determination to complete the project. In his foreword to the American edition he wrote that this work "was my staff and my stay on a path that often led through dark valleys. It was my refuge, my comfort, my home, my symbol of steadfastness, the guarantee of my perseverance in the tempestuous change of things" (*JB* v).

Asked in 1924 to write an introduction to a collection of drawings about the tale of Joseph, Mann remembered Goethe's comments in *Fiction and Truth*: "This natural narrative is most charming, only it seems too short, and one feels inclined to put it in detail."[3] In the years following Mann did just that, and with such success that his secretary in Munich, who typed the first volume from his handwritten manuscript, remarked: "Now, finally, one knows how all that had happened in reality!" Mann reacted with pride that he had succeeded in making this past world come alive, and also with amusement because apparently this "simple woman" could not differentiate between reality and the illusionary world of fiction (*E 5* 186). To construct this atmosphere of realism, he consulted, in addition to the Bible, numerous books on the Old Testament, on Jewish culture and religions, and on myths of Babylonian, Egyptian, and Greek origins. Mann's quest for authenticity led him to undertake journeys to Egypt in 1925 and 1930, and, furthermore, to conduct extensive research on Egyptian art and history.[4] What strikes readers of the tetralogy first are the elaborate, accurate descriptions of the characters and their ancient world. Why this thorough and ambitious commitment? Following in the footsteps of Germany's greatest writer, Goethe, was certainly on Mann's mind since *Death in Venice*. That *Joseph and His Brothers* aspired to greatness from the start becomes evident with its prelude, reminiscent of that to Goethe's magnum opus *Faust*, his "tragedy about mankind" (*E 5* 196). Mann aimed at nothing less than his own "epic about mankind" (*E 5* 189). Surprisingly, he did not mention Dante's *The Divine Comedy*. Yet the prelude to his tetralogy, entitled "Descent into Hell," is an obvious allusion not only to Faust's descent into the mythological world, but also to Dante's first part of his *Divine Comedy*, "The Inferno." Later, in his foreword to the American edition, Mann suggested that the evolution of his novel was also "somehow secretly determined by the recollection of Wagner's grandiose structure" (*JB* xi). Like Wagner's mythological, monumental saga of a family's decline, *The Ring of the Nibelung*, Mann's story about Joseph is presented in a prelude and four parts; like Wagner, he plays with myths, and, also like Wagner, he does so by extensively using leitmotifs.[5]

With *Joseph and His Brothers*, Mann enters the mythical world of Judeo-Christian culture. But he remains loyal to his humorous, sometimes mocking, ironic tone paired with a sympathetic stance toward human shortcomings. Furthermore, old motifs and themes abound. The portrayal of the decadent Egyptian pharaoh who is marked by a vein on his "sickly forehead" (*JB* 944) is reminiscent of Gabriele Klöterjahn in *Tristan*. Illness and the connection to artistic sensibility resurface in Mann's presentation of the Egyptian Mont-kaw; sexual desire as an affliction, a theme in "Little Herr Friedemann," is portrayed in Mut-em-enet who, until Joseph's arrival, lived a life devoted to aestheticism and asceticism. We are reminded of *Death in Venice* when Charon-like figures return in Joseph on various occasions. Undoubtedly, the biblical tale of Joseph and his brothers, a story about a family and their outsider son, would have been less interesting to Mann had it not provided an ideal narrative platform for one of the most prominent themes in Mann's career as a writer: the problematic existence of a narcissistic, creative outsider and the function of creativity.

Like most of Mann's texts, *Joseph and His Brothers* is multifaceted and can be read on various levels. On the realistic level, it is an entertaining version of a biblical tale. On the symbolic level, various themes unfold. For one, the story raises the issue how bourgeois aesthetic, individualistic culture fits into a changing, twentieth-century German world. As pointed out earlier, in his essay "Thoughts in War" Mann had juxtaposed culture with civilization, and creativity, art, aestheticism, and irrationalism with rationality and intellect. This juxtaposition became less rigorous in *Reflections*, where Mann made the point that critical intellect is not excluded from German creative culture, and that "intellect" *and* "nature"—critical, progressive, *and* creative forces together—can lead the way to a new humanity. Its ambassador is the bourgeois artist as Mann described him in 1925: "The poet, in alliance likewise with both forces, nature and intellect, can be called master of mankind" (*GW 9* 186).[6] Mann addresses this desirable combination in the prelude to *The Tales of Jacob*, titled "Descent into Hell." It is the task of the spirit, the intellectual-critical force of life, to embrace the soul, the site of creativity, characterized by "its self-forgetful involvement with form and death" (*JB* 25–26). Thus one aspect of the tetralogy is Mann's question of whether German culture with its aesthetic and life-negating dimension can, together with a rational, intellectual orientation, play a constructive role in German society and find an integration and participation Mann had hoped for, yet had questioned in *The Magic Mountain* and *Disorder and Early Sorrow*.

This German theme is embedded in a timeless, universal one for which the bygone world of the Old Testament provides a perfect background. In his 1936 lecture "Freud und die Zukunft" ("Freud and the Future"), Mann acknowledged that he had undertaken "the step in my subject-matter from the bourgeois and individual to the mythical and typical" (*ETD* 422). In addition, in a speech on the *Joseph* tetralogy in 1942, Mann pointed out that he was most interested in the typical and timeless, "in sum: the mythical. For the typical is already the mythical in as far as it is the primordial norm and form of life, timeless scheme and given formula in which life immerses itself in reproducing its characteristics out of the unconscious" (*E* 5 187). This self-interpretation, as so often is the case with Mann's comments, contains a half-truth. As the prelude to the tetralogy, "Descent into Hell," suggests, myths reveal the essence of the human condition. The narrator, who exists in a specific yet unidentified time and place, invites his readers to travel back with him in time, into the "well of the past" (*JB* 3), to explore the universal nature of man in the realm of myths and legends that provide insights into archetypical human behavior. However, having established this timeless, archetypical world, the narrator also engages in a skeptical assessment of the control the mythical has over life. He considers that, on the one hand, the essential being of man lies outside a specific material world, but that, on the other, man lives in specific historical settings that promote experiences that mold his particular, individual life. Mann had brought forth a similar idea in Hans Castorp's snow vision in *The Magic Mountain*: man participates in the common, "anonymous," as well as in the particular, individual, and creative dimensions of life. Thus, Mann challenges us to doubt the binding authority of myths and raises central questions that transcend cultural and national boundaries. To what extent are human beings predetermined, entrapped in mythical reenactment and in the mythical-typical, and thus unable to make choices? To what extent are they autonomous, and thus responsible for their actions? This set of questions leads to a further, equally ambiguous dimension of the tetralogy: the existence and power of God. In the Book of Genesis the existence of God is beyond doubt. In contrast, Mann's version of the Joseph story from Genesis plays with the dualistic world view of God and his creation, of spirit and life, good and bad, timeless and historical existence. Against this dualistic world view Mann holds a monistic one. The tetralogy leaves open as to whether God exists or whether Abraham has imagined him to exist, and thus also raises the issue of the authority of human creativity.

The Tales of Jacob

The themes of mythical existence and individual freedom, of culture and civilization, of intellectual aloofness and social commitments unfold in the first volume of the tetralogy based on the biblical account of Jacob's betrayal of Esau, his stay at Laban's house, and his marriages to Lea and Rachel, which result in the births of twelve sons and one daughter; his flight from Laban and return to his brother Esau and their reconciliation; the bloodshed in Shechem; and Rachel's and Isaak's deaths. While Mann is faithful to the plot of the biblical story and its chronology, he does not tell it in a chronological form. He starts with Jacob's discovery of his favorite son, the seventeen-year-old Joseph, who is sitting partially clothed beside a well throwing kisses to the moon. Jacob renounces his son's behavior as paganism, reminds him of the abominable practices of the "monkeyland of Egypt" (*JB* 60) and his family's commitment to the Highest God, the God of Abraham. The dialogue between father and son allows Mann to explore concepts and issues of progress and humanism, decadent civilization, and Joseph's veneration of the moon, as well as to cast doubts about the existence of a transcendental deity and Jacob's narrow perspective and dualistic world view. In this discussion, Jacob's accounts of the promiscuity, the sexual rituals, and the death cult of the Egyptians are exaggerated for the sake of praising his monotheistic faith and devotion to an enlightened God. His strong renunciation of foreign customs hints at a lack of tolerance and openness.

Ambiguity toward Jacob, the spiritual leader of Abraham's descendants, characterizes the whole volume. Jacob confesses to his son Joseph that his passion for him and for his deceased mother Rachel prevents him from following in the footsteps of his forefather Abraham, who was willing to sacrifice his son to God. Jacob, unlike Abraham, could not chose faith over love. We are to understand that this love makes Jacob human and resistant to dogmatic, anti-individualistic thinking. Nonetheless, for Jacob, who finds guidance and strength in his complicity with mythical patterns, this deviation causes pangs of consciousness. The vain Joseph tries to put an end to his father's guilt feelings. As a narcissist who covets his father's love and attention, he argues that God himself rejected the human sacrifice of Isaac and accepted the symbolic sacrifice of a lamb. As Joseph further explains, his father acts according to the will of the Highest God who, in Joseph's interpretation, is a progressive god. Joseph's position here becomes that of an opponent of fundamentalist ideas and of one-sided, equivocal truths. For the rhetorically skillful, creative Joseph, myths are open to mutation and modification; they adapt to new circumstances, are open to change, progress, and individual input, and therefore encourage tolerance. Joseph is introduced as a charming, manipulative speaker who combines human and divine will, earthly love and spiritual orientation, creativity and religious authority. Yet his motivation to do so is questionable. He tests his rhetorical skill and intelligence for mere self-aggrandizement.

Creativity is also one of Jacob's attributes. He is a gifted man of "natural spirituality" and "bold dreams" (*JB* 275), and puts his intuitive intellectuality in the service of Abraham's transcendental god and religious spirituality. However, his character is far from perfect. Jacob "had not always played the dignified and heroic rôle in life" (*JB* 41). He is described as a passive, hesitant, even cowardly man. His mother's unwavering determination to elevate him makes it possible that he, and not Esau, receives his father's blessing. After the betrayal, she plans and initiates Jacob's escape to stay with her brother Laban. Jacob prides himself on his passivity because it is connected with freedom and purity (*JB* 158). Despite his awareness of moral wrongdoing, he feels justified in his behavior, "because he was consecrated, because the promise and the blessing handed down from Abraham lay upon him" (*JB* 87–88). That Mann perceives Jacob's intellectual interests as problematic in *The Tales of Jacob* becomes evident in his detailed account of the story of Dinah, the only daughter of Jacob and Lea. In striking deviation from the chronological storyline of the Old Testament, Mann chooses to tell her story before that of her father's marriages to her mother, Lea, and Rachel, and his twenty-five-year stay at Laban's place. In a conscious imitation of Abraham's life, Jacob, having fled with his tribe from Laban, made a covenant with the leader of Shechem, in order to settle and live nearby. When Sichem, the leader's son, falls in love with Dinah and kidnaps her to be his wife, a self-absorbed Jacob protests, but only reluctantly and halfheartedly. He lets his sons act for him. They demand that all Shechemites undergo circumcision before the wedding can take place, a condition that Jacob endorses with "misgiving" (*JB* 114). As Abraham himself and his tribe had followed this demand given by none other than God, he is overcome by "his own pleasure in repetition and recurrence." The novel suggests here that fulfilling mythical patterns is a justification as well as an excuse, because Jacob fears his sons' violence and aggressiveness, and prefers to remain "aloof and innocent" (*JB* 116). He is, as Mann illustrates, quite justified in his fear of his own sons. They betray and kill the men of Shechem. Among their defenseless victims are also many women and children.

Mann's narrator suggests the following as a reason for why the deadly betrayal of the Shechemites appears so early in his account of the biblical events: "For if I unfold the story of the evil and in the end bloody doings of that time, a story inscribed in Jacob's lined and weary old lineaments along with other events that made up the burden of his ancient memories, it is because it forms part of the man's spiritual history, the character of his soul" (*JB* 98). This "spiritual history" is to a large degree a history about an intellectual's flight from reality, decisions, and individual responsibility. To avoid potential conflicts, Jacob visits holy places and communities to discuss with them "the essence of the Only and Most High" (*JB* 107). He feels that his intellectual-religious life, "his mild gaze upon everyday things and spiritual matters" (*JB* 107), justifies his lack of interest in social and political issues. However, in withdrawing repeatedly from the world to meditate about God, he indirectly causes extreme suffering and death, as the story of Dinah exemplifies. This inwardness takes on a symbolic dimension when connected to twentieth-century Germany. Indifference toward the social and political world, combined with an aesthetic way of thinking, characterize the artist and the German *Bildungsbürger* in Mann's fiction and essays written before and during his work on the tetralogy. Thus *The Tales of Jacob* includes a "parable of powerless spirituality,"[7] which turns the novel at this point into a criticism of the educated middle class of the Weimar Republic who subscribed to a humanistic orientation yet remained politically disengaged.[8]

Ambiguity about a spirituality that is based on humanistic tenets yet indifferent to reality also underlies Mann's depiction of Jacob when he stays with his uncle Laban for twenty-five years. Laban is a man whose world is centered on earthly possessions and economic gain. He is called the "clod" (*JB* 152), a reference to his worldly existence in contrast to Jacob's spiritual one. What further characterizes him is his primitive mentality. The world of Laban is backward; his gods demand human sacrifice, a demand underscored by the sacrificial interment of his firstborn son, while still alive, in the foundation of his house to please the gods. Laban's negativity is emphasized by his association with the underworld, his filicide, and his exploitation of Jacob. His betrayal of Jacob when he gives him Lea as a wife, and not, as promised, Rachel, seems cruel. But the narrative insinuates that Jacob, too, is to blame. In one of Jacob's dreams, Anup appears. He is the Egyptian Hades figure whose father, the god Usir, does not notice that during his wedding night the wrong woman is in his bed. Anup remarks: "We are feckless beings, heedless and distracted from birth onwards. Carefulness and foresight are base earthly characteristics, whereas what all has not carefreeness been the cause of in this life?" (*JB* 189) It is this same carelessness and disrespect for reality that explains why Jacob cannot differentiate between Lea and Rachel. With the reference to Usir, Mann also raises the issue that Jacob, eager to follow archetypical behavior, if only semiconsciously, imitates this carelessness.

As in the biblical text, in *The Tales of Jacob*, Rachel, given to Jacob seven days after his marriage to Lea, remains barren for many years. In a novel full of ambiguities, the narrator's suggestion that God punishes Jacob for his indifference to worldly existence is plausible yet not incontestable. True, Jacob is all too insensitive to those around him. In front of his older sons, he privileges and spoils Joseph, thereby condemning them to many years of humiliation and degradation. Yet, the narrative suggests that, because of his creativity and superior, civilized intellect, Joseph deserves to be privileged over his uneducated, coarse, and violent brothers. Jacob's insensitivity is derived in the novel from two contradictory sources, his spiritual orientation and his earthly desires, expressed respectively in his passion for Rachel and Joseph, which makes him blind to reality. These earthly desires often clash with his spirituality. Love, as pointed out earlier, triumphs over faith. Conversely, it is his religious fervor, privileging faith over love, that kills Rachel. Instead of taking her to the nearest town when she is about to give birth, Jacob delays his departure for a few days to build an altar at a site near Beth-el, where he once had an extraordinary vision. Extremely weak, Rachel dies in childbirth at the wayside. The narrator points out Jacob's shortcoming: "He had two passions in life: God and Rachel. Here they came in conflict; and yielding to the spiritual he brought down disaster upon the earthly one" (*JB* 252). But is Jacob really responsible for Rachel's death? The narrator is undecided. On the one hand, he criticizes Jacob because he is too absorbed in spiritual tasks to think of leaving and acts too late: "*At last* he gave the order" (*JB* 254, italics mine). On the other hand, he comments: "Rachel died. God would have it so" (*JB* 249). Individual responsibility and divine will go hand in hand. In the novel Jacob is exonerated as well as found guilty. His spiritual orientation is both right and wrong.

Mann often presents his characters as actors in a play that forces them to act according to the fixed twists and turns of the script. For example, Esau's reaction to Jacob's stealing their father's blessing is to find refuge in a mythical identity: "He wept because it was in his nature, because that was his rôle in life" (*JB* 86). Later the narrator remarks that Jacob had the choice not to give Joseph his mother's robe, a symbol of the rights of the firstborn and his father's blessing, and that, when worn by Joseph, instigates his brothers' jealousy and revenge. Both Jacob and Joseph play a "game" (*JB* 388) to fulfill their mythical destinies. Mann uses the word *Mitschuld* (co-guilt)[9] when he judges Jacob's actions that lead to Joseph's presumed death. Being part of a myth is—paradoxically—an unavoidable and, at the same time, avoidable fate; individuals can make adjustments while participating in the collective experience. *The Tales of Jacob* depicts the power of patterns on the course of history and individual fates, a power that, however, is not absolute: individual autonomy, personal guilt, and responsibility, mythical patterns as well as time-honored attitudes and behavior are often intertwined. If myths were an eternal, irrevocable part of human existence, then the acting out myths, like Laban's act of filicide, would not become morally questionable. The myth of sacrifice is still in place, but in a more humanistic world filicide has been abandoned for symbolic sacrifice. In *The Tales of Jacob*, Mann presents Jacob and his sons as characters whose fate is encoded in their lives, but who nonetheless can make choices, choices that will not change the course of history but will make it more humanistic.

Young Joseph

The tensions between Joseph and his brothers, culminating in their sale of Joseph to Ishmaelite traders, make up the core of *Young Joseph*. These tensions allow Mann to explore further the central themes of the first volume of the tetralogy—

aloofness from worldly concerns, mythical existence, and individual responsibility—and to bring into focus with Joseph the role of the asocial, creative outsider. Well aware of his unusual androgynous beauty and his exceptionally intelligent and creative mind, Joseph has become vain and arrogant and evokes his brothers' anger and envy. The most telling display of this arrogance occurs when he tells them about his dreams. These dreams, in which eleven sheaves of grain bow to the twelfth sheaf, and in which the sun, the moon, and eleven stars bow down before him, are not merely figments of a narcissistic dreamer's imagination, but an artistic prediction of his role as provider in Egypt. In Mann's revision of Joseph's story these two dreams are preceded by another dream in which an eagle takes him to God, and he acquires godlike powers. Again, the dream expresses a narcissist's arrogance, but it also foreshadows Joseph's future leadership role in Egypt, a role neither Joseph nor his humiliated brothers can comprehend at this point in their lives. Readers familiar with the biblical text recognize here the power of the outsider's imagination. At the same time, they are also encouraged to take a sympathetic view of the brothers, who are treated unkindly and unfairly. In order not to turn against the conceited outsider, and thus to escape the mythical pattern of fratricide, the brothers leave town with their herds. The narrative identifies this decision as humanitarian.

In Joseph's fascination with "death magic and under-earthly unreason" (*JB* 278), characteristics of German culture and the German artist are embedded in the novel, characteristics that Mann had introduced in works prior to *Young Joseph*—a clear indication of its symbolic dimensions. Because "dark elements in the composition of his beloved seemed to him to need release and clarification in the intellectual" (*JB* 278), Jacob wants Joseph, in preparation for his future role as bearer of the blessing, to learn how to read and write and become more educated. Jacob acknowledges that the times are changing and that the future spiritual leader needs to be more educated than he is himself. The shift from Jacob's "natural spirituality" and "immediate relations with God" (*JB* 275) to Joseph's acquired knowledge indicates a shift from intuition and creativity to intellectuality and critical reflection, as well as a shift from a spiritual to a life-oriented, secular position. Joseph learns about the rational perception of the world, science, and the world of progress from Jacob's servant, Elizier. He also learns about mythology and the rolling spheres, the world as "cycle of the greatest" and "everlasting recurrence" (*JB* 269), a Nietzschean term that Mann playfully transports into a world thousands of years before Nietzsche's time. Progressive and conservative thinking overlap. Most importantly, Joseph gains the knowledge "that God had given man understanding, in order that he might deal with these sacred matters and make them more consistent" (*JB* 268). In other words, God's creation is neither flawless nor his authority beyond question; it is therefore the responsibility of humans to improve that which already exists. While Elizier teaches Joseph a deeper understanding of the world and the place of the creative individual in that world, he also widens the gap between Joseph and life. Joseph becomes more educated than his brothers, who are farmers and shepherds, and, in doing so, takes on airs—an attitude the novel criticizes yet also justifies. The narrator makes the point that Joseph comprises an extraordinary combination of body and soul, beauty and knowledge. Joseph's self-awareness of this exceptional combination feeds his self-love, an educational by-product Elizier certainly did not intend.

After his lessons with Elizier, Jacob, aware of Joseph's insulting behavior towards his brothers, sends Joseph off to bend in front of them, thus to revoke his self-centered dreams. But by appearing at their herding site in his mother's colored robe, and by addressing his brothers in a patronizing tone, the narcissistic Joseph once again nourishes their resentment against him. Even though the narrator implies that the brothers do not deserve to be constantly submitted to Joseph's arrogance and humiliation and their father's unfair treatment, he nevertheless condemns their subsequent brutality toward Joseph. Like hungry wolves they attack him. The narrator deems their violence to be "a most shameful relapse into savagery. They sank below the level of the human" (*JB* 374). Mann makes explicit that the brothers' animal-like brutality is rooted in archaic, archetypical patterns—Cain's murder of Abel and Lamech's killing of his victim, just as their bloodshed in Shechem had mythical parallels. There the brothers had viewed the massacre as a reenactment of Mardug's victory over the dragon, Tiamat, and thus as a deed legitimized by history. But when they decided to leave their father's dwellings to avoid harming their arrogant brother, and when they, upon Joseph's visit, discuss what to do with him, their resistance to mythical identification and their openness to tolerance and progress become evident. The brothers, as Judah explains, decide against precise imitation: "We lusted to be like Lamech in the song and slay the young man for our hurt. But our customs are not those of the ancient time and of heroic mould. Somewhat we must yield to the present; and lo, instead of killing the youth we could only let him die. Fie upon us, for it was but a bastard thought, begot of the ancient saga and the modern customs!" (*JB* 401) Initially it is their intention to let him die in a dried-up well rather than kill him. Instead, they spare his life and sell him to Ishmaelite traders. Mythical identity and individual autonomy collide; in a variation on the mythical blueprint they find a new, humanistic solution. The act of punishment of the narcissist is in the mythical continuum; the kind of the punishment has changed. Convention and progress are thus intertwined.

Elizier inadvertently taught Joseph arrogance; his brothers' brutality provides quite a different educational experience and lesson. Being beaten by them is a form of initiation. Having temporarily lost his sight due to a bruised eye and to being imprisoned and forsaken in the dark well, Joseph learns to "see" his arrogance and indifference toward others. Previously uncaring, now Joseph "pleaded for the father-heart, he mocked no more, but felt distress and remorse" (*JB* 383). That he even feels sympathy for his "murderers" (*JB* 385), an allusion to Jesus Christ,[10] signals a Joseph who has not only compassion and a social conscience, but also a sense of humility. However, along with his newly gained knowledge that he had loved himself too much, there is, paradoxically, also an affirmation of his arrogant attitude toward his brothers: "He was convinced that God looked further than the pit, that he had far-reaching things in mind as usual and had His eye upon some distant purpose, in the service of which he, Joseph, had been made to drive the brethren to the uttermost" (*JB* 385). Destiny and self-determination, calling and self-calling are intertwined here. Although Joseph knows that he exists to fulfill a future yet to be revealed, this destiny does not absolve him from guilt. While in the well, Joseph thinks about past "errors, perhaps ordained by God, but not on that account less heavy and grievous" (*JB* 387). The fact that despite these past errors—his narcissistic, asocial behavior and insensitivity toward others—Joseph nonetheless will be the future provider, is one of the central paradoxes of the narrative.

Joseph's symbolic death in the well and "resurrection" three days later, when Ishmaelite traders en route to Egypt buy him, are presented as mythical imitation. Implicitly and explicitly Mann includes references to Jesus Christ, as well as to earlier mythical figures such as the Babylonian, Tammuz, the Greek, Adonis, and the Egyptian, Osiris; all four die and return to life. Because Joseph is aware of the mythical dimension of his life and his calling to become a leader, he consciously lives and plays the mythical role.[11] His brothers' actions might have stirred a social awareness in him, but it is the art of performance itself that enthralls Joseph, and which further identifies him as another variant of Mann's illustrious artist figure.

Joseph in Egypt

The third volume of *Joseph and His Brothers* begins with Joseph's self-centered question to the Ishmaelites, "Where are you taking me?" (*JB* 447). The narrative skeleton of this volume is concerned with the sale of Joseph to Potiphar's household and his rise and fall due to the false accusations of Potiphar's wife. While his brothers' actions had led to Joseph's "insight into the deadly error of his former life and a renunciation of it" (*JB* 449), he is far from being modest and from displaying an attitude befitting his status as slave to his Ishmaelite masters. In introducing himself as a person who has experienced death and rebirth—like Tammuz and Osiris, both of whom had been saved—he indicates to them that he is special and once again places himself into a mythical tradition. He even gives himself the name Osarsiph, a word play on Osiris, a further indication that he consciously acts out a mythical existence.

With his question he assumes that the merchants' destination is a result of his presence, rather than a trip planned before they had acquired him from his brothers. The merchant's son accuses Joseph of self-centered thinking, but Joseph replies: "The world hath many centres, one for each created being, and about each one it lieth in its own circle. . . . About thee lieth a universe whose centre I am not but thou art" (*JB* 447). Here Joseph recognizes the individuality of others without diminishing his own special existence. Joseph, the adept forger of witticisms, again displays his rhetorical magic. Whether Mann also sends a first signal of Joseph's future compassion for others must remain open here. Individual and social interests go hand in hand when he argues that the merchants both travel according to their own interests, and simultaneously as tools to get him where destiny has determined him to be. It is the narrator who suggests later, with a humorous undertone, "that the Ishmaelites' entire business was only an extra, and their sole and single significance consisted in the fact that they were bringing the boy Joseph down to Egypt in order to fulfil the ordained" (*JB* 540). From the traders' perspective this is certainly not true. What the narrator, with tongue in cheek, conveys is a belief that the creative individual is meant to assume a leadership role.

With Joseph's arrival at Potiphar's house, the narrator again raises the issue of individual responsibility and fate, of autonomous, free will and determination: "It is uncanny to see the mixture of free will and guidance in the phenomenon of imitation. In the end it is hard to tell whether it is the individual or the destiny that actually follows the pattern and insists upon the repetition. . . . We move in the footsteps of others, and all life is but the pouring of the present into the forms of the myths" (*JB* 551). This perception of history as an interweaving of a fixed past with a fluid present allows for individual impact. Myths are, in the last analysis, not binding, but guiding principles, archetypes of behavior that need not predetermine an individual's life. Mythical patterns and individual choices are not mutually exclusive, as Mann's narrator suggests. "For in repetition there is always change. . . . Life in its play produces changing patterns out of the same material" (*JB* 557).

On his way to the merchants' destination, Potiphar's house, Joseph was fascinated by the urban landscape, the affluence and cultural and political diversity of Egypt. This diversity is represented by the antiprogressive world of Per-Sopd, the primitive, Dionysian world of Per-Bastet, and the humanistic, tolerant world of On, whose cult of Atum-Re is contrasted with the cult of Amun, a nationalistic, conservative movement. The contrast between backward, antihumanistic, irrational ideologies and a progressive ideology appeared earlier in the tetralogy in the dialogue between Joseph and his father, and in the dissimilarities between Laban's and Jacob's orientations. This contrast is continued in Mann's description of the household of Potiphar, where the religious factions of Atum-Re and Amun are represented by Potiphar and the dwarf Dudu, respectively. Potiphar's household is a "microcosm of Egyptian society at large."[12] Moreover, it reflects the central ideological contrasts Mann saw in the Weimar Republic and presented in *The Magic Mountain* (irrationality/barbarism versus rationality/progress). It also alludes to a more recent political development in Germany: the rise of Nazism.

Yet it is not the novel's politics that is most captivating to readers of *Joseph in Egypt*. It is the novel's love story. The biblical account of Joseph's ten-year stay at Potiphar's household briefly mentions Potiphar's wife, her failed attempt to seduce Joseph, and her false accusations. In contrast, Mann devotes approximately fifteen percent of *Joseph and His Brothers* to this episode in Joseph's life. Mann later remarked, "The third 'Joseph' is, due to its erotic content, the most novel-like part" (*E 5* 192). Mann's most obvious invention is giving her a name, Mut-em-enet, and thus an identity and an extensive biography. Why this extraordinary interest in a character who in the Bible, like other characters such as the Ishmaelite traders, only plays a small, albeit significant part in fulfilling Joseph's destiny? The narrator claims that he will correct the false and absurd image of Potiphar's wife, known in popular legend as a nymphomaniac. In all probability, no author before—or after—Mann has told the story of Potiphar's wife in such great detail and with such sympathy. In inventing her story, Mann enters new narrative territory, and, at the same time, returns to a theme familiar from his earlier works: unfulfilled sexuality. Mut's prearranged marriage to the impotent Potiphar forces her into an ascetic and aesthetic existence. She leads the life of a "chaste moon-nun" (*JB* 675) and sings and dances in the service of the Hathoren order. With the appearance of Joseph, Mut can no longer suppress her erotic desires. She falls passionately in love with him; her quiet, respectable life has been shattered: "It is the idea of a catastrophe, the invasion of destructive and wanton forces into an ordered scheme and a life bent upon self-control and a happiness conditioned by it. The saga of peace wrung from conflict and seemingly assured; of life laughingly sweeping away the structure of art; of mastery and overpowering, and the coming of the stranger god" (*JB* 718–19). These sentences bring to mind characters from Mann's earlier œuvre such as Johannes

Friedemann and Gustav Aschenbach. Mut follows in their footsteps when she, too, moves from the ascetic to the life-embracing, and from the Apollonian to the Dionysian.[13]

Mann presents in great detail the story of the suffering Mut experiences as a result of her love for Joseph and her determination to fight her affliction. The novel suggests that if only her husband had sent the handsome Joseph away upon her request this affliction could have been ceased, allowing an honorable ending for Mut. Although aware of the temptations the presence of his slave presents to his wife, Potiphar egotistically demands that he stay. Mut's resistance to her love and passion weakens more and more over a three year period, and culminates in her urging Joseph to sleep with her. Despite her gradual loss of dignity, the narrator expresses empathy for "poor Eni" (*JB* 798), because she had been condemned to live without passionate love and sexuality.[14] In deviation from the Bible, she no longer is simply a vicious woman.

Joseph, the narcissistic, self-centered, beautiful man, who is aware of the influence he has upon the women of the town, does not avoid Mut once she has declared her love. Knowingly he feeds her love frenzy and cruelly plays with her emotions as he had played with those of his brothers. His "pedagogic plan" to free her from her infatuation is a "culpable pretence" (*JB* 792). Joseph's narcissistic desire to be loved again leads him, without considering the consequences, to his guilty behavior. Subsequent events result in Mut becoming equally guilty. With her sexual frustrations mounting and her advances rejected by Joseph, she becomes embittered. She turns into an irrational, vengeful woman, now depicted by Mann as the biblical femme fatale. Falsely accusing Joseph of attempted rape, she brings about his downfall. The narrator, thus far understanding of Mut's behavior, distances himself from her, "not on account of [the accusation's] untruth, which might pass as the garment of the truth; but on account of the demagoguery which she did not scorn to use to rouse the people." To underscore her demagoguery, Mann has Mut imitate Marc Anthony's famous speech in Shakespeare's *Julius Caesar* when she addresses her audience, a group of servants, with "Egyptians! . . . Children of Kemt! Sons of the river and the black earth! . . . Egyptian brothers!" (*JB* 832) The narrator unmasks Mut's attempt to put herself on an equal social footing with the common people as false, and criticizes her attempt to instigate them to take actions against Joseph.

On the realistic level of *Joseph in Egypt,* Mut's story is one of unrequited love and revenge. On the symbolic level, Mut's story contains Mann's rejection of German politics. Her perversion of the truth, coupled with her turning from a rational to an irrational, Dionysian existence, are symbolic of ideological developments in Nazi Germany.[15] In "An Appeal to Reason" Mann had defined

Hitler's nationalism as a movement characteristic of "bacchic excess," of radical antihumanism and irrationality (*OD* 54). Mut's association with the dwarves Dudu and Beknechon, both supporters of the Amun cult, a nationalistic, fanatical, aggressive, and regressive movement, emphasizes that Mann intended to establish affinities between Mut and National Socialism. In *Joseph in Egypt* he criticizes not only its supporters, but also those who passively stand by. Potiphar, who subscribes to tolerance and humanism, could have stopped his wife's Dionysian rapture, but does not act. He thus symbolizes the passive middle class Mann had criticized through his character Jacob in the first volume of the tetralogy.

Arguably, no other part of the tetralogy demonstrates Mann's mastery at telling a story that weaves the political, mythical-universal, and personal-unique so seamlessly into one narrative tapestry as well as his story of Mut. Mann illustrates her multifaceted character and function with numerous allusions to other famous women and fictional characters, including Cleopatra, Isis, the Virgin Mary, Wagner's Kundry from the opera *Parsifal*, Brünhilde, and Isolde, as well as, generally, the biblical whore, the witch, and the femme fatale. Well hidden and skillfully integrated into the political dimension of his story and the mythical tales is an allusion to a passionate love Mann had himself experienced more than thirty years earlier: his unfulfilled love for Paul Ehrenberg. Mut had kept her love a secret, as Mann had his. In the character of Mut the persona of the waiting, desiring woman, a central autobiographical theme in Mann's narratives and fictional plans of the early 1900s (*NB 7–14* 55, 62, 73), returns. That Mann transferred his stigmatized love and suffering to Mut and gave his nonconventional, forbidden desires the mask of a heterosexual relationship, is revealed in a notebook entry from around 1904. This entry includes a poem, five verses long, about an existence devoted to intellectuality and art. It is one of numbness, emptiness, and coldness. This coldness is dispelled by love, to which Mann confesses with the words "I love you! My God . . . I love You!" (*Nb 7–14* 46). Mut becomes Mann's alter ego when she, too, feels saved from "aridity" (*JB* 735)[16] with her passion for Joseph. A further connection between Mann and his female character is established between one of Mann's diary entries about his stigmatized love, "It was there, I had it too, I will be able to tell myself that when I die" (*TB 1940–43* 396),[17] with a passage from the novel where Mut, unable to consummate her love, finds solace in the end with the knowledge "that she had once blossomed and burned, once suffered and loved" (*JB* 989).

While the relationship between Mut and Joseph echoes a very personal story rooted in the author's secret sexual identity, their relationship is simultaneously a play on mythical identities. Embedded in the relationship between Mut and Joseph is the Babylonian myth of Ishtar and Gilgamesh. Ishtar's longing for Gilgamesh is in vain, and, in taking revenge for his rebuff, she asks her father Anu to have Gilgamesh killed. Mut's revenge brings about Joseph's downfall, thereby setting the conditions for Joseph's final rise as Egypt's provider. In his rejection of Mut, Joseph recognizes that he is living out the role of a mythical character. When he cries in a moment of despair, he compares his tears to those of Gilgamesh. Loss and gain, death and resurrection go hand in hand, when Joseph also sees himself as the Egyptian Tammuz who will return to life. Mann has Joseph even create his own myth, that of the repenting son, after his second downfall: "He acknowledged to himself his sin, just as he had done in the first pit, a great year before, and his heart was sore for his father Jacob" (*JB* 856). These examples illustrate that the boundaries between mythical determinations and autonomous, individual decisions are unstable, that the individual, in particular a creative individual like Joseph, can free himself from the entrapments of myths. It is Joseph's vision of his father, a reminder of his higher calling, and not a mythical pattern that leads him to reject temptation. Also, it is his "want of wisdom" (*JB* 856) that brings him down again. Out of free will he has acted irresponsibly, asocially, narcissistically, and thus deserves his punishment.

Joseph the Provider

The final part of the *Joseph* tetralogy, *Joseph the Provider*, written between August 1940 and the winter of 1942/43, tells the story of Joseph's interpretation of the pharaoh's dreams, his rise to power, his wise stewardship of Egypt thereby avoiding famine, and the reunion with his father and brothers. Paralleling *Joseph in Egypt*, mythic reenactment also plays a pivotal role at the beginning of this volume. When asked by the Egyptian prison captain Mai-Sachme about his identity, Joseph replies: "I am he," an allusion to Jesus Christ and his role as savior.[18] Mai-Sachme understands this response as a formula, "a time-honoured revelation of identity, a ritual statement beloved in song and story and play in which the gods had parts" (*JB* 863); consequently he associates the Egyptian river-god, Bata-Hapi, with Joseph. In the Egyptian myth, the young Bata, who had been seduced by the wife of the god Anup and is transformed into Hapi, the bull-god of the Nile and god of fertility, reveals his former identity with the words: "I am Bata, lo, I live still and am the sacred bull of God" (*JB* 866). As provider, Joseph will become "a sort of Nile deity, yes, an incarnation of Hapi himself, the preserver and life-giver" (*JB* 1164). Joseph's identification with an Egyptian fertility-god whose function it is to bring secular blessings, not metaphysical salvation, anticipates his forthcoming turning toward the social realm.

The intelligent, sensitive Mai-Sachme recognizes Joseph's calling as a "bringer of salvation" (*JB* 876). His central function in the novel is to be instrumental in Joseph's elevation, but this function does not explain the extensive description of Mai-Sachme, one of Mann's most likeable characters. Like many of Mann's other less prominent characters—for example Joachim Ziemssen and Raoul Überbein, to name just two—he suffers from unfulfilled love. He confides in Joseph that he was once in love with a young Egyptian girl named Nekhbet. Many years later, he also fell in love with another young girl, with the same intensity and inclination. This girl turned out to be Nekhbet's daughter. Mai-Sachme speculates that he would also love Nekhbet's granddaughter like "her mother and her grandmother, and it will always and for ever be the same love" (*JB* 869). With this continual reincarnation of an object of love, Mann presents a variation on the theme of mythical repetition. Because Mai-Sachme's love can never be realized and does not erupt into uncontrollable passion, he serves as a counter figure to Mut in the novel. Furthermore, he is yet another alter ego of the author.[19] Mai-Sachme's subdued love, about which he would like to write some day, is a fictional rendering of Mann's own covert homosexual love that will return throughout his life, and which he is able to integrate into his fiction throughout his writing career.

The central theme of mythical existence arises again when Joseph introduces himself to Pharaoh Amenhotep with the words: "I am and am not just because I am I. I mean that the general and the typical vary when they fulfil themselves in the particular" (*JB* 937). Here Mann reiterates that mythical and individual identity, past and present, the typical-conventional and the creative-progressive are not separate and exclusive because myth allows for mutation and modification. Joseph presents to Pharaoh Amenhotep the concept of breaking down barriers and bringing together what is deemed to be diametrically opposed: "The pattern and the traditional come from the depths which lie beneath and are what binds us, whereas the I is from God and is of the spirit, which is free. But what constitutes civilized life is that the binding and traditional depth shall fulfil itself in the freedom of God which belongs to the I" (*JB* 937). "Spirit," critical intellect paired with creativity—in the tetralogy a force of progress and change and thus in tension with the status quo—and mythical, earthly existence, a clinging to tradition and order, are interlaced here. They oppose and complement each other like intellect and life, above and below, or like "Light" and "Darkness" (*JB* 907) as Pharaoh names the diametrically opposed spheres of existence. Through Joseph, Mann points out that a socially and morally responsible individual will be able to address both spheres. Mann does not propose their synthesis, rather a mutual recognition and interaction. Bridging the gap will be Joseph's task.

151

With Pharaoh Amenhotep, Mann portrays a progressive, pacifistic intellectual who, like Jacob, favors monotheism and opposes human sacrifice. Of weak physical constitution like many of Mann's artistic and intellectual figures, he subscribes to an aesthetic, contemplative, rather than worldly, pragmatic orientation. His aloofness from the realm of "Darkness," a socially engaged existence associated here with the black, productive soil of the Nile valley, leads to Joseph's rise as Egypt's most influential administrator after he has interpreted the Pharaoh's dreams about seven fertile and seven barren years. With his sophistry and manipulative skills, Joseph proves that he is the one who can mediate between the intellectual realm and worldly concerns, who can convert Amenhotep's progressive, humanistic position into social and political reality. Subsequently, Joseph becomes the "dealer between the spheres and go-between 'twixt above and below" (*JB* 959).

Joseph's position as mediator takes on a mythological dimension when, besides being aligned with the Egyptian mythological figure Hapi, he is also associated with the Greek god Hermes, the worldly and cunning businessman (*E* 5 195).[20] Joseph orders the redistribution of property and land, in particular the expropriation of the big landowners; he strikes a balance between "socialization and freehold occupancy" (*JB* 1169) and combines "crown politics and concern for the little man, a novel, ingenious, an invigorating policy" (*JB* 1165). Probably as a result of Mann's own comments, Joseph's policies have often been compared to Roosevelt's New Deal, introduced to protect the weaker segment of U.S. society in the 1930s.[21] However, Mann's authoritarian Egyptian world, despite some resemblances to Roosevelt's New Deal, is not an allegory of democratic, egalitarian twentieth-century America. With his control over agrarian production and land, Joseph can ensure sufficient production of grain for storage to avoid catastrophe in the seven years of drought. His goal is not political reform and an egalitarian society. He exercises an enlightened despotism. The people of Egypt remain at the mercy of their leaders who, represented by Amenhotep and Joseph, happen to be benign and of humanitarian spirit. Yet their social engagement is limited and ostensibly shrewd at times. The grain is sold at the highest prices to the rich, the less-well-to-do are able to purchase just enough so "that they might not die" (*JB* 1047). The poor, however, receive grain for nothing, a result of Joseph's "human sympathy" and his balanced approach of "largesse and exploitation" (*JB* 1048). In feeding—and not freeing—the poor, Joseph keeps the Pharaoh's labor force alive. And while Joseph has the general physical well-being in mind, not social justice and equality, and uses his reforms to undermine the power and authority of the Pharaoh's enemies, he simultaneously pursues a very personal goal: luring his father and brothers to the filled granaries of Egypt.

A democratic Egypt would have been out of place and time in the biblical world of the *Joseph* tetralogy. But not only narrative consistency and loyalty to the biblical sources made Mann keep a noticeable distance from egalitarianism, one of the building blocks of democracy. While Mann had been an advocate of a social democracy even before Roosevelt's presidency, for instance in his 1932 speech "Goethe als Repräsentant des bürgerlichen Zeitalters" ("Goethe as Representative of the Bourgeois Age"), he never could shed his bourgeois-aristocratic stance, his firm belief in the supreme power of the creative individual and a cultural and political elite, expressed earlier in *Reflections* and best summed up nearly three decades later in an essay published in the United States in the *Atlantic Monthly* in 1944 titled "What is German?": "Democracy is of course primarily a claim, a demand of the majority for justice and equal rights. It is a justified demand from below. But in my eyes it is even more beautiful if it is good will, generosity, and love coming from the top down."[22] In other words, Mann wants to see the educated middle class and its artists play a constructive, engaged role in society, a role he asked this class to fulfill in the Weimar Republic, and which, as the indifference of Jacob as representative of the cultural elite in the first volume of the tetralogy illustrates, it had not performed. With Joseph's role as provider in the last volume, Mann presents symbolically the benign, compassionate leadership of an educated, creative artist-outsider.

Before writing *Joseph as Provider*, Mann had addressed the questionable side of bourgeois artistic existence in "Brother Hitler." In this essay, he establishes an affinity between the bourgeois artist and Hitler because both resent a conformist, integrated life. However, Hitler, with his primitivism, non-intellectuality, and perversion of Germany's culture, is the bad artist who practices an "art uncontrolled by mind, art as black magic" resulting from "brainlessly irresponsible instinct." His art is merely "a brew of darkness" and "a freak of the tellurian underworld." Mann's essay calls for an art that balances darkness and light, and for an artist whose mission it is to be "a winged, hermetic, moon-sib mediator between spirit and life" (*OD* 161). This last phrase contains a direct reference to *Joseph and His Brothers*. At the beginning of the tetralogy, the moon is introduced as a mediator between sun and earth, intellect and life, and Joseph first appears gazing at the moon. At the end of the novel, Joseph becomes a mediator himself. Previously narcissistic, he now is socially oriented and able to put his creativity and intellect in the service of life. Thus the tetralogy, in ending with Joseph as a model leader, can be understood as a text written against the destructive leadership in Nazi Germany.[23]

In various ways, Mann's condemnation of National Socialist ideology is embedded in the narrative structure of *Joseph in Egypt* and *Joseph as Provider*.

Irrationalism and intoxication, embodied in Mut, are also aspects of the societies of Per-Sopd and Per-Bastet. The most influential advocate of reactionary, anti-humanistic forces is the priest of the Amun-cult, Beknechon, whose nationalistic, xenophobic views echo the nationalistic, barbaric dogma of Nazism. With Joseph's leadership and the victory of discipline and humanism in Egypt, Mann presents "a novel of resistance"[24] against Germany's political reality. However, this resistance is not limited to those forces within Germany that celebrate the "orgiastic denial of reason and human dignity" (*OD* 57). *Joseph and His Brothers* is also written against bourgeois aestheticism and arrogance toward the community. The tetralogy starts with Mann's criticism of the alienation of the creative individual from life and the social remoteness of intellectuality, and ends optimistically with an artist-outsider who has learned to participate in life. In his own interpretation, Mann points at the harmony and optimism underlying the text: "In *Joseph* the I returns from wanton absoluteness to the collective, the communality, and the contrast between artistry and bourgeois existence, between isolation and community, individual and collective is suspended in the fairy-tale, as it ought to be suspended in our hopes, our will in the future democracy" (*E 5* 197). Is *Joseph and His Brothers* thus Mann's most optimistic, utopian work?

The author's optimistic assessment of the reconciliation between individual and social goals is not as clear-cut in the novel as his commentary suggests. As the Pharaoh's highest ranking administrator, Joseph had to make drastic adjustments. He had to take on an Egyptian name, marry an Egyptian girl, and dress in an Egyptian fashion. The adolescent Joseph, introduced at the beginning of the novel as aesthetically inclined and arrogant toward the world, has now become completely secularized and assimilated, "severed into the great world" (*JB* 1006). As such, his brothers cannot recognize him when they come to buy grain in Egypt. Joseph himself explains how he has changed from a self-absorbed, arrogant individual to one without extraordinary calling: "For your brother is . . . no harbinger of spiritual salvation. He is just a farmer and a manager" (*JB* 1116).[25] This social, worldly engagement has its price—the loss of artistic creativity, the loss of "soul" mentioned in "Descent into Hell," and of intellectual leadership—and, as such, it is questionable. Because Joseph has become a worldly savior, his father, who still loves Joseph more than any of his other sons, has to deny him the blessing and cannot grant him spiritual leadership. With this denial, Mann indicates that creativity and social responsibility remain at odds.

Written largely during a time when ideological intolerance and the perversion of humanistic ideas and ideals held sway in Germany, a period that culminated in the most destructive war of the twentieth century, *Joseph and His*

Brothers stands out as Mann's most optimistic work. In depicting how individual freedom and creativity can overcome mythical determination, how humanism and rationality can win out over irrational forces, the tetralogy constitutes a counter voice to twentieth century dogmatic beliefs that breed bigotry and violence. Like *The Magic Mountain, Joseph and His Brothers* presents an array of sets of belief and positions—most prominently a spiritual, unworldly, often inhuman, orientation; irrational, nationalistic tenets; narcissistic creativity and social engagement—and refrains from offering ideological directives, and thus from falling into the traps of dogmatism. Instead, *Joseph and His Brothers* is a plea for tolerance and a testimony to Mann's hope that human compassion will prevail. How frail this hope was, however, is apparent in his other, less optimistic narratives written in the late 1930s and early 1940s.

CHAPTER 10

Lotte in Weimar, *The Transposed Heads,* and *The Tables of the Law*

Lotte in Weimar

Mann's diary entries, written at the beginning of his exile in Switzerland in 1933, reveal his deep despair over the loss of the comfortable lifestyle he was accustomed to, over the loss of his home, his homeland, and his direct contact with his readers. The voices of those who had elevated him to Germany's poet laureate became quiet, or even turned against him, under Nazi censorship. What was one of Germany's most honored representatives to do now that he was publicly shunned, with the foundation of his identity gone? The physically and psychologically homeless Mann solved his impasse by identifying with Goethe. What could be more appropriate than to call upon *the* most revered German man of letters and undisputed authority, Goethe, whom Mann had called humanist and citizen of the world in his speech "Goethe as Representative of the Bourgeois Age." The connection to Goethe allowed Mann to adopt an identity that was no longer limited to being a representative of his time, but more broadly to that of a "representative of the bourgeois age." This age, spanning from the fifteenth to the turn of the nineteenth century, so Mann argued, had laid the foundations of German culture, in particular idealistic individualism and humanism. Its "lord and master" (*ETD* 67) was Goethe. It is this classic-humanistic Germany that Mann appropriated for himself when he proclaimed upon his arrival in the United States as an immigrant in 1938: "Where I am, there is Germany."[1] In his new homeland, he made it his task to defend German bourgeois culture, and himself, against the barbarism and irrationality of National Socialism. The national identity that Mann constructed based on Goethe was essentially always a cultural rather than political identity. Its appropriation allowed him to distance himself from current German politics, but it was undermined by Mann's doubts about his understanding of Goethe as the model citizen of the world, the envoy of humanism full of "open-armed welcome to life" (*ETD* 86). These doubts eventually led to a Goethe novel that simultaneously reveres and criticizes the bourgeois artist: *Lotte in Weimar.*

The first step toward approaching the life and work of Goethe are noted in a diary entry of 19 November 1933 where Mann mentions that Charlotte Buff-Kestner's visit to Weimar, as well as a Faust text, are artistic themes that he might pursue. Mann's Faust novel would have to wait another decade. Mann's diary records that he began writing *Lotte in Weimar* (formerly published under the English title *The Beloved Returns*)[2] on 11 November 1936. Certainly not under the anxiety of influence, Mann openly admitted that *Lotte in Weimar* displays his "*imitatio* Goethe's: an identification and *unio mystica* with the father" (*GW 13* 169). The novel is based on an historical anecdote. On 22 September 1816 Charlotte Kestner, the model for Werther's Lotte in Goethe's 1774 epistolary novel, *The Sufferings of Young Werther*, arrived with her daughter Clara in Weimar, where she visited her sister and brother-in-law, Ridel. During their visit, they received an invitation for lunch at Goethe's house. Before Charlotte left Weimar at the end of October, she met Goethe one more time at a social gathering. Goethe also made his seat at the National Theater and his carriage available to Charlotte, but he never accompanied her. According to Clara, Goethe was aloof and surprisingly cold to her mother.

This episode provided an ideal starting point for a story that on the one hand pays tribute to the national writer and on the other shows the dubious asocial side of artistic existence, and thus detracts from holding Goethe up as a model for emulation and identification. Mann's *Lotte in Weimar* begins with Charlotte's arrival at the Elephant Hotel in Weimar, a provincial town in Thuringia (chapter 1). Having barely settled in, she receives one courtesy call after another. The callers are Miss Rose Cuzzle, an English autograph-hunter and sketcher of celebrities and the only fictional character among Charlotte's unexpected visitors; Dr. Friedrich Wilhelm Riemer, Goethe's assistant of thirteen years; Arthur Schopenhauer's sister Adele; and finally, Goethe's son August. They all discuss Goethe with Charlotte, resulting in a plethora of voices that complement as well as contradict each other (chapters 2 to 6). In "The Seventh Chapter," the only chapter given a definite article, Goethe himself appears and, in soliloquy style, reflects upon his life and art. For this chapter Mann resorts generously to Goethe's works, his letters and documented conversations. Chapter 8 describes Charlotte's lunch at Goethe's house. The final chapter breaks with the literary realism of the previous chapters. It is an imaginary, fairy-tale-like scene in which Lotte has a private conversation with Goethe and bids him a kind farewell.

The great authority of the artist and his art upon his readers are illustrated at the very beginning of the novel when the waiter of the hotel, Mager, is presented as an avid, awestruck admirer of Goethe, the Privy Councilor of the Duchy of Saxe-Weimar and "prince of poets" (*LiW* 13). With the petty bourgeois

Mager, Mann aims at a satirical yet kindly portrait of the educated, art-oriented burgher who mistakes fiction for reality. When Mager spreads the news in Weimar, "a hive of court gossip" (*LiW* 56), that Werther's Lotte has arrived in town, he conjures up in everyone's mind the attractive, young country lady of Goethe's *Werther* who sliced bread for her younger siblings and whom Werther loved more than his own life. However, the lady who arrives in Weimar in 1816 is sixty-three years old, no longer slender, and has difficulty preventing her head from shaking. She is addressed with the title of her late husband, "Frau Councilor," according to the custom of the time. Mann's novel is full of people with such titles, and Goethe himself hides behind titles like "Privy Councilor" or "Excellency." What is his true identity? As a writer he has many. But in the world of the provincial town of Weimar, residency of a Grand Duke, he needs the mask of a person of rank, just as Mann needed his. And who is Charlotte Kestner? Is she just the mother of eleven children of whom nine survive? The Frau Councilor? Or Lotte, who experienced with Goethe some of the scenes that are transformed in *The Sufferings of Young Werther* and belong to world literature?

While Mager gets carried away by images of aesthetic origins, Charlotte Kestner wants to be seen as a human, a representative of life, rather than as an artist's artifact. Unlike Manger's admiration for Goethe, hers is less fervent, as she is familiar with the darker sides of the poet's personality. As a young woman, she had rejected Goethe not just because she was already engaged to be married to Kestner, but because Goethe seemed to her to be "inhuman, without purpose or poise" (*LiW* 31). Even so, her identity as Goethe's Lotte comes literally with her accouterments. She has brought along the white dress with pale-red bows that she wore when Goethe used her as the model for Lotte. When she wears the dress at the luncheon at Goethe's house, she tries to rekindle the past and to maintain her identity as the Lotte of the novel. Her attempt is grotesque and ultimately fails. Goethe pretends not to notice it, while her daughter finds it inappropriate. The gap between literature and reality that Mager initially ignores becomes painfully apparent at the end of the novel. One of the principal themes of the novel is this gap.

Another principal theme is the artist's relationship to life. Charlotte returns to Weimar to investigate this relationship further. The visit to her sister is just a convenience to mask her real intention, which is to clarify an "old, never-settled tormenting score" (*LiW* 99). Charlotte needs to know why Goethe fell in love with her despite the fact that she was engaged. She will realize that he loved her precisely because she was engaged. His passion for her had no future, demanded no commitment, and inspired him to write one of the most famous novels of world literature. In Goethe's soliloquy, Mann makes clear that his Goethe figure needs to keep the artificial world of the imagination free from the restrictions of banal and transitory reality. Yet can we, too, agree to his inconsiderate treatment of Lotte's albeit inappropriate attempt to revive the past? Or does his treatment make the gap between literature and human life a cruel one? Charlotte protests the artist's objectification and instrumentalization of human beings by pointing out that human beings do not exist to be tools for others (*LiW* 273). At the same time she is immensely proud to have been immortalized and to have gained such a significant reputation, and that through literature her fame has surpassed that of other women. Goethe's infatuations with these women have yielded "a few lyrics, but no great world-stirring work" (*LiW* 245). With Charlotte's oscillation between attraction to and rejection of the artistic, self-absorbed genius who has brought her eternal fame but is coldhearted, Mann illustrates an ambivalence toward Goethe that is shared by Charlotte's visitors, an ambivalence that underlies the novel as a whole.

Charlotte's encounters and conversations with various visitors are a narrative device to allow Mann to present Goethe's strengths and shortcomings as a human being from various perspectives before his appearance in "The Seventh Chapter." The first visitor is the autograph-hunter Miss Cuzzle, whose obsessive, overexcited admiration for famous people is the subject of Mann's mockery. In using Miss Cuzzle to ridicule those who place too much esteem and authority upon artists, Mann also throws doubts on the artist's own belief in his importance and superiority—thus upon his self-understanding. Miss Cuzzle's visit is followed by that of Dr. Riemer, Goethe's assistant. The historical Riemer wrote a memoir about his services to Goethe, a book that was an important source for Mann. In the novel, Mann uses Riemer's intimate and intelligent knowledge of Goethe to make statements about Goethe's humanity, especially its shortcomings —statements that apply to Mann's opinions about artists' humanity or lack thereof in general. Riemer is highly educated. However, Mann diminishes his intellectual stature by turning him into the caricature of an uncreative scholar and acolyte who admires Goethe's greatness to the point of self-sacrifice, but is full of resentment because of it. In Mann's novel, Riemer's obsequiousness goes so far that he chooses to marry an orphan living in Goethe's family in order to please the "house" of Goethe (*LiW* 58). Other subsequent examples demonstrate that the theme of oppressed eroticism is attached to the house of Goethe.

With Riemer's resentment of Goethe, Mann develops profound insights into the effect that a "great" man has on his human environment. Riemer's ambivalent assessment of Goethe is similar to that of Charlotte. As a human being who is indifferent to the lives of others, Goethe is less than admirable. As an artist and genius whose talents bring immortal fame to mediocre individuals such as

Riemer, he deserves to be venerated. It is Riemer's task in *Lotte in Weimar* to comment upon Goethe as an artist. Behind Riemer's voice stands that of the author, made most apparent when Riemer uses a phrase with which Mann characterizes Joseph in *Joseph and His Brothers*. Goethe is, like Joseph, blessed from above and from below, he lives the extraordinary union "of the greatest intellectual gifts with the most amazing naïveté." This blessing of nature and the spirit is "the blessing of humanity as a whole" (*LiW* 83), but it is also a "curse" (*LiW* 84). Goethe's human greatness leads him to tolerance—an idea Mann had also expressed in "Goethe as Representative of the Bourgeois Age"—but it is a tolerance that results in "a most peculiar coldness, a crushing indifference" and "the neutrality of absolute art" (*LiW* 85). In Riemer's eyes this indifference brings forth a dangerous level of skepticism, irony, and nihilism, destroying any idealism, any belief in freedom and fatherland, even the belief in the meaningfulness of art. This paradox of artistic existence, hovering between humanism and nihilism, is, according to Riemer, mirrored in Goethe's gaze: "It is the gaze of absolute art, which is at once absolute love and absolute nihilism and indifference and implies that horrifying approach to the godlike-diabolic which we call genius" (*LiW* 83). Riemer talks about Goethe, but his observation also points toward Mann and his nihilistic tendencies. This raises a pivotal point. Because Mann conceives of his "*unio mystica*" with Goethe, he must assume that great bourgeois artists share an ambivalent stance toward life and that there is a mythical artistic existence. This assumption allows Mann to project aspects of his own existence on Goethe, turning the latter's life anachronistically into an "*imitatio Mann.*" But Mann's interweaving of his life with that of Goethe goes beyond establishing a secret identity between himself and, indisputably, Germany's greatest artist. It illustrates that *Lotte in Weimar* is not only about Goethe and Mann himself. It is, given Mann's ambivalent portrayal of Goethe as man and artist, both a tribute to and criticism of German artists and their art in their function of representing the nation.

Charlotte's next caller is Adele Schopenhauer, a physically unattractive young woman with a drooping nose, protruding ears, and a puny figure. She does, however, possess remarkable eloquence and wit. Adele represents the new generation that is both patriotic and romantic. With her account of Goethe's disengagement in politics, his abhorrence of political involvement, and his rejection of nationalism, Mann shows the dichotomy between the recognition of the artist as national icon and his rejection of that role, even his inability to fulfill it. Furthermore, Adele's role in the novel is to provide insight into Goethe's relationship with his son. She emphasizes Goethe's egotism, which places exploitation of his son above fatherly love, but she also characterizes him as a man who "was not born to be a tyrant, but rather a friend of humanity" (*LiW* 134), and who loves to make people laugh. When Mann has Adele recount a love story to Charlotte, he reveals that underneath the witty, if unattractive, Adele is a sexually frustrated spinster who can only partake of life and love by talking about it. Her story is about Ottilie von Pogwisch, who, although in love with a soldier, will marry the socially acceptable, but gloomy and dull, August von Goethe, just to be close to his father. She is not in love with August and imagines marrying the father in the guise of his son. Mann implies that she anticipates being immortalized by Goethe in his poetry or prose, and therefore renounces emotional and sexual happiness. That she will be miserable with the young Goethe, that she sacrifices herself just to be near the famous genius, becomes evident in the chapter that follows (chapter 6).

August von Goethe initially comes across as a very unsympathetic character. When he begins his conversation with Charlotte, after he has been waiting in the hotel lobby drinking, he appears to be an alcoholic womanizer. He has a bad temper and dramatically overreacts to Charlotte's dislike for him. His ambivalence is illustrated by the resentment he harbors against his famous father being simultaneously coupled with the pride he feels as his father's son. To be Goethe's son is, as Adele explained earlier, "a high fortune," but at the same time "an oppressive burden, a permanent derogation of one's own ego" (*LiW* 154). Through August, we hear the frustrated voice of Mann's son Klaus, who was never able to free himself from the shadow of his father, and Mann's self-critical assessment of his coldness toward Klaus. August considers his father to be an authoritarian, self-centered person who brings miseries upon all around him, and who expects his son to renounce the right to live his own life, to make sacrifices for a higher goal. He reminds Charlotte of Goethe's *ideé fixe*: "Painful renunciation . . . becomes the pattern and principal theme of life, and all the later renunciations are only a result and repetition of the same thing" (*LiW* 246). Self-renunciation results in callous indifference toward the pain others suffer. As an example of Goethe's merciless character, August mentions Friederike Brion, the young woman who fell passionately in love with his father and who withered away and died when Goethe, the cruel lover, left her. The coldhearted genius who refuses to become part of life will return as a theme in *Doctor Faustus*. August's accusations against the aloof artist who fails on the human level are juxtaposed with Charlotte's reply that Friederike Brion should have mustered the strength and resolution to create a life for herself after Goethe's departure. Her reply, motivated by jealousy, does not diminish the validity of the criticism of the genius.

The first six chapters center on Goethe as a man who makes those around him deeply unhappy, even tyrannizes them. Goethe appears as the "great exploiter and vampire,"[3] but also as one who brings to those associated with him honor, fame, and immortality. "The Seventh Chapter," which includes many quotations by Goethe from various literary and nonliterary sources, shows Goethe from his own perspective. In a quite daring and unexpected narrative move, a "plunge from the myth into the material,"[4] and certainly as a distraction from any preconceived notions, Mann introduces Goethe in a most private situation. Lying in bed, Goethe wakes in a state of sexual arousal having dreamt about a painting of Venus and Adonis. With this scene Mann not only illustrates that Goethe shares with ordinary humanity the same physical reality and biological needs, but he also hints at the displacement of Goethe's sexuality from his life into art. The hermaphroditic dimension of the painting is also an allusion to Mann's transfer of homosexual desires into art. This connection between sexuality and art recurs in chapter 8 when Goethe tells about a young man kissing a glass that is covering a copy of Leonardo da Vinci's head of Charitas. Art provides an outlet for "hot-blooded emotions" aroused by "icily unresponsive matter" (*LiW* 427).

Because Mann found "refuge" in Goethe and in what he perceived to be a national culture and identity standing apart from Nazi Germany, his criticism of Goethe in *Lotte in Weimar* is somewhat surprising. Why would Mann deviate from his earlier assessments of Goethe? Neither his essay "Goethe and Tolstoy" nor his homage to Goethe in his speech of 1932, while commenting negatively upon the "immorality" (*ETD* 83) of the national poet laureate in terms of his relationship to his world, take the criticism as far as the later novel. The reason, as Goethe's soliloquy reveals, lies in Mann's growing self-criticism, voiced in Goethe's own, about a life devoted to art. Goethe enjoys a comfortable, even luxurious lifestyle and concedes that he is pedantic, demanding, and a self-centered elitist. He admits to himself that he has been willing "to betray love and life and human beings to his art!" (*LiW* 318). Goethe's thoughts affirm Riemer's understanding that "icy coldness" (*LiW* 328) is an essential ingredient of artistic greatness. This coldness is again revealed when Mann's Goethe figure does not react to the news of Charlotte's presence, but instead remains preoccupied with a crystal whose inorganic, inanimate, and eternal nature he praises in front of August, and when he talks about something as trivial as haymaking. Goethe is aware of his indifference; more than any of his critics, he scrutinizes his outsider existence—his isolation from the world through social rank and his special creativity, his egocentricity, self-indulgence, and aristocratic detachment from the masses. Of course, Mann's Goethe figure is not meant to be identical with Mann himself. With Goethe's questioning of his artistic existence, Mann engages in a critical self-assessment of his own life. However, accusations are contrasted with justification of the artistic existence. Goethe's creative work, which has earned him his place in the pantheon of German and world literature, is admired; his inhumanity is recognized as a necessary byproduct of geniality. To be a genius is to be a "half-god and prodigy, marvel and monstrum" (*LiW* 324). Mann reveals a Goethe who is aware that his artistic and creative endeavors set him apart, that genius borders on the demonic, but that only detachment from life, freedom from common views and traditions, allow new visions and understandings—a perspective that Mann will reiterate through the humanist Zeitblom in *Doctor Faustus.*

Chapter 8, the encounter between Goethe and Charlotte, sheds further light on the artist's aloofness. Charlotte is disappointed not only because she had hoped for a private conversation with Goethe and instead has to make do with a public luncheon. He is not at all like the Goethe whom Charlotte remembers, the Goethe who had fallen passionately in love with her four decades earlier. Mann unmasks Charlotte's expectations, which are based on a vision of Goethe and his love for her, nourished by the lover's emotional outpourings in *The Sufferings of Young Werther,* as erroneous. But Goethe not only ignores the past when he avoids contact with Charlotte in her white dress; he also avoids Charlotte Kestner, the elderly lady, thereby refusing to acknowledge the unpleasant, decadent side of reality. In this chapter, Mann shows a pompous Goethe ostensibly "lacking sympathy for men and things" (*LiW* 399). At lunch, he ostentatiously takes on the mask of the great writer, wearing his regalia to show off the recognition he has achieved. He plays the role his audience expects from Germany's greatest writer in part because he wants to escape Charlotte's grotesque attempt to resurrect the past. Presenting his public side shuts out any personal, intimate interactions. Conscious of his demonic impact upon others, Goethe challenges his audience with the Chinese proverb, that "the great man is a national misfortune" (*LiW* 418). His audience laughs, somewhat ill at ease, as the artist undermines their belief in his greatness and in his creativity. This creativity is ambivalent in *Lotte in Weimar.* Its outpourings transcend the banality of life, but they also lead to the false identification of fiction with reality.

With Goethe, Mann shows that the great man can be a "misfortune" not only to others, but to himself as well. The genius often victimizes others in order to create extraordinary work, but he is himself a victim of his own striving for greatness. He has become a moody, isolated, and lonely person, suffering from his own greatness. The novel draws a parallel between the sufferings of Goethe and those endured by God, represented by Jesus Christ. Riemer had mentioned that people like he and Charlotte belong to those "upon whom, through him [Goethe], the light of history, legend, and immortality falls as it does upon those about Jesus the Christ" (*LiW* 119). Toward the end of the novel, in his dialogue with Charlotte, Goethe compares himself to a God who sacrifices himself (*LiW*

451). Greatness, egotism, sacrifice, the renunciation of love, and suffering go hand in hand.[5]

Notwithstanding their reservations, all of Goethe's admirers in the novel are convinced of his greatness. So are Mann's readers, even though Mann throws a dubious light upon Goethe's reactions to the political atmosphere that, as the novel suggests, demands conformism. Goethe remains ironically superior when he learns of his scribe's intention to become an ideological turncoat. He even maintains a commanding presence in advocating the suppression of an inopportune writer. More questionable is the effect Goethe's superiority has on his obsequious dinner guests, an effect that makes Charlotte agree with the Chinese saying about the great man being a public misfortune. Is *Lotte in Weimar* a novel that promotes Goethe or discredits him, the reader may thus ask. While the novel up to this point hovers between accusation and justification of the great creative mind, with the final chapter, a narrative tour de force, it becomes a tribute to Goethe the writer and to Goethe's literary production, in spite of, or rather because of his human shortcomings. Up until the last chapter, Mann has narrated his story in a manner that appears realistically possible, even if it does not follow historical events exactly. The last chapter contains a dialogue between Lotte and Goethe that resolves the problems the novel has presented in a poetic, fairy tale–like, comforting manner.

Earlier Goethe had offered Charlotte his box in the Weimar theater and his carriage to fetch her. On her way home, Goethe appears to be riding in the carriage next to her. There are indications, but only a few, that this is not a real scene: Goethe speaks to Charlotte with the same voice with which the young Goethe had read to the young Charlotte forty-four years ago. His hair resembles that of his youth, but it is thinner. He is both old and young; this Goethe is timeless, he is the lover again, and simultaneously the dignity of the nationally recognized man of letters. Other signals that separate this scene from the fictional "reality" of the bulk of the novel are that Goethe, and occasionally even Charlotte, use language from his earlier works—mostly poems—easily recognizable for the German reader. This imaginary Goethe apologizes to Charlotte for having disappointed her in human terms, and Charlotte confesses her jealousy for Friederike Brion. Did Friederike inspire the same kind of love that went into Werther's for Charlotte? Did the real Charlotte's resoluteness, by which she was able to lead her very own life as mother of eleven children, exclude her from serving as the model of the one who was beloved? Friederike was heartbroken when Goethe left her, and ultimately withered away. Does that mean she was able to hold fast to the love of the genius? And what is the value of reality against poetic possibility? To these questions of Charlotte's, the fairytale Goethe replies: "You and she, you are all one in my love—and in my guilt" (*LiW* 449).

Friederike's absolute love and Charlotte's attachment to life, to husband and children, to society, are both aspects of the poet. The fairytale Goethe refuses to place Charlotte's obedience to the demands of a socially useful life above love. Neither is there a preference for the tragic renunciation of real life for the sake of preserving the poetic moment, in spite of the fact that renunciation is a principal theme of Goethe's life.

The renunciation of human life and society by foregoing binding love is a sacrifice, as Goethe suggests in his final sentences. In light of Goethe's comment, "They sacrificed to the god, and in the end the sacrifice was God" (*LiW* 451), is it to be understood as a religious sacrifice for transcendental redemption? Jesus is the self-sacrificed God in the Christian faith. A sacrificed God is also the post-Christian God of Nietzsche's aphorism 125 from *The Gay Science* (1882): God is dead and all of us have killed him.[6] This God was sacrificed for modernity, for humanity's self-determination. The modern, secularized meaning of sacrifice is expressed in Goethe's poem "Selige Sehnsucht" ("Holy Yearning"). During a sexual union at night a moth flies into a burning candle. It becomes the symbol of death and renewal, of man's freedom and self-redemption. The writer, as the fairytale Goethe explains in reference to himself, is both the moth that sacrifices itself and the candle that provides the light and is consumed in the process. The ultimate renunciation is the poet's sacrifice of his humanity for a poetic world that transcends the banality of human existence.

Lotte in Weimar is a novel about the ambiguity of human creativity. If creativity aims at human greatness it must leave the comfort zone of an integrated existence. But this comfort zone would sink into banality without human creativity. This transcending power of creativity is once again addressed at the conclusion of the novel. Mager, who himself shows signs of aging, offers his arm to support Charlotte Kestner while leading her back to the hotel from the carriage, and observes that to help Werther's Lotte from Goethe's carriage is "buchenswert," meaning worthy of being put in a book. (The translation renders *buchenswert* as "It ought to be put down" [LiW 453].) But Mann did not merely mean what Mager may possibly record in a diary. "Buchenswert," worthy of being put in a book, this book, is the contrast between the elderly, transitory Charlotte and Werther's youthful Lotte who, in another book, will stay forever young.

Lotte in Weimar illustrates that the artist, lacking human qualities such as consideration and compassion for others, is highly suspect, and that his relationship to the world does not set a good example for human interactions.[7] What is not questionable, though, is the artist's authority as a critical voice.[8] When Goethe lectures his lunch guests about the Jews in Germany, about their irony and wit, their advanced level of education in medicine and the arts, and overall considerable contributions to civilization, and when he condemns the anti-Semitism at Eger, he is the voice of humanism and reason. Here Goethe becomes also the mouthpiece of Mann, who has spoken out against the anti-Semitism of Nazi Germany. Through Goethe, Mann contrasts German culture with Germany's new, sinister movement, full of "arrogant conceit" and "all sorts of hypocrisy and fatherland rubbish and bigoted, malcontent croaking" (*LiW* 310–11), and expresses his revulsion against Nazi-Germany:

> That they so love cloudy vapouring and berserker excesses, repulsive; wretched that they abandon themselves credulously to every fanatic scoundrel who speaks to their baser qualities, confirms them in their vices, teaches them nationality, means barbarism and isolation. . . . They look with jaundiced eyes on those whom foreigners love and respect, seeing in them the true Germany. No, I will not appease them. They do not like me —so be it, I like them neither, we are quits. What I have of Germany I will keep—and may the devil fly away with them and the philistine spite they think is German! They think they are German—but I am. (*LiW* 330–31)

The autobiographical dimension of Goethe's political comments becomes even more evident with the following sentence in *Lotte in Weimar*: "For their best always lived in exile among them; and in exile only, in dispersion, will they develop all the good there is in them for the healing of the nations, and become the salt of the earth" (*LiW* 339). These words by Goethe, who himself had not lived in exile, are Mann's comment about himself. *Lotte in Weimar* is thus an "exile work sui generis"[9] as it reiterates Mann's claim "Where I am, there is Germany."

Mann assumed that in exile he could sustain the Germany that is "freedom, is culture, universality, love" (*LiW* 331), while barbarism and antihumanism ran rampage in Germany. The act of writing itself became a home for Mann, and a constant reminder of his cultural identity when writing about Goethe and German culture. But, as his portrait of Goethe suggests, Mann also understood his voice to be that of a lonely man who has lost direct contact with his native audience, and whose tirades against antihumanism might fall on deaf ears. Goethe's loneliness is certainly the fate of the great artist, but it is also a reflection of Mann's fate in exile.

The Transposed Heads: A Legend of India

Perhaps it was the sense of alienation, coupled with the recognition of having overestimated the artist's influence that made Mann reluctant to continue with his *Joseph* tetralogy and its underlying optimism about the artist-leader's authority and social compassion. Rather than returning, as planned, to *Joseph and His Brothers* after the completion of *Lotte in Weimar*, he found yet another diversion in the fall of 1939: the world of Indian mythology introduced to him by two books he had recently read, Heinrich Zimmer's *Maya: Der indische Mythos* (Maya: the Indian myth), from 1936, and *Die indische Weltmutter* (The Indian world mother), from 1939. In *Die indische Weltmutter*, he discovered the story of two friends who decapitate themselves in the temple of the Goddess Kali. Commanded by the Goddess, the wife of one of the friends puts the heads back on but interchanges the bodies. The story does not clearly state that the young woman entertains adulterous thoughts while doing so. These are explicit in Goethe's 1809 novel *Die Wahlverwandtschaften* (*Elective Affinities*), and the 1819 ballad about the exchange of heads and bodies titled "Des Paria Gebet" ("The Pariah"). Both are works Mann knew well. Thus, Mann's aim to follow in the artistic footsteps of his "father" Goethe, and his need to cling to German culture while in exile, appear to be contributing factors in writing his "Indian novella," *Die vertauschten Köpfe* (*TB 1937–1939* 500) between January and July 1940, while he and his family resided in Princeton and Southern California.

Mann wrote his version of the Indian story in the style of a fairy tale, told with much humor and irony, focusing on sexual frustrations and the yearning for a full life. At its center lies the relationship between two friends, the intellectual, physically delicate and refined Schiradaman and the athletic, life-oriented Nanda. After decapitating themselves in the temple of the World Mother, Schiradaman's pregnant wife Sita, at the command of the Goddess, replaces the heads on the torsos, thereby restoring them to life. However, she transposes them, half intentionally, half unintentionally, as she had been longing for Nanda's strong body. An ascetic rules that Sita's husband is now Schiradaman's head with Nanda's body, to the delight of Sita and to the disappointment of Nanda. Initially Sita enjoys her "new" husband, but to her dismay the coexistence of the intellectual and the physical cannot be sustained. Nanda's body, controlled by Schiradaman's head, becomes weak, befitting that of an intellectual, while Schiradaman's body, controlled by Nanda's head, becomes more athletic. A few years after the birth of her son Samadhi, Sita visits Nanda and makes love to him, justifying her adultery by telling herself that her lover has her husband's body. The dilemma as to who is Sita's husband reaches its deadly conclusion. Adherence to the moral conventions that condemn polyandry leads both friends to kill each other simultaneously. As customs prescribe, Sita burns on their funeral pyre. Samadhi becomes the reader to the king.

Sita's transposition of the heads symbolizes the yearning to erase the chasm between spirit and nature, art and life, a yearning Mann had addressed through many of his earlier artist figures as well as in various essays . In "Goethe and Tolstoy" Mann depicted "the sentimental longing—of the sons of spirit for nature, of the sons of nature for spirit" that would result in a higher unity of spirit and nature and in "humanitas" (*ETD* 174). The union of nature and spirit remains a utopian model in the essay. In *The Transposed Heads* "the world's goal is union between spirit and beauty," but it is unattainable, as the narrator points out: "This tale of ours is but an illustration of the failures and false starts attending the effort to reach the goal."[10] The gradual change of the bodies reaffirms the separation between spirit and life. Although the offspring Samadhi displays both physical beauty and intellectuality, he is neither the embodiment of the synthesis of life and spirit, nor is he a mediator like Joseph. Samadhi's existence is conspicuously removed from life. His shortsightedness restricts him from seeing and participating in life. While Joseph's beauty and creativity allows him to become a leader and socially integrated, Samadhi's intellectual talents are put to a limited, uncreative use. He reads out loud to the king what others have written.

Similar to Mann's earlier tales of passion, such as those in *Death in Venice*, the Chauchat episode in *The Magic Mountain*, and Mut's story in the *Joseph and His Brothers*, love and desire defy conventions and ethics in *The Transposed Heads*; they are subversive, destructive forces. In contrast, and thus an indication of Mann's play with perspectives, the story of *The Transposed Heads* illustrates that serving civilization and protecting one's honor as a dignified, respected member of society triumphs over the individualistic, selfish fulfillment of primordial sexual desires. However, the narrative is far from endorsing a civilization whose customs demand, besides submission to rigid sexual politics, Sita's painful and gruesome death on the funeral pyre. Mann presents both the cruelty of conventions and the individual's desire to adhere to them without taking sides.

The Tables of the Law

The request to write a contribution for an American collection of stories critical of Nazi Germany provided Mann with yet another diversion from completing the *Joseph* tetralogy. First published in English in 1943 under the title "Thou Shalt Have No Other Gods Before Me," *Das Gesetz* (*The Tables of the Law*) is based on the story of Moses who teaches the Hebrews about the invisible god Jahwe and leads them out of their Egyptian serfdom to nearby Mount Sinai where he receives God's Ten Commandments. Outraged that the people adore a golden calf during his absence, he destroys their idol with the stone tablets, then returns to Mount Sinai to rewrite the commandments.

Like the *Joseph* tetralogy, *The Tables of the Law* is an amusing, witty revision of a biblical tale, a showcase of Mann's mastery of playing with words and

168

fables. With humor, Mann undermines the authority of the Bible when he suggests that Jawhe is nothing more than a convenient figment of Moses's imagination, and that the Egyptians' punishment for enslaving the Hebrews is not the result of divine interference but of natural causes. When Moses is concerned about the beauty of the letters on the tablets rather than about the content of the commandments, Mann pokes fun at aestheticism. Nonetheless, behind this entertaining story about mankind's past lurks a critical assessment of contemporary issues. Since the loss of the First World War, and the subsequent Treaty of Versailles, the Germans saw themselves as a humiliated people. Hitler's success was largely due to his promise to lead Germany out of its humiliation. The Hebrews endured similar humiliation under Egyptian rule; Moses becomes their leader because he promises liberation. Like Hitler, he shakes his fists when addressing his audience and withholds the truth about his true intentions to gain their support. Analogous to Hitler, he sees himself as a messiah figure who brings his chosen people a new religion and uses aesthetic means to manipulate his followers. He relies on propaganda and demagoguery; one of his loyal supporters, his half-sister Miriam, composes a song praising God and his glorious destruction of their enemies. The narrative voice, implicitly inviting the reader to compare this with Nazi marches and drum beating, comments laconically: "It must be imagined sung to the timbrel" (*Tables* 22). Violence and terror are part and parcel of Moses's rule to achieve his agenda. He does not shy away from ordering killings, and displays racism and intolerance.[11]

In his essay "Brother Hitler" Mann established affinities between the bourgeois artist and Hitler. Mann was possibly familiar with the proclamation by Goebbels, Nazi minister of propaganda, that it was Hitler's task "to form a people out of the raw material man."[12] Mann compares Moses's work of changing the Hebrews' customs and morals to that of a sculptor who turns a raw boulder into a work of art. Despite these parallels between Hitler and Moses, underscored by Moses's striking willingness to kill all enemies, even Hebrews, who disobey his orders, there are also decisive differences. By giving Moses the facial features of the Italian artist Michelangelo, Mann places his Moses in the tradition of Western European humanism—and his own artist figures. Reminiscent of Tonio Kröger, Moses is of mixed origin, half Egyptian, half Hebrew—an outsider—and, unlike Hitler, obsessed with the desire for the "spiritual, the pure, the holy" (*Tables* 1).

Above all what sets Moses apart from Hitler are his intentions as leader. When he frees the Hebrews from their Egyptian serfdom he also wants to free them from their existence driven by desire and instinct and lead them to an intellectual, morally disciplined, civilized life. Moses is the bringer of a life-affirming humanism, not a destructive force. The Ten Commandments are not simply religious norms, they are "the moral law in general, man's civilization" (*SN* 16). Moses's task is not an easy one, in light of the fact that Mann paints a rather negative picture of humankind in the story. They are a mob without morality, intellect, and rationality. Whenever their basic physical needs are not met during their flight from Egypt, they turn against their leader. In order to bring humanity and culture to the mob, Mann provides Moses with two powerful, ruthless men, comparable to Hitler's henchmen, to enforce his leadership, his laws and order. The narrative suggests that use of violence and terror against the enemies of humanity, even against one's own people, is justified, because without brutal force human moral progress is impossible. Terror is the only pedagogical tool for the Hebrews to learn their lessons in civilization. Fearing Moses's "avenging angel," who would drive them into the desert, that is to say, into death, if they were to neglect his prohibitions, they obey: "All the things that Moses forbade came to seem frightful to them. At first this was so only in connection with the punishment; but after a while the thing itself came to be thought of as an evil" (*Tables* 40). Fear of punishment leads to an acceptance of new moral standards, and a bad conscience if these standards are violated. But fear cannot be the foundation of civilization and humanism.

Mann's optimistic assessment that morality and rationality will guide, and even dominate, human behavior is counterbalanced by substantial doubts that they have become ingrained in flesh and blood. In the absence of intellectual leadership and disciplinary power, human beings relapse into primitive rites. The Hebrew community regresses to barbaric behavior; Dionysian rapture, incest, murder, and idolatry reign when Moses goes to Mount Sinai to receive God's Ten Commandments. When Moses returns from the mountain a second time with new tablets inscribed with the commandments, he conveys to the community God's knowledge that "His commands will not be obeyed, but will be rebelled against over and over again" (*Tables* 62). In the end, Mann's tale is thus overshadowed by doubts that the rational forces of life can win over nature and Dionysian forces. In light of the political and historical developments in the early 1940s that saw a return to barbarism, the victory of irrational and Dionysian forces over humanism and rationality, Mann's skepticism certainly was warranted.

In the vein of *Joseph and His Brothers*, *The Tables of the Law*, described by Mann as a "postlude" (*SN* 15) to the tetralogy, despite the fact that the tetralogy had not yet been completed, continues with the presentation of the artist-leader figure with good intentions. At the same time, the story destabilizes the boundaries between good and bad leaders. Moses's inhuman actions in the name of humanism overshadow his moral leadership and make him both a counter figure and a complementary figure to Hitler. Furthermore, his tyrannical means are not the only questionable side to his character. Despite his social engagement that brought an end to the Hebrews' slavery and his love for life, mainly expressed on the personal level by his attraction to his black concubine, he remains distanced from life. When he destroys the first set of commandments by smashing them on the golden calf, he not only does so out of anger and in order to destroy the idol, but because of his high aesthetic standards. Because his letters were not perfect, he erases not only his inferior artistic product but its moral message, the blueprint of Western civilization. Mann rectifies this slip into aestheticism. As the second set of stone tablets satisfies Moses' artistic standards, he can give his moral lecture based on their content and demonstrate his social responsibility at the end of the narrative.

Writing during his exile provided Mann with an aesthetic refuge from an antihumanistic, destructive warmongering world that disregarded human dignity, compassion, and freedom. Although Mann had lost his German readership and had had to witness the perversion of Germany's bourgeois-humanistic culture and (self-)destruction from his American exile, he continued writing, therefore keeping the memories of this culture alive and securing the continuation of bourgeois German culture. With humor and irony, Mann describes in *Lotte in Weimar*, *The Transposed Heads*, and *The Tables of the Law* the deficit of love, the flaws of human nature, the questionable nature of artistic authority, and the enrichment of the world through creativity. Mann did not shy away from a self-accusatory stance with his acknowledgment of the amoral leadership of the artist. Yet with their underlying call for humanism, compassion, and tolerance, these narratives are also narratives of resistance. Their existence is testimony to Mann's belief that the artist, despite all his shortcomings, can be a servant to humanity. This belief, infused with skepticism, will be austerely challenged in *Doctor Faustus*.

CHAPTER 11

Doctor Faustus

Ever since *Buddenbrooks*, Mann had warned the educated middle class of the dangers of life-negating aestheticism, their distance from life and lack of love. And ever since his speech "The German Republic," he had tried to be the voice of reason and humanism, and to convince them to accept and support democracy, the political guarantor of the future of bourgeois humanistic and individualistic culture. The exiled author, who enjoyed respect in the United States as an advocate and representative of the German humanistic tradition, must certainly have been disappointed that many among those readers who had elevated him to Germany's poet laureate in the 1920s would turn away from him after 1933. Others had simply begun to ignore his voice, while still others had even become supporters of what Mann derogatorily referred to as "the mob." Mann felt morally and intellectually superior to those enthralled by the voices of antireason and antiliberalism, yet he also wondered whether he was really so different from them. Throughout his long career, Mann had always been skeptical toward his artistic, creative existence. In *Lotte in Weimar* he defended the independence of art and the artist, assuming that only freedom from social and moral responsibility fosters creativity and a deeper understanding of reality, and thus allows art to become a symbol and proponent of unadulterated humanity. However, the narrative had also demonstrated the questionable side of the pursuit of creativity, as it can lead to a narcissistic, inhuman distancing from life.

On 23 May 1943, burdened by this disappointment and by self-doubts, Mann began writing *Doktor Faustus* (*Doctor Faustus*). With this novel he revisited familiar themes and issues, among them art and disease, love and death, repressive bourgeois morality, the path from an ascetic, Apollonian to a self-destructive life, the social and political irresponsibility of the critical intellect, and an unbound creativity indifferent to life. His plan to use the old German Faust myth to explore these themes did not just grow out of the rise of National Socialism and the self-destructive path of the German nation. It can be traced back to an old idea from around 1904 that Mann had about an artist: "*Novella or for 'Maja'* character of the syphilitic artist: as Dr. Faust and prescribed to the devil. The poison takes effect as intoxication, stimulus, inspiration; in enraptured enthusiasm he is allowed to create ingenious, wonderful works, the devil guides him. Finally, *the devil gets him*: paralysis" (*NB 7–14* 121–22). This note suggests a narrative that focuses on the artist as outsider. When Mann reread it in 1943 much had changed—and not only as far as German history and politics were concerned. By 1943 Mann no longer saw the artist (and himself) merely as a social outsider of extraordinary talents and creativity rebelling against a bourgeois, stifling existence; he was now the artist as representative of Germany and its culture. Thus, writing about an artist's fate had to become a reflection of a collective, national experience. Germany's embrace of irrational, barbaric forces provided the ultimate provocation for Mann as a German and as a German artist. Interweaving an artist's fate, and thus his own, with that of his nation was a significant challenge, a challenge that he was ready to undertake with *Doctor Faustus*, a novel that, according to Mann's comment in *The Story of a Novel,* has as its subject "the flight from the difficulties of a cultural crisis into the pact with the devil, the craving of a proud mind, threatened by sterility, for an unblocking of inhibitions at any cost, and the parallel between pernicious euphoria ending in collapse with the nationalistic frenzy of Fascism" (*SN* 30).

To distance himself from the all-too-personal subject matter, Mann employs a narrator, Serenus Zeitblom, both to tell the story of his artist (and Mann's Faust figure), the composer Adrian Leverkühn, and, simultaneously, to describe Germany's path to antihumanism and destruction. Zeitblom, a humanist and retired teacher of classical philology, starts writing his chronicles of Leverkühn's life on the same day Mann begins to write the novel. Although Zeitblom shares with his author his love for the composer and strong resentment of Germany's ideological and political developments under Nazism, Zeitblom is not identical with Mann. Living withdrawn from public life and limited by his middle-class perspectives and values, Zeitblom is often the target of Mann's irony. Zeitblom's chronicle goes back to his schooldays, when Adrian Leverkühn became his school friend. To the disappointment of Zeitblom, the relationship between both was always distant, due to Leverkühn's coldness, cynicism, and arrogance. Nonetheless, Zeitblom is fascinated by Leverkühn, who, after briefly studying theology, becomes a composer dedicated solely to his art, while Zeitblom enters a conventional bourgeois existence. Zeitblom reminisces about Leverkühn's days as a student, his connection to a group of reactionary students known as the Winfried circle, his introduction to music, and burgeoning striving for artistic greatness during the years before the First World War. Leverkühn has extraordinary talents and insights that warrant Zeitblom's—and the reader's—admiration. Dissatisfied with his music, he is in search of inspiration, which comes in the form of a woman, the syphilitic prostitute Hetaera Esmeralda. Reluctantly Zeitblom tells of his friend's sexual encounter with her in Pressburg, Hungary. Mann uses this encounter as symbolic of the pact with the devil. It brings about the ensuing disease that stimulates Leverkühn to overcome the stagnation from which bourgeois art and his own production suffer. In chapter 25, the central chapter of the novel, Mann presents Leverkühn's imagined dialogue with the devil, in which the latter promises an artistic breakthrough provided that Leverkühn does not love. To keep this provision, Mann's artist suppresses and sacrifices love for artistic greatness. Leverkühn lives only for his art, yet yearning for love and life subsists. A brief homosexual relationship with the violinist Rudi Schwerdtfeger, a half-serious contemplation of marriage, and the love for his sister's young son, Nepomuk Schneidewein, which results in his nephew's death because Leverkühn broke the pact with the devil, disrupt an otherwise reclusive existence. As his music engenders an international reputation among specialists, Leverkühn's pact seems to be fulfilled, his fate sealed. However, this fate becomes uncertain with the presence—or more precisely, the absence—of Frau von Tolna, a Hungarian aristocrat and an enigmatic figure who remains invisible throughout the novel. Mann implies a secret identity between Frau von Tolna and Hetaera Esmeralda. Because the relationship between Leverkühn and Frau von Tolna/Hetaera Esmeralda is based on the condition that they never meet, he can love her without endangering her life, thereby resisting and fulfilling the provision of the pact.

Parallel to his story of Leverkühn's extraordinary life, Zeitblom also tells about the world of the educated middle class in Munich, their enthusiasm for war and fantasies about the destruction of bourgeois society before and after the First World War, their lack of engagement for democratic and liberal ideals, and their leaning toward nationalistic, irrational forces after the war. Zeitblom's portrayals of individual fates and personal tragedies that reflect the absence of love in this world are accompanied by descriptions of an increasingly antihumanistic, totalitarian, and sinister Germany. At the same time, Leverkühn composes barbaric, dissonant music, evoking the annulment of humanism. Leverkühn's career as a composer ends in 1930 when his disease leads him to insanity. He dies ten years later. At the time of the German defeat, in 1945, Zeitblom ends his chronicles asking his readers to pray for his friend and for Germany.

Mann's own account of the genesis and progress of the novel in *The Story of a Novel* reveals that at this time in his career he was perturbed by his reputation as a traditionalist writer whose work enjoys "popularity" (*SN* 91), and that he might be rated as inferior to avantgardists like James Joyce. Mann was touched "with a strange intensity" by a critic's comment on Joyce's modernistic style, which stated that "the best writing of our contemporaries is not an act of creation, but an act of evocation, peculiarly saturated with reminiscences," (*SN* 91), presumably because he had high hopes that with the completion of his new novel now underway he would be recognized as one of the preeminent modernist writers of his time. Like Joyce's *Ulysses* with regard to Homer's Ulysses, *Doctor Faustus* is a work of evocation. The novel is based on the Faust myth of the old chapbook about Faust (1587)[1] that had challenged many illustrious minds, among them Christopher Marlowe, Johann Wolfgang von Goethe, and the French composer Charles Gounaud, to present their own interpretations of the story of the ambitious Faust who had sold his soul to the devil to gain knowledge and power. Mann's Faust figure, Adrian Leverkühn, is a type and a construct rather than an individual. And yet he is much more. His life is not only based on a fictional figure, but also on real persons, including both Martin Luther (1483–1546), Mann himself, and Friedrich Nietzsche, one of the most prominent models. Various aspects of Nietzsche's life, as told by his friend Paul Deussen, are transferred to Leverkühn's life: Nietzsche's brothel experience in Cologne where he hits a few notes on the piano before running out, his contraction of syphilis, his artistic creativity followed by megalomania, and, at the end, his insanity and childlike helplessness. Both Nietzsche and Leverkühn die at the age of fifty-five. Mann chose to impose some of Nietzsche's real-life experiences on his fictional character because he understood Nietzsche to be a representative of an existence, a mood, and an intellectual climate described in his 1947 essay "Nietzsche's Philosophy in the Light of Contemporary Events." Mann interprets Nietzsche's life as one of deepest solitude, isolation, and renunciation, of suffering and intoxication. The philosopher's thinking is "absolute geniality, unpragmatical in the extreme, devoid of any pedagogical responsibility, profoundly unpolitical; it is in truth *without* any relation to life."[2] This concisely summarizes Leverkühn's life.

It is not only with Leverkühn as a synthetic character that Mann breaks down the traditional boundaries between fiction and reality. Throughout the novel, the distinction between the real and the imagined world are blurred. For example, the composer Gustav Mahler and the German conductors Bruno Walter and Otto Klemperer are all mentioned, as are the cities of Halle, Leipzig, and Palestrina. Mann's description of the fictional Kaisersaschern, where Leverkühn spends much of his youth, evokes Aachen, Lübeck, Naumburg, and Nürnberg, thereby infusing contemporary German history with elements from the Holy Roman Empire of the German Nation. Many of the names Mann found in Luther's letters, such as Zeitblom and Ölhafen, are appropriated to summon up a Lutheran atmosphere reminiscent of Germany during the Reformation. Leverkühn's invisible sponsor, Frau von Tolna, evokes Frau von Meck, a friend of the composer Peter Ilyich Tchaikovsky (1840–1893). The philosopher Theodor W. Adorno appears as a scholar in Leverkühn's dialogue with the devil. Many of the characters in the novel are based on real people that Mann knew from Munich and Germany's cultural life of the 1920s, and on members of Mann's own family. The fictional family Rodde shares facets of the lives of Mann's immediate family; like Mann's mother, Frau Senator Rodde, a widow, moves to Munich. Clarissa Rodde is an actress, like Mann's sister Carla; both Clarissa and Carla commit suicide by taking potassium cyanide. The fate of Mann's sister Julia is reflected in that of Inez Rodde. Both try to escape their bourgeois predicaments with morphine. Inez becomes a murderess and ends up in an insane asylum. Julia Mann committed suicide. Nepomuk Schneidewein's model is Mann's favorite grandchild, Fridolin.

As in earlier works, Mann's own life is projected in *Doctor Faustus* in numerous ways. Mann had called the novel an "arcanum and confession" (*SN* 32). First, Mann interweaves his stigmatized desires into the narrative. The violinist Rudi Schwerdtfeger resembles Mann's friend Paul Ehrenberg, his object of secret sexual longings some four decades prior. Inez Rodde's love for the violinist, the love of an older woman for a younger man, is a version of Mut's relationship to Joseph in *Joseph and His Brothers*. Second, his doubts about the social irresponsibility and immorality of artistic existence permeate the novel and make it his most radical, self-accusatory testimony to his own life as an artist. Third, as mentioned earlier in the context of James Joyce, Mann had reservations about his own artistic achievements, the illusionary character of bourgeois art and its future. His self-doubts are voiced in Leverkühn's comment in his conversation with the devil: "What falls prey to criticism is the outward show of the bourgeois work of art" (*DF* 257). Leverkühn is by no means identical to Mann. He is a composer, not a man of letters. Yet aspects of Mann's own art, foremost among them the autobiographical dimensions and montage technique, are present in Leverkühn's music. Just as *Doctor Faustus* is an amalgamation of various stories and lives, and thus a novel of multiple voices and multilayered meanings, so is Leverkühn's music. Leverkühn uses for his compositions works by Dante, Shakespeare, Brentano, Verlaine, Blake, Keats, Klopstock, and the chapbook, suspiciously not by Goethe, in his attempt to annul the illusionary works of bourgeois culture. Montage in *Doctor Faustus*, as Mann has pointed out, is an attempt to transcend the realm of fictionality, to "shake off" the illusionary character of art (*Br 3* 16). What Mann leaves unmentioned is that montage allows for a proliferation of meaning; due to its intertextuality, *Doctor Faustus* is a polyphonic novel in which a multitude of voices—ergo, the absence of a single authorial voice—leads not only to a multifaceted text, but also to unresolvable tensions and ambiguities.

Since its publication in 1947, the novel has challenged readers and interpreters. It has been discussed as a historical novel about Germany, a novel about the crisis of twentieth century art, as a Nietzsche and Faust novel, as a novel about crime and punishment, sin and redemption, a novel hovering between realism and modernism,[3] and more recently, and in light of the publication of Mann's diaries, as a radical autobiography.[4] The by now countless interpretations on this most controversial novel have been as contradictory as the work itself. Whether Germany's path to Nazism is a result of cultural heritage or of political and economic developments, remains open to discussion. Similarly, many other issues remain unresolved. Is the novel a masterpiece and Mann's "greatest" work,[5] or is it too German in its theme and scope, thus lacking the universal appeal of *The Magic Mountain* and the *Joseph* tetralogy?[6] Is it permissible to reduce such a complex era of German history, one that involves Nazi Germany, to an analog of the Faust myth and the psyche of one extraordinary individual?[7] Has Mann turned away from Goethe and the German humanistic-classicistic tradition and followed the chapbook?[8] Or is Goethe's *Faust* constitutive, and the intertextuality between Goethe's drama and Mann's novel an indication of Mann's ambition to achieve a Goethe-like fame?[9] Is Mann's diabolic artist at the end condemned, like his precursor in the chapbook, or is he, like Goethe's Faust, redeemed through the love of a woman? Concomitantly, is Germany condemned or not? Is the novel a renunciation or affirmation of bourgeois art? Finding answers to these questions leads to the core of this multifaceted novel; yet these answers cannot aim at definiteness, as that would violate the novel's most salient aspects: its play with ambiguities and its openness. To recognize these ambiguities and their implications is the goal of the discussion of the novel that follows, centering on Mann's representation of Germany, the artist's creativity in crisis, and *Doctor Faustus* as a love story.

Germany in *Doctor Faustus*

The novel covers a time span in German history characterized by sweeping ideological, social, and political transformations—Wilhelmian Germany, the First World War, the Weimar Republic, Nazi Germany, and the Second World War. In *Reflections*, Mann had identified Germany as a cultural nation represented by the educated burgher, the quintessential German. This perspective also informs *Doctor Faustus*. At the center of the novel is the culturally oriented segment of German society consisting of students and academics, artists and dilettantes, aristocrats and social parvenus. For years, under the influence of the Marxist critic Ernst Fischer,[10] *Doctor Faustus* was targeted as a novel that does not do justice to the totality of Germany, that emphasizes its cultural traditions at the cost of underestimating the extent to which social and economic forces, national and international politics, shape the history of Germany. Such criticism overlooks the underlying intention of the novel: to explore to what extent the German middle class—that had not heeded Mann's warnings about the dangers of aestheticism and antiliberal thoughts—has failed in preventing the formation of National Socialism and its rise to power, and, furthermore, to undertake a soul-searching, self-critical examination about what Mann as a bourgeois artist has or has not done in light of Germany's path to antihumanism.

In exploring these questions, Erich Kahler's 1937 study, *Der deutsche Charakter in der Geschichte Europas* (*The German Character in the History of Europe*),[11] had a decisive influence upon the shaping of *Doctor Faustus*. Kahler, a close friend and neighbor of the Manns in Princeton from 1938 to 1941, provided Mann with a characterological history of Germany. Kahler argues that because Germany lacked a clearly defined historical and political entity and national coherence until 1871, it can only be defined in terms of its intellectual and cultural history. He sees in the encounter of primitive, isolated Germanic tribes with the Roman Empire, the highest civilization at that time, the foundation for the subsequent and continual interplay between two powerful poles, between paganism and Christianity, barbarism and humanism. Germany's oscillation between inwardness, political immaturity, radical nationalism, and a European spirit continues with the emergence of Martin Luther and Protestantism on the one hand, and the secular ideals of humanism of the Weimar Classical period on the other. For Kahler, Luther is the prototype of the German burgher who is indifferent to worldly, political, and social concerns. Thus Germanness embodies nationalism and self-absorption, and, simultaneously, cosmopolitanism. With National Socialism, and its revival of Germanic pagan cults, the German disposition for nationalism and barbarism gains an overwhelming preeminence.

For more than three decades, Mann himself presented a twofold image of Germany. Subsequently, Kahler's explications on the duality of the German character in the late 1930s can be regarded as substantiating and enhancing Mann's earlier conceptions. In *Reflections* Mann had praised German inwardness. A decade later, in the 1926 essay "Lübeck als geistige Lebensform" ("Lübeck as an Intellectual Form of Life"), Mann had high hopes for the German character now defined as "cosmopolitanism" (*E 3* 37). With this definition, Mann does not reverse *Reflections*. Rather, it indicates his understanding, which is reflected in *Doctor Faustus*, of Germany as a nation with a dual identity. The composite town of Kaisersaschern symbolizes German universalism as well as the atmosphere and mentality of the late Middle Ages, a Germanness defined in the novel as "a psychological state threatened by the poison of loneliness, by eccentricity, provincial standoffishness, neurotic involution, unspoken Satanism" (*DF* 326).

Kahler's influence is also traceable in one of Mann's speeches, written in 1945 while *Doctor Faustus* was in progress, "Deutschland und die Deutschen" ("Germany and the Germans"). In this speech Mann sketches "the story of German 'inwardness.'"[12] While Germany has a tradition of openness to the world, going back to the Holy Roman Empire of the German Nation, it remained simultaneously world-shy, introverted, and provincial as a result of Luther's Protestant movement. Luther had proliferated a nonpolitical concept of freedom and became an advocate of indifference to social and worldly affairs. Luther's world was also indebted to the medieval world of the irrational; there is "a secret union of the German spirit with the Demonic,"[13] best illustrated by the pact between the scholastic Faust and the devil. This German belief in irrational, demonic forces was revived during the romantic period and became a counterforce to Germany's openness, humanism, and the rationality of the Age of Enlightenment. Mann correlates romanticism to an "antiquarianism . . . of soul that feels very close to the chthonian, irrational, and demonic forces of life."[14] It is this romanticism, with its embrace of the past and its return to folklore, its snubbing of rationality and celebration of the morbid, and its "seduction to death," that the Nazis appropriated: "Reduced to a miserable mass level, the level of a Hitler, German Romanticism broke out into hysterical barbarism, into a spree and a paroxysm of arrogance and crime." It should be noted that Mann does not condemn German culture and romanticism categorically here; he denounces its distortion and abuse by the Nazis. Mann concludes that there are not two Germanys, an evil and a good one, but only one, whose best qualities have been perverted by devilish cunning: "Wicked Germany is merely good Germany gone astray, good Germany in misfortune, in guilt, and ruin." Concomitantly, Mann cannot dissociate himself from the evil Germany responsible for the death and sufferings of millions: "It is all within me."[15] Acknowledging this kinship with the evil Germany, turns "Germany and the Germans" into a document of radical self-criticism.

Mann's notion that Germany's culture plays a part in the rise of National Socialism and in Germany's downfall, and his recognition that Nazism is not necessarily deviant but an outgrowth of German intellectual and cultural history, initially met with resistance from those who prided themselves as belonging to the so-called Inner Emigration[16] and the cultural establishment of postwar Germany. When Germany grew more open to self-exploration and self-criticism, a discernible shift became noticeable in discussions on Mann's novel—a recognition that *Doctor Faustus* has contributed valuable insights into the interaction between German culture and history.[17]

This interaction is addressed in *Doctor Faustus* when Mann introduces prophecies of cultural regression and of barbaric intoxication, and discussions about Germany's path into isolating nationalism and antiliberalism through conversations among students and among the members of upper-class salons in Munich with whom Leverkühn and Zeitblom interact in the early 1900s. The Christian fraternity "Winfried," joined by Leverkühn while he is a theology student in an attempt to combat his distance from life, subscribes to anticivilizatory, nationalistic ideas. With their call for a new unifying order, their acceptance of a social system open to demonic forces, their glorification of the primitive and of *Blut und Boden* (blood and soil) mysticism, they provide the ideological breeding ground for the National Socialists. A "new world of anti-humanity" (*DF* 300) is also hypothesized in the gatherings at the salons of the Roddes and Schlaginhaufens in Munich, in the months before the beginning of the First World War. The educated burghers gather in elegant, ornate rooms decorated with valuable art works and surround themselves with decadent aristocrats in a vain attempt to reconstruct the atmosphere of the late nineteenth century, and to create the illusion of stability in a drastically changing epoch. While being entertained by Wagner's music, intellectuals such as Dr. Chaim Braisacher indulge in imagining a world bereft of bourgeois-liberal values, seemingly oblivious to the fact that such notions chip away at the foundations of their own bourgeois world and their affluent lifestyle. With arrogance and malicious delight, they project a world of barbarism and intolerance, indifferent to the fact that their intellectual frivolity smacks of social irresponsibility and provides a vehicle for antihumanistic forces. What is so striking in Mann's presentation of his educated burghers —and what reminds us of *Buddenbrooks*—is the absence of love. Mann also displays this absence in his presentation of the intellectuals of Munich who meet after the end of the First World War in the salon of Sixtus Kridwiss. The enormous sacrifice of human life on European battlefields has not shaken up these intellectuals in the least; rather, it has desensitized them to utmost violence and human suffering. They reveal a blatant disregard for individual life and dignity, the achievements of culture, enlightenment, and humanity, and indulge in imagining a new world: "It was an old-new, revolutionarily atavistic world, in which values linked to the idea of the individual (such as, let us say, truth, freedom, justice, reason) were sapped of every strength and cast aside" (*DF* 387). This vision anticipates the antiliberal, antihumanistic world of National Socialism.

Mann's bitterness and disappointment in the educated middle class that had ignored his voice, resonates in his sometimes unsympathetic portrayal of them. Yet they are not vicious people in the novel as they understand their predictions of the end of bourgeois society and the suspension of bourgeois-Christian morality to be nothing more than an intellectual game, an amusing aesthetic exercise. The guests in Kridwiss's salon applaud the dilettante poet Daniel Zur Höhe because his vision of terrorism and brutality is "beautiful": "It was 'beautiful' in a cruel and utterly beauty-bound way, in that unconscionably detached, jesting, irresponsible spirit that poets in fact allow themselves" (*DF* 383). It does not concern them that their aesthetic constructions of brutal, destructive worlds can become a reality whereupon the very economic privileges and bourgeois-liberal cultural traditions that allow them their cherished freedom of thought would evaporate. Here Mann unmasks the bourgeois tendency to be antibourgeois, a tendency that is not particularly German in character but a trait of unrestricted creativity in pluralistic societies. At the beginning of the twenty-first century, Mann's critical assessment of the escape into aesthetic constructions by the German middle class has by no means only historical value. Today's worldwide popular cultures, in evoking violent, destructive worlds, have an effect upon cheering audiences mesmerized by apocalyptic visions similar to that of Mann's bourgeois culture upon his characters. Seen from this angle, *Doctor Faustus* is a surprisingly contemporary, transnational novel.

In *Doctor Faustus*, the irresponsible play with aesthetic constructs to renounce the bourgeois world, so as to break out of a world of stagnation and ennui, is but one aspect of bourgeois self-destructiveness brought about by a lack of compassion and love. The other aspect is degeneration—decline and death—also familiar from *Buddenbrooks*. After her husband's death in Bremen in northern Germany, the widow Rodde decides to move to Munich with her daughters Inez and Clarissa to lead a libertine, bohemian existence. Like Thomas Buddenbrook, she becomes a victim of physical decline, losing both her teeth and hair. The rest of her life is spent quietly and uneventfully in a reclusive village in Bavaria. The life of her daughter Inez takes a more dramatic and tragic turn. Initially yearning for bourgeois stability and a luxurious lifestyle, Inez had married the academic Helmut Institoris, who provides her with a stately house, "a model home of German bourgeois culture" (*DF* 345). As in *Buddenbrooks*, bourgeois security implies the absence of love and sexual frustration. Mann signals the repressive nature of this world by mentioning that provocative or seditious literature and art are excluded. Inez seeks and finds a passionate life, fed by aesthetic images of romantic love and suffering, in her extramarital affair with the violinist Rudi Schwerdtfeger. She kills him when he ends their relationship, and thus ruins her bourgeois existence. While the novel elicits understanding for Inez's flight from a repressive world, her ensuing conduct is reprehensible. Her passion is a consuming affliction, an uncontrollable intoxication, familiar from earlier characters in Mann's fiction such as Aschenbach and Mut. Because her love is described as a man's love for a woman, and because Rudi Schwerdtfeger looks like Paul Ehrenberg, Mann again secretly conveys his own emotional suffering from his stigmatized desire as well as his rejection of these desires when he presents them as irrational and self-destructive.

Clarissa Rodde's fate is the most tragic of the three Roddes. She hates the hypocrisy of bourgeois existence. Living with the illusion that she is a talented actress, she tries in vain to become successful. Her escape into aestheticism, combined with a romantic yearning for death fed by art exemplified by her collection of skulls, one of which is used to store deadly poison, stands in contrast to her need for a secure bourgeois existence. Her attempt to marry an industrialist from Alsace fails when he finds out that she has had a previous love affair, and is thus of morally questionable character. Neither accepted as an actress nor in the formalized world of bourgeois values, she commits suicide by ingesting poison. With her fate, Mann illustrates how strict moral standards win out over love and compassion.

All these events are narrated from the point of view of Zeitblom, who has lived reclusively since 1934 after retiring from his profession as a high school teacher to avoid having to support Nazi policies. While writing his chronicles about his friend's life and Germany's path into barbarism and terror, he is afraid that his sons, who do not share their father's abhorrence of the regime, might find his manuscript and inform the Gestapo. His reluctance to go into details about Germany's current situation, instead merely hinting at acts of terror such as the Nazis' burning of books and their brutality in prisons, should not be interpreted as cowardly. With Zeitblom, "a harmless and simple soul, well meaning and timid" (*SN* 31), Mann paints a realistic picture of life under deadly terror in the early 1940s for those who were not born to be heroes. That is not to say that Mann makes him immune to criticism. Zeitblom's conduct represents the German burghers' inability to resist as well as their failure to resist.

Zeitblom prides himself as being a "descendant of the German humanists" and an opponent of the demonic forces in life (*DF* 6). They have no place in his worldview and he presents himself as a pedantic classicist and humanist, "having never felt the slightest inclination boldly to seek out the intimacy of those nether powers, or worse, wantonly to challenge them, or to give them so much as my little finger when they have approached me with temptation" (*DF* 6). Nonetheless, he admits that German culture unfolds under the "fruitful contact" (*DF* 11) with the demonic, that it is an immanent, vital component of culture. However, Zeitblom's humanism comes under scrutiny when he makes the point that he never agreed "fully" (*DF* 10) with the *Führer* and his paladins on their anti-Semitic policies, suggesting that the gap that Zeitblom erects between himself and the Nazis, between humanism and an inhuman, barbaric orientation, is not as wide as Zeitblom would like us to believe. When Zeitblom narrates that his father's pharmacy, named "Blessed Messengers," supplies Adrian Leverkühn's father with the necessary ingredients to "speculate the elements" (*DF* 16), thus following in the footsteps of medieval alchemists who practiced black magic, Mann informs his readers that humanism is not impervious to the demonic.

What makes Zeitblom sympathetic to readers is the fact that he is appalled by the antiliberal tendencies of his peers and does not participate in the evocation of the new world of irrationalism and barbarism in which the Kridwiss circle indulges. We can side with Mann's narrator when he reacts with revulsion to their sinister enthusiasm for their visions of the demise of the bourgeois-liberal world. Zeitblom's presence provides a counterbalance to the other members of his class in the novel and attests to the fact that Mann's presentation of the educated middle class is not one-sided. At the same time, Mann submits his narrator to criticism. As Zeitblom does not want to be a spoilsport, he decides "to join in the general merriment" and to offer "a smiling, intellectually amused recognition of what was now or was yet to be" (*DF* 387). In this scene, Mann exposes Zeitblom as acting socially irresponsibly by remaining silent. Despite his cosmopolitanism and humanistic perspective, he, too, is guilty of aestheticizing brutality and violence when he deems the blood on the lips of the dying Rudi Schwerdtfeger to be "touchingly beautiful" (*DF* 472). Like his peers, Zeitblom participates, albeit unintentionally, in the demise of his bourgeois liberal world.

The burghers' embrace of aestheticism, coupled with their lack of interest in both shaping their social and political world and assuring the survival of bourgeois humanism, suggest that with *Doctor Faustus* Mann has written a novel about the end of German bourgeois society. Zeitblom's comment at the end of the novel points toward this understanding: "Oh Germany, you are perishing, and I remember your hopes!" (*DF* 408) But his apocalyptic prophecy, which coincides with Germany's defeat and capitulation in 1945, cannot be taken literally. In writing his novel, Mann presupposes as readers the educated, aesthetically oriented burghers who did not disappear in 1945, but were instead in charge of the political and cultural developments in West Germany. *Doctor Faustus* is not about their demise; it is an accusation against those who have privileged art over social engagement and have allowed the demonic sphere and the tenor of antipolitics of Germany's cultural heritage to dominate. Moreover—and therein lies an optimistic dimension of the novel—it is an appeal for social responsibility that Mann reiterates in Leverkühn's speech at the end of the novel.

In a letter from September 1949, Mann disclosed that *Doctor Faustus* incorporates an "exposure of my own life" (*DüD 3* 99). The affinity between

Mann's narrator Zeitblom and Mann himself, so visibly established with the identical starting date of writing, is part of this exposure. While Zeitblom is not a competent, experienced man of letters and admits to "artistic inadequacies and lack of control" (*DF* 7), he shares his author's cultural orientation and his position as an observant bystander, appalled and yet spellbound at the same time. Through Zeitblom, Mann raises the questions whether he, too, has become guilty of having remained aloof, whether Germany's bourgeois artists and their audiences, presumed to be the stewards of German humanism, missed their opportunity to provide an antidote to barbarism and irrationalism, and whether their culture ultimately failed to guarantee human freedom and dignity. The self-accusatory tenor and evocation of mea culpa is, however, undercut toward the end of *Doctor Faustus*. Quite recognizably, the voice of the exiled author speaks through Zeitblom who, living in inner exile, despondently utters: "Germany . . . this unhappy land, is alien to me, utterly alien, precisely because I, certain of its ghastly end, held myself apart from its sins, hid from them in my solitude. Must I not ask if I was right in doing so?" (*DF* 529) Being a passive bystander, in contrast to the perpetrators of violence, does not, as Mann's criticism of the educated burghers illustrates, absolve him from guilt. But something else does— Zeitblom's unceasing, unwavering loyalty to "one painfully important man. . . . It is as if this loyalty may well have made up for my having fled in horror from my country's guilt" (*DF* 529). This loyalty to the artist and his art is shared by Mann himself. Steadfastly devoted to his craft, Mann continued "producing *Kultur*" (*Letters* 481) and kept up the tradition of bourgeois art in writing *Doctor Faustus*, a novel that sustains what it criticizes. This paradox becomes most apparent in Mann's ambivalent presentation of the artist Adrian Leverkühn.

Creativity in Crisis

Leverkühn, to whom Zeitblom devotes so much of his time and emotion, is related to Mann's earlier artist figures and characters, as well as to Mann himself. Leverkühn's father is intellectually oriented, his mother sensitive and of musical ancestors. During childhood and adolescence, Leverkühn sets himself apart from the rest with his superior intelligence, arrogance, and coldness. When he starts to learn to play the piano at the age of fifteen, migraine headaches, a symbol for outsiderness, set in. In vain, Leverkühn resists his artistic inclinations when he studies theology to humiliate and punish himself for his coldness. His path toward artistic greatness is told with admiration and concern. *Doctor Faustus* is Mann's first fictional text with detailed accounts of artistic productions and the artist's striving to create the original work—a striving that, paradoxically, is self-centered yet self-sacrificing, narcissistic yet self-destructive.

In order to succeed in his attempt to create innovative music, Leverkühn has to overcome three hurdles. The first is of a social nature; withdrawal from life and love is imperative for ingenious art. The second is of artistic nature; artistic production has become stagnant, "the means of art had turned stale and were exhausted by history" (*DF* 144) and, subsequently, the existing conventions and musical tools only allow parody of existing music. The third hurdle relates to the social function of art; bourgeois art is irresponsible because it is illusion, and Leverkühn questions "whether, given the current state of our consciousness, our comprehension, and our sense of truth, the game is still permissible, still intellectually possible, can still be taken seriously; whether the work as such, as a self-sufficient and harmonically self-contained structure, still stands in a legitimate relation to our problematical social condition, with its total insecurity and lack of harmony" (*DF* 192). Zeitblom is frightened by his friend's thoughts, but not only, as he suggests, because it could impede and undermine Leverkühn's artistic existence. Mann unmasks Zeitblom's existence devoted to aestheticism through Leverkühn's following comment: "The work! It's a sham, something the bourgeoisie wants to believe still exists" (*DF* 192).

As in Mann's earlier works, such as "Little Herr Friedemann," Wagner's music appears in *Doctor Faustus* as the epitome of art as illusion. When Leverkühn condemns traditional music as "copulation with the mob, as thrown kisses and posturing at galas, as a bellows for emotional surges" (*DF* 144), he renounces the manner by which Wagner's operatic world communicates with its audience. Leverkühn abhors performance and representation; he does not desire to reach a contemporary audience with his esoteric music. His early music is meant to be as un-Wagnerian and as un-German as possible, "not even remotely akin to that mythic pathos and demonic natural world" (*DF* 174). Full of mocking, persiflage, and parody, his first compositions are based on texts by Dante Alighieri, William Shakespeare's *Love's Labor's Lost* and *The Tempest*, and poetry by William Blake, John Keats, and Paul Verlaine. Leverkühn's reclusiveness, counterbalanced by his interest in foreign texts, represents the two opposing sides of German culture. He embodies "the old-fashioned German provincialism of Kaisersaschern, and an explicit cosmopolitanism . . . an eccentric reticence to deal with the world and an inner need for the wide world beyond" (*DF* 175). Paradoxically, Leverkühn's openness to the world attests to both his German cosmopolitanism as well as his German inwardness. In his selection of works from Verlaine, whose poetry stood under the influence of German romanticism, Leverkühn focuses on themes of demonic and evil nature, of decadence and death. Thus his attempt to break out of German traditions into Western European cultures is halfhearted at times, and is later forsaken when he turns to German texts, in particular the chapbook of Faust.

In his depiction of Leverkühn's artistic development and his compositions, Mann was assisted by Theodor W. Adorno, another German émigré living in Southern California. From Adorno, Mann had learned that the emancipation of tonal music from traditional forms and musical organizations had reached its highest point with Beethoven's late compositions, that all creative possibilities had been explored and exhausted. In his 1948 book, *Philosophy of Modern Music*, which Mann knew prior to its publication, Adorno explains how this stagnation was overcome by Arnold Schönberg (1874–1951). Schönberg saw the solution in rejecting the illusionary character of bourgeois works of art, an idea Mann transfers to Adrian Leverkühn when the latter makes the point that the self-contained work is no longer permissible. Schönberg's artistic career, divided by Adorno in three phases, starts out with the imitation of tradition, followed by parody of tradition, and third, the breakthrough to atonal, twelve-tone music. The last two phases also define Leverkühn's artistic development.

Mann's most ambitious and daring artist figure is not satisfied with his first compositions. In his quest for innovative modes of expression, Leverkühn envisions a new music with a strict organization, because bourgeois artistic freedom "has begun to coat talent like a mildew and is showing signs of sterility" (*DF* 203). Intrigued by the musical system of Johann Conrad Beissel (1691–1768) and his primitive laws of music, in which mathematics and magic, the demonic and order, form a symbiotic unity like the magic square in Albrecht Dürer's "Melancholia," Leverkühn pursues a music subordinated to "law, rule, coercion, system" (*DF* 203). The music he subsequently develops is based on Schönberg's dodecaphony. It is a music built on a set row of notes that the composer must use to create his own variations and derivatives. The subordination of his artistic free will and affirmation of creative freedom exist simultaneously. This music is totalitarian and free, regressive and progressive. Leverkühn intends to dismantle the illusion of bourgeois art. As he points out to Zeitblom, his innovative music no longer strives for harmony and melody, but the audience will instead hear the systematic order, its underlying laws and the regularity to which the composition adheres and "the perception of it would provide an unknown aesthetic satisfaction" (*DF* 206).

Breaking through conventions and taking creativity to new heights comes at a high price in *Doctor Faustus*. Occasionally Leverkühn suffers from severe headaches; and despite his contempt for the world and unwavering commitment to his art, he sometimes yearns for love and human companionship. However, his greatest sacrifice to art is his life and the sale of his soul, his pact with the devil, who in exchange promises innovative compositions for a remaining life span of twenty-four years. In the modern, twentieth-century world, the devil of the old

Faust legend is an anachronistic figure. Thus Mann has his Faust character contract syphilis. In lieu of the traditional devil figure, the inspiring disease will bring "upliftings and illuminations, experiences of release and unshackling" (*DF* 246), artistic triumph interrupted by periods of pain. All this the devil promises Leverkühn during their conversation in Palestrina, Italy. That this conversation, symbolic of the traditional sealing of the pact in Faust myths, is Leverkühn's delusion, becomes apparent when his apparition of the devil changes first to his old teacher Schleppfuss, and then to a music critic whom Mann modeled on Adorno. In return for the composer's soul, the devil offers Leverkühn music freed from the shackles of prudence and reason, music that will go beyond the conventional, self-contained, illusionary work that allows identification: "Only what is not fictitious, not a game, is still permissible—the unfeigned and untransfigured expression of suffering in its real moment" (*DF* 256). The devil's pledge culminates in the promise of artistic breakthrough: "You will lead, you will set the march for the future, lads will swear by your name. . . . It is not merely that you will break through the laming difficulties of the age—you will break through the age itself, the cultural epoch, which is to say, the epoch of this culture and its cult, and dare a barbarism" (*DF* 258). With hindsight we subsequently realize that Leverkühn's music does not reach the popularity his diabolic guest envisions; it will however have barbaric, expressive elements and go beyond conventional music.

With his bold compositions written after his stay in Palestrina, Leverkühn gains a reputation as an avant-garde, esoteric composer. His *Cosmic Symphony*, *Gesta Romanorum*, and *Apocalipsis cum figuris* are recognized by a small circle of music lovers as pacesetting contemporary creations. His intellectual organization of notes allows him to break the boundaries of traditional musical forms and genres; he succeeds in turning against "the aesthetic kind of theater that had been part of the bourgeois circle of life." With uneasiness, Zeitblom observes that in Leverkühn's work "the dramatic form was being superseded by the epic, music drama being transformed into oratorio, opera drama into opera cantata" (*DF* 391). Zeitblom clings to art as illusion and play, yet opens up to his friend's first major, highly paradoxical work, *Apocalipsis cum figuris*, of which Mann's novel gives a fascinating account. It consists of simple choruses juxtaposed with refined polyphonic songs, primitive instruments, and highly sophisticated orchestral music, thus embracing bloody barbarism and bloodless intellectuality (*DF* 393). Wagnerian extensive cadences, beguiling, mesmerizing melodies luring listeners into a world of love and death, stand in contrast to Leverkühn's extensive use of glissandi, sliding tones that are the very first primitive musical expressions of mankind. These glissandi place the work into a world of antihumanistic, anticultural, even demonic forces; they herald the return to a barbaric world—one which the Kridwiss circle, at the time that Leverkühn composes the work, embraces profusely in their imagination. While this work is life-negating by invoking an era of barbarism and apocalyptic pandemonium, Zeitblom understands it as a work full of longings for a soul. Hellish laughter, presented through a mayhem of cacophonous sounds, is counterbalanced by a children's chorus, dissonant but of enrapturing quality. Harmony is used to represent the infernal, the apocalyptic; dissonance conveys the pious. The chorus takes on the traditional function of the orchestra, and vice versa. What intrigues Zeitblom most about this disturbing work is the "mystery of identity" (*DF* 397). Leverkühn uses the same notes and sequences for the world of the destructive-demonic that he uses to portray the angels. This paradoxical correspondence fuses good and evil. Zeitblom recognizes the work as a story of sin and redemption. Because of his emotional reaction to it and his reception of the work as a daring, self-reflective paragon of bourgeois art, Mann raises doubts as to whether Leverkühn has achieved the artistic breakthrough for which he has sold his soul.

Leverkühn's last and most ambitious work, *The Lamentations of Doctor Faustus*, composed between 1927 and 1930 and presented vividly by Mann's artistry with words and paradoxical phrases, is a far cry from Wagner's melodic, seductive music. The whole composition is based on twelve-tone music and Leverkühn's "strictest work, a work of utmost calculation . . . simultaneously purely expressive" (*DF* 512). The words "For I die as both a wicked and good Christian" (*DF* 511) are the central theme of the cantata. In contrast to the mathematical, rigid structure of the work and its cold intellectuality and mechanical quality stand highly emotional elements—the lamentations, the refusal to be saved, the rejection of reconciliation and the excruciating hopelessness that redemption is possible. *The Lamentations of Doctor Faustus* is Leverkühn's most self-critical work. In it he condemns himself because he has taken his artistic freedom too far. It is a testimony to his utmost despair that he will descend into hell, but also to his speculation for redemption and mercy. With its hovering between despair and transcendence of despair, between the justification for condemnation and the hope for salvation, this highly ambivalent final opus ends.

The Lamentations of Doctor Faustus is a highly expressive work with primitive elements—the innovative work that the devil had promised Leverkühn. Zeitblom assumes that Leverkühn has reached the breakthrough with this composition, which, in terms of the Faustian dimension of the novel, would imply Leverkühn's certain condemnation. Yet Zeitblom's judgments cannot always be trusted. *The Lamentations of Doctor Faustus*, intended by Leverkühn to be the "revocation" (*DF* 514) of bourgeois-humanistic art, is a reversal of Ludwig van Beethoven's Ninth Symphony. Leverkühn's work begins rather than ends with a choral movement. As Beethoven's Ninth Symphony, a quintessential piece of bourgeois musical tradition, provides a reflected framework for the intended new artistic expression, this tradition is kept alive. Mann allows Zeitblom to resort to established aesthetic criteria to understand and interpret the cantata. Zeitblom correlates it to Beethoven's, as well as to Claudio Monteverdi's works, a subtle hint by Mann that Leverkühn's last composition is rooted in and meant to illustrate both the nationalistic and the cosmopolitan nature of Germanness. Zeitblom also comments on Leverkühn's use of the chapbook and the Bible, pivotal texts about condemnation and salvation in Western cultures. Intrinsic to the illusionary character of art, that Leverkühn attempts to overcome and for which he forswore life, love, and his soul, is its communication with the audience. However, with Zeitblom's reactions, Mann points out that Leverkühn's work partakes in the tradition of realistic, communicative art despite its atonality and anticonventional structure. It is music "liberated as language" (*DF* 512).

There is another, salient dimension to the work that makes us question its radical departure from the tradition it wants to take back. At the end of *The Lamentations of Doctor Faustus*, one group of instruments after another steps back, the last note is a slowly fading high G: "Then nothing more. Silence and night. But the tone, which is no more, for which, as it hangs there vibrating in the silence, only the soul still listens, and which was the dying note of sorrow— is no longer that, its meaning changes, it stands as a light in the night" (*DF* 515). The cantata ends with a high G, a symbol for a plea for grace. Analogous to Beethoven's Ninth Symphony, which glides into the simple melody of joy after the fortissimo development of the fourth movement, Leverkühn's *Lamentations of Doctor Faustus* ends on a simple, positive note. Leverkühn has not overcome tradition: "Simultaneous mockery and glorification of something fundamental, a painful, ironic remembrance of tonality, of the tempered scale, of traditional music itself" (*DF* 194), characteristic of his early works, are also present at the very end of his creative life. The end of bourgeois art has not, in fact, come. Ironically, Leverkühn, the most severe critic of the bourgeois artist and art in Mann's novel, becomes its (albeit reluctant) preserver.

Mann's intoxicated artist figure responds to the crisis of creative sterility with irresponsible, cerebral music that scoffs at humanity. Paralleling Leverkühn's coldness and his aesthetic play with barbaric themes is Germany's descent into inhuman, barbaric politics. Leverkühn's compositions capture the atmosphere of Germany's recent past, present, and near future. The *Cosmic Symphony*, composed before the beginning of the First World War while the burghers in the salons of Munich, tired of their stagnant bourgeois world evoke a new world of antihumanism to amuse themselves, is a piece full of mockery and nihilism. *Apocalipsis cum figuris* and *The Lamentations of Doctor Faustus* echo the barbarism and guilt of the time. This parallelism highlights both the dangerous social and political implications of aestheticism as well as the destructive temptations of bourgeois art—and Mann's accusations against the German bourgeoisie, its artists, and himself. Does this mean that the novel advocates the end of bourgeois art? It would seem so when Leverkühn, aware of his own social irresponsibility, already imagines during the First World War an art that is no longer "ersatz religion" (*DF* 339), but instead an art that will be a "servant of a community," "art without suffering, psychologically healthy, that confides without solemnity, that trusts without sorrow, an art that is on a first-name basis with humanity" (*DF* 339). In his final speech Leverkühn accuses himself of social indifference and the failure "prudently to act that among men such order be established that may again prepare lively soil and honest accommodation for the beautiful work" (*DF* 524). What is so striking about Mann's inclusion of this sentence is that it implies a resistance to the elimination of the "beautiful," the aesthetic work. Rather Mann suggests here the establishment of a society that can appreciate bourgeois art while being committed to society. Thus, in the end, a utopian hope is revealed in what appeared, on the surface, to be an extremely pessimistic, dark novel.

Mann reclaims the aesthetic work by accentuating that the problem of Germany's historical and political calamity is not art itself, but the producers and consumer of art: Leverkühn and the German educated burghers like Zeitblom who favor an artistic orientation over political and social engagement, and look upon reality with arrogance and apathy. Mann himself was far from renouncing aesthetic pleasures. Diary entries both during and shortly after the period in which he wrote *Doctor Faustus* reveal that he himself listened passionately to Wagner's operas (see, for example, entries from 14 September 1944, 29 November 1944, and 22 February 1948), whereas his composer Leverkühn renounced them. It is part of the proliferation of meaning that *Doctor Faustus* can be understood as Mann's (albeit reluctant and half-hearted) homage to Wagner's grand aesthetic constructs. Amongst the numerous allusions to Wagner's operas is Zeitblom's (and Mann's) understanding of Germany's downfall as "twilight of the gods" (*DF* 185).[18] Like Wagner's bygone Germanic world, Mann's modern German world is a site of love and death, sin and a pledge for redemption. Despite the use of montage and his play with fiction and reality to break down the illusionary character of *Doctor Faustus*, and despite the strong criticism of aestheticism and self-accusations, the novel also attests to Mann's adherence to aestheticism. This ambivalence is reflected in the depiction of his asocial artist, Leverkühn, who, while deserving condemnation, is nonetheless worthy of love.

A Love Story

To suggest that *Doctor Faustus* is also a love story might at first seem perplexing, as the apparent absence of love and the diabolic intoxication of both the artist and Germany are central themes of the novel. Mann's analogy between Leverkühn and Germany, between a self-centered, sarcastic artist, characterized by "coldness" (*DF* 8),[19] and a nation catering to barbarism and human destruction, hinges on this absence of love. The Germany of the Nazi era in *Doctor Faustus* is neither capable nor worthy of love, unlike Leverkühn, who is loved as well as being capable of love. Thus Mann disrupts Leverkühn's function as a symbol for Germany. Neither Zeitblom's chronicles nor Mann's novel *Doctor Faustus* itself would exist without love for this cold artist. In *The Story of a Novel,* Mann confessed that he had never loved a fictional character as much as Adrian Leverkühn, with the possible exception of Hanno Buddenbrook, that he was "infatuated with his 'coldness,' his remoteness from life, his lack of 'soul'" (*SN* 89). This love is transferred to Zeitblom, who confesses that his diligent work on his friend's biography is a labor of love. Zeitblom's relationship to Leverkühn represents the fascination of the German burgher, as well as Mann's own fascination with the aesthetically oriented, great artist who is willing to devote his life and lose his soul to art, and whose aloofness and hubris he accepts and, indeed, expects.

Behind Zeitblom's love for the asocial artist and his esoteric art lies an intensity of emotion and jealousy that suggests another "radical confession" (*SN* 154), namely that of homosexual love. By writing about these sublimated forbidden desires, Mann creates a further link with his narrator. Zeitblom's secret sexual identity is alluded to early in the text. He married his wife Helene not out of love, but out of "a need for order in my life and a desire to conform to ethical standards" (*DF* 12). Although she is his sole companion in his reclusive life and his love for her cannot be doubted, Zeitblom devotes only a few lines to her existence—mainly to praise her qualities as housewife and cook. Zeitblom's ignoring her presence is as striking as his reluctance to write about the non-heterosexual love of others for Leverkühn. Zeitblom is jealous of Rüdiger Schildknapp and Rudi Schwerdtfeger, who spend extended periods of time with Leverkühn abroad; furthermore, both are allowed to address Leverkühn with "du," the familiar, personal form of "you," a closeness Zeitblom, Leverkühn's most loyal friend, was never privileged to share.[20] Zeitblom, who otherwise likes to speculate about episodes in Leverkühn's life he himself had not witnessed —for example Leverkühn's encounter with the prostitute Hetera Esmeralda— provides very little information about Leverkühn's homosexual relationship with Rudi Schwerdtfeger. The gaps in Zeitblom's narrative are telling; he unmasks his own repressions by not writing about nontraditional sexuality. Unlike earlier characters with stigmatized desires such as Aschenbach and Mut, Zeitbloms's love remains discreet and reserved, like that of Mann himself.

Because arrogance and coldness are a predisposition of artistic greatness, the only provision of the pact seems to suit Leverkühn's character perfectly: "Love is forbidden you insofar as it warms. Your life shall be cold—hence you may love no human being" (*DF* 264). But Mann's Faust figure does not always abide by the condition of the pact. His love for Schwerdtfeger, and later his love for his young nephew Nepomuk, is warm—thus both must die. Repeatedly Leverkühn reaches out to others, thus he remains the true son of Kaisersaschern who is diabolic and inward-oriented as well as cosmopolitan and life-embracing. When Leverkühn visits the prostitute Hetaera Esmeralda, to intentionally contract syphilis and so to trigger the chemical changes that result in artistic intoxication, *Doctor Faustus* breaks down the antagonism between love and art. Parallel to the ambivalence of Leverkühn's compositions, the sexual encounter is the "dialectical unity of good and evil" (*DF* 114); "love and poison" become a "mythological unity" (*DF* 165) in which Leverkühn selfishly satisfies sexual desires and artistic ambitions yet also gives love to the prostitute. She reciprocates by displaying compassion and love when she warns him of her infected body. Four years after his encounter with Hetaera Esmeralda in Pressburg, Leverkühn explains to Zeitblom that every sensual act implies tenderness and love. Because Leverkühn, who tends to be sarcastic and introverted, now speaks openly and honestly about himself and confesses his love, we cannot doubt his words. Zeitblom notably avoids looking directly at Leverkühn. He does not want to expose his own love for the artist.

Leverkühn's love for Hetaera Esmeralda never dwindles; encoded in his music is the sequence of notes H-E-A-E-Es (the note H is equivalent to B in English), a reference to the absent beloved. Hetaera Esmeralda returns in the novel as the enigmatic Frau von Tolna, whose ring he wears. By now a woman of affluence, she supports the artist who once showed her love in order to help him gain international recognition, and allows him to stay at her country estate during her absence. This agreement, under which direct contact is prevented, thereby avoiding the "warm" love that the pact forbids, is a protection for Esmeralda/Frau von Tolna. Their relationship is, as Mann had commented, "a means of circumventing the devil's proscription of love, commandment of coldness"

(*Letters* 494). This love is a narrative element that allows Mann to open up the possibility of salvation for his artist. A Hungarian musicologist explains to Leverkühn that someone guided his attention to Leverkühn's music, someone "from a sphere higher than academia, from the sphere of love and faith, in a word, by the eternal feminine" (*DF* 410). With these words Mann alludes to the final two verses of Goethe's *Faust*, "The Eternal-Feminine / Draws us on high."[21] Goethe's Faust preys on Gretchen's love for him, causes her insanity and the death of their child, as well as that of her brother. Nonetheless, he is worthy of redemption. Although Mann has repeatedly made the point that his Faust narrative is not based on Goethe's *Faust*,[22] Frau von Tolna's love for Leverkühn indisputably connects Mann's *Doctor Faustus* to Goethe's drama. Goethe's Faust is saved in the end because of a woman's love. So, too, might Mann's Faust be, but not only due to Esmeralda's/Frau von Tolna's love. In a remarkable departure from literary tradition based on a heterosexual paradigm, it is a man's unconventional, unfaltering love, that of Zeitblom for Leverkühn, that here suggests that the demonic musician also deserves redemption.[23]

When Leverkühn gives his final speech about his sins and guilt, he imitates the Faust of the chapbook, whose descent into hell is certain. But Goethe's *Faust* is called upon one more time in *Doctor Faustus* to undermine any certainty. In Goethe's drama, the choir of angels proclaims: "Whoever strives in ceaseless toil, / Him we may grant redemption."[24] Adrian Leverkühn admits that he has been a sinner and "a votary of Devilish concupiscence, yet notwithstanding did diligently and steadfastly apply [himself] as a worker, never roistering" (*DF* 525). Can a bourgeois work ethic, which the demonic artist shares with Mann himself, redeem Leverkühn? Mann's novel oscillates between the chapbook and Goethe's *Faust*, between condemnation and redemption at the end. To add to the ambiguity, Mann brings into play a less obvious literary source. Toward the end of his speech, Leverkühn speculates that his sinful life, although not deserving forgiveness, must be a "provocation for eternal goodness" (*DF* 526). In the epilogue of Shakespeare's comedy *The Tempest*, Prospero asks for indulgence:

> And my ending is despair
> Unless I be reliev'd by prayer,
> Which pierces so that it assaults
> Mercy itself, and frees all faults.

With his reference to Shakespeare, Mann leaves the strictly German, provincial world of the Faust myth and evokes Leverkühn's cosmopolitanism, his openness to the world that deserves salvation. Yet this is not the final word on Leverkühn's fate. Upon the conclusion of his deliberations, Leverkühn opens his arms, a reference to the sufferings of Christ, and "suddenly, as if pushed" (*DF* 527), he falls from his piano stool onto the floor. Has the devil claimed his soul after twenty-four years, or will grace save him? Is Adrian Leverkühn the artist who takes the sins of his society upon himself, or is he the diabolic artist who ends up in hell? With Zeitblom's prayer for mercy for Adrian Leverkühn, as well as Germany, the novel ends. Perhaps the humanist Zeitblom, quite familiar with Shakespeare's comedy, remembers Prospero's request for prayer and, at the same time, Mann sends us a signal that German culture has the potential to resurrect its promise of cosmopolitanism.[25] The reader is left with a multitude of voices and a polyphonic novel that makes neither salvation nor condemnation a certainty.[26]

CHAPTER 12

The Holy Sinner, The Black Swan, and Confessions of Felix Krull, Confidence Man

The Holy Sinner

Mann began his next work of fiction, *Der Erwählte* (*The Holy Sinner*), in January 1948. The narrative is based on the same legend from the medieval collection of stories, *Gesta Romanorum*, used by Leverkühn in *Doctor Faustus* as the basis of an opera for marionettes. It is, as Zeitblom remarks, an "exuberantly sinful, simple and grace-filled story" (*DF* 336) about forbidden, stigmatized love. Mann's adaptation tells of the incest of aristocratic twins, Wiligis and Sibylla, which results in the birth of a son who is cast out upon the sea in a cask. Also contained in the cask is an ivory tablet that reveals his noble and sinful origins. The infant is rescued, educated in a monastery, and given the name Grigorss. Throughout his childhood, Grigorss is treated as an outsider by his peers. When the abbot reveals the content of the tablet to his intelligent and handsome student, Grigorss decides to become a knight, to search for his parents, and atone for their guilt. Providence has it that his ship drifts to the shores of his homeland and that he marries Sibylla. The narrative suggests that both mother and son withhold their intuitive knowledge of their blood relationship and thus become guilty of incest. When Sibylla finds the tablet, their relationship ends. As penitence for their illicit love, Grigorss maroons himself for seventeen years on a rock surrounded by rough waters and exposed to the elements. During this time, his body is transformed into a hedgehog-like creature. During the same time, Sibylla becomes an altruistic woman and serves the community with humility. Miraculously, Grigorss regains his human shape after a vision has brought officials from the Vatican to him. Elevated to Pope Gregorius, he absolves his penitent mother and wife, who had undertaken a pilgrimage to Rome, from her sins and serves as a great pope for the rest of his life. In sum, *The Holy Sinner* is a fairy tale–like story in which the moral and social outcast finds a socially responsible existence. It thus provides a counterpoint to Mann's previous novel, *Doctor Faustus*.

In *Death in Venice*, Aschenbach becomes famous with works Mann himself never finished. Now Mann follows in the footsteps of Leverkühn with his version of a medieval legend. In addition to the *Gesta Romanorum*, Hartmann von Aue's *Gregorius*, Wolfram's *Parsifal*, Gottfried von Strassburg's *Tristan*, Wagner's mythological worlds, and the life of Jesus Christ provide the main sources for Mann's variation.[1] Moreover, Mann resorts to his own works for sources; stigmatized desire and incest, the outsider motif, and a reference to mythical existence in *Joseph and His Brothers* are among the many allusions to his own work. His narrator, the Irish monk Clemens, comments that "the life of man follows well-tried patterns" (*HS* 16). The extensive integration of direct and indirect quotations into *The Holy Sinner* illustrates Mann's artistic gift of borrowing from various texts and traditions to create what could be called a symphonic work of art of Western culture. Mann himself thought of *The Holy Sinner* as the last and final literary evocation of an old myth and legend, as a farewell to the culture that had shaped his world and Western civilization (*GW 11* 691). Alternatively, one can understand Mann's text as a revival of some central texts of Western civilization, which is itself on the brink of self-destruction, and as a lighthearted play with its narratives and traditions after his darker, more critical exploration of them in *Doctor Faustus*.

Given Mann's unwarranted, yet lingering, reputation as a traditional, realistic writer, it must be stressed that by employing intertextuality and self-referentiality in *The Holy Sinner*, Mann challenged traditional notions of authorship and authority, and therefore created a postmodern text before postmodernism became a literary fashion. Its intertextual character makes *The Holy Sinner* overtly a fictional text that rejects the illusionary character of art and escape into aestheticism, and that reminds us of Leverkühn's notion in *Doctor Faustus*, that the illusionary character of the bourgeois work of art is no longer permissible. In order to destroy this illusion, Mann resorts to another postmodern narrative component: the self-reflective text. When all the church bells of Rome are ringing at the beginning, the text poses the question: "Who is ringing the bells?" It is "the spirit of story-telling" (*HS* 8). This spirit invents and controls the course of the story and the fate of individual characters. To underscore its authority, Mann makes it, with a humorous undertone, responsible for the death of Wiligis. Because Mann gives this spirit sole decision over life and death, guilt and grace, his version of the Gregorius legend steps decisively away from the religious legend. No longer is it divine order and mercy—God's might—that decides human fate, but the power of creativity. In other words, Mann juxtaposes the creativity of the modern, secular world with the religious authority of the Middle Ages to which his characters submit themselves. Unquestionably, Mann pokes fun at the authority of religion. Yet the authority of creativity is not binding. Creativity is a playful force that can challenge orientations but does not claim to become a substitute for religion.

The spirit of storytelling, and, ergo, creativity, is embodied in the narrator, Clemens, who writes the story while residing in St. Gall, Switzerland, at some unspecified time. That he exists outside time and is a product of the imagination like the ringing church bells, becomes obvious in his language. Mann enhances his German text with words from Latin, Old High German, Old English, and Old French, and uses archaic as well as modern phrases to erase the boundaries of place and time. The story contains a number of amusing discrepancies and anachronisms. For example, Grigorss could have neither read a book nor played soccer in the Middle Ages. His mother/wife Sibylla lives in the era of chivalry and *Minne* (courtly love) of the Middle Ages; the historical Gregory the Great was Pope in Rome from 590 to 604 A.D. Mann's thorough, conscientious striving for authenticity, exhibited in his detailed research about Egypt and its culture for the *Joseph* tetralogy, is replaced in *The Holy Sinner* by his obvious resistance to historical accuracy in order to remind his readers of the fictionality of the text.

Its playful character has brought about diverse, contradictory reactions among critics. *The Holy Sinner* has been understood as a humorous rendering of literary patterns and myths, a "language game of grandiose dimensions,"[2] as Mann's "most lucid, most amusing text,"[3] and, in contrast, as "a very serious religious book."[4] All these interpretations can be substantiated by the text. As Mann's play with various literary sources, various languages, and the self-referential elements suggests, it is a humorous, lighthearted story, spiked with elements of parody and self-parody, and, furthermore, an antidote to the Faust novel. Mann himself referred to the narrative as a "playful stylistic novel" (*GW 11* 691). However, in spite of all the jokes and travesties, it has serious underpinnings, because Mann attempted to conserve the religious core of the legend, its Christianity and the idea of sin and mercy. Its serious dimension unfolds with Mann's characterization of the sinners. Here he returns to motifs from his early narratives. Both of Grigorss's parents, Wiligis and Sibylla, bear a scar on their forehead from chicken pox. These markings remind us of the light-blue, pulsating vein on Gabriele Klöterjahn's forehead in *Tristan.* Just as the twins Siegmund and Sieglinde Aarenhold in "The Blood of the Walsungs," the twins Wiligis and Sibylla in *The Holy Sinner* feel that nobody is equal to them. Wiligis admits: "Pride . . . was our sin, and that in all the world we would hear of no one else but just of us very special children" (*HS* 46). This narcissistic love isolates them from the world and drives them to incest. After the death of Wiligis, Sibylla clings to this same self-centered love. To atone for her incest, Sibylla has sworn to chastity; her refusal to marry an aristocrat leads to war, and to the gradual political and economic decline of her principality and the prolonged suffering of her subjects. Narcissism is also Grigorss's sin. Extraordinarily handsome, intelligent, with the scar of stigmatized desire on his forehead, a mark that his mother fails to recognize, he gives in to the forces of antireason when he marries her. Thus, as in *Death in Venice*, the Dionysian wins over the Apollonian. However, this victory is short-lived. The marriage ends. In Grigorss's and his mother's/wife's minds—and probably also in the minds of many of Mann's readers—their incestuous behavior is the ultimate sin against human laws and Christian morality, since both are, albeit initially subconsciously, aware of their blood relationship.[5]

However, the narrative is far from unequivocal when it comes to passing moral judgment on stigmatized sexuality. In a striking deviation from Hartmann von Aue's *Gregorius*, the twins' incest in Mann's version does not start out as a rape, but as a consensual attraction and seduction. Subsequently, its sinfulness and its certain condemnation in the medieval legend are reduced. Throughout the narrative, Clemens, whose acknowledgment of papal authority is undermined by his resistance to strict doctrine, voices his sympathy for the sinners. He knows that, according to Christian standards, their incestuous behavior should be unpardonable. But when he gives more weight to Wiligis's killing of a dog on the first night of his incest with his sister than to the incestuous behavior itself, he indicates tolerance. Mann tells us with humor that a dog is the only victim of forbidden desires. The underlying notion that the fulfillment of these individual desires generally should be acceptable as long as others are not harmed or negatively impacted, belongs to its serious tone and reveals a central aspect of *The Holy Sinner*: Mann's rebellion against moral rigidity.

Certainly *The Holy Sinner* does not advocate incest. Rather the story challenges the authority of moral taboos and their enslavement of the bourgeois world and Western civilization. That incest itself is not the target of Mann's criticism becomes apparent in light of the fact that it is presented as the result of a deeper sin: self-love and indifference to society. Grigorss, the "Chosen One" as the original German title refers to him, is able to shed both of these when he is elevated to the papal throne. He becomes the enlightened Pope Gregorius and ideal leader in the service of life, the embodiment of tolerance and forgiveness. Narcissism gives way to empathy and selfless devotion to the community. In this regard, *The Holy Sinner* can be read as a postwar text with an underlying optimistic tenor. Out of a world governed by atavistic forces rises a humane world governed by intellect. Yet, is it a "profoundly optimistic novel"?[6] Pope Gregorius's devotion to life is best described as *agape*, a brotherly, unselfish love for life. This compassionate love stands between cold intellect and life, but it cannot eradicate the abyss between these two spheres. Gregorius's life is bound to celibacy and the erasure of individual desires; it must remain a life without intimate love. What have been presented as irreconcilable, antagonistic forces throughout Mann's œuvre, remain so even in a humorous story like *The Holy Sinner*.

The autobiographical elements within *The Holy Sinner* reveal it to be a story about self-denial. Like previous texts, it too contains Mann's secret confession of his homosexual desires. With the relationship between Sibylla and Grigorss, Mann presents yet another variation of an older woman's infatuation for a young man. Mann creates in his writing a forbidden liaison that he denied himself when Grigorss and Sibylla commit incest. Their self-imposed punishment for the transgression of moral law lies in their renunciation of their elevated social status and privileged existence. Because Mann's repression of his own homosexual desires was always interrelated to his fears of losing his bourgeois recognition and existence, a price too high for him to pay, their fate serves as a warning to Mann not to heed to his own passions. At the same time, the story voices resistance against moral taboos with its appeal for tolerance.

In his lecture "Meine Zeit" ("My Time"), presented in Chicago in 1950 while Mann was working on *The Holy Sinner*, Mann characterized his life as one of "guilt, indebtedness, guiltiness" in reference to his aloofness as artist; thus he is tortured by Christian self-doubts and self-criticism, remnants of a protestant-bourgeois upbringing. His desire for "making amends, cleansing and justification" (*E 6* 160) also has Christian roots. In *The Holy Sinner*, Mann confesses to his guilt of narcissism. But the narrative should not be mistaken for Mann's religious confession or as testimony to an old man's conversion from a secular, often nihilistic stance to Christian credo; the faith and prayers of his monk, like Zeitblom in *Doctor Faustus* a simple and somewhat frightened character, are not Mann's own. Grigorss's penitence and subsequent turn toward the social realm are also not Mann's. As grace and redemption are given to the sinners by the spirit of story telling, ergo the realm of art and aestheticism, Mann implicitly expresses his hope to redeem himself through his art. Mann's repentance is his constant striving for literary greatness that he pursues with unrelenting diligence, a striving that had also characterized Adrian Leverkühn and might have brought him redemption.

The Black Swan

Mann reacted in April 1951 to a mixed review of *The Holy Sinner* with the following words, written in his diary: "Correct its characterization as a late work, sum, something absolutely final, most extreme after which nothing more can come" (*TB 1951–1952* 43). But he did continue. Mann began writing his last story *Die Betrogene* (*The Black Swan*) in Pacific Palisades in May 1952 and finished it, despite being distracted by occasional illness and depression, in Zurich, Switzerland, in March 1953. Probably anticipating critical comments, he called it a "problematic product" (*GW 11* 529) and an "experiment" (*GW 11* 530). Initially, his skeptical assessment was shared by many of his readers. Since the 1980s, and deservedly so, Mann's last completed piece of short fiction and "beyond doubt, [his] most often and most persistently misunderstood work,"[7] has gained noticeably in reputation and scholarly interest.[8]

With *The Black Swan*, Mann takes us back in time. Some years after the First World War, the central character, Rosalie von Tümmler, a fifty-year-old Rhenish widow, falls passionately in love with Ken Keaton, a young American war veteran and the English tutor of her son Eduard. During an excursion to a castle, she declares her love to him. Their plan to pursue an intimate tryst within the next twenty-four hours is shattered when Rosalie hemorrhages a few hours after the excursion. She is diagnosed with terminal cancer and dies a few weeks later. According to Mann's diary, the conception of this narrative goes back to an anecdote told by Katia Mann in April 1952. An older aristocratic woman in Munich falls head over heels in love with her son's private tutor. This unexpected passion brings back what she perceives as her menstruation and an overall feeling of rejuvenation. Tragically, this alleged return to biological womanhood turns out to be a result of cancer of her reproductive organs. Intrigued by this story, Mann speculated how it could end: "death or suicide due to deepest insult by nature or renunciation and the peace of the grave" (*TB 1951–1952* 198–99). His rendering of the story will conclude with his protagonist's conciliation with nature and the peace of death.

Katia Mann's anecdote provided the basic plot for her husband's story, a "story of a deception, of a bitter trick by nature, suffered by a good child of nature" (*GW 11* 529), as Mann himself described *The Black Swan*. But this anecdote certainly would have been of no interest to him had it not had the potential to complement and reflect upon his other works, to be one of his "postludes" (*Br 3* 306), a self-reflective text that presents previous themes and motifs in a different, mostly diametrically opposed light. Mann returns to the biblical realm of the *Joseph* tetralogy when Rosalie von Tümmler compares herself to the biblical figure Sarah from the Old Testament, who finally becomes pregnant after years of infertility. The themes of desire, love, and death had been at the core of *The Transposed Heads*. As in *Disorder and Early Sorrow*, written nearly three decades earlier, Mann turns to the German upper middle class of the 1920s. But Mann also enters new and untested fictional territory. Rather than the more familiar Munich, the locality of Katia's anecdote and longtime residence of the Mann family, *The Black Swan* takes place in Düsseldorf, a city Mann had visited about twenty-five years earlier and knew only marginally. Obliging his usual need for details, briefly abandoned in *The Holy Sinner*, Mann consulted various local sources to achieve an authentic presentation of Düsseldorf and its surroundings. Additionally he made inquiries about ovarian and uterine cancer. The love of an older woman for a young man less than half her age, the focus on menstruation and menopause, and the detailed clinical description of cancerous female reproductive organs were taboo topics in literature (and German society) in the 1950s, and certainly Mann provided an unexpected story and no easy reading for his audiences. Initially readers and critics alike were sensitive to or avoided discussion of these taboos, and even questioned the story's literary merits.[9]

What might have been more shocking than any of these is the taboo unrecognized for over three decades. Mann's diary entries reveal that the relationship between the older widow and the young, handsome American, Ken Keaton, serves as a mask for Mann's homosexual desires for the resident of Düsseldorf, Klaus Heuser, whom the author, then fifty-two years old like his fictional character Rosalie, had met on the North Sea island of Sylt in 1927 and had been in contact with until 1935. In September 1935, in reference to Heuser, Mann mentions his "passion, the last variation of a love which probably will not ignite again" (*TB 1935–1936* 173). In February 1942, another entry about his stigmatized love can be found: "It was there, I had it too, I will be able to tell myself that when I die" (*TB 1940–43* 396). Mann's choice of Düsseldorf as the setting for the story is a strong indication that Klaus Heuser was on his mind when he wrote *The Black Swan*. Also on his mind was another, more recent infatuation, that with the waiter Franz Westermeier, whom Mann had met in the Hotel Dolder in Zurich, Switzerland, in July 1950: "Once again this, once again love" (*TB 1949–50* 213).[10] Rosalie von Tümmler, whose desire for Keaton is explicitly compared in the narrative to that of a man in erotic pursuit of a young woman, can be interpreted as a fictional projection and encoding of Mann's secret homosexual inclinations and desires. As in previous works, a secret identity between the author and his female character exists in this story.

A second anecdote also stirred Mann's imagination as a potential vehicle for use in transferring homosexual to heterosexual desires. Nearly half a century earlier, Mann had considered fictionalizing an event in Goethe's life, the love of the aging Goethe for a young girl, Ulrike von Levetzow, in Marienbad. Presumably as a result of his own advancing years, Mann felt the need to counterbalance his fear of losing the ability to experience love and passion by keeping in mind

Goethe's late passion. Again, it was love not sanctioned by society so much as love in general that grabbed Mann's imagination. To what extent he was preoccupied with, and perhaps even fixated on passionate, forbidden love in old age, and to what extent he rejected this disruption of his detached, disciplined, and representational life, becomes apparent in two essays written before *The Black Swan*," "Die Erotik Michelangelos" (Michelangelo's eroticism), from 1950, and "Bernard Shaw," from 1951.

In "Die Erotik Michelangelos," Mann argues that the Italian artist, whose homosexuality he acknowledges, was a blessed person because even in old age he could love and sexually desire another human being, be it man or woman, without expecting love in return (*GW 9* 788). That Mann thinks highly of the artist's strength to enjoy his object of love visually and to aestheticize it, has autobiographical roots. The artist as voyeur remains within the boundaries of moral conventions. In view of the Westermeier episode, it becomes apparent that Mann is hiding behind the mask of Michelangelo in this essay in order to write about his own ability to simply admire the objects of his forbidden desire while refraining from physical contact. Mann reveled in his feelings of love for Franz Westermeier, but also rejected them. To his diary he divulges that, even if the opportunity had presented itself, he would never have been able to engage in an affair.[11] The statement that most strikingly reflects Mann's projection of himself onto Michelangelo comes at the end of the essay: "[Michelangelo] has always cursed love as evil, as affliction and sweet poison, while clinging to it like to no other. It was the foundation of his creativity, his inspiring genius, the motor, the glowing driving force of his super-masculine, nearly also superhuman works" (*GW 9* 792–93). The same holds true for most, if not all of Mann's writings. But there is also another, opposite driving force that Mann acknowledges in "Bernard Shaw."

In his obituary for George Bernard Shaw (1856–1950), Mann again mentions Goethe's passion for the young Ulrike von Levetzow, this time in order to contrast a state of passion and intoxication with an existence devoted to asceticism, aestheticism, a life of "coldness" dominated by "sobriety and salad-diet" (*GW 9* 802). Such an existence Mann finds embodied in the Irish writer.[12] While the Michelangelo essay had revealed Mann's sympathy for sensual passions and desires, his deliberations on Shaw emphasize his high esteem for a life of dispassionate rigor and resolute work ethic. Thus, with these two texts, Mann oscillates between affirmation and renunciation of forbidden love and artistic detachment, and so follows a pattern characteristic of his whole work: the establishment of opposing perspectives to come to terms with the paradoxes in his own life. Both perspectives reverberate in *The Black Swan*.

Rosalie von Tümmler follows in the mythical paths Mann set up for many of his characters. With earlier characters, such as Gustav Aschenbach, Mut, and Sibylla, she shares an infatuation for a younger man and the sudden impact of passion upon a rather monotonous existence.[13] Nonetheless, Rosalie stands out in a peculiar way. She is a housewife, characterized by "simplicity and cheerfulness" and "love for Nature" (*BS* 5), hence a rare protagonist in Mann's fictional world more frequently inhabited by alienated artists and burghers, intellectuals and dilettantes, full of contempt for life. She is one of those "dull" individuals frowned upon by artists like Tonio Kröger, and even by Mann himself, because, as Tonio Kröger put it so poignantly half a century earlier, "Emotion, warm, heartfelt emotion, is invariably commonplace and unserviceable" (*Stories* 155–56). Rosalie's "warm heart" (*BS* 5) and "simple-heartedness" (*BS* 15), coupled with a vivid imagination, lead her to some distorted views of reality. She claims that her husband died a hero's death at the beginning of the First World War, although in reality he was killed in an automobile accident. Regarding Keaton, who was wounded and lost a kidney, she says that he has "sacrificed one of his kidneys on the altar of his fatherland" (*BS* 73). With her name, a reference to her favorite flower, the rose, Mann underscores her "rosy" outlook on life, her sentimental revelry in nature, and obsession with love. Yet her assumed closeness to nature cannot prevent her from a false assessment of nature, culminating in misconceptions about her own body. Not surprisingly, Mann does not spare the good-natured Rosalie from his irony and a nonidealistic and nihilistic counterpoint. Outside Rosalie's perspective, nature and life are cruel, indifferent, and, above all, destructive. Mann's clinical description of cancerous organs and cells is devoid of any romanticism and awe, reminiscent of his detached accounts of Hanno's hideous, deadly disease in its final stages in *Buddenbrooks* and of Nepomuk Schneidewein's meningitis in *Doctor Faustus*.

The object of Rosalie's infatuation is Ken Keaton, a carefree American abroad in the 1920s, whose alliterated name recalls that of Hans Hansen. With Keaton having only one kidney, Mann also establishes a connection to Rudi Schwerdtfeger in *Doctor Faustus*. The intertextual link to the bisexual Schwerdtfeger is a coded signal for the homosexual subtext of *The Black Swan*. It is likely that Keaton, in addition to representing an object of Mann's forbidden desires, also voices the author's frustrations with American politics in the late 1940s and early 1950s. Keaton resents his homeland, its money- and success-oriented world, its obsessive churchgoing, its immense mediocrity, and, most importantly, its lack of historical atmosphere. Yet the intellectual validity of Keaton's critical stance toward his homeland is placed in a questionable light, as is Mann's sympathy for his character. Keaton's love of history and his enthusiasm for Europe are naive and superficial. Not only his "ingenuousness" (*BS* 72), but also his parasitic existence, make him an unlikable character. Like Schwerdtfeger, Keaton sponges off of others and exploits his charm. He is aware of the effect of his presence upon the older, middle-class women in Düsseldorf and has entertained a love affair with one of them before his encounter with Rosalie. *The Black Swan* is far from passing a moral judgment upon Keaton's sexual adventures. What Mann suggests with Keaton's intellectual deficits and parasitic life, however, is that the young handsome American is unworthy of Rosalie's unadulterated feelings. Towards the end of the narrative, Mann displays a blatant disregard for the American. Keaton is not given an opportunity to speak when Rosalie confesses her passion to him and suggests a rendezvous. When she is hospitalized and dying, Keaton has disappeared from the story. Not only does Mann insinuate that falling in love, rather than the fulfillment of love, is the pivotal and most treasured experience for Rosalie and for Mann himself. Both the overall negative portrayal of Keaton and the character's sudden unannounced exit from the story line throw doubts upon Rosalie's object of affection, and thus the affection itself.

In his presentation of Rosalie's love for Keaton, Mann creates an intricate web of themes and motifs with regard to love, life, and death. Repeatedly, life and death are interwoven. The few budding branches of an old oak tree grow from its diseased, decaying trunk. A little mound of excrement smells of musk, thus signaling the simultaneous presence of love and death. With Keaton's presence, sexual desire, the joy of love, and youthful life—as well as death—appear in Rosalie's life. Her assumed regained fertility makes her feel alive, yet this feeling is paradoxically attained through the final stages of a deadly carcinoma.[14] The thematic constellation of life, love, and death becomes prevalent when the narrative presents the excursion on the Rhine River, Wagner's mythical landscape, to the fictional Holterhof castle (based on Benrath castle near Düsseldorf). Rosalie's improvised song about the wind on the Rhine, while the boat carries her, her children, and Keaton toward their destination, refers back to the beginning of the story when she reveres the wind as an aid to pollination. The tune reflects the hope Rosalie has found in love and renewed fertility.[15] Mann counters Rosalie's life-affirming attitude with the presence of the bearded, red-haired boatman who takes the group up the river. He is associated with the devil and Charon, who leads his passengers to the underworld. The boatman from *Death in Venice* also comes to mind, in particular, since Rosalie talks about "taking off in a gondola" (*GW 8* 938).[16] More allusions to classical Greek, Roman, and Christian literature that evoke death follow. After leaving the boat, the party walks on a "damp footpath across a meadow" (*BS* 121), an allusion to the Asphodel Fields that Odysseus crosses on his way to the underworld.[17] Rather than the white swans, which in the

Ovidean tradition are the birds of love and which often symbolize illicit love,[18] black swans, messengers of death, appear. One of these majestic birds hisses angrily at Rosalie when she refuses to part with the bread intended for them. This change from reserved and arrogant, self-controlled elegance to instinctive, desire-driven, greedy aggression anticipates Rosalie's loss of countenance when she is alone in the castle with Keaton, declaring her love and deep longing for him. In the swan episode, the narrative furthermore hints at the identity of life and death with Christian symbolism. Jesus Christ breaks bread during the Last Supper before his death, which is to lead to eternal life. Rosalie eats some of the bread, which is symbolic of life yet intended for the black swans, the birds of love and death. A few weeks later Rosalie dies.

Mann's meshing of love and death continues with the description of the rococo Holterhof castle. Statues of Apollo and his muses, and Pan and his nymphs evoke a world of erotic liberty. Death reveals itself in the coldness that greets the guests upon their entering the castle. The dilapidated walls suggest decay and morbidity. Eros and thanatos are joined when the guide opens secret doors. Behind the first door is the torso of a man who "smiled down into space over his goat's beard, priapic and welcoming" (BS 130). Priapus is the god of male procreative powers. Behind another secret door is a passageway that leads into darkness and exhales an odor of mold and death. In this atmosphere of death, Rosalie confesses her love to the young American. Sitting on a sofa in an alcove, they are surrounded by a tapestry with "billing pairs of doves" (BS 132), signifying love. Besides the sofa stands a wooden statue of amour holding a torch, signifying death.[19]

In this "dead pleasure chamber," Rosalie rejects the sexual advances of Keaton: "Go away, stop it, you devil. I will be yours, but not in this mould" (BS 133). However, in addressing her beloved jokingly as "devil," Rosalie mocks the conventional moral perspective that, at that time, did not condone an intimate relationship between an older woman and a young man. Unknown to Rosalie, Keaton does indeed turn out to be a "devil." According to the doctor's medical diagnosis that an outside force has stimulated healthy cells to transform into carcinomatoid cells, he exerts a harmful influence. That a deadly end is looming is hinted at when Rosalie symbolically dies a Liebestod in the castle crypt. In allusion to Isolde's bending down to the body of her beloved before her own death in the final scene of Wagner's Tristan and Isolde, Rosalie embraces Keaton and nearly "would have sunk to the ground before him" (BS 132).

With the disclosure of Rosalie's incurable cancer just hours after this romantic scene in the castle and her forthcoming death, Mann prevents the transgression of bourgeois social and moral paradigms. This is not the first time this happens in Mann's fiction. Both *Death in Venice* and the Mut episode in the *Joseph in Egypt* deny their characters sexual fulfillment; on the other hand, *The Holy Sinner* does not shy away from portraying stigmatized desires. Does Mann take a conservative, even moral, position in *The Black Swan* when he kills off his character, thus robbing her of the opportunity to pursue her sexual "deviant" interests? The answer cannot be unequivocal in light of textual evidence from *The Black Swan* and autobiographical information. Mann's diary entries about his encounter with Franz Westermeier reveal his ambiguity toward a homosexual relationship: "Banal activity, aggressiveness, the experiment how far he would be willing does not belong to my life that demands secrecy. . . . Shrinking back from *a reality whose possibility of happiness would be highly doubtful" (TB 1949–1950* 214). Internalized bourgeois values, a realistic assessment that a stigmatized relationship is doomed to fail, and, above all, Mann's need to be respected and revered by his bourgeois readers, provide sufficient reasons for restraint on the personal as well as artistic level. The unfulfilled desire in *The Black Swan* echoes Mann's own self-denial and abstinence. Yet, typical of Mann's ambivalence throughout his life and career, he recognizes and submits himself to the social and moral entrapments of his bourgeois milieu while simultaneously escaping them. Rosalie's death signifies not merely the avoidance of a scandalous life and stigmatized sexuality. One of Mann's diary entries suggests that Rosalie's death becomes a substitute for, and tool to overcome, his own death wish: "Immediacy of the wish to die because I can no longer endure the yearning for the 'godly boy' (not necessarily is it this one)" (*TB 1949–1950* 239).[20] Death provides an escape from alienating, restrictive norms. Wishing to die means the rejection and abandonment of a life of normalcy; thus it implies a willingness to submit oneself to the "forbidden" sphere.

While the masking of stigmatized sexual desires enticed Mann to write *The Black Swan*, there is even more to the story when we also consider the role of Rosalie's daughter, the artist-outsider Anna. The German title, "The Betrayed Woman," refers to Rosalie, but it can also be applied to her daughter. Nature has denied Anna the traditional roles of wife and mother, as she was born with a clubfoot; she therefore joins Mann's long list of stigmatized characters. Her physical handicap has turned her into a serious and intellectual person, and despite a disappointing love affair that has left her cold and detached from life, she has not lost the ability to be compassionate. Her caring nature is displayed in her relationship to her mother, to whom Anna provides a contrasting foil in the story. Anna, associated with winter, the season of nature's death and inactivity, resents nature. She is the voice of cool intellect, of reason and pragmatism in the story. Because of their differences, Anna and Rosalie share a secret identity similar to that of Leverkühn and Zeitblom. Anna stands for that part of the author who has distanced himself and taken flight into art where he can encode his alienation from society and problematic relationship to sexuality. Rosalie embodies Mann's own renaissance of passion in old age and his love for a young man. Thus *The Black Swan* displays in two seemingly very different characters contrasting aspects of the single persona of their author and succeeds in bringing together the two most taxing facets of Mann's life, the discreet management and coding of transgressive sexual desires on the one hand, and coming to terms with the nature and function of his creativity on the other.

The constellation Leverkühn-Zeitblom, the relationship between artist and burgher and their discussions on art, resonates in the relationship between Anna and her mother. Reminiscent of Serenus Zeitblom, Rosalie expects aesthetic pleasure and illusion from art. In her opinion, art should reflect and enhance the beauty of nature and touch the heart. Rosalie suggests that Anna should captivate the visual beauty and scent of lime trees on canvas, thus rendering the invisible in nature visible in a "synesthetic" art (*BS* 22). But Anna, the modernist artist, rejects her mother's aesthetic needs. Spiral-like lines, cones, and circles on a gray-yellow background make up Anna's intangible rendering of evening wind and trees and deny identification. Her art alludes to Wassily Kandinsky's (1866–1944) abstract, nonfigurative paintings with their nonnaturalistic colors. It also echoes the totally calculated music of Leverkühn as she subscribes to mathematical, highly symbolic structures. A further affinity between Anna and the Faustian musician is that Mann confers a Leverkühnian thought about the end of bourgeois illusionary art upon Anna: "The state of the times and of art no longer permits it" (*BS* 9). Anna produces art that resists identification and the construction of illusionary worlds. Yet, in its abstractions aimed at negating the beauty of nature and life, her art encourages detachment from reality.

In two major aspects Mann's last completed novel, *Doctor Faustus*, provides a backdrop to the fictional landscape of *The Black Swan*. First, Mann revisits the relationship between artist and society. Mann had called Anna his "best character,"[21] presumably, because she combines what have been irreconcilable states of being throughout Mann's work: the artist-outsider existence and the caring, socially responsible existence. With Anna, who is detached as an artist yet caring and tolerant as a human being, Mann retracts his harsh criticism of the asocial artist. However, the outsider existence of the artist remains unchallenged. A sexual, romantic life is denied to the physically stigmatized Anna.

The second intertextual link between *The Black Swan* and *Doctor Faustus* concerns the motif of mercy. Adrian Leverkühn asks for mercy because narcissistic retreat from society and the renunciation of love are absolutely necessary to produce the innovative, extraordinary work. In *Doctor Faustus* mercy carries religious overtones; Adrian Leverkühn challenges God's mercy as He has given him the talent to produce ingenious work and to pursue it relentlessly. In *The Black Swan*, the notion of mercy is brought back to a monistic, nonmetaphysical level when Rosalie sees mercy in the way nature operates. When her illusions of renewed life are shattered, she feels blessed nonetheless and keeps her countenance. Rosalie claims that she has experienced "not a lie, but goodness and mercy" (*BS* 140). To have been granted the illusion of life in death, to have understood that without death there is no life, and that both are necessarily and harmoniously intertwined, is the lesson Rosalie takes to her grave. Rosalie dies reconciled with life's eternal circle of life and death. Is this reconciliation a truly happy ending? Her notion that the trick nature plays on her is a blessing reminds us of her "rosy," distorted view of reality. Thus the reader, skeptical throughout the story of Rosalie's judgment and perspective, is warned not to see in her perception that of the author nor to derive from it the story's final message. The doubts cast on Rosalie's unequivocal acceptance of nature and Anna's unfulfilled existence overshadow the reconciliatory chord that Mann attempts to strike in an attempt to come to terms with his own alienated existence as artist, with his frustrated love, and with the finality of his own life.

Confessions of Felix Krull, Confidence Man

After *The Holy Sinner*, Mann returned to an earlier, uncompleted manuscript about a confidence man that he had begun writing in January 1910. Interrupted first by *Death in Venice* and then by *The Magic Mountain* in 1913, Mann did not resume the manuscript until 1951; but he again repeatedly put it aside for other works, among them *The Black Swan*. The project was never finished. *Confessions*, arguably Mann's funniest and most entertaining novel, finally appeared in 1954 as a fragment.

The beginning of *Confessions* presents the confessor and first person narrator, Felix Krull, a man in his forties who had previously been in prison and who promises his readers a truthful account of his life as an impostor. The motif of the criminal and impostor can be traced in Mann's œuvre back to "The Joker" and *Tonio Kröger*. In both texts this motif is tied to the depiction of the bourgeois artist. In Nietzsche's writings Mann had found support in his reservations about artistic existence as dubious,[22] reiterated in the 1907 sketch "Im Spiegel" (In the mirror). There Mann both characterized the artist as a "notorious charlatan" (*E 1* 101) who sometimes pretends to a bourgeois existence and strikes compromises for life's conveniences, and questioned the authority and respect bestowed upon the artist. In *Confessions*, Mann reduces the artist to an impersonator and fraud.

Felix Krull is born to a privileged existence as the only son of a champagne maker in the Rhine Valley near Mainz a few years after the founding of the German Empire in 1871. This existence is, however, short-lived. Bankruptcy forces his fraudulent, frivolous father into suicide. Together with his mother and much older sister Olympia, an actress of debatable talent, Krull moves to Frankfurt. After lying his way out of military service in one of Mann's most comic scenes, and receiving a brief education in love by the prostitute Rosa, Krull leaves for Paris to work in a hotel. The profits from stolen jewelry allow him to lead a secret, double life. Away from work he is a dandy, and at work he is a servant attending to menial tasks. Due to his charm and good looks, he soon advances to the position of waiter. With humor, and a tendency toward self-aggrandizement, Krull recounts an amorous encounter with a hotel guest, Madame Houpflé, the owner of the jewelry he stole. She is one of Mann's voices in the novel that, in praising the beauty of young men, expresses Mann's own homosexual longings. Another voice is that of the Scottish homosexual, Lord Kilmarnock (in the English translation, Lord Strathbogie), who exhibits some of Mann's physical characteristics and whose sexual advances Krull declines. Krull is then approached by the Marquis de Venosta, nicknamed Loulou, whose parents intend to send him on a one-year journey around the world to break off his love affair with a socially inferior yet very charming Parisien. The Marquis suggests Krull should assume his identity and travel in his place, an enticing offer that, with the promise of being able to enjoy a privileged existence, Krull cannot refuse. In the guise of Loulou, Krull takes a train to Lisbon, Portugal, where he meets Professor Kuckuck. Kuckuck introduces him to the high society of Lisbon, and to his wife and beautiful daughter. The novel ends with the seduction of Felix Krull by Madame Kuckuck.

One source that might have served as an inspiration for Mann's *Confessions*, were the popular memoirs of the thief Georges Manolescu, *A Prince of Thieves*, from 1905. However, the principal factor in Mann's decision to write about "the illusionary form of existence" (*A Sketch of My Life* 42–43) was, as in some earlier works, to follow in the footsteps of and compete with Germany's greatest writer, Goethe. Initially, *Confessions* was planned as a fictional autobiography, an imitation and parody of Goethe's semiautobiographical *Fiction and Truth*, with the intention to use the criminal artist figure to undermine the authority, dignity, and importance that the German educated burghers bestowed upon their artists. With Krull's life of fraud and incarceration, Mann's novel also parodies the German bildungsroman, which depicts personal growth and the education of an asocial individual to social engagement. In contrast to the genre's ideal protagonist, Krull's character is static, without internal developments. His confessions testify to his narcissism and lack of human compassion. Vanity and pride in his "whole career of fraud" (*FK* 48), the need to entertain himself and his readers with his criminal and sexual escapades, and to justify his actions and lifestyle motivate Krull to write his memoirs. Because they serve his need for self-aggrandizement and self-affirmation, a pedagogical or moral message does not transpire throughout the story.

As is the case throughout Mann's works, autobiographical elements abound in *Confessions*. Krull is born around the same time as Mann. Mann hated school; Krull rejects the despotism and dullness of the Wilhelmian school system. The death of Mann's father facilitated his desire to escape bourgeois existence. The death of Krull's father allows Krull to move from the "cramped and odious native place" to "the great world" (*FK* 69). Both Mann and Krull create illusions with their artistic talents. Krull's double life is a reference to Mann's own. Krull likes to appear in disguise or pretend to be someone else; Mann's bourgeois, representational, heterosexual existence covers up his innermost secrets—his homosexual disposition. And both share a rejection of the world that admires them and whose admiration they nonetheless seek. Aspects of Mann's life are also reflected by other characters in the novel. The writer Diana Houpflé, who loves young men, is yet another mask for Mann. So is Lord Kilmarnock, who, notably, exhibits some external traits of Mann. With the Scots' psychological portrait, Mann provides brief, fleeting glimpses into the wretched life of a homosexual living under repressive bourgeois Christian mores—and thus into his own. These parallels and affinities are not meant to suggest that Mann is identical with Krull or any of the other characters. The transgression of conservative sexual norms as displayed by these characters' sexual adventures and open attitudes was never Mann's own. And, of course, unlike Krull, Mann was neither a thief nor an imposter. He merely projects some of his own desires and fears upon these characters, together with his profound doubts about his own existence and that of the bourgeois artist who leads a life of "merry-making" (*E 1* 101) and seduces his audience to embrace a world of lies and deception.

Because the artist-narrator is identified at the very beginning of the novel as a criminal and imposter, Mann sends his readers a dual message: do not trust the narrator and do not trust artists. However, readers, assumed by Krull to be from among "the best houses" (*FK* 58)—in other words, educated burghers and members of the upper classes—are manipulated by Mann to be almost immediately smitten by the intelligent, attractive man, despite the fact that Krull does not share their moral code. A central function of Mann's fiction and art in general transpires here: the seductive, liberating power of creativity that nourishes our desire to transcend a restrictive existence and to enter a realm of irresponsibility, and, simultaneously, to question our existence. With his story, Krull sets his readers up to admire and sympathize with his lifestyle by illustrating how tawdry and full of hypocrisy the real world, ergo the readers' world, is. Krull, the son of "an upper-class though somewhat dissolute family" (*FK* 3), grew up in a world of deceptions and fraud. His father betrays not only his clients by selling tainted champagne, but also his wife by his liasons with maids and prostitutes. Krull's godfather, Schimmelpreester, is called "Herr Professor," but has no right to hold an academic title. He is a painter of little talent; what talent he has he puts to use in designing labels for bottles of faux-champagne—a humorous allusion to art as illusion and fraud.

Pretense and make-believe dominate in Mann's *Confessions*. Krull's father encourages his son to pretend to play the violin in front of an audience while the real violinist is hidden behind the orchestra. The older Krull not only initiates his talented son into the art of fraud, but also nourishes his need for admiration and success. During a visit to a theater, he teaches him that people want to escape from the ordinariness of their lives, that reality is hideous and disgusting, and that artistic illusion makes life tolerable. On stage, the performance and appearance of the actor Müller-Rosé are captivating; life is beautiful. In contrast, off stage and without makeup, Müller-Rosé is repulsive. His body is covered with disgusting pimples, his features are ugly, his behavior is vulgar. Assisting in the lesson that life is unsightly and mundane is Schimmelpreester, who turns Krull into a "costume head" (*GW 7* 313).[23] In making Krull wear different costumes, he introduces him to alternative identities and lives and reinforces his yearning to escape his "real" life. After his costume sessions, Krull feels "gloom, disillusion, and boredom" (*FK* 47). He comes to reject everyday reality, the bourgeois, humdrum, and sheltered life that the majority enjoys.

Readers can hardly disagree with Krull's aversion to reality. The world Mann portrays has nothing to offer to an extraordinarily attractive, talented young man but mediocrity. Mann insinuates that, by reading his stories, the readers themselves are dissatisfied with their ordinary lives and thus put on "costumes," just like Krull. These they find by escaping into the realm of fictional worlds. Implicitly, Mann tells his readers that they need the artist and his storytelling, even if he is a liar, an imposter, and motivated by selfish reasons. That people want to forget the dullness of existence is accentuated in *Confessions* by the many visits of Mann's characters to artistic worlds—the theater, the circus, the bullfighting arena—and by mentioning the novels that Madame Houpflé writes to relieve her audience from the burdens of reality.

In the memoirs of the thief Manolescu, Mann found the motto, *Mundus vult decipi* (the world wants to be deceived), which he wrote down in his notebook and which might have confirmed him in his notion that the artist's existence as a creator of illusionary worlds is justified. In the same notebook entry, we find another important thought for understanding the novel: "The world, this horny and stupid harlot wants to be deceived—and that is a godly construction, because life itself is based on fraud, on delusion, it would run dry without illusion. Vocation of art."[24] These sentences reveal Schopenhauer's influence upon the genesis of *Confessions*. Following his view, Mann presents the world as illusion and life as meaningless. *Confessions* further echoes Schopenhauer's philosophy when Krull contemplates that knowledge of the insignificance of existence can lead to nihilistic indifference and indolence, or, alternatively, to the need to pretend that the world and its inhabitants are indeed important. A world without "appearance and dream" (*FK* 356) is not worth inhabiting. In order not to sink into existentialist despair and lethargy, Krull decides to create illusions and to consider "the world a great and infinitely enticing phenomenon" (*FK* 13). In the absence of a transcendental meaning of life or the hope of salvation, Krull's pretense that life is meaningful has only one goal: the pursuit of hedonistic pleasures.

With *Confessions*, Mann takes his readers on the humorous journey of a young man's mastery of disguise, simulation, and impersonation. In one of the most memorable scenes of the novel, Krull stands in front of the military medical examiner. To avoid being drafted and having to relinquish an existence of anarchic freedom, Krull pretends to have an epileptic attack:

> My head rolled and several times it twisted almost entirely around just as if Old Nick were in the act of breaking my neck; my shoulders and arms seemed on the point of being wrenched out of their sockets, my hips were bowed, my knees turned inward, my belly was hollowed, while my ribs seemed to burst the skin over them; my teeth were clamped together; not a single finger but was fantastically bent into a claw. And so, as though stretched on a hellish engine of torture, I remained for perhaps two thirds of a minute (*FK* 100–101).

Krull's victory over the military authorities is not only amusing to read; it also contains a serious, critical dimension. On the one hand, Mann ridicules the imposter artist; on the other, he mocks the German authorities and their representatives, the educated burghers who fall prey to the make-believe of art. That Krull's artistic talents have subversive powers, even a devilish dimension, is suggested by Mann, but he does not dwell on it either here or elsewhere in the novel. Instead, the novel focuses on the luck and success in everything Krull undertakes. Whether he steals jewelry, fools the authorities, seduces women, or uses his beauty and charm to advance in the ranks of hotel employment, nothing in his life goes wrong. The world is a big playground and always at his disposal. Emotionally, Krull remains on the outside; he is irresponsible and inconsiderate, indifferent to the impact his actions might have upon others. However, Mann's psychological profile of this narcissistic artist-outsider does not draw the reader's condemnation, only admiration for his skills as a trickster, and, indirectly, on a symbolic level, for the bourgeois artist. Krull's selfish actions bring happiness to others. For example, Diana Houpflé, who earlier in the novel was a victim of Krull's robbery, finds sexual ecstasy in his embrace and forgives the thief. Indeed, she wants to be robbed of more of her jewelry. The Marquis benefits from Krull's impersonation of him, because he is free to continue his relationship with his lover in Paris.

In *Tonio Kröger*, Mann made the point that the artist carries within himself "a thousand possible ways of life, although at the same time privately aware that none of them was possible at all" (*Stories* 150). Life similarly holds copious possibilities for Krull; without responsibilities, obligations, and emotional ties, leading a "foundationless existence" (*FK* 355), he enjoys absolute freedom under constantly changing masks and circumstances. When he rejects Lord Kilmarnrock's offer to become his homosexual partner in exchange for a comfortable life and perhaps a rich inheritance, Krull does not decline the generous offer based on narrow bourgeois sexual morality; rather he does so because he does not want to be stuck in one role and lose his freedom. Any emotional engagement and responsibility toward others is alien to him, as is the imprisonment in one identity. That Krull lacks a fixed identity is most obvious when Mann refers to Krull's open sexuality. He is attracted to twins, male and female, and dreams of embracing both. Unstable or uncertain sexual identity is a reoccurring motif throughout the novel. For example, the circus artiste Andromache is depicted as hermaphroditic, and Schimmelpreester's delight in seeing Felix dress and undress suggests a homoerotic interest. With his androgynous appearance, Krull is sexually appealing to both women and men who neither desire a man nor a woman but "some extraordinary being" (*FK* 118). Houpflé calls Krull "*mignon* in livery" (*FK* 172), a reference to the young Mignon in Goethe's *Wilhelm Meister*, who, when dressed in boys' clothes, appears as an androgynous being. Undoubtedly, Mann was also aware of the meaning of the word *mignon* in French, a derogatory term for a feminine homosexual. Houpflé also refers to Krull's legs as being like those of Hermes (*FK* 175). The association of Krull with the Greek god

Hermes further underscores Krull's destabilized identity. Hermes is the god of thieves and thugs, of form and beauty, the god of travelers, and the mediator between the world of life and death, the god who continually crosses boundaries.

Whereas Felix Krull's sexual ambiguity was present in the novel from the beginning, the connection to the multifaceted god Hermes in his parody of artistry was added by Mann in the 1950s. In bestowing a mythical dimension upon his character that embeds the individual in a broader social and cultural context, Mann expands the story of the individualistic, German confidence man to one about the universal dimensions of life. Krull's existence is not the only one of mythical proportions in the novel. The third book of *Confessions* leads more and more into a mythical realm. The Kuckuck family represents Olympic gods,[25] and toward its end, the novel turns into a "humorous play with gods" and a "parodistic Pantheon."[26] In the last episodes of the novel, the criminal aspects of Krull's character are less prominent, and other characters are presented in greater detail. With Professor Kuckuck's explications about the origins of the universe, the novel becomes more philosophical, and turns to fundamental aspects and questions of life. This is not to say that Mann abandons the parodistic, light-hearted story about the individualistic, morally questionable artist for a grave depiction of the *condition humane*.[27] Like Joseph in the *Joseph* tetralogy, who has mythical depth but nevertheless remains a symbol of the asocial artist turned social leader, Krull remains the self-centered artist figure who presumably will continue his fraudulent existence after his tryst with Madame Kuckuck, as his later life as a prisoner suggests.

The fusing of existentialist and artistic issues in the novel is developed with the conversation between Krull and Professor Kuckuck on a train. The name Kuckuck, German for cuckoo, is a signal to the reader not to take this character and his deliberations too seriously. Mann bestows upon him traits of Schopenhauer; Kuckuck espouses the latter's speculations about the evolution from inorganic to organic matter, from the realm of minerals to human beings. Each individual aspect of life is a manifestation of the will to live, a blind never-ending desire. Being is a temporary existence between nothing and nothing, without the possibility of transcendental redemption and grace evoked in *Doctor Faustus* and *The Holy Sinner*. Despite Kuckuck's conviction that in the end there is "Nothingness" (*FK* 272), we should not perceive him as a nihilist. Rather Mann lets him believe in carpe diem, a variation of the motto that had governed the life of Krull's father, "Freut euch des Lebens" (*FK* 7, "Enjoy life"). What makes life interesting and worth living is that it is only an episode between non-existence and death. Transitoriness of life gives "worth, dignity, and charm" to it. With the thought that "Being was not Well-Being; it was joy and labour" and deserves our "universal sympathy" (*FK* 276–77), Kuckuck acknowledges that suffering cannot be excluded from the love for life.

In *Buddenbrooks* Mann introduced Schopenhauer's idea that life is suffering. Thomas Buddenbrook yearned for death and dissolution of individuality to escape an alienated existence that forced him to play an unwanted role as a bourgeois merchant. Suffering from life seems to be the least likely theme of *Confessions*, a novel that, unlike any other of Mann's works, celebrates the enjoyment of life, sexual fulfillment, and happiness. In fact, in contrast to Thomas Buddenbrook, Krull is not forced into a self-alienating existence; overtly, his relationship to life is of an erotic, hedonistic nature. The self-censorship that informed some of Mann's earlier works, with its submission to moral and sexual boundaries, has now given way to creative freedom that embraces life denied in reality, turning imagination into a tool of unrestricted liberation. In *Confessions*, Mann lives out his fantasies. Consequently, the novel can be understood as Mann's fictional erasure of his lifelong suffering from sexual repression. Yet Krull's desire to sleep points at a suspicious weariness of life and a counter motif to individual self-fulfillment in the novel. The inclusion of the sleep motif suggests an ambivalence in Krull's character. On the one hand, Krull is highly narcissistic and individualistic; on the other, he desires, like Thomas Buddenbrook, to suspend his individuality and to become part of an amorphous whole. This ambivalence becomes apparent in Mann's presentation of the nature of Krull's role playing. Assuming various identities is a sign of individual creativity, but it is also a rejection of individuality. The narrative reveals that Krull's masks express a need for abandonment of anarchic freedom and individuality when Krull assumes the identity of the Marquis de Venosta. Krull welcomes the opportunity to displace his "worn-out self" temporarily; he is pleasantly surprised that with his change of identity comes, as he says, "a sort of emptying out of my inmost being—that is, I had to banish from my soul all memories that belonged to my no longer valid past" (*FK* 258). The imitation and usurpation of another's identity erases the boundaries between individual and other; the "real I" (*FK* 230) is no longer a separable, identifiable entity.

Just as masquerade and the adoption of masks allow for the erasure of individuality, so does sexuality in *Confessions*. Paradoxically, Krull's lust for life, most explicitly embodied in the sexual act, exposes his suffering from life. Krull praises the union of two separate bodies as "the greatest possible closeness, intimacy, and commingling" leading to the "wordless primordial condition" (*FK* 83). In his conversation with Zouzou, Professor Kuckuck's attractive daughter, he argues that it is love that liberates human beings from their loneliness, that it releases them from their suffering "in this world of separateness and isolation"

(*FK* 364). Krull's deliberations cannot always be trusted, however. To seduce Zouzou, he resorts to theatrical charm and outrageous lies about his compassion for poor children, whose filthy, lice-infested hair he stroked with ungloved hands. Yet his notion that love erases loneliness cannot be dismissed as yet another lie. When he dreams about love earlier in the novel, he dreams about "primal indivisibility and indeterminateness" (*FK* 81). His yearning for closeness and obliteration of individuality while at the same time satisfying his lust for life, is displayed at the end when "primordial forces" (*FK* 384) bring him ecstasy in the arms of Zouzou's mother. This escape from life, however, stands in stark opposition to his desire to write about his life and his hedonistic love for life. Self-renunciation and self-affirmation stand side by side.

With *Confessions*, Mann revisits some of the central contradictions of his whole life's work. In the figure of the dazzling, yet criminal imposter Krull, Mann displays his oscillation between justification and disapproval of the artistic existence, between glorifying a life without social obligations, a life of sexual freedom beyond oppressive moral boundaries, and rejecting it. The novel hovers between nihilism and the belief that life is worth living despite suffering and self-denial. What seems beyond doubt is the hope that art and artistic creativity will always have a place in the world. This hope is voiced in Krull's question: "What would become of life and what would become of joy—without which there can be no life—if appearance . . . no longer counted for anything?" (*FK* 379)

Throughout his artistic career, Mann's homosexuality, pervasive in all of his works, was a profound source of his creativity. His last fictional works, discussed in this chapter, demonstrate once more how he used his creativity to camouflage and sublimate his unfulfilled desires and voice his resistance to anti-individualistic, repressive moral paradigms. Certainly his homosexual sensibility made Mann often contemptuous of life and frequently led to a self-accusatory stance, most apparently in his early stories with their satirical, often vitriolic depiction both of society and the outsider's existence. But, paradoxically, it is this same sensibility that made Mann engage in life, uncover its antihumanistic dimensions, and look beyond his personal sufferings at the deficit of love and humanity in society in his writings. In other words, Mann was able to interweave the narcissistic, intimately personal impulses that fed his writing, with a humanistic perspective and a plea for a better, more tolerant world. Mann's strength as an artist and as a human being largely derived from his capability not to yield to the temptations of the stigmatized and creative outsiders of his fiction, who could not free themselves from despising life and who remained marginalized or were defeated by life. Instead, Mann turned toward life, and offered, even in his most nihilistic and pessimistic portrayals of human existence, resistance to the destructive forces of life, most prominently displayed in the motto from *The Magic Mountain,* *"For the sake of goodness and love, man shall grant death no dominion over his thoughts"* (*MM* 487).

For various reasons, this love for life was never unproblematic. Mann's selfish drive for artistic distinction and fame, a self-centeredness that is under scrutiny throughout his writings, his nihilistic streak that once again resonates in his last novel, and his lifelong doubts whether a tolerant human community harboring the creative, nonconformist outsider could ever exist, provided a counterforce to his affirmation of life. Mann was reserved about his affirmation of life; his fiction always voiced ambivalence. But he also spoke out, most strikingly when he demanded engagement for a humane and humanistic world to defeat Nazism. That Mann never tied his humanism to political agendas made him enemies on both sides of the ideological spectrum. But throughout his life, he refused to subscribe to dogma and any ideology, understanding all too well the duality of ideologies as liberators and tyrants of mankind.

Beyond doubt, Mann has enriched the twentieth-century literary landscape with his vast body of literature that, in both its copiousness and its multifaceted structure, its masterly command of language and style and craftsmanship in every detail, is without equal and has secured a place among the classics for several of his works. Also indisputable is Mann's pivotal position as a figure whose insights, although those of an outsider with elitist leanings, into German and European culture and history will continue to promote debates about cultural legacies and the interrelatedness of culture and politics. Last but by no means least, his writings allow us an understanding of the sexual politics of his time and beyond, and raise our awareness of the sufferings caused by intolerance, be they caused by narrow-minded morality or ideology. The recently published revelations from the diaries have resulted in a new perception and exposure of Mann the writer and Mann the person, and, subsequently, have led to a flood of biographies and new translations of Mann's major novels and narratives. This new understanding will surely lead to a greater recognition of some of Mann's lesser known works such as *The Holy Sinner* and *The Black Swan,* and a continuing interest in insightful and accurate translations of his texts.

What Mann's intimate disclosures cannot alter are passages and episodes in his writings that have captured his readers' imagination for decades. Among them are the school episode in *Buddenbrooks;* Tonio Kröger's fear of becoming like a gypsy in a green wagon; Gustav Aschenbach's casting his last glance upon Tadzio in *Death in Venice;* the door-slamming Clavdia Chauchat and Hans Castorp's outing in the snow in *The Magic Mountain;* the moving scene of Joseph's reunion with his father and brothers in *Joseph and His Brothers*; Adrian Leverkühn's final speech and playing of his last composition in *Doctor Faustus*; and Krull's performance in front of the military medical examiner in *Confessions*. Mann has created a multifaceted array of glimpses into human joys and sorrows that have become part of the twentieth-century literary heritage because they encapsulate the essence of human life and experience and, therefore, reflect Mann's fascination and compassion for life that are often veiled and contested in his works, but never erased. Today, this compassion might have become more perceptible with the publication of the diaries, but it was always present, just perhaps insufficiently appreciated. As Hermann Hesse wrote in his obituary for Thomas Mann, "For all his honors and success, he has been much misunderstood. For decades the German public at large failed utterly to see what a great heart, what loyalty, responsibility, and capacity for love lay behind his irony and virtuosity. Those qualities will keep his work and his memory alive long after these troubled times have passed away."[28]

Notes

Chapter 1

1. Mann burned his diaries written prior to 1918, and in 1945, while living in Pacific Palisades, California, he also destroyed those written between 1922 and 1932. A selection of diary entries in English translation is offered in Thomas Mann, *Diaries 1918-1939*, selection and foreword by Hermann Kesten, translated by Richard and Clara Winston (New York: Harry N. Abrams, 1982).

2. Since Mann's mother was herself a "foreigner," nationality is not a convincing reason in Mann's case.

3. Quoted in Helmut Koopmann, "Lotte in Amerika, Thomas Mann in Weimar: Erläuterungen zum Satz 'Wo ich bin, ist die deutsche Kultur,'" *Wagner-Nietzsche-Thomas Mann: Festschrift für Eckhard Heftrich*, eds. Heinz Gockel, Michael Neumann, and Ruprecht Wimmer (Frankfurt am Main: Vittorio Klostermann, 1993), 330.

4. Published in Thomas Mann, *Order of the Day: Political Essays and Speeches of Two Decades*, trans. H. T. Lowe-Porter, Agnes E. Meyer, and Eric Sutton (New York: Alfred Knopf, 1937; reprint, Freeport, N.Y.: Books for Libraries Press, 1969), 69–82.

5. Quoted and translated in Donald Prater, *Thomas Mann: A Life* (Oxford and New York: Oxford University Press, 1995), 248. The German epistle, "Ein Brief von Thomas Mann," is published in *E 4* 169–74. It should be noted that, in quoting from the homosexual poet von Platen, Mann not only addresses his outsider life as an exiled author, but also his outsider existence as a man with a hidden, stigmatized desire.

6. According to Hermann Kurzke, Mann's bibliography lists over three hundred nonfiction texts between 1937 and 1945 (*Thomas Mann: Life As a Work of Art: A Biography*, trans. Leslie Willson [Princeton and Oxford: Princeton University Press, 2002], 417).

7. This did not stop him from accusing America of "ignorance and maliciousness" (*TB 1940–1943* 315) because it did not focus all its war efforts on the destruction of Nazi Germany. Mann's criticism is based on unreasonable expectations, and his failure to recognize that U.S. foreign policies and interests were not, and could not be, identical with the hopes of the German exile. This example serves to illustrate clearly how much Mann was "a German in America."

8. Donald Prater, in emphasizing Mann's narcissistic nature, comments, "The judgement is inescapable that he regarded others, whether family, friends, or more distant strangers, as mere appendages to his own life and work, to be handled from his Olympian height" (*Thomas Mann: A Life*, 263).

9. Hermann Kurzke calls Mann "the uncrowned king of literary emigration" (*Thomas Mann: Life As a Work of Art*, 456).

10. Also taking part in this flight were Lion and Martha Feuchtwanger, and Franz and Alma Werfel.

11. Quoted in Kurzke, *Thomas Mann: Life As a Work of Art*, 465.

12. Thomas Mann, *Thomas Mann's Addresses: Delivered at the Library of Congress 1942–1949* (Washington, D.C.: Library of Congress, 1963), 25.

13. Frido Mann, "Das Verhältnis von Thomas Mann und seiner Familie zu Deutschland," *Thomas Mann Jahrbuch* 10 (1997): 30.

Chapter 2

1. Since 1988, two volumes with new translations of most of Mann's stories and novellas, from "The Will to Happiness" to *Death in Venice*, have become available: *Death in Venice and Other Stories by Thomas Mann*, trans. David Luke (New York: Bantam Books, 1988) and *Thomas Mann: Death in Venice and Other Tales*, trans. Joachim Neugroschel (Harmondsworth: Penguin Books, 1999). As the content of these volumes differs, the quotations in this chapter are from both volumes.

2. Michael Wieler, "Der französische Einfluß: Zu den frühesten Werken Thomas Manns am Beispiel des Dilettantismus," *Thomas Mann Jahrbuch* 9 (1996): 184–85.

3. A detailed interpretation on Schopenhauer influences and references in the narrative is offered by Edo Reents, "Von der Welt als Vorstellung zur Welt als Wille: Schopenhauer und Thomas Manns *Enttäuschung*," *Thomas Mann Jahrbuch* 8 (1995): 209–40.

4. Mann's story of a cripple who renounces life and becomes devoted to art and aestheticism might have been influenced by a character in Theodor Fontane's novel *Effie Briest* (1895), the apothecary Alonzo Gieshübler.

5. Karl Werner Böhm, *Zwischen Selbstzucht und Verlangen: Thomas Mann und das Stigma Homosexualität* (Würzburg: Königshausen & Neumann, 1991), 179–80.

6. Hans R. Vaget, *Thomas Mann: Kommentar zu sämtlichen Erzählungen* (Munich: Winkler, 1984), 35.

Chapter 3

1. Thomas Mann, "Ein Nachwort" (*GW 11* 546–49), from 1905.

2. Thus Henry Hatfield's statement that *Buddenbrooks* depicts "the decay of [Mann's] own family as a subject"—though it has influenced the reception of the novel considerably—must be taken with caution (*Thomas Mann* [Norfolk: New Directions Books, 1951], 35).

3. In *Reflections of a Nonpolitical Man*, Mann also states that he had experienced "the process of the loss of burgherly nature in an all too intimately psychological, completely unpolitical way" (*R* 103).

4. Most likely Mann was influenced by Nietzsche's ironic suggestion in *The Case of Wagner* to transfer Wagner's mythological story into a bourgeois setting.

5. For a detailed account on the intertextuality between *Buddenbrooks* and *The Ring of the Nibelung* see Hans R. Vaget, "Thomas Mann und Wagner: Zur Funktion des Leitmotivs in *Der Ring des Nibelungen* und *Buddenbrooks*," *Literatur und Musik: Ein*

Handbuch zur Theorie und Praxis eines komparatistischen Grenzgebietes, ed. Steven Paul Scher (Berlin: Erich Schmidt Verlag, 1984), 326–47.

6. Richard Sheppard, "Realism Plus Mythology: A Reconsideration of the Problem of 'Verfall' in Thomas Mann's *Buddenbrooks*," *Modern Language Review* 89 (1994): 929; also Judith Ryan, "*Buddenbrooks*: Between Realism and Aestheticism," in *The Cambridge Companion to Thomas Mann*, ed. Ritchie Robertson (Cambridge: Cambridge University Press, 2002), 132.

7. Is the decline "ultimately the work of Fate"? (Sheppard, "Realism Plus Mythology," 916). In contrast to Sheppard, I suggest an interpretation of the novel that understands fate as a contributing factor to the decline, not the central one.

8. See Erich Heller's influential chapter on *Buddenbrooks* in *The Ironic German: A Study of Thomas Mann* (London: Secker and Warburg, 1958) and T. J. Reed, *Thomas Mann: The Uses of Tradition* (Oxford: Clarendon Press, 1974; reprint, New York: Oxford University Press, 1996), 82.

9. A recent translation of Gabriele Reuter's novel, *From a Good Family*, trans. Lynne Tatlock (Columbia, S.C.: Camden House, 1999) now makes this novel also available to American readers.

10. Reuter, *From a Good Family*, 14.

11. Reuter's novel contributed extensively to Mann's conception of *Buddenbrooks*. For example, Agathe Heidling's uncle Gustav violates bourgeois principles when he marries a woman of questionable morality and therefore becomes the black sheep of the family (*From a Good Family*, 14). A similar fate strikes Christian in *Buddenbrooks*. On intertextual links between *Buddenbrooks* and *From a Good Family* see also Herbert Lehnert, "Tony Buddenbrook und ihre literarischen Schwestern," *Thomas Mann Jahrbuch* 15 (2002): 47–48.

12. *GW 1* 204–5. Woods's translation is missing the world "nearly" (compare *B* 181). Hardly ever has Tony received from critics and readers more than sympathy. For example, Reed writes: "What would a closer inspection of her inner life add? Only a confirmation that there is virtually no further substance beneath her familiar mannerisms, her repeated and usually derivative phrases" (*Thomas Mann: The Uses of Tradition*, 55–56). Nearly twenty years later, this negative image still dominates. For example, Claus Tillmann states that Tony lacks ambiguity and complexity (*Das Frauenbild bei Thomas Mann: Der Wille zum strengen Glück* [Wuppertal: Deimling, 1991], 42). Feminist scholars, however, have adopted an alternative reading of Tony. See Elizabeth Boa, "*Buddenbrooks*: Bourgeois Patriarchy and *fin-de-siècle* Eros," in *Thomas Mann: Modern Literatures in Perspective*, ed. Michael Minden (London and New York: Longmann, 1995), 125–42.

Chapter 4

1. Mann to Otto Grautoff, 27 July 1897, *Thomas Mann: Briefe an Otto Grautoff 1894–1901 und Ida Boy-Ed 1903–1928*, ed. Peter de Mendelssohn (Frankfurt am Main: Fischer, 1975), 97.

2. Dostoyevsky's narrative "The Landlady" (1847), in which a beautiful young woman visits a sick outsider and intellectual, might also be a source.

3. The town can be identified as Lübeck, while the description of the apartment is based on Mann's apartment in Munich.

4. Paul de Mendelssohn, *Der Zauberer: Das Leben des deutschen Schriftstellers Thomas Mann*, vol. 1 (Frankfurt am Main: S. Fischer, 1996), 628.

5. The quotation is from Savonarola according to Hans R. Vaget (*Thomas Mann: Kommentar zu sämtlichen Erzählungen*, 100).

6. *GW 8* 235–36; Luke's translations of "wishes" for "Willen" and "that is the law of nature" for "so will es ja die Natur" (*Stories* 109–10) fail to fully capture Mann's implied reference to Schopenhauer's "will" to life.

7. Friedrich Nietzsche, *The Birth of Tragedy and other Writings*, trans. Ronald Speirs, eds. Raymond Geuss and Ronald Speirs (Cambridge: Cambridge University Press, 1999), 40.

8. In a letter to Heinrich Mann from 13 February 1901, Thomas Mann wrote that "literature is death"; in other words, art leads away from life (*HM/TM* 46).

9. In a letter to Kurt Martens Mann wrote on 28 March 1906, that "*Tonio Kröger* is a confession of love for life which verges on the inartistic in its overtness and directness" (*Letters* 48).

10. Hermann Kurze points out that Mann found this biblical passage in Eckermann's conversations with Goethe, and that this passage was quoted with reference to the poet August von Platen who lacks love (*Thomas Mann: Epoche-Werk-Wirkung* [Munich: Beck, 1985], 102–3). Thus the quotation from *Tonio Kröger* can be understood as Mann's skeptical assessment of his character's declaration of love.

11. For the ambivalent ending of *Tonio Kröger*, see also Wolfgang Schneider, *Lebensfreundlichkeit und Pessimismus: Thomas Manns Figurendarstellung* (Frankfurt am Main: Vittorio Klostermann, 1999), 50.

12. See Hans Wysling, "Zu Thomas Manns 'Maja'-Projekt," in *Quellenkritische Studien zum Werk Thomas Manns*, eds. Paul Scherrer and Hans Wysling (Bern: Francke 1967), 23–47; Böhm, *Zwischen Selbstzucht und Verlangen*, 182–85, 197–215.

13. The numerous striking parallels between "Bliss" and these notes are listed in Böhm, *Zwischen Selbstzucht und Verlangen*, 184–85.

14. The sketch is based on Mann's attending a lecture organized by the poet and Stefan George pupil Ludwig Darleth (1870–1948) on Good Friday 1904.

15. Richard Wagner, *The Valkyrie*, 1.3.

16. A limited edition was first published in 1921; since 1958, the year of the first edition of Mann's collected works, it has been included in all subsequent editions.

17. Neither the extremely ugly Frau Aarenhold, nor the totally unsophisticated Herr Aarenhold nor the decadent Aarenhold twins match the Pringsheims. See also Gerhard Kaiser, "Thomas Manns *Wälsungenblut* und Richard Wagners *Ring*," *Thomas Mann Jahrbuch* 12 (1999): 251–52.

18. Vaget, *Thomas Mann: Kommentar zu sämtlichen Erzählungen*, 156.

Chapter 5

1. Often *Royal Highness* has been omitted from literature about Mann's work. More recent examples are *Thomas Mann: Romane und Erzählungen*, ed. Volkmar Hansen (Stuttgart: Reclam, 1993) and *The Cambridge Companion to Thomas Mann*, ed. Ritchie Robertson (Cambridge and New York: Cambridge University Press, 2002).

2. In contrast to Friedemann, in Mann's story "Little Herr Friedemann," Über-bein does not succumb to sexual passion. Yet, he too commits suicide because his life, completely devoted to form and discipline, proves to be equally empty and meaningless.

3. Böhm suggests that Überbein's short-lived relationship to the white woman "neutralizes" the teacher's homosexual orientation (Böhm, *Zwischen Selbstzucht und Verlangen*, 301).

4. In his portrayal of Axel Martini, Mann might have had Nietzsche in mind. Mann knew about the contrast between Nietzsche's unstable health, his ascetic life, and his glorification of the strong, Dionysian life in his writings (*GW 10* 364–65).

5. Katia Mann was of Jewish descent. Mann made concessions to his readers of Wilhelmian Germany in not marrying his fictional highness to a Jewish woman; this is an indication that he wanted to communicate with his readers, not alienate them, and also an indication of the anti-Semitic atmosphere of the time.

6. Helmut Jendreieck, *Thomas Mann: Der demokratische Roman* (Düsseldorf: Bagel, 1977), 215. See also Herbert Lehnert, *Thomas Mann: Fiktion, Mythos, Religion* (Stuttgart: Kohlhammer, 1965), 88–89.

7. The translation "exotic childlike face" (*RH* 305) does not capture the sense of self-alienation Mann conveys in this scene.

8. Reinhard Baumgart, *Das Ironische und die Ironie in den Werken Thomas Manns* (Munich: Hanser, 1964), 130; Hans Mayer, *Thomas Mann* (Frankfurt am Main: Suhrkamp, 1980), 79.

9. Mann calls him an American "money man" (*NB 7–14* 90).

Chapter 6

1. In this figure we find, according to Werner Frizen, "a complete death dance of Asian-European death and devil mythology" (*Thomas Mann: Der Tod in Venedig* [Munich: Oldenbourg, 1993], 25). A detailed explanation of mythological sources is also provided by Ehrhard Bahr, *Thomas Mann: Der Tod in Venedig* (Stuttgart: Reclam, 1991), 12–13.

2. For a further discussion of the ambivalence and tensions see Herbert Lehnert, "Historischer Horizont und Fiktionalität in Thomas Manns *Der Tod in Venedig*," in *Wagner-Nietzsche-Thomas Mann*, 259*ff*.

3. The German original is "ein erhöhtes Leben" (*GW 8* 457). Luke's otherwise very sensitive translation misses the religious overtones with his translation "an inten-sified life" (*Stories* 206).

4. Thus I can only partially agree with Dorrit Cohn who wrote, "This narrator is for discipline, dignity, decorum, achievement, and sobriety, against disorder, intoxication, passion, and passivity. In short, he volubly upholds within the story a heavily rationalistic and moralistic cultural code." ("The Second Author of 'Der Tod in Venedig,'" in *Probleme der Moderne*, eds. Benjamin Bennett, Anton Kaes, William J. Lillyman [Tübingen: Max Niemeyer Verlag, 1983], 227). Cohn's essay has since been reprinted in *Thomas Mann: Death in Venice*, ed. Clayton Koelb (New York: Norton, 1994), 178–95.

5. In Nietzsche's *The Birth of Tragedy*, Dionysian celebrations center around "an excess of sexual indiscipline" (20).

6. Lehnert, *Thomas Mann: Fiktion, Mythos, Religion*, 108.

7. Werner Frizen, "Fausts Tod in Venedig," in *Wagner-Nietzsche-Thomas Mann*, 247–48.

8. Ibid., 229.

9. Hans R. Vaget, "Die Erzählungen," in *Thomas-Mann-Handbuch*, ed. Helmut Koopmann (Stuttgart: Kröner, 1990), 589.

10. For example, Reed sees in Aschenbach's love for Tadzio primarily Mann's rendering of Plato's *Symposium* and a version of Diotima's idea on beauty (*Thomas Mann: The Uses of Tradition*, 161–62). An interpretation focused on stigmatized sexuality informs Robert Tobin's essay "Why Is Tadzio a Boy? Perspectives on Homoeroticism in *Death in Venice*," in *Thomas Mann: Death in Venice*, ed. Clayton Koelb, 207–32.

11. Böhm, *Zwischen Selbstzucht und Selbstverlangen*, 322.

12. Vaget, "Die Erzählungen," 581.

13. Lehnert, "Historischer Horizont und Fiktionalität in Thomas Manns *Der Tod in Venedig*," 268.

14. That the "will to form" is a counterforce to chaos and evidence that *Death in Venice* is a "break out from negativity" is Peter Pütz's central argument in "Der Ausbruch aus der Negativität. Das Ethos im *Tod in Venedig*," *Thomas Mann Jahrbuch* 1 (1988): 8.

15. Esther H. Lesér, *Thomas Mann's Short Fiction: An Intellectual Biography,* ed. Mitzi Brunsdale (London and Toronto: Fairleigh Dickinson University Press, 1989), 163.

Chapter 7

1. Mann to S. Fischer, 22 August 1914, quoted in de Mendelssohn, *Der Zauberer*, vol. 2, 1605.

2. Mann shared this view with many of his contemporary intellectuals and writers, among them Gerhart Hauptmann, Robert Musil, and Hermann Hesse.

3. These words, meaning "humanism," "reason," and "song," appear in French in the German original.

4. Mann makes the point that the king was a misogynist and not sexually attracted to women, judging by his contempt for Europe's most powerful women at that time, France's Madame Pompadour, Russia's Czarina Elizabeth, and Austria's Empress Maria Theresia.

5. Privately, Mann also admitted to this subversive element of the essay. He wrote to Ernst Bertram that he feared a scandal upon its publication, "because the king is seen with a fairly inopportune skepticism." Quoted in Gerhard Kluge, "Friedrich, der König von Preussen, in Essays von Thomas und Heinrich Mann und der Bruderkonflikt," *Thomas Mann Jahrbuch* 12 (1999): 271.

6. Mann to Paul Amann, 3 August 1915, quoted in Thomas Mann, *Letters to Paul Amann 1915–1952,* trans. Richard and Clara Winston, ed. Herbert Wegener (Middletown, Conn.: Wesleyan University Press, 1960), 45.

7. Ibid., 39.

8. Upon Mann's minor revisions in the manuscript for a new edition, conservatives reacted with anger and accused him—incorrectly—of falsifying the original. Their real motif was revenge for Mann's speech "The German Republic" in 1922. See also Walter D. Morris, "Introduction" (*R* xii).

9. Quoted in Hermann Kurzke, *Thomas Mann: Epoche-Werk-Wirkung* (Munich: Beck, 1985), 144–45.

10. Most likely Mann was familiar with Burke's arguments, even if he did not read his famous essay until 1920, as Dieter Borchmeyer points out in "Politische Betrachtungen eines angeblich Unpolitischen," *Thomas Mann Jahrbuch* 10 (1997): 92–93.

11. *R* 357. Mann never parted from his idea of benign authority, as his Joseph novels, completed in 1943, affirm.

12. This passage appears in a similar wording in Mann's notebook (*NB 7–14* 239) and is to be identified as Mann's response to his brother's essay on Zola.

13. Dieter Borchmeyer, "Politische Betrachtungen eines angeblich Unpolitischen," 90.

14. See Herbert Lehnert and Eva Wessell, *Nihilismus der Menschenfreundlichkeit: Thomas Manns "Wandlung" und sein Essay Goethe und Tolstoi* (Frankfurt am Main: Vittorio Klostermann, 1991), 16–17.

15. Eckhard Heftrich, *Vom Verfall zur Apokalypse* (Frankfurt am Main: Vittorio Klostermann, 1982), 144.

16. On the ambivalence of "The German Republic" see also Lehnert and Wessell, *Nihilismus der Menschenfreundlichkeit*, 101–10.

17. A lucid introduction to the genesis of the speech and to the differences between speech and essay is presented by Clayton Koelb in *Thomas Mann's "Goethe and Tolstoy:" Notes and Sources*, ed. Clayton Koelb (University: University of Alabama Press, 1984), 1–35. Quotations from the speech from 1921 in my chapter are from this volume. Quotations from the extended version are from *ETD*.

18. Clayton Koelb, *Goethe and Tolstoy*, 250

19. Reed, *Thomas Mann: The Uses of Tradition*, 286.

20. Ibid., 287. Reed did not have access to the notes and diary entries when he came to this conclusion. Having access to these, Clayton Koelb made the correct argument that the essay's "basic thrust and its central arguments" (Koelb, *Goethe and Tolstoy*, 10) existed since 1921.

21. Lehnert and Wessell, *Nihilismus der Menschenfreundlichkeit*, 165.

22. Koelb, *Goethe and Tolstoy*, 250.

23. Mann's "conception of Germany and of its role in the cultural and political development does not change" (Koelb, *Goethe and Tolstoy*, 15).

Chapter 8

1. For an in-depth analysis of *The Magic Mountain* see the collection of essays, *A Companion to Thomas Mann's Magic Mountain*, ed. Stephen D. Dowden (Columbia, S.C.: Camden House, 1999), which provides new insights into the novel's complexity and modernity.

2. Reed, *Thomas Mann: The Uses of Tradition*, 226.

3. For detailed accounts on the affinities between *The Magic Mountain* and *Death in Venice* see Reed, *Thomas Mann: The Uses of Tradition*, 229–30; Eva Wessel, "Der Zauberberg," in *Thomas Mann: Romane und Erzählungen*, ed. Volkmar Hansen (Stuttgart: Reclam, 1993), 124–25; Kurzke, *Thomas Mann: Epoche-Werk-Wirkung*, 193.

4. Mann to S. Fischer, 22 August 1914, quoted in Paul de Mendelssohn, *Der Zauberer*, vol. 1, 988.

5. Mann, *Letters to Paul Amann 1915–1952*, 41.

6. Wessell, "Der Zauberberg," 132.

7. Mann, *Letters to Paul Amann*, 87.

8. Mann, *Briefe an Otto Grautoff 1894–1901 und Ida Boy-Ed 1903–1928*, 207.

9. A detailed account of their ideological positions offers Børge Kristiansen, *Unform-Form-Überform: Thomas Manns Zauberberg und Schopenhauers Metaphysik*. Copenhagen: Akademisk Forlag, 1978.

10. It is also a reconciliatory gesture aimed at his brother Heinrich whose ideological leanings Thomas Mann had criticized in *Reflections of a Nonpolitical Man*.

11. Hermann Kurzke interprets Settembrini as a character who is not interested in truth but in the "will to power, for self-aggrandizement und competitive capability" (*Thomas Mann: Epoche-Werk-Wirkung*, 200).

12. Settembrini thus reminds us of civilization's literary man who supports a war in the service of civilization (*R* 42).

13. Settembrini's affection for Castorp can be understood as homoerotic since he cares for Castorp throughout the novel and is jealous when Castorp falls in love with Clavdia Chauchat.

14. Similar thoughts are expressed by Mann himself (*E 6* 174); thus Castorp becomes here the author's voice.

15. The affinities and differences between Naphta and the Conservative Revolution are presented in Hans Wisskirchen, *Zeitgeschichte im Roman: Zu Thomas Manns Zauberberg und Doktor Faustus* (Bern: Francke, 1986), 76*ff*.

16. Herbert Lehnert, "Leo Naphta und sein Autor," *Orbis Litterarum* 37 (1982): 65.

17. For a reading of Clavdia Chauchat as a femme fatale see Hans Wysling, "Der Zauberberg," in *Thomas-Mann-Handbuch*, 406; see also Frederick A. Lubich, "Thomas Mann's Sexual Politics—Lost in Translation," *Comparative Literature Studies* 31 (1994):

114, and Stephen D. Dowden, "Mann's Ethical Style," in *A Companion to Thomas Mann's Magic Mountain*, 26–27.

18. Wysling, "Der Zauberberg," 406–7.

19. Helmut Koopmann, *Der klassisch-moderne Roman in Deutschland: Thomas Mann, Alfred Döblin, Hermann Broch* (Stuttgart: Kohlhammer, 1983), 54.

20. Friedrich Nietzche, *The Birth of Tragedy*, 23.

21. Hans Wisskirchen defines this as "the synthesis of democratic sympathy for life and Romantic affection for death" (*Zeitgeschichte im Roman*, 102).

22. Wysling, "Der Zauberberg," 416–17. Reed calls Peeperkorn "the most enigmatic character in the book and the most controversial, eliciting flatly contradictory judgments" (*Thomas Mann: The Uses of Tradition*, 258).

23. On music in *The Magic Mountain* see Reed, *Thomas Mann: The Uses of Tradition*, 266–67, and David Blumberg, "From Muted Chords to Maddening Cacophony: Music in *The Magic Mountain*," in *A Companion to Thomas Mann's Magic Mountain*, 80–94.

24. Recent discussions on Castorp's education include the essays by Joseph P. Lawrence, "Transfiguration in Silence: Hans Castorp's Uncanny Awakening," in *A Companion to Thomas Mann's Magic Mountain*, 1–13, and by Michael Neumann, "Ein Bildungsweg in der Retorte: Hans Castorp auf dem Zauberberg," *Thomas Mann Jahrbuch* 10 (1997): 133–48.

25. Neumann, "Ein Bildungsweg in der Retorte," 143.

26. Koopmann, *Der klassisch-moderne Roman in Deutschland*, 74.

27. A lucid study of this paradox can be found in Lehnert and Wessell, *Nihilismus der Menschenfreundlichkeit*.

28. Mann, *Briefwechsel mit Autoren*, ed. Hans Wysling (Frankfurt am Main: S. Fischer, 1988), 269.

29. Mann, *Death in Venice and Seven Other Stories*, trans. H. T. Lowe-Porter (New York: Vintage, 1989), 187.

30. The accuracy of Mann's depiction of the antihumanistic, intolerant atmosphere was affirmed with the ban of the text in Italy.

31. Mann, *Death in Venice and Seven Other Stories*, 166.

32. Ibid., 162.

33. Ibid., 172.

34. Kurzke, *Thomas Mann: Life As a Work of Art*, 328.

Chapter 9

1. The first references to the plans for a story about Joseph can be dated back as early as 1922, as Herbert Lehnert suggests in "Der sozialisierte Narziss: *Joseph und seine Brüder*," in *Thomas Mann: Romane und Erzählungen*, ed. Volkmar Hansen (Stuttgart: Reclam, 1993), 186.

2. The first American edition in one volume, entitled *Joseph and His Brothers*, appeared in 1948.

3. Mann, *A Sketch of My Life*, trans. H. T. Lowe-Porter (New York: Alfred Knopf, 1960), 66.

4. Alfred Grimm, *Joseph und Echnaton: Thomas Mann und Ägypten* (Mainz: Verlag Philipp von Zabern, 1992); Hermann Kurzke, *Mondwanderungen: Wegweiser durch Thomas Manns Joseph-Roman* (Frankfurt am Main: Fischer, 1993).

5. Eckhard Heftrich presents a detailed analysis of direct and indirect references to Wagner's operas in his book *Geträumte Taten: "Joseph und seine Brüder,"* (Frankfurt am Main: Vittorio Klostermann, 1993).

6. A comprehensive account of Mann's oscillating perspective on culture and civilization, creativity and intellect is provided by Lehnert, "Der sozialisierte Narziss," 194*ff.*

7. Dierk Wolters, *Zwischen Metaphysik und Politik: Thomas Manns Roman "Joseph und seine Brüder" in seiner Zeit* (Tübingen: Niemeyer, 1998), 165.

8. Wolters writes, "Thomas Mann constructs here the autobiographical conflict of a nonpolitical inwardness under pressure" (*Zwischen Metaphysik und Politik*, 181).

9. *GW 4* 642. The translation "responsibility" (*JB* 430) does not imply a sharing of guilt like the German word.

10. Jesus asks God to forgive his murderers (Luke 23:34).

11. In a letter to Ernst Bertram from 12 December 1926, Mann wrote that he had intended Joseph to be a kind of mythical con-man who identifies himself with his predecessors.

12. Raymond Cunningham, *Myth and Politics in Thomas Mann's "Joseph und seine Brüder"* (Stuttgart: H.-D. Heinz, 1985), 100.

13. Manfred Dierks shows various parallels between Aschenbach and Mut in *Studien zu Mythos und Psychologie bei Thomas Mann* (Frankfurt am Main: Vittorio Klostermann, 1972), 192. See also Wolters, *Zwischen Metaphysik und Politik*, 259.

14. Cf. William McDonald, *Thomas Mann's Joseph and His Brothers: Writing, Performance, and the Politics of Loyalty* (Rochester, N.Y.: Camden House, 1999), 205. "Though hardly a feminist, Mann can expose patriarchy's cruelties even as he keeps the image of the father at the center of his narrative."

15. Dierks, *Studien zu Mythos und Psychologie bei Thomas Mann*, 194.

16. The German original "Dürre und Starre" (*GW 5* 1113) is closer to the diary entry.

17. This diary entry will be further discussed in connection with Mann's story *The Black Swan* (see Chapter 12).

18. The German version "Ich bin's" (*GW 5* 1308) is an obvious allusion to Jesus Christ (Mark 14:62 and Matthew 14:27).

19. In a diary entry Mann compares his love for Paul Ehrenberg with Mut's affliction (*TB 1933–1934* 411). Mann's feelings for Karl Heuser, more restrained and without youthful intensity, are reflected in Mai-Sachme's more controlled love.

20. Mann himself mentioned in a lecture on the novel that Joseph adopts "the role of Hermes" (*E 5* 195).

21. In his introduction to the American complete edition of *Joseph and His Brothers* Mann wrote: "For it is the mask of an American Hermes, a brilliant messenger of

shrewdness, whose New Deal is unmistakably reflected in Joseph's magic administration of national economy" (*JB* xiii). See also Heftrich, *Geträumte Taten*, 473–74, and Wolters, *Zwischen Metaphysik und Politik*, 302–9, on the comparison between Roosevelt's politics and those in *Joseph as Provider*.

22. Mann, *"What is German?,"* *Atlantic Monthly* 5 (May 1944): 83. The German version, titled "Schicksal und Aufgabe," was also published in 1944.

23. Raymond Cunningham understands Joseph as "a fictional portrayal of an anti-Hitler" (*Myth and Politics*, 203) and as "the champion of Mann's political ideals" (205).

24. Kurzke, *Thomas Mann: Epoche-Werk-Wirkung*, 255.

25. "Economist" and not "manager" is the better translation for the German "Volkswirt" (*GW 5* 1687).

Chapter 10

1. *New York Times*, 22 February 1938; quoted in Hans R. Vaget, "Schlechtes Wetter, gutes Klima: Thomas Mann in America," in *Thomas-Mann-Handbuch*, 68.

2. Originally published under the title *The Beloved Returns* (1940), the most recent reprint of Lowe-Porter's translation has adopted the original title. The translation itself, however, has not been modified.

3. Reinhard Baumgart, "Joseph in Weimar—Lotte in Ägypten," *Thomas Mann Jahrbuch* 4 (1991): 85.

4. Werner Frizen, "'Wiedersehn—ein klein Kapitel.' Zu *Lotte in Weimar,*" *Thomas Mann Jahrbuch* 11 (1998): 184.

5. For a detailed discussion on Goethe as mythical and in particular Christ-figure see Friedhelm Marx, "'Die Menschwerdung des Göttlichen.' Thomas Manns Goethe-Bild in *Lotte in Weimar,*" *Thomas Mann Jahrbuch* 10 (1997): 113–32.

6. Friedrich Nietzsche, *The Gay Science*, trans. Josefine Nauckhoff, ed. Bernard Williams (Cambridge: Cambridge University Press, 2001), 119–20.

7. Eckhart Kleßmann writes, "Greatness and genius, as this novel tells us, come at the price of terrible loneliness and the state of aloneness, from which qualities such as love, kindness, warmth are more and more eliminated" ("Lotte in Weimar," *Thomas Mann Jahrbuch* 4 [1991]: 55).

8. See also Herbert Lehnert: "Besides respect and sympathy for Goethe stands the doubt about the authority of the great author as a possibility of humanistic orientation" ("Dauer und Wechsel der Autorität: 'Lotte in Weimar' als Werk des Exils," in *Internationales Thomas-Mann-Kolloquium 1986 in Lübeck* [Bern: Francke Verlag, 1987], 48).

9. Koopmann, "Lotte in Amerika, Thomas Mann in Weimar," 338.

10. Mann, *The Transposed Heads: A Legend of India*, trans. H. T. Lowe-Porter (New York: Vintage Books, 1959), 98.

11. Jacques Darmaun, "*Das Gesetz*—Hebräische Saga und deutsche Wirklichkeit," in *Thomas Mann: Romane und Erzählungen*, ed. Volkmar Hansen (Stuttgart: Reclam 1993), 282.

12. Goebbels as quoted in Frederick A. Lubich, "'Fascinating Fascism': Thomas Manns 'Das Gesetz' und seine Selbst-de-Montage als Moses-Hitler," *German Studies Review* 14 (1991): 559.

Chapter 11

1. A chapbook is a small book of popular tales hawked by "chapmen," an archaic word for peddlers or merchants.

2. Mann, *Thomas Mann's Addresses*, 100.

3. Herbert Lehnert and Peter C. Pfeiffer, eds., *Thomas Mann's "Doctor Faustus"*: *A Novel at the Margin of Modernism* (Columbia, S.C.: Camden House, 1991) is devoted to this debate.

4. Eckhard Heftrich, "*Doktor Faustus*: Die radikale Autobiographie," in *Thomas Mann 1875–1975. Vorträge in München—Zürich—Lübeck*, eds. Beatrix Bludau, Eckhard Heftrich, and Helmut Koopmann (Frankfurt am Main: S. Fischer, 1977), 135–54.

5. Reed, *Thomas Mann: The Uses of Tradition*, 402.

6. Henry Hatfield, *From 'The Magic Mountain:' Mann's Later Masterpieces* (Ithaca, N.Y.: Cornell University Press, 1979), 134.

7. Martin Travers criticizes Mann's "essentialist view of the German 'psyche,' his over-valorization of individual agency, which has its origins in the Great Man view of history, and a teleological concept of historical change that is read through the literary trope of tragedy" ("Thomas Mann, *Doctor Faustus*, and the Historians: The Function of 'Anachronistic Symbolism,'" in *The Modern German Historical Novel: Paradigms, Problems, and Perspectives*, eds. David Roberts and Philip Thomson [New York and Oxford: Berg, 1991], 159).

8. Ritchie Robertson argues, "Mann makes virtually no use of Goethe's *Faust*" ("Accounting for History: Thomas Mann, *Doctor Faustus*," in *The German Novel in the Twentieth Century: Beyond Realism*, ed. David Midgley [Edinburgh: Edinburgh University Press, 1993], 130). This view is, as I demonstrate at the end of this chapter, disputable.

9. A close analysis of this intertextuality is presented in Eva Bauer Lucca's book *Versteckte Spuren: Eine intertextuelle Annäherung an Thomas Manns Roman "Doktor Faustus"* (Wiesbaden: Deutscher Universitätsverlag, 2001).

10. Ernst Fischer, "*Doktor Faustus* und die deutsche Katastrophe: Eine Auseinandersetzung mit Thomas Mann," in *Kunst und Menschheit* (Wien: Globus, 1949), 35–97.

11. To my knowledge, the book has not been translated into English. Eric Kahler's series of lectures on Germany, published posthumously as *The Germans*, eds. Robert and Rita Kimber (Princeton: Princeton University Press, 1974), incorporates its central themes and arguments. See also Hans R. Vaget, "Erich Kahler, Thomas Mann und Deutschland: Eine Miszelle zum *Doktor Faustus*," in *Ethik und Ästhetik: Werke und Werte in der Literatur vom 18. bis zum 20. Jahrhundert. Festschrift für Wolfgang Witkowski*, ed. Richard Fisher (Frankfurt am Main: Lang, 1995), 509–18.

12. Mann, *Thomas Mann's Addresses*, 64.

13. Ibid., 51.

14. Ibid., 61.

15. Ibid., 64–65.

16. The term applies to Germans like the fictional Zeitblom who silently resisted by not participating in public life.

17. Initially, Mann's perception that German bourgeois, humanistic culture was instrumental in the success of National Socialism, raised not only a few eyebrows, but also protest. That this culture, in particular nineteenth-century German Romanticism, can lead to Nazi ideas and ideals, has become more acceptable since the "Historiker-streit" (historians' dispute) in the 1970s in the Federal Republic of Germany, and is a central argument in J. P. Stern's *Hitler: The Führer and the People* (Berkeley and Los Angeles: University of California Press, 1975).

18. For a detailed account of intertextual links between Wagner's operas and *Doctor Faustus* see Matthias Schulze, "Immer noch kein Ende: Wagner und Thomas Manns *Doktor Faustus,*" *Thomas Mann Jahrbuch* 13 (2000): 195–218.

19. The English translation by Woods (*DF* 8) does not italicize the word as the German original does.

20. Despite the fact that Mann establishes a secret identity between Rüdiger Schildknapp and Rudi Schwertfeger in giving them the same initials, an intimate homosexual relationship of Adrian Leverkühn with Rüdiger Schildknapp cannot be assumed. Schildknapp does not have to die.

21. Johann Wolfgang von Goethe, *Faust*, trans. Walter Arndt (New York: Norton, 2001), lines 12110–11.

22. See, for example, *DüD 3* 278.

23. See also George Bridges, "Sublimation in Thomas Mann's *Doctor Faustus*: Love's Labor Lost," *Monatshefte* 91 (1999): 38.

24. Goethe, *Faust,* lines 11936–37.

25. Whether this cosmopolitanism will resurface, remains uncertain in Mann's fiction; it is a certainty in Mann's brief article "Das Ende" (The end, 1945) in which he expresses his faith that in the future Germany will be able to mobilize its "best forces" (*GW 12* 950), so that it can participate in establishing a better world for mankind.

26. On the openness of Leverkühn's fate see also Susan von Rohr Scaff, *History, Myth, and Music: Thomas Mann's Timely Fiction* (Columbia, S.C.: Camden House, 1998), 149–54.

Chapter 12

1. Hans Wysling identified more than twenty sources and direct and indirect quotations in "Thomas Manns Verhältnis zu den Quellen: Beobachtungen am 'Erwählten,'" *Quellenkritische Studien zum Werk Thomas Manns*, eds. Paul Scherrer and Hans Wysling (Bern: Francke, 1967), 258–324.

2. Helmut Koopmann, "Der Erwählte," *Thomas-Mann-Handbuch*, 513.

3. Ruprecht Wimmer, "Der sehr große Papst: Mythos und Religion im *Erwählten*," *Thomas Mann Jahrbuch* 11 (1998): 97.

4. Renate Böschenstein, "*Der Erwählte*—Thomas Manns postmoderner Ödipus?" *Colloquium Helveticum* 26 (1997): 81.

5. These self-references evoke the ambiguities with which earlier texts have looked upon the breaking of sexual conventions; they are not merely "a mechanical restatement" of earlier themes and motifs as Reed notes in *Thomas Mann: The Uses of Tradition*, 403.

6. Koopmann, "Der Erwählte," 503.

7. Hans R. Vaget, *Thomas Mann. Kommentar zu sämtlichen Erzählungen*, 303.

8. See Alan D. Latta, "The Reception of Thomas Mann's *Die Betrogene*: Part II, The Scholarly Reception," *Internationales Archiv für Sozialgeschichte der deutschen Literatur* 18 (1993): 123–56.

9. Alan D. Latta, "The Reception of Thomas Mann's *Die Betrogene*: Tabus, Prejudices, and Tricks of the Trade," *Internationales Archiv für Sozialgeschichte der deutschen Literatur* 12 (1987): 237–72.

10. For further discussion of possible blueprints for Ken Keaton and the Westermeier episode, see James Northcote-Bade, "'Noch einmal also dies': Zur Bedeutung von Thomas Manns 'letzter Liebe' im Spätwerk," *Thomas Mann Jahrbuch* 3 (1990): 139–48.

11. Mann condemns André Gide's aggressive homosexual conduct, and asserts that he himself would never reveal his homosexual desires to a young man to avoid embarrassment for both (*TB 1951–1952* 115).

12. Mann could not know how distorted his portrayal of Shaw is, as Shaw's diaries, published later, reveal a personality deviating from his public image.

13. Thus one must be careful to trust Mann's own interpretation that *The Black Swan* should not be seen in light of *Death in Venice* (*GW 11* 529).

14. The observations of Adrian Leverkühn's father, Jonathan Leverkühn, in *Doctor Faustus* about the ambivalence of nature, that a crocus can be mistaken for a meadow-saffron, come to mind in view of Rosalie's own deception.

15. Later in the story Mann reverses the motif of the wind as life-bringing agent. Rosalie has been "impregnated" from afar, when Dr. Muthesius refers to an external stimulation of ovarian cells as the cause of her cancer.

16. The English translation is "to set sail" (*BS* 117), thus fails to capture the mythological undertone.

17. Homer, *The Odyssey,* bk. 11, line 615.

18. Ovid, *Metamorphoses*, bk. 10, line 708; *Ars Amatoria*, bk. 3, line 810.

19. Titus Heydenreich gives a detailed explanation of this ambivalent world signifying love and death in "Eros in der Unterwelt: Der Holterhof-Ausflug in Thomas Manns Erzählung *Die Betrogene*," *Interpretation und Vergleich: Festschrift für Walter Pabst*, ed. Eberhard Leube (Berlin: Erich Schmidt Verlag, 1972), 92.

20. The "dieser" here refers to an Argentinian tennis player whom Thomas Mann had observed in St. Moritz.

21. *DüD 3* 520.

22. For example, in *Human, All Too Human*, part 1, aphorism 188, Nietzsche writes: "The conception of the artist as deceiver, once grasped, leads to important discoveries" (*Human, All Too Human*, trans. Paul V. Cohn [New York: Russell & Russell, 1964], 101).

23. The translation "trying on costumes" (*FK* 47) does not convey the notion that with each costume Felix Krull also changes his "head," implying that he changes identity externally as well as internally.

24. Quoted in Hans Wysling's seminal study of the novel, *Narzissmus und illusionäre Existenzform. Zu den Bekenntnissen des Hochstablers Felix Krull* (Bern and Munich: Francke, 1982), 417.

25. A detailed account of the mythological dimension of *Confessions* can be found in Wysling, *Narzissmus und illusionäre Existenzform*, 254–69.

26. Ibid., 269.

27. I cannot share Wysling's interpretation that *Confessions* completely moves away from a depiction of a precarious artistic existence to a novel exploring the possibilities and boundaries of human existence in a serious tone at the end (*Narzissmus und illusionäre Existenzform*, 271), because parody and humor, and in particular Mann's half-serious presentation of Kuckuck, provide a counterbalance to its serious underpinnings.

28. *The Hesse/Mann Letters: The Correspondence of Hermann Hesse and Thomas Mann 1910–1955*, eds. Anni Carlsson and Volker Michels, trans. Ralph Manheim (New York: Harper & Row, 1975), 167.

Bibliography

The following bibliography contains a selection of Thomas Mann's publications in German and English, and a list of selected critical literature, published mainly over the last two decades. This list includes most works cited in this study as well as additional titles.

Selected German Works by Thomas Mann

Briefe 1889–1936. Ed. Erika Mann. Frankfurt am Main: S. Fischer, 1962.

Briefe 1937–1947. Ed. Erika Mann. Frankfurt am Main: S. Fischer, 1963.

Briefe 1948–1955 und Nachlese. Ed. Erika Mann. Frankfurt am Main: S. Fischer, 1961–1965.

Briefe an Otto Grautoff 1894–1901 und Ida Boy-Ed 1903–1928. Ed. Peter De Mendelssohn. Frankfurt am Main: S. Fischer, 1975.

Essays, 6 vols. Eds. Hermann Kurzke and Stephan Stachorski. Frankfurt am Main: S. Fischer, 1993–1997.

Dichter über ihre Dichtungen, 3 vols. Ed. Hans Wysling and assisted by M. Fischer. Munich: Heimeran, and Frankfurt am Main: S. Fischer, 1975–1981.

Gesammelte Werke in Dreizehn Bänden. Frankfurt am Main: S. Fischer, 1974.

Notizbücher 1–6. Eds. Hans Wysling and Yvonne Schmidlin. Frankfurt am Main: S. Fischer, 1991.

Notizbücher 7–14. Eds. Hans Wysling and Yvonne Schmidlin. Frankfurt am Main: S. Fischer, 1992.

Tagebücher 1918–1921. 1933–1934. 1935–1936. 1937–1939. 1940–1943. Ed. Peter de Mendelssohn.

Tagebücher 1944–1946. 1946–1048. 1949–1950. 1951–1952. 1953–1955. Ed. Inge Jens. Frankfurt am Main: S. Fischer 1977–1995.

Selected Works by Mann in English Translations

The Black Swan. Trans. Willard R. Trask. New York: Alfred Knopf, 1954.

Buddenbrooks: The Decline of a Family. Trans. John E. Woods. New York: Alfred Knopf, 1993.

The Coming Victory of Democracy. Trans. Agnes E. Meyer. New York: Alfred Knopf, 1938.

Confessions of Felix Krull, Confidence Man. Trans. Denver Lindley. New York: Vintage International, 1992.

Death in Venice and Other Stories by Thomas Mann. Trans. David Luke. New York: Bantam Books, 1988.

Death in Venice and Other Tales. Trans. Joachim Neugroschel. Harmondsworth: Penguin Books, 1999.

Death in Venice and Seven Other Stories. Trans. H. T. Lowe-Porter. Vintage International, New York 1989.

Diaries, 1918–1939. Trans. Richard and Clara Winston. Ed. Herman Kesten. London: Robin Clark, 1984.

Doctor Faustus: The Life of the German Composer Adrian Leverkühn As Told by a Friend. Trans. John E. Woods. New York: Vintage International, 1999.

Essays of Three Decades. Trans. H. T. Lowe-Porter. New York: Alfred Knopf, 1948.

The Hesse/Mann Letters: The Correspondence of Hermann Hesse and Thomas Mann, 1910–1955. Eds. Anni Carlsson and Volker Michels. Trans. Ralph Manheim. Foreword by Theodore Ziolkowski. New York: Harper & Row, 1975.

The Holy Sinner. Trans. H. T. Lowe-Porter. New York: Alfred Knopf, 1951.

Joseph and His Brothers. Trans. H. T. Lowe-Porter. New York: Alfred Knopf, 1948.

Letters of Thomas Mann, 1889–1955. Selected and trans. Richard and Clara Winston. New York: Alfred Knopf, 1971.

Letters of Heinrich and Thomas Mann, 1900–1946. Trans. Don Reneau with additional translations by Richard and Clara Winston. Ed. Hans Wysling. Berkeley and Los Angeles: University of California Press, 1998.

Letters to Paul Amann, 1915–1952. Trans. Richard and Clara Winston. Ed. Herbert Wegener. Middletown, Conn.: Wesleyan University Press, 1960.

Lotte in Weimar: The Beloved Returns. Trans. H. T. Lowe-Porter. Introduction by Hayden White. Berkeley and Los Angeles: University of California Press, 1990.

The Magic Mountain. Trans. John E. Woods. New York: Alfred Knopf, 1999.

Order of the Day. Trans. H. T. Lowe-Porter, Agnes E. Meyer, and Eric Sutton. 1937. Reprint, New York: Alfred Knopf, 1969.

Past Masters and Other Papers. Trans. H. T. Lowe-Porter. 1933. Reprint, New York: Freeport, 1968.

Reflections of a Nonpolitical Man, Trans. Walter D. Morris. New York: Frederick Ungar, 1983.

Royal Highness. Trans. A. Cecil Curtis. London: Minerva, 1997.

A Sketch of My Life. Trans. H. T. Lowe-Porter. New York: Alfred Knopf, 1960.

The Story of a Novel: The Genesis of "Dr. Faustus." Trans. Richard and Clara Winston. New York: Alfred Knopf, 1961.

The Tables of the Law. Trans. H. T. Lowe-Porter. New York: Alfred Knopf, 1945.

Thomas Mann's Addresses: Delivered at the Library of Congress, 1942–1949. Washington, D.C.: Library of Congress, 1963.

Thomas Mann's "Goethe and Tolstoy": Notes and Sources. Ed. Clayton Koelb. University: University of Alabama Press, 1984. Includes translation of speech of 1921.

The Transposed Heads: A Legend of India. Trans. H. T. Lowe-Porter. New York: Vintage, 1969.

Selected Critical Works

Books and Monographs

Bahr, Ehrhard. *Thomas Mann: Der Tod in Venedig.* Stuttgart: Reclam, 1991.

Bauer Lucca, Eva. *Versteckte Spuren: Eine intertextuelle Annäherung an Thomas Manns Roman "Doktor Faustus."* Wiesbaden: Deutscher Universitätsverlag, 2001.

Beddow, Michael. *Thomas Mann: "Doctor Faustus."* Cambridge: Cambridge University Press, 1994. Analyzes the complex structure of the plot, explores the novel's principal historical, theological, psychological, and musical themes, the Faust tradition, impact of Nietzsche, and the reception of the novel after its publication in Germany.

Berlin, Jeffrey B., ed. *Approaches to Teaching Mann's Death in Venice and Other Short Fiction.* New York: Modern Language Association of America, 1992. Resource for teachers and students interested in background materials, general introductions to Mann's early stories and critical studies of *Death in Venice.*

Bloom, Harold, ed. *Thomas Mann.* New York: Chelsea House Publishers, 1986. A collection of distinguished essays published between 1931 and 1983.

Böhm, Karl Werner. *Zwischen Selbstzucht und Verlangen: Thomas Mann und das Stigma Homosexualität.* Würzburg: Königshausen and Neumann, 1991. Studies homosexual subtexts in Mann's fiction from early works to *The Magic Mountain.*

Cunningham, Raymond. *Myth and Politics in Thomas Mann's "Joseph und seine Brüder."* Stuttgart: H.-D. Heinz, 1985. Discusses the *Joseph* tetralogy as a critical commentary on Nazi Germany.

Dierks, Manfred. *Studien zu Mythos und Psychologie bei Thomas Mann.* Frankfurt am Main: Vittorio Klostermann, 1972.

Dowden, Stephen D., ed. *A Companion to Thomas Mann's The Magic Mountain.* Columbia, S.C.: Camden House, 1999. Ten essays on Mann's novel exploring its multidimensionality.

Fetzer, John Francis. *Music, Love, Death, and Mann's Dr. Faustus.* Columbia, S.C.: Camden House, 1990. Explores the interdependence of music, love, and death to emphasize the novel's complexity, ambiguities, and taunting evasiveness.

———. *Changing Perceptions of Thomas Mann's Doctor Faustus: Criticism, 1947–1992.* Columbia, S.C.: Camden House, 1996. Presents history of critical perceptions and shifts in understanding *Doctor Faustus* with extensive chronological bibliography from 1947–1995.

Frizen, Werner. *Thomas Mann: Der Tod in Venedig.* Munich: Oldenbourg, 1993. A well informed introduction to the novella including discussion on mythical dimensions, and the influence of Goethe and Wagner on Mann.

———. *Bekenntnisse des Hochstaplers Felix Krull.* Munich: Oldenbourg 1999. Detailed analysis of genesis, narrative structure and main motifs.

Grimstad, Kirsten J. *The Modern Revival of Gnosticism and Thomas Mann's Doktor Faustus.* Rochester, N.Y.: Camden House; 2002. Relationship of *Doctor Faustus* to Gnosticism.

Hansen, Volkmar, ed. *Thomas Mann. Romane und Erzählungen*. Stuttgart: Reclam, 1993.

Härle, Gerhard, ed. *"Heimsuchung und süßes Gift": Erotik und Poetik bei Thomas Mann*. Frankfurt am Main: S. Fischer, 1992.

Hatfield, Henry. *From "The Magic Mountain." Mann's Later Masterpieces*. Ithaca, N.Y.: Cornell University Press, 1979. A lucid study of Mann's fiction and essays since *The Magic Mountain*, discussing Mann's artistic craftsmanship, his nondogmatic moralism and turning toward politics in his later writings.

Heftrich, Eckhard. *Vom Verfall zur Apokalypse*. Frankfurt am Main: Vittorio Klostermann, 1982. A very detailed study of the influences of Wagner's operas on the *Joseph* tetralogy.

———. *Geträumte Taten: "Joseph und seine Brüder."* Frankfurt am Main: Vittorio Klostermann, 1993.

Heftrich, Eckhard and Helmut Koopmann. *Thomas Mann und seine Quellen. Festschrift für Hans Wysling*. Frankfurt am Main: Vittorio Klostermann, 1991.

Heilbut, Anthony. *Thomas Mann: Eros and Literature*. New York: Alfred Knopf, 1995. Based on a solid knowledge of German cultural history, Heilbut's biography provides a portrait of Mann as a homosexual unable to come out, as the author of homoerotic fiction, and the reluctant husband who values bourgeois respectability. Heilbut's biography ends with the period succeeding *The Magic Mountain*.

Koopmann, Helmut, ed. *Thomas-Mann-Handbuch*. Stuttgart: Kröner, 1990. To date the most extensive study of Mann's writings by the most prominent Thomas Mann scholars.

Kurzke, Hermann. *Thomas Mann: Epoche-Werk-Wirkung*. Munich: Beck, 1985.

———. *Thomas Mann: Life As a Work of Art: A Biography*. Trans. Leslie Willson. Princeton and Oxford: Princeton University Press, 2002. Extensive biography based on Mann's own information from letters, diaries, and other self-revelations.

Lehnert, Herbert. *Thomas Mann: Fiktion, Mythos, Religion*. Stuttgart: Kohlhammer, 1965.

Lehnert, Herbert and Peter C. Pfeiffer, eds. *Thomas Mann's "Doctor Faustus": A Novel at the Margin of Modernism*. Columbia, S.C.: Camden House, 1991. Openness and ambiguities of the novel are underlying assumptions of most essays in the collection.

Lehnert, Herbert, and Eva Wessell. *Nihilismus der Menschenfreundlichkeit: Thomas Manns "Wandlung" und sein Essay Goethe und Tolstoi*. Frankfurt am Main: Vittorio Klostermann, 1991.

Lesér, Esther H. *Thomas Mann's Short Fiction: An Intellectual Biography*. Ed. Mitzi Brunsdale. London and Toronto: Fairleigh Dickinson University Press, 1989. Combines a close reading of Mann's stories with Mann's intellectual and artistic development. Extensive bibliography.

Luft, Klaus Peter. *Erscheinungsformen des Androgynen bei Thomas Mann*. New York: Peter Lang, 1998.

McDonald, William E. *Thomas Mann's "Joseph and His Brothers": Writing, Performance, and the Politics of Loyalty*. Rochester, N.Y.: Camden House, 1999. Establishes connections between the novel, Mann's essays, and public appearances.

McMullin, Peter. *Childhood and Children in Thomas Mann's Fiction*. Lewiston: Edwin Mellen Press, 2002.

Mendelssohn, Paul de. *Der Zauberer: Das Leben des deutschen Schriftstellers Thomas Mann*. 3 vols. Frankfurt am Main: S. Fischer, 1996. Extensive biography until 1918. Years 1918 through 1933 in fragments.

Meyer, Martin. *Tagebuch und spätes Leid. Über Thomas Mann*. Munich: Carl Hanser, 1999. Interpretation of the diaries as documents revealing Mann's oscillation between self-doubts and political engagement, narcissism and social responsibility.

Minden, Michael, ed. *Thomas Mann*. London and New York: Longman, 1995. Introduction to historical and cultural contexts of Mann's writings. Collection of essays includes contemporary reactions to Mann's writings and essays on *Buddenbrooks*, *The Magic Mountain*, and *Doctor Faustus*.

Moulden, Ken, and Gero von Wilpert, eds. *Buddenbrooks-Handbuch*. Stuttgart: Alfred Kröner Verlag, 1988. Explores central themes of *Buddenbrooks*, sources, background, and the reception of the novel.

Nolte, Charlotte. *Being and Meaning in Thomas Mann's "Joseph" Novels*. London: W. S. Maney and Son, 1996. A close study applying Jungian concepts of myth and archetype to shed light on Joseph and mythic consciousness.

Northcote-Bade, James *Die Betrogene aus neuer Sicht: Der autobiographische Hintergrund zu Thomas Manns letzter Erzählung*. Frankfurt am Main: R. G. Fischer, 1994.

Pörnbacher, Karl. *Thomas Mann: Mario und der Zauberer*. Stuttgart: Reclam, 1996.

Prater, Donald. *Thomas Mann: A Life*. Oxford and New York: Oxford University Press, 1995. Excellent biography based on detailed facts of Mann's life. Mann's homosexual disposition acknowledged but, in contrast to Heilbut's biography, not as central driving force in Mann's life.

Reed, T. J. *Thomas Mann: The Use of Tradition*. 1974. Reprint, Oxford: Clarendon Press, 1996. Standard work in English on Mann's fiction and its cultural backgrounds.

Ridley, Hugh. *Thomas Mann: Buddenbrooks*. Cambridge: Cambridge University Press, 1987. Explores the personal and historical background of the novel, its major themes and narrative techniques.

———. *The Problematic Bourgeois: Twentieth Century Criticism on Thomas Mann's Buddenbrooks and The Magic Mountain*. Columbia, S.C.: Camden House, 1994. Discusses the reception of both novels in light of changing critical paradigms and political trends.

Scaff, Susan von Rohr. *History, Myth, and Music: Thomas Mann's Timely Fiction*. Columbia, S.C.: Camden House, 1998. Focus on Mann's major novels to trace the importance Mann bestows on creativity for human existence and survival. Impact of Wagner, Nietzsche, Weber, and Tillich on Mann's novels also discussed.

Schneider, Wolfgang. *Lebensfreundlichkeit und Pessimismus: Thomas Manns Figurendarstellung*. Frankfurt am Main: Vittorio Klostermann, 1999.

Stock, Irvine. *Ironic out of Love: The Novels of Thomas Mann*. Jefferson, N.C., and London: McFarland, 1994.

Swales, Martin. *Buddenbrooks: Family Life as a Mirror of Social Change*. New York: Twayne, 1991. Introduces the complexity of the novel and puts it in the context of both German and European realistic literature.

Treitel, Ilona. *The Dangers of Interpretation: Art and Artist in Henry James and Thomas Mann*. New York: Garland Publishing, 1996.

Vaget, Hans R. *Thomas Mann: Kommentar zu sämtlichen Erzählungen*. Munich: Winkler, 1984.

Wiegmann, Hermann. *Die Erzählungen Thomas Manns*. Bielefeld: Aisthesis Verlag, 1992.

Wisskirchen, Hans. *Zeitgeschichte im Roman: Zu Thomas Manns "Zauberberg" und "Doktor Faustus."* Bern: Francke, 1986.

Wolters, Dierk. *Zwischen Metaphysik und Politik: Thomas Manns Roman "Joseph und seine Brüder" in seiner Zeit*. Tübingen: Niemeyer, 1998.

Wysling, Hans. *Narzissmus und illusionäre Existenzform: Zu den Bekenntnissen des Hochstablers Felix Krull*. Bern and Munich: Francke, 1982.

Extensive Presentation of the Sources, Meaning and Reception of Mann's Narratives

Articles

Boa, Elizabeth. *"Buddenbrooks*: Bourgeois Patriarchy and *fin-de-siècle* Eros." In *Thomas Mann: Modern Literatures in Perspective*, edited by Michael Minden, 125–42. London and New York: Longmann, 1995. Feminist reading of *Buddenbrooks* as a novel aimed at a critique of patriarchy.

Borchmeyer, Dieter. "Repräsentation als ästhetische Existenz. *Königliche Hoheit* und *Wilhelm Meister*: Thomas Manns Kritik der formalen Existenz." *Recherches Germaniques* 13 (1983): 105–36.

Böschenstein, Renate. *"Der Erwählte*—Thomas Manns postmoderner Ödipus?" *Colloquium Helveticum* 26 (1997): 71–101.

Bridges, George. "Thomas Mann's *Mario und der Zauberer*: 'Aber zum Donnerwetter! Deshalb bringt man doch niemand um!'" *German Quarterly* 64 (1991): 501–17. Interprets the novella as a psychological allegory that serves Mann as an aesthetic tool to renounce his homosexual inclinations.

———. "Sublimation in Thomas Mann's *Doctor Faustus*: Love's Labor Lost." *Monatshefte* 91 (1999): 28–44. Focuses on Zeitblom's relationship to Leverkühn based on Zeitblom's repressed stigmatized desires.

Brinkley, Edward S. "Fear of Form: Thomas Mann's *Death in Venice*." *Monatshefte* 91 (1999): 2–27. Reads Mann's novella as a modern text deconstructing traditional notions of homosexual identity.

Cohn, Dorrit. "The Second Author of 'Der Tod in Venedig.'" In *Probleme der Moderne*, edited by Benjamin Bennett, Anton Kaes, and William J. Lillyman, 223–45. Tübingen: Max Niemeyer Verlag, 1983. Reprinted in *Thomas Mann: Death in Venice*. A

Norton Critical Edition, edited by Clayton Koelb, 178–95. New York: Norton, 1994. Discusses relationship between narrator and Aschenbach and growing critical distance.

Darmaun, Jacques. "*Das Gesetz*—Hebräische Saga und deutsche Wirklichkeit." In *Thomas Mann: Romane und Erzählungen*, edited by Volkmar Hansen, 270–93. Stuttgart: Reclam, 1993.

Eisenstein, Paul. "Leverkühn as Witness: The Holocaust in Thomas Mann's *Doktor Faustus*." *German Quarterly* 70 (1997): 325–46. Explores Leverkühn's art as a mirror of historical suffering.

Elsaghe, Yahya. "Zur Sexualisierung des Fremden im *Tod in Venedig*." *Archiv für das Studium der neueren Sprachen und Literaturen* 234 (1997): 19–32.

Feuerlicht, Ignace. "Thomas Mann and Homoeroticism." *Germanic Review* 57 (1982): 89–97. Discusses Mann's relationship to Paul Ehrenberg and Klaus Heuser and the sublimation of homosexual desires in some of Mann's writings.

Frizen, Werner. "Fausts Tod in Venedig." In *Wagner-Nietzsche-Thomas Mann. Festschrift für Eckhard Heftrich*, edited by Heinz Gockel, Michael Neumann, and Ruprecht Wimmer, 228–53. Frankfurt: Vittorio Klostermann, 1993.

———. "'Wiedersehn—ein klein Kapitel.' Zu *Lotte in Weimar*." *Thomas Mann Jahrbuch* 11 (1998): 171–202.

Furst, Lilian R. "Re-reading *Buddenbrooks*." *German Life and Letters* 44 (1991): 317–29. Discusses *Buddenbrooks* as a realistic and symbolic novel.

Hansen, Volkmar. "Lotte in Weimar." In *Thomas Mann: Romane und Erzählungen*, 228–69.

Heydenreich, Titus. "Eros in der Unterwelt: Der Holterhof-Ausflug in Thomas Manns Erzählung *Die Betrogene*." In *Interpretation und Vergleich: Festschrift für Walter Pabst*, edited by Eberhard Leube, 79–95. Berlin: Erich Schmidt Verlag, 1972.

Hoffmeister, Werner. "Thomas Manns *Unordnung und frühes Leid*: Neue Gesellschaft, neue Geselligkeit." *Monatshefte* 82 (1990): 157–76. Interprets the story in terms of its social and political dimensions.

Kaiser, Gerhard. "Thomas Manns *Wälsungenblut* und Richard Wagners *Ring*." *Thomas Mann Jahrbuch* 12 (1999): 251–52.

Kamla, Thomas A. "Thomas Mann's 'Gefallen': États d'âme and the Bahrian New Psychology." *German Quarterly* 66 (1993): 510–23. Explores impact of Hermann Bahr's psychology on aesthetic sensibility of Mann's protagonist.

Karasek, Hellmuth. "Königliche Hoheit." *Thomas Mann Jahrbuch 4* (1991): 29–44.

King, John S. "'Most Dubious': Myth, the Occult, and Politics in the *Zauberberg*." *Monatshefte* 88 (1996): 217–36. Close interpretation of the chapter "Most Dubious" to shed light on the novel's conclusion.

Kleßmann, Eckhart. "Lotte in Weimar." *Thomas Mann Jahrbuch 4* (1991): 45–57.

Koopmann. Helmut. "'Doktor Faustus' als Widerlegung der Weimarer Klassik." In *Internationales Thomas-Mann-Kolloquium*, edited by Cornelia Bernini, Thomas Sprecher, and Hans Wysling, 92–109. Bern: Francke, 1987.

———. "Der Erwählte." In *Thomas-Mann-Handbuch*, edited by Helmut Koopmann, 498–515. Stuttgart: Kröner, 1990.

————. "Warnung vor Wirklichem: Zum Realismus bei Thomas Mann." In *Wegbe-reiter der Moderne*, edited by Helmut Koopmann and Clark Muenzer, 68–87. Tübingen: Niemeyer, 1990.

————. "Lotte in Amerika, Thomas Mann in Weimar." In *Wagner-Nietzsche-Thomas Mann*, 324–42.

Kowalik, Jill Anne. "'Sympathy with Death': Hans Castorp's Nietzschean Resentment." *German Quarterly* 58 (1985): 27–48. Questions the notion that *The Magic Moun-tain* is a novel of development.

Kraft, Herbert. "Goethe 1939: Thomas Manns Roman *Lotte in Weimar*." In *Wagner-Nietzsche-Thomas Mann*, 310–23.

Latta, Alan D. "The Reception of Thomas Mann's *Die Betrogene*: Tabus, Prejudices, and Tricks of the Trade." *Internationales Archiv für Sozialgeschichte der deutschen Literatur* 12 (1987): 237–72.

————. "The Reception of Thomas Mann's *Die Betrogene*: Part II: The Scholarly Reception." *Internationales Archiv für Sozialgeschichte der deutschen Literatur* 18 (1993): 123–56.

Lehnert, Herbert. "Die Dialektik der Kultur. Mythos, Katastrophe und die Kontinuität der deutschen Literatur in Thomas Manns 'Doktor Faustus.'" In *Schreiben im Exil*, edited by Stephan Alexander and Hans Wagener, 95–108. Bonn: Bouvier, 1985.

————. "Dauer und Wechsel der Autorität: 'Lotte in Weimar' als Werk des Exils." In *Internationales Thomas-Mann-Kolloquium 1986 in Lübeck*, 30–52.

————. "Idyllen und Realitätseinbrüche: Ideologische Selbstkritik in Thomas Manns *Die vertauschten Köpfe*." In *Zeitgenossenschaft. Festschrift für Egon Schwarz*, edited by Paul Michael Lützeler, Herbert Lehnert, and Gerhild Scholz Williams, 123–39. Frankfurt am Main: Athenäum, 1987.

————. "Der sozialisierte Narziß: *Joseph und seine Brüder*." In *Thomas Mann: Romane und Erzählungen*, 186–228.

————. "Historischer Horizont und Fiktionalität in Thomas Manns *Der Tod in Venedig*." In *Wagner-Nietzsche-Thomas Mann*, 254–78.

————. "Tony Buddenbrook und ihre literarischen Schwestern," *Thomas Mann Jahr-buch* 15 (2002): 35–53.

Lubich, Frederick A. "'Fascinating Fascism': Thomas Manns 'Das Gesetz' und seine Selbst-de-Montage als Moses-Hitler." *German Studies Review* 14 (1991): 553–73.

————. "Thomas Mann's Sexual Politics—Lost in Translation." *Comparative Literature Studies* 31 (1994): 107–27. Points out the need for faithful translations of Mann's œuvre to make available his ambivalent and multifaceted presentations of sexuality.

Mahadevan, Anand. "Switching Heads and Cultures: Transformation of an Indian Myth by Thomas Mann and Girish Karnad." *Comparative Literature* 54 (2002): 23–42. An interesting, non-Western approach as Mahadevan examines the adaptation of an eleventh-century Indian parable in Mann's *The Transposed Heads* and in Karnad's play *Hayavadana*.

Mann, Frido. "Das Verhältnis von Thomas Mann und seiner Familie zu Deutschland." *Thomas Mann Jahrbuch 10* (1997): 27–35.

Marx, Friedhelm. "Thomas Mann und Nietzsche: Eine Auseinandersetzung in *Königliche Hoheit*." *Deutsche Vierteljahrsschrift für Literaturwissenschaft und Geistesgeschichte* 62 (1988): 326–41.

———. "'Die Menschwerdung des Göttlichen.' Thomas Manns Goethe-Bild in *Lotte in Weimar*." *Thomas Mann Jahrbuch* 10 (1997): 113–32.

Northcote-Bade, James. "'Noch einmal also dies': Zur Bedeutung von Thomas Manns 'letzter Liebe' im Spätwerk." *Thomas Mann Jahrbuch* 3 (1990): 139–48.

Ohl, Hubert. "Riemers Goethe: Zu Thomas Manns Goethe-Bild." *Jahrbuch der deutschen Schillergesellschaft* 27 (1983): 381–95.

Parkes-Perret, Ford B. "Thomas Mann's Silvery Voice of Self-Parody in *Doctor Faustus*." *Germanic Review* 64 (1989): 20–30. Investigates Zeitblom's love for Leverkühn and Zeitblom as Mann's parodistic alter ego.

Petersen, Jürgen. "Die Märchenmotive und ihre Behandlung in Thomas Manns Roman 'Königliche Hoheit.'" *Sprachkunst* 4 (1973): 216–30.

Pütz, Peter. "Der Ausbruch aus der Negativität. Das Ethos im *Tod in Venedig*." *Thomas Mann Jahrbuch* 1 (1988): 1–11.

Reents, Edo. "Von der Welt als Vorstellung zur Welt als Wille: Schopenhauer und Thomas Manns *Enttäuschung*." *Thomas Mann Jahrbuch* 8 (1995): 209–40.

Robertson, Ritchie. "Accounting for History: Thomas Mann, *Doktor Faustus*." In *The German Novel in the Twentieth Century: Beyond Realism*, edited by David Midgley, 128–48. Edinburgh: Edinburgh University Press, 1993.

Ryan, Judith. "*Buddenbrooks*: Between Realism and Aestheticism." *The Cambridge Companion to Thomas Mann*, edited by Ritchie Robertson, 119–36. Cambridge: Cambridge University Press, 2002.

Sauer, Paul Ludwig. "Das 'vernünftige Märchen' Thomas Manns: Der Roman 'Königliche Hoheit' im Spannungsfeld zwischen Volksmärchen und Kunstmärchen." *Blätter der Thomas Mann-Gesellschaft Zürich* 23 (1989–90): 31–49.

Scaff, Susan von Rohr. "The Dialectic of Myth and History: Revision of Archetypes in Thomas Mann's Joseph Novels." *Monatshefte* 82 (1990): 177–93. Explores the role of myth and archetypes as forces of stability in human history.

———. "The Duplicity of the Devil's Pact: Intimations of Redemption in Mann's *Doktor Faustus*." *Monatshefte* 87 (1995): 151–69. Argues that the authority of the devil's pact is debatable and neither Leverkühn's redemption nor his condemnation a certainty at the end.

Schulze, Matthias. "Immer noch kein Ende: Wagner und Thomas Manns '*Doktor Faustus*.'" *Thomas Mann Jahrbuch* 13 (2000): 195–218.

Sheppard, Richard. "Realism Plus Mythology: A Reconsideration of the Problem of 'Verfall' in Thomas Mann's *Buddenbrooks*." *Modern Language Review* 89 (1994): 916–41. Explores the mythological dimensions of the novel to question traditional perceptions of *Buddenbrooks* as a realistic novel.

Siefken, Hinrich: "Goethe 'spricht.' Gedanken zum siebten Kapitel des Romans *Lotte in Weimar.*" In *Thomas Mann und seine Quellen: Festschrift für Hans Wysling*, edited by Eckhard Heftrich and Helmut Koopmann, 224–49. Frankfurt: Vittorio Klostermann, 1991.

Tobin, Robert. "Why is Tadzio a Boy? Perspectives on Homoeroticism in *Death in Venice.*" In *Thomas Mann: Death in Venice*, edited by Clayton Koelb, 207–32. New York: Norton, 1994. Explores in detail relationship between sexuality and textuality.

Travers, Martin. "Thomas Mann, *Doctor Faustus* and the Historians: The Function of 'Anachronistic Symbolism.'" In *The Modern German Historical Novel: Paradigms, Problems and Perspectives*, edited by David Roberts and Philip Thomson, 145–59. New York and Oxford: Berg, 1991. Raises doubts about Mann's historiography.

Tumanov, Vladimir. "Jacob as Job in Thomas Mann's *Joseph und seine Brüder.*" *Neophilologus* 86 (2002): 287–302. Treatment of Jacob and his relationship to Job based on sources in rabbinic literature.

Vaget, Hans R. "Amazing Grace: Thomas Mann, Adorno, and the Faust Myth." In *Our Faust. Roots and Ramifications of a Modern German Myth*, edited by Reinhold Grimm and Jost Hermand, 168–89. Madison: University of Wisconsin Press, 1987.

———. "Erich Kahler, Thomas Mann und Deutschland. Eine Miszelle zum *Doktor Faustus.*" In *Ethik und Ästhetik: Werke und Werte in der Literatur vom 18. bis zum 20. Jahrhundert: Festschrift für Wolfgang Wittkowski zum 70. Geburtstag*, edited by Richard Fischer, 509–18. Frankfurt am Main: Peter Lang, 1995.

———. "Confession and Camouflage: The Diaries of Thomas Mann." *Journal of English and Germanic Philology* 96 (1997): 567–90. Discusses diaries as Mann's self-exposure of homosexuality and establishes connections to Mann's fiction, and also looks at their merit as historical documents.

Wallinger, Sylvia: "'Und es war kalt in dem silbernen Kerzensaal, wie in dem der Schneekönigin, wo die Herzen der Kinder erstarren.' Gesundete Männlichkeit—gezähmte Weiblichkeit in Thomas Manns *Königliche Hoheit* und *Wälsungenblut.*" In *Der Widerspenstigen Zähmung*, edited by Sylvia Wallinger and Monika Jonas, 235–57. Innsbruck: Institut für Germanistik, Universität, 1986.

Wessell, Eva. "*Der Zauberberg.*" In *Thomas Manns Romane und Erzählungen*, 121–50.

Wieler, Michael. "Der französische Einfluß. Zu den frühesten Werken Thomas Manns am Beispiel des Dilettantismus." *Thomas Mann Jahrbuch* 9 (1996): 173–87.

Wimmer, Ruprecht. "'AH, ÇA C'EST BIEN ALLEMAND, PAR EXEMPLE!' Richard Wagner in Thomas Manns *Doktor Faustus.*" In *Wagner-Nietzsche-Thomas Mann*, 49–68.

———. "Der sehr große Papst: Mythos und Religion im *Erwählten.*" *Thomas Mann Jahrbuch* 11 (1998): 91–107.

Wysling, Hans. "Thomas Manns Verhältnis zu den Quellen. Beobachtungen am 'Erwählten.'" In *Quellenkritische Studien zum Werk Thomas Manns*, edited by Paul Scherrer and Hans Wysling, 258–324. Bern: Francke, 1967.

———. "Zu Thomas Manns 'Maja'-Projekt." In *Quellenkritische Studien zum Werk Thomas Manns*, 23–47.

———. "Königliche Hoheit." In *Thomas-Mann-Handbuch*, 385–95.

Index

Unless otherwise indicated, all titles in quotation marks or italics refer to Mann's works.